# OLD ENGLISH GRAMMAR

BY

JOSEPH WRIGHT

PH.D., D.C.L., LL.D, LITT.D.
FELLOW OF THE BRITISH ACADEMY
EX-PROFESSOR OF COMPARATIVE PHILOLOGY IN THE
UNIVERSITY OF OXFORD

AND

ELIZABETH MARY WRIGHT

THIRD EDITION

OXFORD UNIVERSITY PRESS

*Oxford University Press, Walton Street, Oxford OX2 6DP*
*London Glasgow New York Toronto*
*Delhi Bombay Calcutta Madras Karachi*
*Kuala Lumpur Singapore Hong Kong Tokyo*
*Nairobi Dar es Salaam Cape Town*
*Melbourne Auckland*
*and associates in*
*Beirut Berlin Ibadan Mexico City Nicosia*

*Published in the United States by*
*Oxford University Press, New York*

*First published 1925*
*Reprinted 1934, 1945, 1950, 1954,*
*1961, 1967, 1972 and 1975*
*First published in paperback 1982*



*British Library Cataloguing in Publication Data*
*Wright, Joseph*
*Old English grammar. –3rd ed.*
*1. Anglo-Saxon language–Grammar*
*I. Title II. Wright, Elizabeth Mary*
*429'.5 PE131*
*ISBN 0-19-811942-9*

*Printed in Hong Kong*

# PREFACE TO THE FIRST EDITION

In writing this Grammar we have kept steadily in view the class of students for whom the Series of Grammars was originally planned. As it is not intended for specialists, some details of more or less importance have been intentionally omitted, but we venture to think that the present volume contains all that the ordinary student will require to know about the subject. The student who thoroughly masters the book will not only have gained a comprehensive knowledge of Old English, but will also have acquired the elements of Comparative Germanic grammar. But from our long experience as teachers of the subject, we should strongly recommend the beginner not to work through the phonology at the outset, but to read Chapter I and sections 47-53, and then to learn the paradigms, and at the same time to read some easy texts such as are to be found in any of the Old English Readers. This is undoubtedly the best plan in the end, and will lead to the most satisfactory results. In fact, it is in our opinion a sheer waste of time for a student to attempt to study in detail the phonology of any language before he has acquired a good working knowledge of its vocabulary and inflexions.

In selecting examples to illustrate the sound-laws we have tried as far as possible to give words which have been preserved in Modern English. A comparison of the Index to the Grammar with an Old English Dictionary would show that we have thus included nearly all the simple words which have been preserved in the modern language. Our object in doing this was to enable the student to lay a solid foundation for his further study of historical English grammar, and to provide a basis for the next volume of the Series, which will deal with Middle English.

Although this Grammar makes no pretence of being an exhaustive work, yet it is by far the most complete Grammar that has hitherto been written in our own language, and the first to deal with the subject in a strictly scientific manner. We gratefully acknowledge the help we have derived from the learned articles and books by that splendid band of German Anglisten which has done so much to throw light upon the history and philology of our language in all its stages. On pp. xiv–xv will be found a select list of the books which we have found most useful, but it is our pleasant duty to mention here our special indebtedness to the works of Bülbring, Cosijn, and Sievers.

In conclusion, we wish to express our sincere thanks to the Controller of the University Press for his great kindness in complying with our wishes in regard to special type, and to the Press Reader for the excellent manner in which he has read the proofs.

JOSEPH WRIGHT.
ELIZABETH M. WRIGHT.

OXFORD,
*January*, 1908.

# PREFACE TO THE SECOND EDITION

THE rapidity with which the first edition of this Grammar has been exhausted, seems to indicate that there is a real need for a Series of historical and comparative Grammars specially designed to meet the requirements of students. In our opinion the writers of grammars of modest dimensions are often more anxious to provide material useful to their colleagues than handbooks suitable to the needs of their students.

For reasons stated in the preface to the first edition we have rigidly preserved the original plan and scope of the grammar, and although the old numbering of the paragraphs has remained the same, a careful examination of the grammar and index will show that the whole has been thoroughly revised. There can hardly be any doubt that all practical teachers of the subject will agree that it is far better and easier for the student to take early West Saxon as the standard for Old English, and to group around it the chief deviations of the other dialects, than to start with a grammar which treats all the dialects as being of equal importance. For us to have treated the subject in the latter manner would have defeated the very object with which the grammar was written.

In conclusion we wish to express our heartiest thanks to the writers of the critical and helpful reviews of the first edition, which appeared in the *Archiv für das Studium der neueren Sprachen und Literaturen*, vol. cxxv (by Professor Björkman); *Athenaeum* for April 18, 1908; *Beiblatt zur Anglia* for July, 1910 (by Professor Pogatscher); *Deutsche*

*Literaturzeitung* for May 22, 1909 (by A. Eichler); *Literaturblatt für germanische und romanische Philologie*, 1908, cols. 279–81 (by Professor Jordan); *Revue Critique* for July 23, 1908 (by Professor Doin).

JOSEPH WRIGHT.
ELIZABETH M. WRIGHT.

OXFORD,
*December*, 1913.

# PREFACE TO THE THIRD EDITION

THIS new edition of the Grammar has been thoroughly revised. Some paragraphs have been entirely rewritten, and many others have been improved in various ways. We have, however, thought it advisable to preserve the same arrangement of the material as in the previous editions.

JOSEPH WRIGHT.
ELIZABETH M. WRIGHT.

OXFORD,
*February*, 1925.

# CONTENTS

# SELECT LIST OF BOOKS USED

*Brugmann, Karl.* Kurze vergleichende Grammatik der indogermanischen Sprachen. Strassburg, 1904.

*Bülbring, Karl D.* Altenglisches Elementarbuch (Lautlehre). Heidelberg, 1902.

*Cosijn, P. J.* Altwestsächsische Grammatik. Haag, 1883-6.

*Dieter, Ferdinand.* Laut- und Formenlehre der altgermanischen Dialekte. Leipzig, 1900.

*Hall, John R. Clark.* A concise Anglo-Saxon Dictionary for the use of students. London, 1894.

*Holthausen, Ferdinand.* Altsächsisches Elementarbuch. Heidelberg, 1899.

*Kaluza, Max.* Historische Grammatik der englischen Sprache. Erster Teil. Berlin-Schöneberg, 1906.

*Kluge, Friedrich.* Geschichte der englischen Sprache (Paul's Grundriss der germanischen Philologie, vol. i, pp. 925–1166, Strassburg, 1904).

Urgermanisch: Vorgeschichte der altgermanischen Dialekte. Strassburg, 1913.

Nominale Stammbildungslehre der altgermanischen Dialekte. Halle, 1899.

*Koch, Friedrich C.* Die Satzlehre der englischen Sprache. Cassel, 1878.

*Mayhew, A. L.* Synopsis of Old English Phonology. Oxford, 1891.

*Noreen, Adolf.* Altisländische und altnorwegische Grammatik unter Berücksichtigung des Urnordischen. Halle, 1903.

Geschichte der nordischen Sprachen, besonders in altnordischer Zeit. Strassburg, 1913.

Abriss der urgermanischen Lautlehre. Strassburg, 1894.

*Pogatscher, Alois.* Zur Lautlehre der griechischen, lateinischen und romanischen Lehnwörter im Altenglischen. Strassburg, 1888.

*Sievers, Eduard.* Angelsächsische Grammatik. Halle, 1898.

*Streitberg, Wilhelm.* Urgermanische Grammatik. Heidelberg, 1896.

*Sweet, Henry.* The Student's Dictionary of Anglo-Saxon. Oxford, 1897.

*Toller, T. Northcote.* An Anglo-Saxon Dictionary, based on the manuscript collections of the late Joseph Bosworth. Oxford, 1882–1898. And Supplement, 1908.

*Walde, Alois.* Die germanischen Auslautgesetze. Halle, 1900.

*Wright, Joseph.* An Old High German Primer. Oxford, 1906.
Grammar of the Gothic Language. Oxford, 1910.
The English Dialect Grammar. Oxford, 1905.
Comparative Grammar of the Greek Language. Oxford, 1912.

# ABBREVIATIONS

| | | | | |
|---|---|---|---|---|
| Dor. | = Doric | | MHG. | = Middle High German |
| Fr. | = French | | NE. | = New English |
| Germ. | = Germanic | | NHG. | = New High German |
| Goth. | = Gothic | | Nth. | = Northumbrian |
| Gr. | = Greek | | OE. | = Old English |
| Hom. | = Homer | | OHG. | = Old High German |
| Indg. | = Indo-Germanic | | O.Icel. | = Old Icelandic |
| instr. | = instrumental | | O.Ir. | = Old Irish |
| Ken. | = Kentish | | OS. | = Old Saxon |
| Lat. | = Latin | | Prim. | = Primitive |
| loc. | = locative | | Skr. | = Sanskrit |
| ME. | = Middle English | | WS. | = West Saxon |

The asterisk * prefixed to a word denotes a theoretical form, as OE. **dæg**, *day*, from Prim Germanic * **đaȝaz.**

# INTRODUCTION

§ 1. OLD English is a member of the West Germanic division of the Germanic (Teutonic) branch of the Indo-Germanic family of languages. This great family of languages is usually divided into eight branches :—

I. **Aryan,** consisting of: (1) The Indian group, including Vedic (the language of the Vedas), classical Sanskrit, and the Prākrit dialects. (2) The Iranian group, including (*a*) West Iranian (Old Persian, the language of the Persian cuneiform inscriptions, dating from about 520–350 B. C.); (*b*) East Iranian (Avesta—sometimes called Zend-Avesta, Zend, and Old Bactrian—the language of the Avesta, the sacred books of the Zoroastrians).

II. **Armenian,** the oldest monuments of which belong to the fifth century A. D.

III. **Greek,** with its numerous dialects.

IV. **Albanian,** the language of ancient Illyria. The oldest monuments belong to the seventeenth century.

V. **Italic,** consisting of Latin and the Umbrian-Samnitic dialects. From the popular form of Latin are descended the Romance languages: Portuguese, Spanish, Catalanian, Provençal, French, Italian, Raetoromanic, Roumanian or Wallachian.

VI. **Keltic,** consisting of: (1) Gaulish (known to us by Keltic names and words quoted by Latin and Greek authors, and inscriptions on coins); (2) Britannic, including Cymric or Welsh, Cornish, and Bas Breton or Armorican (the oldest records of Cymric and Bas Breton date back to the eighth or ninth century); (3) Gaelic, including Irish-Gaelic, Scotch-Gaelic, and Manx. The oldest monuments are the old Gaelic ogam inscriptions which probably date as far back as about 500 A. D.

VII. **Baltic-Slavonic,** consisting of: (1) The Baltic division, embracing (*a*) Old Prussian, which became extinct in the seventeenth century, (*b*) Lithuanian, (*c*) Lettic (the oldest records of Lithuanian and Lettic belong to the sixteenth century); (2) the Slavonic division, embracing: (*a*) the South-Eastern group, including Russian (Great Russian, White Russian, and Little Russian), Bulgarian, and Illyrian (Serbian, Croatian, Slovenian); (*b*) the Western group, including Czech (Bohemian), Sorabian (Wendish), Polish and Polabian.

VIII. **Germanic,** consisting of:—

(1) **Gothic.** Almost the only source of our knowledge of the Gothic language is the fragments of the biblical translation made in the fourth century by Ulfilas, the Bishop of the West Goths.

(2) **Old Norse** (Scandinavian), which is sub-divided into two groups: (*a*) East Norse, including Swedish, Gutnish, and Danish; (*b*) West Norse, including Norwegian, and Icelandic.

The oldest records of this branch are the runic inscriptions, some of which date as far back as the third or fourth century.

(3) **West Germanic,** which is composed of:—

(*a*) High German, the oldest monuments of which belong to about the middle of the eighth century.

(*b*) Low Franconian, called Old Low Franconian or Old Dutch until about 1200.

(*c*) Low German, with records dating back to the ninth century. Up to about 1200 it is generally called Old Saxon.

(*d*) Frisian, the oldest records of which belong to the fourteenth century.

(*e*) English, the oldest records of which belong to about the end of the seventh century.

NOTE.—1. A few of the chief characteristics of the Germanic languages as compared with the other branches of the Indo-

Germanic languages are: the first sound-shifting or Grimm's law (§§ **229–34**); Verner's law (§ **238**); the development of the so-called weak declension of adjectives (§ **421**); the development of the preterite of weak verbs (§ **520**); the use of the old perfect as a preterite (§ **481**).

2. The most characteristic differences between Gothic and Old Norse on the one hand, and of West Germanic on the other, are: the West Germanic gemination of consonants (§§ **254–6**); the loss of final **z** which arose from Indo-Germanic **s** by Verner's law (§ **252**); the West Germanic development of prim. Germanic **ww** (§ **90**), **jj** (§ **275**); the form of the second pers. sing. pret. indicative of strong verbs (§ **481**). Gothic and Old Norse preserved the old perfect ending, as Goth. Old Norse **namt**, *thou tookest*, but OE. **nōme**, OS. OHG. **nāmi**. In the West Germanic languages the **-t** was only preserved in the preterite-present verbs, as OE. **wāst**, OS. **wēst**, OHG **weist**, *thou knowest*.

3. The most characteristic difference between High German and the other Germanic languages is: the High German sound-shifting (§ **230**).

§ **2**. The division of a language into fixed periods must of necessity be more or less arbitrary. What are given as the characteristics of one period have generally had their beginnings in the previous period, and it is impossible to say with perfect accuracy when one period begins and another ends. For practical purposes Old English may be conveniently divided into two periods: early OE. from about 700 to 900; and late OE. from 900 to 1100.

§ **3**. The oldest records of OE. exhibit clearly defined dialectal peculiarities which have been treated in some detail in the phonology, so that the student can easily collect together for himself the chief characteristics of each dialect. In this grammar early West Saxon is taken as the standard for OE., and is treated in greater detail than the other dialects. In using OE. poetry for grammatical purposes the student should remember that it was for the most part originally written in the Anglian dialect, but that it has come down to us chiefly in late West Saxon copies which contain many Anglian forms. OE. is usually divided into four dialects: (*a*) Northumbrian, embracing the district between the Firth of Forth and the Humber. (*b*) Mercian, between the Humber and the Thames. (*c*) West Saxon, south of the Thames, except Kent and Surrey. (*d*) Kentish, embracing Kent and Surrey. Northumbrian and Mercian are often classed together and called Anglian.

Even in the oldest recorded OE. there was of course no such thing as a uniform Northumbrian, Mercian, West Saxon, or Kentish dialect. Within each principal division there must have been some or many sub-dialects, and this is one of the main reasons why we find certain phonological peculiarities in texts ascribed to one or other of the four principal dialects. So-called phonological irregularities sometimes also arose from copyists introducing into manuscripts forms peculiar to their own dialect, or in transcribing manuscripts from one dialect into another they sometimes left dialect forms peculiar to their original; and in transcribing manuscripts from e. g. early WS. into late WS. forms belonging to the older period were often copied.

NOTE.—A detailed comparison of late OE. phonology with that of the Modern dialects would doubtless show that the dialects of Sussex and East Anglia were closely related to the dialect of Kent in the OE. period. This is not the place for such a comparison, so one example must suffice here. The change of **ȳ** to **ē** (§ **132**, Note) in late OE. is always regarded as a special Kentish peculiarity, but the same sound-change must also have taken place in Sussex and East Anglia, where OE. **ȳ** has regularly become **ī** (through the older stage **ē**) in the Modern dialects, as **līs** (OE. **lȳs**), *lice*; **mīs** (OE. **mȳs**), *mice*; whereas had **ȳ** simply been unrounded to **ī** in the late OE. period of these dialects, the Modern forms would have been ***lois** and ***mois**. See also § **112**, Note I.

# PHONOLOGY

## CHAPTER I

### ORTHOGRAPHY AND PRONUNCIATION

§ **4**. OE. was written in the British modified form of the Latin alphabet with the addition of þ and ƿ (= **w**) from the runic alphabet. Vowel length was mostly omitted in writing, but in the case of long vowels it was sometimes represented by doubling the vowel or by using the diacritic sign ´, as **huus, hús,** *house.* The sign ¯, placed over vowels, is used in this grammar to mark long vowels and diphthongs. The account of the pronunciation given below is only approximately accurate. It is impossible to ascertain with perfect certainty the exact pronunciation of any language in its oldest period.

#### A. The Vowels.

§ **5**. The OE. vowel-system was represented by the six elementary letters **a, e, i, o, u, y,** the ligatures **æ, œ,** and the digraphs **ea, eo, io,** and **ie,** the digraphs having the value of diphthongs. See § **6**. They all had both a short and a long quantity.

**a** had the same sound as the **a** in NHG. **ab, gast,** as **dagas,** *days*; **habban,** *to have*; **hagol,** *hail*; **hara,** *hare.* **a** before nasals was probably a low-back-wide vowel like the **â** in Fr. **pâte** and the **a** as pronounced in many Scotch dialects in such words as **ant, man,** which English people often mistake for **o** especially when lengthened. In OE. it was accordingly often written **o** and may be pronounced like the **o** in NE. **not,** as **band, bond,** *he bound*; **land, lond,**

*land*; **lang, long,** *long*; **mann, monn,** *man*; **nama, noma,** *name*. See § **59**.

**ā** had the same sound as the **a** in NE. **father,** as **ān,** *one*; **bān,** *bone*; **rāp,** *rope*; **twā,** *two*; **cnāwan,** *to know*; **māwan,** *to mow*; **sāwan,** *to sow*.

**æ** had the same sound as the **a** in NE. **hat,** as **dæg,** *day*; **fæder,** *father*; **fæstan,** *to fasten*; **hæfde,** *he had*; **mægden,** *maiden*.

**ǣ** had the same sound as the **ai** in NE. **air,** and the è in French **père,** as **dǣd,** *deed*; **sǣd,** *seed*; **wǣpen,** *weapon*; **clǣne,** *clean*; **hǣlan,** *to heal*; **lǣdan,** *to lead*; **sǣ,** *sea*.

**e** had the same sound as the **e** in NE. **west, end,** as **etan,** *to eat*; **fell,** *skin*; **helpan,** *to help*; **segl,** *sail*; **ende,** *end*; **here,** *army*; **mete,** *meat*; **exen,** *oxen*.

**ē** had the same sound as the **e** in NHG. **reh,** as **hēr,** *here*; **cwēn,** *queen*; **fēdan,** *to feed*; **grēne,** *green*; **tēþ,** *teeth*.

**i** had the same sound as the **i** in NE. **sit,** as **fisc,** *fish*; **sittan,** *to sit*; **þing,** *thing*; **niman,** *to take*.

**ī** had the same sound as the **i** in NHG. **ihn,** and nearly the same sound as the **ee** in NE. **feed,** as **līf,** *life*; **mīn,** *my*; **tīd,** *time*; **fīf,** *five*; **sīþe,** *scythe*.

**o** had the same sound as the **o** in NHG. **Gott,** and was nearly like the **o** in NE. **not,** as **col,** *coal*; **coren,** *chosen*; **dohtor,** *daughter*; **nosu,** *nose*; **oxa,** *ox*. See **a** above.

**ō** had the same sound as the **o** in NHG. **Bote,** as **brōþor,** *brother*; **grōwan,** *to grow*; **mōdor,** *mother*; **mōna,** *moon*; **sōna,** *soon*; **gōs,** *goose*; **ōþer,** *other*; **þōhte,** *he thought*.

**u** had the same sound as the **u** in NE. **put,** as **duru,** *door*; **full,** *full*; **hungor,** *hunger*; **lufian,** *to love*; **guma,** *man*; **þunor,** *thunder*.

**ū** had the same sound as the **u** in NHG. **gut,** and nearly the same sound as the **oo** in NE. **food,** as **cū,** *cow*; **hūs,** *house*; **sūr,** *sour*; **ūt,** *out*; **mūþ,** *mouth*; **ūs,** *us*.

**œ** had the same sound as the **ö** in NHG. **Götter,** as dat. **dœhter,** *to a daughter*; **œle,** *oil*; **œxen,** *oxen.*

**œ̄** had the same sound as the **ö** in NHG. **schön,** as **bœ̄c,** *books*; **dœ̄ma(n),** *to judge*; **cwœ̄n,** *queen.*

**y** had the same sound as the **ü** in NHG. **mütter,** as **brycg,** *bridge*; **cyning,** *king*; **scyld,** *guilt*; **þyncan,** *to seem.*

**ȳ** had the same sound as the **ü** in NHG. **grün,** as **brȳd,** *bride*; **mȳs,** *mice*; **wȳscan,** *to wish*; **ȳþ,** *wave.*

It is difficult to determine what was the precise pronunciation of the **a, e, o** in the second element of diphthongs. In these combinations they had the function of consonants and may be pronounced as very short unstressed **ă, ĕ, ŏ.** The first element of the diphthongs **ea, ēa** was a very open sound like the **æ** in OE. **fæder,** and the **a** in NE. **hat,** but the **e** in the diphthongs **eo, ēo** was like the **e** in NE. **bed** or like the close **é** in French **été.** In the long diphthongs each of the elements was longer than in the short diphthongs.

**ea** = **æ** + **ă,** as **eall,** *all*; **healdan,** *to hold*; **earm,** *arm*; **heard,** *hard*; **eahta,** *eight*; **weaxan,** *to grow*; **geat,** *gate.*

**ēa** = **ǣ** + **a,** as **dēaþ,** *death*; **hēafod,** *head*; **hlēapan,** *to leap*; **slēan,** *to slay*; **gēar,** *year*; **scēap,** *sheep*; **nēah,** *near*; **strēa,** *straw.*

**eo** = **e** + **ŏ,** as **meolcan,** *to milk*; **heorte,** *heart*; **steorra,** *star*; **sweostor,** *sister*; **geolo,** *yellow.*

**ēo** = **ē** + **o,** as **cēosan,** *to choose*; **dēop,** *deep*; **þēof,** *thief*; **sēon,** *to see*; **cnēo,** *knee.*

**ie** = **i** + **ĕ,** as **giest,** *guest*; **ieldra,** *older*; **ierfe,** *inheritance*; **hliehhan,** *to laugh*; **giefan,** *to give*; **hierde,** *shepherd*; **siehþ,** *he sees*; **cnieht,** *boy.*

**īe** = **ī** + **e,** as **hīeran,** *to hear*; **gelīefan,** *to believe*; **hīehra,** *higher*; **cīesþ,** *he chooses*; **līehtan,** *to give light*; **nīewe,** *new.*

**io** = **i** + **ŏ,** as **liornian,** *to learn*; **mioluc, miolc,** *milk*; **miox,** *manure.*

**īo** = **ī**+**o**, as **līode**, *people*; **þīostre**, *dark*; **sīon**, *to strain*; **þīon**, *to thrive*.

§ **6**. From what has been said above we arrive at the following OE. vowel-system:—

| | |
|---|---|
| Short vowels | **a, æ, e, i, o, u, œ, y** |
| Long ,, | **ā, ǣ, ē, ī, ō, ū, œ̄, ȳ** |
| Short diphthongs | **ea, eo, ie, io** |
| Long ,, | **ēa, ēo, īe, īo** |

NOTE.—1. **æ** was often written **ae**, and **e** in the oldest records. In the oldest period of the language there must have been two short **e**-sounds, viz. **e** = Germanic **e** (§ **80**), and **e** = the i-umlaut of **æ** (§ **55**), the latter probably being more open than the former, but the two sounds seem to have fallen together at a very early date, and are accordingly not distinguished in this grammar. Some scholars distinguish them by writing the former **e** and the latter **ę**. And in like manner they also sometimes distinguish the **o** = Germanic **o** (§ **42**), and the **o** = Germanic **a** before nasals (§ **59**), by writing the former **o** and the latter **ǫ**. In late OE. **e, y** were often written for **æ, i** and vice versa. In Ken. **ǣ̆** was sometimes written in mistake for **ē̆**, as **ætan** = **etan**, *to eat*; **hǣr** = **hēr**, *here*. In late Nth. **æ, œ, y** were sometimes written **ai, oi, ui**. **œ, œ̄**, (§ **47**), written **oe** in OE. manuscripts, were best preserved in the Anglian dialects. They were unrounded to **e, ē** in WS. about the end of the ninth and in Ken. about the end of the tenth century. Long **ī** was sometimes written **ig** finally and occasionally also medially, as **hig** = **hī**, *they*; **bigspell** = **bīspell**, *parable*. The **ō** in words like **gōs**, *goose* (§ **61**), and **mōna**, *moon* (§ **121**), must originally have been an open **ō** like the **a** in NE. **all**, but it fell together with Germanic long close **ō** (§ **128**) at an early period. The diphthong **ē̆a** was sometimes written **æa, æo** in the oldest records. **ē̆o** was often written for **ī̆o** in the oldest WS. For **ē̆o**, of whatever origin, Nth. often has **ē̆a**; and Ken. often has **ī̆a** (**ya**) for WS. **ē̆a, ē̆o, ī̆o**. In late WS. the combinations **ǣw, ēw**, of whatever origin, were often written **ēaw, ēow**. The combination **ēaw** was occasionally written **ēuw, ēuu, ēu, ēw** in Anglian. **ie** and **īe** occur chiefly in WS. After **ī̆e** had regularly become **ī̆** in WS. the **ī̆e** was sometimes wrongly written for old **ī̆**.

2. A diphthong may be defined as the combination of a sonantal with a consonantal vowel. It is called a falling or a rising diphthong according as the stress is upon the first or the second element. The OE. diphthongs were generally falling diphthongs, but the diphthongs, which arose from the influence of initial palatal **c, g,** and **sc** upon a following palatal vowel, were originally rising diphthongs which at a later period became falling diphthongs through the shifting of the stress from the second to the first element of the diphthong. See § **51**.

## B. The Consonants.

§ **7.** The OE. consonant-system was represented by the following letters :—**b, c, d, f, g, h, k, l, m, n, p, r, s, t, þ (ð), *w, x.**

**v** (written **u**) and **z** (= **ts**) were very rarely used except occasionally in late loanwords. **c, cc, nc, sc ; g, ng ;** and **h** (except initially), **hh** were guttural or palatal according to the sound-law stated in § **309.** On the vocalic liquids and nasals in OE. see § **219**.

Of the above letters **b, d, m, n, p, t** had the same sound-values as in Modern English. The remaining consonants require special attention.

**c.** Guttural **c,** sometimes written **k** in the oldest records, was pronounced nearly like the c in NE. **could.** Palatal **c** (often written **ce** before a following guttural vowel) was pronounced nearly like the **k** in NE. **kid.** In the OE. runic alphabet the two **k**-sounds had separate characters. Some scholars assume that palatal **c** and **sc** were pronounced like the **ch** and **sh** in NE. **church ; ship, fish.** Examples of guttural **c** are : **bucca,** *he-goat* ; **cēlan,** *to cool* ; **cnēo,** *knee* ; **sprecan,** *to speak* ; **cyssan,** *to kiss* ; **bōc,** *book* ; **weorc,** *work* ; **drincan,** *to drink* ; **þancian,** *to thank* ; and of palatal **c : cēosan,** *to choose* ; **cinn,** *chin* ; **cīese,** *cheese* ; **bēc,** *books* ; **crycc,** *crutch* ; **benc,** *bench* ; **þenc(e)an,** *to think* ; of **sc : sceal,** *shall* ; **scēap,** *sheep* ; **scōh,** *shoe* ; **wascan,** *to wash* ; **fisc,** *fish* ; See §§ **309, 312.**

**f**. Initially, finally, and medially before voiceless consonants, also when doubled, **f** was a voiceless spirant like the **f** in NE. **fit, shaft,** as **fæder,** *father*; **fōt,** *foot*; **ceaf,** *chaff*; **hrōf,** *roof*; **geaf,** *he gave*; **sceaft,** *shaft*; **pyffan,** *to puff*. Medially between voiced sounds it was a voiced spirant (often written **b** in the oldest records) nearly like the **v** in NE. **vine, five,** as **giefan,** *to give*; **hafaþ,** *he has*; **seofon,** *seven*; **wulfas,** *wolves*; **hræfn,** *raven*; **lifde,** *he lived*. See §§ **229,** Note 5, **293.**

**g** was used to represent several different sounds: (*a*) a guttural and a palatal explosive; (*b*) a guttural and a palatal spirant which had separate characters in the OE. runic alphabet. The palatal explosive and the palatal spirant were often written **ge** before a following guttural vowel with **e** to indicate the palatal nature of the **g**.

Before guttural vowels initial **g** was a guttural explosive and was pronounced like the **g** in NE. **good,** but in the oldest OE. it was a guttural spirant = the **g** often heard in NHG. **sagen** (cp. § **314**), as **gāst,** *spirit*; **god,** *God*; **gold,** *gold*. Before palatal vowels initial **g** was a palatal spirant nearly like the **j** in NHG. **jahr** and the **y** in NE. **ye, you,** as **geaf,** *he gave*; **giefan,** *to give*; **giest,** *yeast*; **geoc,** *yoke*.

Medial **gg** was always a guttural explosive like the **g** in NE. **good,** as **dogga,** *dog*; **frogga,** *frog*; **stagga,** *stag*. Medial and final **cg** was a palatal explosive nearly like the **g** in NE. **get,** as **lecg(e)an,** *to lay*; **secg(e)an,** *to say*; **brycg,** *bridge*; **wecg,** *wedge*. The **g** in medial and final **ng** was a guttural or a palatal explosive, the former being nearly like the **g** in NE. **longer,** as **sungon,** *they sang*; **hungor,** *hunger*; **lang,** *long*; and the latter nearly like the **g** in NE. **finger,** as **lengra,** *longer*; **streng,** *string*; **þing,** *thing*.

Medial intervocalic **g** was a guttural or a palatal spirant, the former being nearly like the **g** in NHG. **sagen,** as **boga,** *bow*; **fugol,** *bird*; **lagu,** *law*; and the latter nearly like the g in NHG. **siegen**, as **bīeg(e)an**, *to bend*; **fæger**, *fair*; **hyge**, *mind*.

NOTE.—1. Some scholars assume that palatal **cg** and **ng** were pronounced **dž**, and **ndž** where **dž** = the j in NE. **just**. See § **319**, Note.

2. ʒ is generally used for **g** in OE. manuscripts and printed texts, and often also in grammars. In this grammar ʒ is only used to represent the prim. Germanic voiced spirant (§ **229**, Note 5).

**h**. Initial **h** (except in the combination **hw**) was an aspirate like the **h** in NE. **hand**, as **habban**, *to have*; **heard**, *hard*; **hūs**, *house*; **hlūd**, *loud*. Initial **hw** was pronounced χ**w** like the **wh** in many Scotch dialects, as **hwā**, *who?*; **hwǣte**, *wheat*. In all other positions **h**, including **hh**, was a guttural or palatal spirant, the former being like the ch in NHG. **nacht, noch**, as **dohtor**, *daughter*; **eahta**, *eight*; **tiohhian**, *to think, consider*; **sulh**, *plough*; **feorh**, *life*; **dāh**, *dough*; **troh**, *trough*; and the latter like the ch in NHG. **nicht, ich**, as **flyht**, *flight*; **siehþ**, *he sees*; **nēah**, *near*; **hliehhan**, *to laugh*. In the oldest records final **h** was sometimes written **ch**, as **elch** = **eolh**, *elk*; **salch** = **sealh**, *willow*.

**k** was sometimes used to express the guttural c (see above), as **kynn**, *race, generation*; **kyning**, *king*; **knēo**, *knee*; See § **309**.

**l**. In Northumbrian and the greater portion of the Mercian district, **l** was pronounced like the **l** in NHG. and in standard NE., but in West Saxon, Kentish, and parts of the southern portion of Mercia, it was a reverted sound formed by the under surface of the tip of the tongue being turned to the hard palate which imparted to the sound a kind of guttural quality. This explains why breaking (§§ **49, 63**) took place in WS. and Ken. before **l**+consonant, but not in Anglian. The reverted **l** is still preserved in the dialects of the southern and south-western counties. Examples are : **lǣdan,** *to lead* ; **folc,** *folk* ; **fugol,** *bird* ; **eall,** *all* ; **healdan,** *to hold* ; **meolcan,** *to milk.*

**r** was trilled in all positions as in Modern Scotch, as **rīdan,** *to ride* ; **duru,** *door* ; **word,** *word* ; **fæder,** *father.* In West Saxon, Kentish, and parts of the southern portion of Mercia, it was reverted like **l** (see above), which accounts for breaking taking place before **r** + consonant more regularly in WS. and Ken. than in Anglian, as **earm,** *arm* ; **heard,** *hard* ; **eorþe,** *earth* ; **liornian,** *to learn.*

**s.** Initially, finally, medially before voiceless consonants, and when doubled, **s** was a voiceless spirant like the **s** in NE. **sit,** as **sealt,** *salt* ; **sunu,** *son* ; **standan,** *to stand* ; **sweostor,** *sister* ; **hūs,** *house* ; **īs,** *ice* ; **cyssan,** *to kiss.* Medially between voiced sounds, it was a voiced spirant like the **s** in NE. **rise,** as **bōsm,** *bosom* ; **cēosan,** *to choose* ; **nosu,** *nose* ; **ōsle,** *ousel.*

**þ.** Initially, medially when doubled, and finally **þ** was a voiceless spirant like the **th** in NE. **thin,** as **þencan,** *to think* ; **þēof,** *thief* ; **moþþe,** *moth* ; **bæþ,** *bath* ; **mūþ,** *mouth.* Medially between voiced sounds, it was a voiced spirant like the **th** in NE. **then,** as **baþian,** *to bathe* ; **brōþor,** *brother* ; **eorþe,** *earth* ; **fæþm,** *fathom.*

Initial **þ** was written **th** until about 900 in imitation of Latin. Afterwards it was written **ð,** and **þ** (borrowed from the runic alphabet). And the voiced spirant was often written **d** in imitation of the contemporary Latin pronunciation.

**w** does not occur in OE. manuscripts, but was represented by **uu, u** until about the year 900, later by **ƿ** borrowed from the runic alphabet. In late Nth. it was sometimes represented by **wu, v,** and before **ă, ǣ̆, ĕ** by **wo, vo, uo, o.** It had the same sound-value as the **w** in NE. **wet,** as **wæter,** *water* ; **sweltan,** *to die* ; **wlanc,** *proud* ; **sāwol,** *soul.*

**x** was pronounced like the **x** in NE. **six,** as **rīxian,** *to rule* ; **siex,** *six* ; **weaxan,** *to grow* ; **āxian,** *to ask.*

§ **8**. From what has been said above we arrive at the following OE. consonant-system:—

| | | Labial. | Inter-dental. | Dental. | Guttural. | Palatal. |
|---|---|---|---|---|---|---|
| *Explosives* | Voiceless | **p, pp** | | **t, tt** | **c, cc** | **c, cc** |
| | Voiced | **b, bb** | | **d, dd** | **g, gg** | **g, cg** |
| *Spirants* | Voiceless | **f, ff** | **þ, þþ** | **s, ss** | **h, hh** | **h, hh** |
| | Voiced | **f** | **þ** | **s** | **g** | **g** |
| *Nasals* | | **m, mm** | | **n, nn** | **n** | **n** |
| *Liquids* | | | | **l, ll; r, rr** | | |
| *Semi-vowel* | | **w** | | | | |

To these must be added the aspirate **h**, and **x**. The double consonants were pronounced long as in Modern Italian and Swedish, thus **habban** = **hab·ban,** *to have*; **swimman** = **swim·man**, *to swim*, see §§ **258–9**. From the above table it will be seen that the OE. alphabet was very defective, insomuch as each of the letters **c, f, g, h, n, s,** and **þ** was used to represent two or more sounds. In order to distinguish the gutturals from the palatals in writing some scholars place a dot over the latter, as **ċ, ġ, ḣ, ṅ.**

### Stress (Accent).

§ **9**. By accent in its widest sense is meant the gradation of a word or word-group according to the degree of stress or of pitch with which its various syllables are uttered. Although strictly speaking there are as many different degrees of accent in a word or word-group as there are syllables, yet for ordinary purposes it is only necessary to distinguish three degrees, the principal accent, the secondary accent, and the weak accent or, as it is generally termed, the absence of accent. The secondary accent is as a rule separated from the principal accent by at least one intervening syllable.

All the Indo-Germanic languages have partly pitch (musical) and partly stress (expiratory) accent, but one or other of the two systems of accentuation always predominates in each language, thus in Sanskrit and Old Greek the accent was predominantly pitch, whereas in the oldest periods of the Italic dialects, and the Keltic and Germanic languages, the accent was predominantly stress. The effect of this difference in the system of accentuation is clearly seen in Old Greek and the old Germanic languages by the preservation of the vowels of unaccented syllables in the former and by the weakening or loss of them in the latter. In the early period of the parent Indg. language, the stress accent must have been more predominant than the pitch accent, because it is only upon this assumption that we are able to account for the origin of the vowels **ĭ, ŭ**, **ə** (§ **16**, Note 1), the liquid and nasal sonants (§§ **34–7**), and the loss of vowel often accompanied by a loss of syllable, as in Greek gen. *πα-τρ-ός* beside acc. *πα-τέρ-α*; *πέτ-ομαι* beside *ἐ-πτ-όμην*; Gothic gen. pl. **aúhs-nē** beside acc. ***aúhsa-ns.** It is now a generally accepted theory that at a later period of the parent language the system of accentuation became predominantly pitch, which was preserved in Sanskrit and Old Greek, but which must have become predominantly stress again in prim. Germanic some time prior to the operation of Verner's law (§ **238**).

The quality of the prim. Indg. syllable-accent was of two kinds, the 'broken' or acute and the 'slurred' or circumflex. The former was a rising and the latter a rising-falling accent. Long vowels with the acute accent were bimoric and those with the circumflex trimoric, that is long vowels with the circumflex accent were about half as long again as those with the acute accent. All original long vowels including the first element of long diphthongs had the acute accent. The circumflex accent was unoriginal and arose in prim. Indo-Germanic in the following manner:—
(*a*) From the contraction of vowels, as **-ā̃s,** from **-ā-es** in the nom. plural of **ā**-stems, as Skr. **vŕkās,** *she-wolves,* from an

original form ***wlqā + es,** cp. Goth. **gibōs,** *gifts*; **·ō̃s** from **·o·es** in the nom. plural of **o**-stems, as Skr. **vṛ́kās,** Goth. **wulfōs,** from an original form ***wlqo + es,** *wolves*; **·ā̃i** from **·ā·ai** in the dat. singular of **ā**-stems, as Gr. θεᾷ from an original form ***dhwesā + ai,** *to a goddess,* cp. Goth. **gibái,** *to a gift*; **·ō̃i** from **·o·ai** in the dat. singular of **o**-stems, as Gr. θεῷ from an original form ***dhweso + ai,** *to a god.* (*b*) When a short vowel disappeared after a long vowel, as in the gen. singular of **ā**-stems, as Gr. θεᾶς from an original form ***dhwesāso,** *of a goddess.* (*c*) When a medial long diphthong lost its second element, as in the acc. sing. Gr. Doric βῶν, Vedic **gā́m** (= metrically **gaam**), from ***gō̃m,** older ***gṓum,** *ox, cow*; Gr. Ζῆν, *Zeus,* Vedic **dyā́m** (= metrically **dyaam**), *sky, day,* from ***djē̃m,** older ***djḗum.** (*d*) The same change from the acute to the circumflex accent also took place in prim. Indo-Germanic when a final nasal or liquid disappeared after a long vowel, as Lithuanian **akmũ** (= ō̃), *stone,* beside Gr. ἡγεμών, *leader*; Goth. **tuggō** (= ·ō̃), *tongue,* beside **guma** (= ·ōn), *man*; Lithuanian **motẽ** (= ·ẽ), *wife,* beside Gr. πατήρ, *father.* This distinction in the quality of the syllable-accent was preserved in prim. Germanic in final syllables containing a long vowel, as is seen by the difference in the development of the final long vowels in historic times according as they originally had the 'broken' or the 'slurred' accent. See § **217**.

In the parent Indo-Germanic language the chief accent of a word did not always fall upon the same syllable, but was free or movable as in Sanskrit and Greek, cp. e.g. Gr. nom. πατήρ, *father,* voc. acc. πάτερ, πατέρα; Skr. **ḗmi,** *I go,* pl. **imás,** *we go.* This free accent was still preserved in prim. Germanic at the time when Verner's law operated, whereby the medial or final voiceless spirants became voiced when the vowel immediately preceding them did not bear the chief accent of the word (§ **238**).

At a later period of the prim. Germanic language, the chief accent of a word became confined to the root- or stem-syllable. This confining of the chief accent to the root-syllable was the cause of the great weakening—and eventual loss—which the vowels underwent in unaccented syllables in the prehistoric period of the individual Germanic languages (§§ **212–23**). And the extent to which the weakening of unaccented syllables has been carried in some of the Modern Germanic dialects is well illustrated by such sentences as, **as et it mǫən,** *I shall have it in the morning*; **ast ə dunt if id kud,** *I should have done it if I had been able* (West Yorks.).

§ **10.** The rule for the accentuation of uncompounded words is the same in Old English as in the oldest period of the other Germanic languages, viz. the chief stress fell upon the stem syllable and always remained there even when suffixes and inflexional endings followed it, as **beran,** *to bear*; **dagas,** *days.* **grēting,** *greeting*; **hǣlnes,** *salvation*; **hǣriht,** *hairy*; **handlung,** *handling*; **mistig,** *misty.* **hlēapettan,** *to leap up*; **ierringa,** *angrily*; **lēofosta,** *dearest.* **hēafodu,** *heads*; **lǣnere,** *lender*; **sealfian,** *to anoint*; **wundrode,** *he wondered.* **berende,** *bearing*; **cyningas,** *kings*; **grimettan,** *to rage.* **gædeling,** *companion*; **heofonisc, heofonlic,** *heavenly.* **æþele,** *noble*; **hetele,** *hostile*; **macode,** *he made*; **nerede,** *he saved.* **æþelingas,** *noblemen*; **fultumian,** *to help*; **huntigestre,** *huntress*; **maþelode,** *he spoke.* The position of the secondary stress in trisyllabic and polysyllabic words fluctuated in OE., and with the present state of our knowledge of the subject it is impossible to formulate any hard and fast rules concerning it.

In compound words it is necessary to distinguish between compounds whose second element is a noun or an adjective, and those whose second element is a verb. In the former case the first element had the chief accent in the parent Indg. language; in the latter case the first element had or had not the chief accent according to the position of the verb in the sentence. But already in prim. Germanic the second element of compound verbs nearly always had the chief accent; a change which was mostly brought about by the compound and simple verb existing side by side. This accounts for the difference in the accentuation of such pairs as **ándgiet,** *intelligence*: **ongíetan,** *to understand*; **ándsaca,** *adversary*: **onsácan,** *to deny*; **bī́gang,** *practice*: **begángan,** *to practise*; **órþanc,** *device*: **āþéncan,** *to devise*; **ū́þgenge,** *fugitive*: **oþgángan,** *to escape*; **wíþersaca,** *opponent*: **wiþsácan,** *to oppose*.

§ **11.** As has been stated above, compound words, whose second element is a noun or an adjective, had originally the chief stress on the first syllable. This simple rule was preserved in OE., as **ācbēam,** *oak-tree*; **æftergield,** *additional payment*; **brȳdguma,** *bridegroom*; **cornhūs,** *granary*; **dēaþstede,** *death-place*; **fēowergield,** *fourfold payment*; **frēomǣg,** *free kinsman*; **gēardagas,** *days of yore*; **godbearn,** *godchild*; **lārhūs,** *school*. **æfterboren,** *posthumous*; **æþelcund,** *of noble origin*; **ārfæst,** *virtuous*; **brynehāt,** *burning hot*; **gearowyrdig,** *eloquent*; **īsengrǣg,** *iron-grey*; **mōdwlanc,** *proud*; **wordsnotor,** *eloquent*. Nouns like **ālī́efednes,** *permission*, **onfángennes,** *reception*, **ongíetennes,** *understanding*, **ongínn,** *beginning*, &c., are no exception to the rule, because such nouns were formed direct from the corresponding verbs: pp. **ālī́efed, onfángen, ongíeten,** inf. **ongínnan.**

§ **12.** Already in the oldest period of the language many nouns and adjectives were formed from verbs containing an inseparable particle, and accordingly had the chief stress on the second element, as **bebod,** *command*; **bebyrignes,** *burying*; **bedelfing,** *digging round*; **begang** beside **bī́geng,** *practice*; **behāt,** *promise*; **behēfe,** *suitable*; **belāf,** *remainder*; **belimp,** *occurrence*; **forbod,** *prohibition*; **for-**

**gietol,** *forgetful*; **forhæfednes,** *temperance*; **forlor, forlorennes,** *destruction*; but **fórwyrd,** *ruin*. In like manner the prefix **ge-** was already unaccented in the oldest period of the language—probably partly also in prim. Germanic—and therefore words compounded with it had the chief stress on the second element, as **gebann,** *decree*; **gebed,** *prayer*; **gebrōþor,** *brethren*; **gefeoht,** *fight*; **gefēra,** *companion*; **gesceaft,** *creation*; **geþeaht,** *counsel, thought*; **gewider,** *bad weather, storm*; **ge-æþele,** *congenial*; **gecoren,** *chosen*; **gecynde,** *innate, natural*; **gedēfe,** *befitting*; **gelīc,** *alike*; **gemǣne,** *common*; **gemyndig,** *mindful*; **gesund,** *healthy*; **gefyrn,** *long ago*.

§ **13.** In compound nouns the chief secondary stress was upon that syllable of the second element which would have the chief stress if it were used alone, as **brȳ́dgùma,** *bridegroom*; **fḗowergìeld,** *fourfold payment*; **géarowȳ̀rdig,** *eloquent*. For further examples, see above. But compounds which were no longer felt as such did not have a strong secondary stress upon the second element, as **ēorod** from **eoh + rād,** *troop of cavalry*; **hlāford** from **hlāf + weard,** *lord*.

§ **14.** In the oldest period of the language, the compound verbs had the chief stress upon the second or first element according as the first element was inseparable or separable, as **becúman,** *to become*; **behéaldan,** *to behold*; and similarly **gebǣran,** *to behave*; **gehātan,** *to name*; **forbēodan,** *to forbid*; **forgiefan,** *to forgive*; **geondsēon,** *to survey*; **geondþencan,** *to consider*; **oþberstan,** *to break away*; **oþfeallan,** *to fall off*; **tōberstan,** *to burst asunder*; **tōdǣlan,** *to divide*. **ætíewan,** *to exhibit*; **ætníman,** *to deprive*; and similarly **oferswīþan,** *to overcome*; **oferweorpan,** *to overthrow*; **underberan,** *to support*; **underniman,** *to comprehend*; **þurhþȳrelian,** *to pierce through*; **þurhwunian,** *to abide continuously*; **wiþfōn,** *to grasp at*; **wiþmetan,** *to compare*; **ymbbindan,** *to bind round*; **ymbhweorfan,** *to revolve*.

Verbs like **ándswarian,** *to answer,* **ándwyrdan,** *to answer,* **fúltumian,** *to support,* **ṓrettan,** *to fight,* are no exception to the rule, because such verbs were formed direct from the nouns: **ándswaru, ándwyrde, fúltum, ṓret.** Examples of separable verbs are: **ǽftersprecan,** *to claim*; **ǽfterfolgian,** *to pursue*; **bī́standan,** *to support*; **bī́libban,** *to live by*; and similarly **eftcierran,** *to turn back*; **eftflōwan,** *to flow back*; **foregangan,** *to precede*; **forescēawian,** *to foresee*; **ūpræ̅ran,** *to raise up*; **ūpiernan,** *to run up*; **incuman,** *to come in*; **midwunian,** *to live together*; **ongēanfealdan,** *to fold back*; **tōdōn,** *to put to*; **ūtdrīfan,** *to drive out*; **ūtflōwan,** *to flow out.*

§ **15.** In compound adverbs the first element had the chief or secondary stress according as it was the more or less important element of the compound, as **éal(l)mæ̅st,** *almost*; **éalneg** from **ealne + weg,** *always*; **éalswā,** *quite so*; but **onwég,** *away*; **tōgǽdere,** *together*; **þæ̅rínne,** *therein.*

# CHAPTER II

## THE PRIMITIVE GERMANIC EQUIVALENTS OF THE INDO-GERMANIC VOWEL-SOUNDS

§ **16.** The parent Indo-Germanic language had the following vowel-system:—

| | |
|---|---|
| Short vowels | **a, e, i, o, u, ə** |
| Long ,, | **ā, ē, ī, ō, ū** |
| Short diphthongs | **ai, ei, oi, au, eu, ou** |
| Long ,, | **āi, ēi, ōi, āu, ēu, ōu** |
| Short vocalic | **l, m, n, r** |

NOTE.—1. The short vowels **i, u, ə,** the long vowels **ī, ū,** and vocalic **l, m, n, r** occurred originally only in syllables which did not bear the principal accent of the word.

The short vowels **i, u,** and vocalic **l, m, n, r** arose from the loss of **e** in the strong forms **ei, eu, el, em, en, er,** which was caused by the principal accent having been shifted to some other syllable in the word, cp. § **229**, Note 3.

2. **ə**, the quality of which cannot be precisely defined, arose from the weakening of an original **ā**, **ē**, or **ō**, caused by the loss of accent. It is generally pronounced like the final vowel in German **Gabe** and in NE. **litter**.

3. **ī** and **ū** were contractions of weak diphthongs which arose from the strong forms **eiə**, **āi**, **ēi**, **ōi**; **euə**, **āu**, **ēu**, **ōu** through the loss of accent. The **e** in **eiə**, **euə** had disappeared before the contraction took place. See § **9**.

4. Besides the ordinary long vowels **ā**, **ē**, **ō** with the 'broken' or acute accent the parent Indg. language had also the three long vowels **ā̃**, **ē̃**, **ō̃** (also sometimes written **â**, **ê**, **ô**) with the 'slurred' or circumflex accent. The former were bimoric and the latter trimoric in length. The difference between the two kinds of long vowels was still preserved in final syllables in the oldest historic period of the separate Germanic languages, see § **217**.

5. Diphthongs only occurred before consonants and finally. When a diphthong came to stand before a vowel its second element belonged to the following vowel, as **ĕit**, **ĕut**, **tĕi**, **tĕu**, but **tĕ-je**, **tĕ-we**.

6. Strictly speaking the combination **a**, **e**, or **o** + nasal or liquid is also a diphthong, because the history and development of such combinations are precisely parallel with those of the diphthongs **ai**, **ei**, **oi**, and **au**, **eu**, **ou**.

7. The long diphthongs were shortened before consonants in the prehistoric period of all the European languages, and they then had the same further development as the original short diphthongs. In this grammar no further account will be taken of them in stem-syllables. For their treatment in final syllables see § **217**.

8. In philological works the vocalic liquids and nasals are often written **l̥**, **m̥**, **n̥**, **r̥** in order to distinguish them from consonantal **l**, **m**, **n**, **r**. Upon theoretical grounds it used to be assumed that the parent Indg. language also had long vocalic nasals and liquids, but scholars are now generally agreed that the forms which were supposed to contain these sounds admit of an entirely different explanation, see Wright, *Greek Grammar*, § **68**.

§ **17**. **a** (Lat. **a**, Gr. *α*) remained, as Lat. **ager**, Gr. *ἀγρός*, Goth. **akrs**, O.Icel. **akr**, OS. **akkar**, OHG. **ackar**, OE.

**æcer**, *field, acre*; Gr. ἅλς, Lat. gen. **salis**, Goth. O.Icel. OS. **salt**, OHG. **salz**, OE. **sealt** (§ 64), *salt*; Lat. **aqua**, Goth. **aƕa**, OS. OHG. **aha**, OE. **ēa** from ***eahu**, older ***ahu** (§ 70), *water, river*.

§ 18. **e** (Lat. **e**, Gr. ε) remained, as Lat. **ferō**, Gr. φέρω, *I bear*, O.Icel. **bera**, OS. OHG. OE. **beran**, *to bear*; Lat. **edō**, Gr. ἔδομαι, *I eat*, O.Icel. **eta**, OHG. **eʒʒan**, OS. OE. **etan**, *to eat*; Lat. **pellis**, Gr. πέλλα, OS. OHG. **fel**, OE. **fell**, *skin, hide*.

§ 19. **i** (Lat. **i**, Gr. ι) remained, as Gr. Hom. ϝίδμεν, Goth. **witum**, O.Icel. **vitum**, OS. **witun**, OHG. **wiʒʒum**, OE. **witon**, *we know*, cp. Lat. **vidēre**, *to see*; Lat. **piscis**, Goth. **fisks**, O.Icel. **fiskr**, OS. **fisk**, OHG. OE. **fisc**, *fish*; Lat. **vidua** (adj. fem.), *bereft of, deprived of*, Goth. **widuwō**, OS. **widowa**, OHG. **wituwa**, OE. **widewe**, *widow*.

§ 20. **o** (Lat. **o**, Gr. ο) became **a** in stem-syllables, as Lat. **octō**, Gr. ὀκτώ, Goth. **ahtáu**, OS. OHG. **ahto**, OE. **eahta** (§ 68), *eight*; Lat. **hostis**, *stranger, enemy*, Goth. **gasts**, OS. OHG. **gast**, OE. **giest** (§ 73), *guest*; Lat. **quod**, Goth. **ƕa**, O.Icel. **hvat**, OS. **hwat**, OHG. **hwaʒ**, OE. **hwæt**, *what*. See § **218**, 1.

§ 21. **u** (Lat. **u**, Gr. υ) remained, as Gr. κυνός (gen. sing.), Goth. **hunds**, O.Icel. **hundr**, OHG. **hunt**, OS. OE. **hund**, *dog, hound*; Gr. θύρā, OS. **duri**, OHG. **turi**, OE. **duru**, *door*; Skr. **bu-budhimá**, *we watched*, Gr. πέ-πυσται, *he has inquired*, Goth. **budum**, O.Icel. **buðum**, OS. **budun**, OHG. **butum**, OE. **budon**, *we announced, offered*.

§ 22. **ə** became **a** in all the Indo-Germanic languages, except in the Aryan branch, where it became **i**, as Lat. **pater**, Gr. πατήρ, O.Ir. **athir**, Goth. **fadar**, O.Icel. **faðer**, OS. **fader**, OHG. **fater**, OE. **fæder**, *father*, Skr. **pitár-** (from ***pətér-**), *father*; Lat. **status**, Gr. στατός, Skr. **sthitás**, *standing*, Goth. **staþs**, O.Icel. **staðr**, OS. **stad**, OHG. **stat**, OE. **stede**, prim. Germanic ***stađiz**, *place*.

§ 23. **ā** (Lat. **ā**, Gr. Doric ᾱ, Attic, Ionic η) became **ō**, as

Lat. **māter**, Gr. Dor. μάτηρ, O.Icel. **mōðer**, OS. **mōdar**, OHG. **muoter**, OE. **mōdor**, *mother*; Gr. Dor. φράτηρ, *member of a clan*, Lat. **frāter**, Goth. **brōþar**, O.Icel. **brōðer**, OS. **brōthar**, OHG. **bruoder**, OE. **brōþor**, *brother*; Lat. **fāgus**, *beech*, Gr. Dor. φᾱγός, *a kind of oak*, Goth. **bōka**, *letter of the alphabet*, O.Icel. OS. **bōk**, *book*, OE. **bōc-trēow**, *beech-tree*.

§ **24**. Indg. **ē** (= Lat. **ē**, Gr. η) remained; it was a long open sound and is generally written **ǣ** (= Goth. **ē**, O.Icel. OS. OHG. **ā**, OE. (WS.) **ǣ**) in works on Germanic philology in order to distinguish it from the long close **ē** which arose in prim. Germanic, see §§ **38**, Note, **125**. It should be noted that the two sounds were kept apart in all the Old Germanic languages except Gothic. Examples of Indg. **ē** are: Lat. **ēdimus**, Goth. **ētum**, O.Icel. **ātum**, OS. **ātun**, OHG. **āʒum**, OE. **ǣton**, *we ate*; Lat. **mēnsis**, Gr. μήν, *month*, Goth. **mēna**, O.Icel. **māne**, OS. OHG. **māno**, OE. **mōna** (§ **121**), *moon*; Goth. **ga-dēþs**, O.Icel. **dāð**, OS. **dād**, OHG. **tāt**, OE. **dǣd**, *deed*, related to Gr. θή-σω, *I shall place*.

§ **25**. **ī** (Lat. **ī**, Gr. ῑ) remained, as Lat. **su-īnus** (adj.), *belonging to a pig*, Goth. **swein**, O.Icel. **svīn**, OS. OHG. OE. **swīn**, *swine*, *pig*; Lat. **sīmus**, OS. **sīn**, OHG. **sīm**, OE. **sī-en**, *we may be*.

§ **26**. **ō** (Lat. **ō**, Gr. ω) remained, as Gr. πλωτός, *swimming*, Goth. **flōdus**, O.Icel. **flōð**, OHG. **fluot**, OS. OE. **flōd**, *flood*, *tide*, cp. Lat. **plōrāre**, *to weep aloud*; Gr. Dor. πώς, Goth. **fōtus**, O.Icel. **fōtr**, OHG. **fuoʒ**, OS. OE. **fōt**, *foot*; Goth. **dōms**, O.Icel. **dōmr**, OHG. **tuom**, OS. OE. **dōm**, *judgment*, *sentence*, related to Gr. θωμός, *heap*.

§ **27**. **ū** (Lat. **ū**, Gr. ῡ) remained, as Lat. **mūs**, Gr. μῦς, O.Icel. OHG. OE. **mūs**, *mouse*; Lat. **sūs**, Gr. ῦς, OHG. OE. **sū**, *sow*, *pig*; Goth. **fūls**, O.Icel. **fūll**, OHG. OE. **fūl**, *foul*, related to Lat. **pūteō**, *I smell bad*, Gr πύθω, *I make to rot*.

§ **28**. **ai** (Lat. **ae**, Gr. *αι*, Goth. **ái**, O.Icel. **ei**, OS. **ē**, OHG. **ei** (**ē**), OE. **ā**) remained, as Lat. **aedēs**, *sanctuary*, originally *fire-place*, *hearth*, Gr. *αἴθω*, *I burn*, OHG. **eit**, OE. **ād**, *funeral pile*, *ignis*, *rogus*; Lat. **aes**, Goth. **áiz**, O.Icel. **eir**, OHG. **ēr**, OE. **ār**, *brass*, *metal*, *money*; Lat. **caedō**, *I hew*, *cut down*, Goth. **skáidan**, OS. **skēdan**, **skēđan**, OHG. **sceidan**, OE. **scādan**, **sceādan** (§ **133**, Note 3), *to divide*, *sever*.

§ **29**. **ei** (Lat. **ī** (older **ei**), Gr. *ει*) became **ī**, as Gr. *στείχω*, *I go*, Goth. **steigan** (**ei** = **ī**), O.Icel. **stīga**, OS. OHG. OE. **stīgan**, *to ascend*; Gr. *λείπω*, *I leave*, Goth. **leiƕan**, OS. OHG. **līhan**, OE. **lēon** from ***līohan**, older ***līhan** (§ **127**), *to lend*; Lat. **dīcō**, *I say*, *tell*, Gr. *δείκνῡμι*, *I show*, Goth. **ga-teihan**, *to tell*, *declare*, OS. **af-tīhan**, *to deny*, OHG. **zīhan**, OE. **tēon**, *to accuse* (§ **127**).

§ **30**. **oi** (O.Lat. **oi** (later **ū**), Gr. *οι*, Goth. **ái**, O.Icel. **ei**, OS. **ē**, OHG. **ei** (**ē**), OE. **ā**) became **ai** (cp. § **20**), as Gr. *οἶδε*, Goth. **wáit**, O.Icel. **veit**, OS. **wēt**, OHG. **weiȥ**, OE. **wāt**, *he knows*; O.Lat. **oinos**, later **ūnus**, Goth. **áins**, O.Icel. **einn**, OS. **ēn**, OHG. **ein**, OE. **ān**, *one*, cp. Gr. *οἰνή*, *the one on dice*; Gr. *πέ-ποιθε*, *he trusts*, Goth. **báiþ**, O.Icel. **beið**, OS. **bēd**, OHG. **beit**, OE. **bād**, *he waited for*.

§ **31**. **au** (Lat. **au**, Gr. *αυ*, Goth. **áu**, O.Icel. **au**, OS. **ō**, OHG. **ou** (**ō**), OE. **ēa**) remained, as Lat. **auris**, Goth. **áusō**, OS. OHG. **ōra**, OE. **ēare**, *ear*; Lat. **augeō**, Gr. *αὐξάνω*, *I increase*, Goth. **áukan**, O.Icel. **auka**, OS. **ōkian**, OHG. **ouhhōn**, OE. **ēacian**, *to add*, *increase*.

§ **32**. **eu** (O.Lat. **ou** (later **ū**), Gr. *ευ*, Goth. **iu**, O.Icel. **jō** (**jū**), OS. OHG. **eo**, later **io**, OE. **ēo**) remained, as Gr. *γεύω*, *I give a taste of*, Goth. **kiusan**, O.Icel. **kjōsa**, OS. OHG. **kiosan**, OE. **cēosan**, *to test*, *choose*; Gr. *πεύθομαι* (see § **230**, 8), *I inquire*, Goth. **ana-biudan**, *to order*, *command*, O.Icel. **bjōða**, OS. **biodan**, OHG. **biotan**, OE. **bēodan**, *to offer*; O.Lat. **doucō**, later **dūcō**, *I lead*, Goth. **tiuhan**, OS. **tiohan**, OHG. **ziohan**, OE. **tēon** (§ **139**), *to* *lead, draw.* Prim. Germanic **eu** was still preserved in old Germanic proper names found in ancient authors, as **Teutomērus, Reudigni**; in the oldest Norse runic inscriptions, as **-leubaR,** *dear*; and in the oldest OE. glosses, as **steupfædær,** later **stēopfæder,** *stepfather.* See § **44.**

§ **33. ou** (O.Lat. **ou** (later **ū**), Gr. *ου*, Skr. **ō,** Goth. **áu,** O.Icel. **au,** OS. **ō,** OHG. **ou** (**ō**), OE. **ēa**) became **au** (cp. § **20**), as prim. Indg. ***roudhos,** Goth. **ráuþs,** O.Icel. **rauðr,** OS. **rōd,** OHG. **rōt,** OE. **rēad,** *red,* cp. Lat. **rūfus,** *red*; prim. Indg. ***bhe-bhoudhe,** Skr. **bu-bṓdha,** *has waked,* Goth. **báuþ,** O.Icel. **bauð,** OS. **bōd,** OHG. **bōt,** OE. **bēad,** *he offered.*

§ **34. m** (Lat. **em,** Gr. *α, αμ*) became **um,** as Gr. *ἀμο-* (in *ἀμόθεν, from some place or other*), Goth. **sums,** O.Icel. **sumr,** OS. OHG. OE. **sum,** *some one*; Gr. *ἑκατόν*, Lat. **centum** (with **n** from **m** by assimilation to the dental, and similarly in the Germanic languages), Goth. OE. OS. **hund,** OHG. **hunt,** *hundred,* all from a prim. form ***kmtóm;** acc. sing. Lat. **pedem,** Gr. *πόδα*, Goth. **fōtu** (§ **211,** I), *foot.*

§ **35. n** (Lat. **en,** Gr. *α, αν*) became **un,** as Lat. **commentus** (pp.), *invented, devised,* Gr. *αὐτό-ματος, acting of one's own will,* Goth. **ga-munds,** OHG. **gi-munt,** OE. **ge-mynd** (§ **112**), *remembrance,* prim. form. ***mntós** (pp.) from root **men-,** *think*; acc. pl. Gr. *πόδας*, Goth. **fōtuns,** *feet*; OS. **wundar,** OHG. **wuntar,** OE. **wundor,** *wonder,* cp. Gr. *ἀθρέω* from **ϝαθρέω*, *I gaze at.*

§ **36. r** (Lat. **or,** Gr. *αρ, ρα*) became **ur, ru,** as OHG. **gi-turrum,** OE. **durron,** *we dare,* cp. Gr. *θαρσύς* (*θρασύς*), *bold, θαρσέω, I am of good courage*; dat. pl. Gr. *πατράσι*, Goth. **fadrum,** OHG. **faterum,** OE. **fæd(e)rum,** *to fathers*; Lat. **porca,** *the ridge between two furrows,* OHG. **furuh,** OE. **furh,** *furrow*; Skr. **va-vrtimá,** *we have turned,* O.Icel. **urðom,** OS. **wurdun,** OHG. **wurtum,** OE. **wurdon,** *we became.*

§ **37.** **l** (Lat. **ol, ul,** Gr. αλ, λα) became **ul, lu,** as Goth. **fulls,** O.Icel. **fullr,** OHG. **vol,** OS. OE. **full,** prim. form ***plnós,** *full*; Goth. **wulfs,** O.Icel. **ulfr,** OHG. **wolf,** OS. OE. **wulf,** prim. form ***wlqʷos,** *wolf*.

Note.—If we summarize the vowel-changes which have been stated in this chapter, it will be seen that the following vowel-sounds fell together:—**a, o,** and **ə**; original **u** and the **u** which arose from Indg. vocalic **l, m, n, r**; **ī** and **ei**; **ā** and **ō**; **ai** and **oi**; **au** and **ou.**

## CHAPTER III

## THE PRIMITIVE GERMANIC VOWEL-SYSTEM

§ **38.** From what has been said in §§ **17–37,** we arrive at the following vowel-system for the prim. Germanic language:—

| | |
|---|---|
| Short vowels | **a, e, i, u** |
| Long ,, | **ǣ, ē, ī, ō, ū** |
| Diphthongs | **ai, au, eu** |

Note.—Besides **ǣ** (= Indg. **ē,** § **24**) prim. Germanic also had a long close **ē** which arose from various sources. The two sounds fell together in Gothic, but were kept apart in all the other languages. Apart from the **ē** in the preterite of a small number of the seventh class of strong verbs (§§ **512–14**), and in a few Latin loanwords, it only occurs in a few words. Its chief sources seem to be:—(*a*) From the Indg. long diphthong **ēi** which regularly stood in ablaut relation to **ī**, as Goth. O.Icel. OS. OE. **hēr,** OHG. **hēr,** later **hear, hiar, hier,** *here*: Goth. **hi-drē,** OE. **hi-der,** *hither*; OE. **cēn,** OHG. **kēn,** later **kean, kian, kien,** *torch*: OE. **cīnan,** *to crack*; OHG. **zēri,** &c., *beautiful*: OS. OE. **tīr,** O.Icel. **tīrr,** *renown, glory, splendour*; OS. **mēda,** OE. **mēd,** OHG. **mēta,** &c., Indg. ***mēizdhā**: Goth. **mizdō,** OE. **meord,** Gr. μισθός, *pay, reward.* (*b*) Latin loanwords, as OE. **bēte,** OHG. **biezza,** Lat. **bēta,** *beetroot*; Goth. **mēs,** OE. **mēse,** OHG. **meas, mias,** vulgar Latin **mēsa,** *table.* (*c*) The pret. of a small number of the seventh class of strong verbs (§§ **512–14**), as O.Icel. OS. OE. **hēt,** OHG. **hiaz,** beside Goth. **haíhait,** *he called*; O.Icel. OS. OE. **lēt,** OHG.

**liaʒ**, beside Goth. **laílōt**, *he let*. For a comprehensive article on the subject, see Feist, Paul-Braune's *Beiträge zur Geschichte der deutschen Sprache und Literatur*, vol. xxxii, p. 447 ff.

§ **39**. This system underwent several modifications during the prim. Germanic period, i. e. before the parent language became differentiated into the various separate Germanic languages. The most important of these changes were :—

§ **40**. **a** + **ŋχ** became **āχ**, as Goth. OS. OHG. **fāhan**, O.Icel. **fā**, OE. **fōn** (§ **139**), from ***faŋχanan**, *to catch, seize*, cp. Lat. **pangō**, *I fasten*; Goth. **þāhta**, OS. **thāhta**, OHG. **dāhta**, OE. **þōhte** (inf. **þencan**), from older ***þaŋχta**, ***þaŋχtō-**, *I thought*, cp. O.Lat. **tongeō**, *I know*. Every prim. Germanic **ā** in accented syllables was of this origin. Cp. § **23**.

Note.—The **ā** in the above and similar examples was still a nasalized vowel in prim. Germanic, as is seen by its development to **ō** in OE. The **ī** (§ **41**) and **ū** (§ **43**) were also nasalized vowels in prim. Germanic. According to Professor Björkman in *Herrig's Archiv*, vol. cxxv p. 189 these prim. Germanic nasalized vowels have been preserved in some Scandinavian dialects down to the present day.

§ **41**. **e** became **i** under the following circumstances :—

1. Before a nasal + consonant, as Goth. OS. OE. **bindan**, O.Icel. **binda**, OHG. **bintan**, *to bind*, cp. Lat. **of-fendimentum**, *chin-cloth*, **of-fendix**, *knot, band*, Gr. *πενθερός*, *father-in-law*; Lat. **ventus**, Goth. **winds**, O.Icel. **vindr**, OHG. **wint**, OS. OE. **wind**, *wind*; Gr. *πέντε*, Goth. **fimf**, O.Icel. **fim(m)**, OHG. **fimf**, **finf**, OE. **fīf** (§ **97**), *five*; and similarly in early Lat. loanwords, as OE. **minte**, OHG. **minza**, Lat. **menta**, **mentha**, *mint*; OE. **gimm**, OHG. **gimma**, Lat. **gemma**, *gem*. This explains why OE. **bindan**, *to bind*, and **helpan**, *to help*, belong to the same ablaut-series. See § **226**.

This **i** became **ī** under the same conditions as those

by which **a** became **ā** (§ **40**), as Goth. **þeihan,** OS. **thīhan,** OHG. **dīhan,** OE. **þēon** (§ **127**), from ***þiŋχanan,** older ***þeŋχanan,** *to thrive*; and similarly OHG. **sīhan,** OE. **sēon,** *to strain*; OHG. **fīhala,** OE. **fēol,** *file*; OHG. **dīhsala,** OE. **þīxl** (**þīsl**), *wagon-pole, shaft.* The result of this sound-law was the reason why verbs of the type ***þiŋχanan** passed from the third to the first class of strong verbs (§ **492**) in the prehistoric period of all the Germanic languages, cp. the isolated pp. OS. **gi-thungan,** OE. **ge-þungen,** *full-grown.*

2. When followed by an **i, ī,** or **j** in the next syllable, as Goth. OS. OHG. **ist,** OE. **is,** from ***isti,** older ***esti** = Gr. ἔστι, *is*; OHG. **irdīn,** *earthen,* beside **erda,** *earth*; Goth. **midjis,** O.Icel. **miðr,** OS. **middi,** OHG. **mitti,** OE. **midd,** Lat. **medius,** from an original form ***medhjos,** *middle*; OS. **birid,** OHG. **birit,** *he bears,* from an original form ***bhéreti,** through the intermediate stages ***ƀéređi, *ƀériđi, *ƀíriđi,** beside inf. **beran**; O.Icel. **sitja,** OS. **sittian,** OHG. **sizzen,** OE. **sittan,** from an original form ***sedjonom,** *to sit*; and similarly O.Icel. **liggja,** OS. **liggian,** OHG. **liggen,** OE. **licgan,** *to lie down.*

This sound-law accounts for the difference in the stem-vowels of such pairs as OE. **feld** (OHG. **feld**), *field*: **gefilde** (OHG. **gifildi**), *a plain*; **feþer,** *feather*: **fiþere,** *wing*; **weder** (OHG. **wetar**), *weather*: **gewider** (OHG. **giwitiri**), *storm*; **heord** (OHG. **herta**), *herd*: **hierde** (OHG. **hirti**), *shepherd*; **helpan,** *to help*: **hilpst, hilpþ** (OHG. **hilfis, hilfit**); **beran,** *to bear*: **bir(e)st, bir(e)þ** (OHG. **biris, birit**), and similarly in the second and third person singular of the present indicative of many other strong verbs; pp. **legen, seten**: inf. **licgan,** *to lie down,* **sittan,** *to sit.*

3. In unaccented syllables, except in the combination **-er** when not followed by an **i** in the next syllable, as OE. **fēt,** older **fœ̄t,** from ***fōtiz,** older ***fōtes,** *feet,* cp. Gr. πόδες,

*feet.* Indg. **e** remained in unaccented syllables in the combination **-er** when not followed by an **i** in the next syllable, as acc. OS. **fader,** OHG. **fater,** OE. **fæder,** Gr. *πατέρα, father*; OE. **hwæþer,** Gr. *πότερος, which of two.*

§ **42.** **i,** followed originally by an **ă, ŏ,** or **ē** in the next syllable, became **e** when not protected by a nasal + consonant or an intervening **i** or **j,** as O.Icel. **verr,** OS. OHG. OE. **wer,** Lat. **vir,** from an original form ***wiros,** *man*; OHG. OE. **nest,** Lat. **nīdus,** from an original form ***nizdos.** In historic times, however, this law has a great number of exceptions owing to the separate languages having levelled out in various directions, as OE. **spec** beside **spic,** *bacon*; OHG. **lebara** beside OE. **lifer,** *liver*; OHG. **leccōn** beside OE. **liccian,** *to lick*; OHG. **lebēn** beside OE. **libban,** *to live*; OHG. **quec** beside OE. **cwic,** *quick, alive.*

§ **43.** **u,** followed originally by an **ă, ŏ, ē,** or the combination **-eno-** (cp. §§ **218,** 2, **483**) in the next syllable, became **o** when not protected by a nasal + consonant or an intervening **i** or **j,** as OS. **dohter,** OHG. **tohter,** OE. **dohtor,** Gr. *θυγάτηρ, daughter*; O.Icel. **ok,** OHG. **joh,** OE. **geoc** (§ **110**), Gr. *ζυγόν, yoke*; OHG. **got,** OS. OE. **god,** from an original form ***ghutóm,** *god*; OHG. OE. **gold,** *gold,* beside OHG. **guldīn,** OE. **gylden,** *golden*; pp. OS. **giholpan,** OHG. **giholfan,** OE. **geholpen,** *helped,* beside pp. OS. **gibundan,** OHG. **gibuntan,** OE. **gebunden,** *bound*; pp. OS. **gibodan,** OHG. **gibotan,** OE. **geboden,** *offered,* beside pret. pl. OS. **budun,** OHG. **butum,** OE. **budon,** *we offered.* Every prim. Germanic **o** in accented syllables was of this origin. Cp. § **20.**

This sound-law accounts for the difference in the stem-vowels of such pairs as OE. **cnotta,** *knot*: **cnyttan** from ***knuttjan,** *to tie*; **coss,** *a kiss*: **cyssan,** *to kiss*; **corn,** *corn*: **cyrnel,** *kernel*; **fox**: **fyxen,** *she-fox*; **god**: **gyden** (OHG. **gutin**), *goddess*; **hold,** *gracious*: **hyldo** (OHG.

**huldī**), *grace, favour*; pret. **bohte, worhte**: inf. **bycgan,** *to buy,* **wyrcan,** *to work.* It was best preserved in OHG. In O.Icel. OS. and OE. we often find **u** where we should expect **o**. The **u** in these cases was partly due to levelling out in various directions and partly to the influence of neighbouring sounds, especially an **f, w, m,** or **n** (see §§ **108–9**), as O.Icel. **fullr,** OS. OE. **full,** beside OHG. **fol,** *full*; O.Icel. **ull,** OE. **wull(e)**, beside OHG. **wolla,** *wool*; O.Icel. **numenn,** OS. **ginuman,** OE. **numen,** beside O.Icel. **nomenn,** OHG. **ginoman,** *taken*; O.Icel. **hunang,** OE. **hunig,** beside OS. **honeg,** OHG. **honang,** *honey.*

**u** became **ū** under the same conditions as those by which **a** and **i** became **ā** and **ī**, as pret. third pers. singular Goth. **þūhta,** OS. **thūhta,** OHG. **dūhta,** OE. **þūhte,** beside inf. Goth. **þugkjan,** OS. **thunkian,** OHG. **dunken,** OE. **þyncan,** *to seem*; Goth. **ūhtwō,** OS. OHG. OE. **ūhta,** *daybreak, dawn*; OHG. **fūhti,** OE. **fūht,** *damp.*

§ **44.** The diphthong **eu** became **iu** when the next syllable originally contained an **i, ī,** or **j**, cp. § **41** (2), but remained **eu** when the next syllable originally contained an **ă, ŏ,** or **ē** (cp. § **32**). The **iu** remained in Goth. OS. and OHG., but became **jū** (**ȳ** by **i**-umlaut) in O.Icel., and **īo** (**īe** by **i**-umlaut) in OE., as Goth. **liuhtjan,** OS. **liuhtian,** OHG. **liuhten,** OE. **līehtan,** *to give light*: OE. **lēoht,** *a light*; O.Icel. **dȳpt,** OS. **diupi,** OHG. **tiufī,** OE. **dīepe,** *depth*: OE. **dēop,** *deep*; OS. **liudi,** OHG. **liuti,** OE. **līode,** *people*; OS. **kiusid,** OHG. **kiusit,** O.Icel. **kȳs(s)**, OE. **cīesþ,** *he chooses*: OE. **cēosan,** *to choose.* See § **138.**

§ **45.** From what has been said in §§ **40–4,** it will be seen that the prim. Germanic vowel-system had assumed the following shape before the Germanic parent language became differentiated into the various separate languages:—

| | | |
|---|---|---|
| Short vowels | **a, e,** | **i, o, u** |
| Long ,, | **ā, ǣ, ē,** | **ī, ō, ū** |
| Diphthongs | **ai, au,** | **eu, iu** |

The following table contains the normal development of the above vowel-system in Goth. O.Icel. OS. OHG. and OE. stem-syllables :—

| P. Germ. | Goth. | O.Icel. | OS. | OHG. | OE. |
|---|---|---|---|---|---|
| **a** | **a** | **a** | **a** | **a** | **æ** |
| **e** | **i** | **e** | **e** | **e** | **e** |
| **i** | **i** | **i** | **i** | **i** | **i** |
| **o** | **u** | **o** | **o** | **o** | **o** |
| **u** | **u** | **u** | **u** | **u** | **u** |
| **ā** | **ā** | **ā** | **ā** | **ā** | **ō** |
| **ǣ** | **ē** | **ā** | **ā** | **ā** | **ǣ** |
| **ē** | **ē** | **ē** | **ē** | **ia, (ie)** | **ē** |
| **ī** | **ei** | **ī** | **ī** | **ī** | **ī** |
| **ō** | **ō** | **ō** | **ō** | **uo** | **ō** |
| **ū** | **ū** | **ū** | **ū** | **ū** | **ū** |
| **ai** | **ái** | **ei** | **ē** | **ei** | **ā** |
| **au** | **áu** | **au** | **ō** | **ou** | **ēa** |
| **eu** | **iu** | **jō** | **eo, (io)** | **eo, (io)** | **ēo** |
| **iu** | **iu** | **jū** | **iu** | **iu** | **īo** |

Note.—The table does not include the sound-changes which were caused by umlaut, the influence of neighbouring

**consonants**, &c. For **details** of **this kind** the student should consult the grammars of the separate languages. But as we shall have occasion to make use of many Gothic, OS. and OHG. forms in this grammar, the following points should be noted here :—

1. Goth. **i** and **u** were broken to **aí** (= short open **e**) and **aú** (= short open **o**) before **r**, **h**, and **ƕ**, as **baíran**, OE. **beran**, *to bear*; **saíƕan**, OHG. **sehan**, *to see*; **baíriþ**, OHG. **birit**, *he bears*; **saíƕiþ**, OHG. **sihit**, *he sees*; pp. **baúrans**, OE. **boren**, *borne*; **daúhtar**, OE. **dohtor**, *daughter*; **waúrms**, OHG. **wurm**, *serpent, worm*; **sauhts**, OHG. **suht**, *sickness*. Gothic **ei** was a monophthong and was pronounced like the ī in the other Germanic languages. Germanic **ai** and **au** remained in Gothic, but they are generally written **ái** and **áu** in order to distinguish **them** from the short vowels **aí** and **aú**.

2. **a** was the only vowel which underwent **i**-umlaut in OS. and OHG., as sing. **gast**, pl. **gesti** = Goth. **gasteis**, *guests*; OS. **sendian**, OHG. **senten** = Goth. **sandjan**, *to send.* When it is necessary for phonological reasons to distinguish between this **e** and Germanic **e**, the latter is written **ë** in this book, as **bëran**, *to bear.*

3. Prim. Germanic **ai** became **ē** in OHG. before **r**, **w**, and old **h**, as **ēr**, *before* = **Goth**. **áir**, *soon*; **ēht** = Goth. **áihts**, *possession*; gen. **snēwes**, **Goth**. nom. **snáiws**, *snow.*

4. **Prim. Germanic au** became **ō** in OHG. before the consonants **d**, **t**, **ʒ**, **s**, **n**, **r**, **l**, and old **h**, as **tōd** = Goth. **dáuþus**, *death*; **kōs** = Goth. **káus**, *he chose*; **hōh** = Goth. **háuhs**, *high.*

# CHAPTER IV

## THE OLD ENGLISH DEVELOPMENT OF THE PRIM. GERMANIC VOWELS OF ACCENTED SYLLABLES

§ **46**. Before entering upon the history of the separate Germanic vowels in OE. it will be well to state and illustrate here several phenomena which concern the OE.

vowels in general. For the chronological order in which the sound-changes took place see § **53** and Note.

### I. Umlaut (Mutation).

§ **47**. Umlaut is of two kinds: Palatal and Guttural. Palatal umlaut, generally called **i**-umlaut, is the modification (palatalization or fronting) of an accented vowel through the influence of an **ĭ** or **j** which originally stood in the following syllable. This process took place in prehistoric OE.—probably in the sixth century—and the **ĭ** or **j** had for the most part already disappeared in the oldest OE. records. The **i**, which remained, mostly became **e** at an early period (§ **215**, Note), so that for the proper understanding of the forms which underwent **i**-umlaut it is necessary to compare them with the corresponding forms of some other Germanic language, especially with the Gothic. The result of **i**-umlaut is generally the fronting of guttural (back) vowels, as **a** to **e**, **u** to **y**. It rarely consists in the raising of front vowels, as in **æ** to **e**, **ĕa** to **ĭe**. The simple vowels and diphthongs which underwent **i**-umlaut in OE. are: **a(o)**, **æ**, **o**, **u**; **ā**, **ō**, **ū**; **ea**, **io**; **ēa** and **īo**.

**a(o)** > **e** (but **æ** in the oldest period), as **benc** from ***baŋkiz**, *bench*; **ende**, Goth. **andeis**, *end*; **lengra**, OHG. **lengiro**, *longer*; **lengþ(u)** from ***laŋgiþu**, *length*; pl. **menn**, prim. Germanic ***manniz**: sing. **mann**, *man*; **sendan**, Goth. **sandjan**, *to send* (§ **60**).

**æ** > **e**, as **bedd**, Goth. **badi**, *bed*; **bet(e)ra**, Goth. **batiza**, *better*; **hebban**, Goth. **hafjan**, *to raise*; **here**, Goth. **harjis**, *army*; **lecgan**, Goth. **lagjan**, *to lay* (§ **55**).

**o** > **e** (older **œ**), as dat. **dehter** from ***dohtri**, beside nom. **dohtor**, *daughter*; **ele**, Lat. **oleum**, *oil*; **exen**, *oxen*, beside **oxa**, *ox* (§ **107**).

**u** > **y**, as **bycgan**, Goth. **bugjan**, *to buy*; **cyning**, OHG. **kuning**, *king*; **cynn**, Goth. **kuni**, *race, generation*; **gylden**,

OHG. **guldīn,** *golden*; **þyncan,** Goth. **þugkjan,** *to seem* (§ **112**).

**ā** > **ǣ,** as **dǣlan,** Goth. **dáiljan,** *to divide*; **ǣnig,** *any*: **ān,** *one*; **hǣlan,** Goth. **háiljan,** *to heal*; **hǣþ,** Goth. **háiþi,** *heath* (§ **134**); **lǣwan** from ***lāwjan,** Goth. **lēwjan,** *to betray* (§ **120**).

**ō** > **ē** (older **œ̄**), as **bēc** from ***bōkiz,** *books*; **dēman,** Goth. **dōmjan,** *to judge*; **fēt,** OHG. **fuozzi,** *feet*; **sēcan,** Goth. **sōkjan,** *to seek* (§ **129**). **wēnan** from ***wōnjan,** older ***wǣnjan,** Goth. **wēnjan,** *to hope*; **cwēn** from ***kwōni-,** older ***kwǣniz,** Goth. **qēns,** *queen, wife* (§ **122**). **ēhtan** from ***ōhtjan,** *to persecute*; **fēhþ,** *he seizes,* beside inf. **fōn** (§ **118**). **ēst** from ***ōsti-,** older ***anstiz,** Goth. **ansts,** *favour*; **tēþ,** prim. Germanic ***tanþiz,** *teeth* (§ **62**).

**ū** > **ȳ,** as **mȳs** from ***mūsiz,** *mice*; **brȳcst** from ***brūkis,** *thou enjoyest,* **brȳcþ** from ***brūkiþ,** *he enjoys,* beside inf. **brūcan** (§ **132**). **cȳ** from ***kū-iz,** *cows* (§ **130**). **cȳþan** from ***kūþjan,** older ***kunþjan,** *to make known*; **dȳstig,** *dusty* (§ **114**).

**ea** > **ie** (later **i, y**), as **fiellan** from ***fealljan,** older ***falljan,** *to fell*; **ieldra,** Goth. **alþiza,** *older* (§ **65**). **ierfe,** Goth. **arbi,** *inheritance*; **iermþu,** OHG. **armida,** *poverty* (§ **67**). **scieppan,** Goth. **skapjan,** *to create* (§ **73**). **hliehhan,** Goth. **hlahjan,** *to laugh*; **wiexþ,** OHG. **wahsit,** *it grows* (§ **69**).

**io** > **ie** (later **i, y**), as **hierde,** OHG. **hirti,** *shepherd*; **ierre,** OHG. **irri,** *angry*; **siehst,** OHG. **sihis,** *thou seest*; **siehþ,** OHG. **sihit,** *he sees*; **wiersa,** OHG. **wirsiro,** *worse* (§ **99**).

**ēa** > **īe** (later **ī, ȳ**), as **gelīefan,** Goth. **galáubjan,** *to believe*; **hīehsta,** Goth. **háuhista,** *highest*; **hīeran,** Goth. **háusjan,** *to hear* (§ **136**). **cīese,** Lat. **cāseus,** *cheese*; **nīehsta** from ***nēahista,** *nearest* (§ **123**). **stīele,** Germanic stem-form ***staχlja-,** *steel* (§ 71). **wīelisc,** prim. Germanic ***walχiskaz,** *foreign* (§ **64**, Note 1).

**īo > īe** (later **ī, ȳ**), as **cīesþ** from ***kīosiþ**, older ***kiusiþ**, *he chooses*; **tīehþ** from ***tīohiþ**, *he draws*; **līehtan**, Goth. **liuhtjan**, *to give light* (§ **138**). **līehtan** from ***liōhtjan**, older ***līχtjan**, *to lighten, make easier*; **līehþ** from ***līohiþ**, OHG. **līhit**, *he lends* (§ **127**). **frīend**, prim. Germanic ***frijōndiz**, *friends* (§ **104**).

§ **48.** Guttural umlaut is the modification of an accented vowel (**a, e, i**) through the influence of a primitive OE. guttural vowel (**u, ŏ, a**) in the next syllable, whereby a guttural glide was developed after the vowels **a, e, i**, which then combined with them to form the diphthongs **ea, eo, io**. This sound-change took place about the end of the seventh century. As a rule umlaut only took place before a single consonant. When the vowel which caused umlaut was **u**, it is called **u**-umlaut, and when **ŏ**, or **a**, it is called **o/a**-umlaut.

**u**- and **o/a**-umlaut of **a** only took place in Mercian, as **featu**, *vats*, **heafuc**, *hawk*, **steapul**, *pillar*, **steaþul**, *foundation*, beside **fatu, hafoc, stapol, staþol** in the other dialects. **fearan**, *to go*, **fearaþ**, *they go*, **feata**, *of vats*, beside **faran, faraþ, fata** in the other dialects. See § **78.**

**u**-umlaut of **e** and **i**, and **o/a**-umlaut of **i** took place in Ken. before all single consonants, in Anglian before all single consonants except gutturals (**c, g**), but in WS. only before labials and liquids, as **eofor** (OHG. **ebur**), *boar*; **heol(o)stor** from older **helustr**, *hiding place*; **heorut**, *hart*. **meodu**, *mead* (*drink*), **eosol**, *donkey* = WS. **medu, esol**. Ken. **breogo**, *prince* = WS. and Anglian **brego**, see § **92**. **mioluc**, *milk*; **cliopung**, *calling*. **siodu**, *custom*, **sionu**, *sinew* = WS. **sidu, sinu**. Ken. **siocol**, *sickle*, **stiogol**, *stile* = WS. and Anglian **sicol, stigol**, see § **101**. **liofast**, *thou livest*. **nioma(n)**, *to take*, **niomaþ**, *they take*, **wiotan**, *to know* = WS. **niman, nimaþ, witan**. Ken. **stiocian** from ***stikōjan**, *to prick* = WS. and Anglian **stician**, see §§ **92–3, 102**.

**o/a**-umlaut of **e** did not take place in WS. In Ken. it took place before all single consonants and in Anglian before all single consonants except gutturals, as **beoran,** *to bear,* **eotan,** *to eat,* **feola,** *many* = WS. **beran, etan, fela.** Ken. **weogas,** *ways,* **spreocan,** *to speak* = WS. and Anglian **wegas, spreca**(n), see § **93.**

## 2. Breaking (Fracture).

§ **49.** Breaking is due to the influence of an **l, r,** or **h** + consonant, or single **h,** upon a preceding vowel (Germanic **a, e, i; ǣ, ī**) whereby a guttural glide was developed between the vowel and the consonant, which then combined with the vowel to form a diphthong. For the reason why breaking took place before **l** and **r** + consonant more regularly in WS. and Ken. than in Anglian, see § **7.** In the examples given below we shall confine ourselves chiefly to WS.

**a** (**æ**) > **ea,** as **ceald,** Goth. **kalds,** *cold*; **healdan,** Goth. **haldan,** *to hold* (§ **64**); **bearn,** Goth. **barn,** *child*; **heard,** Goth. **hardus,** *hard* (§ **66**); **eahta,** Goth. **ahtáu,** *eight*; **weaxan,** Goth. **wahsjan,** *to grow*; **seah,** OHG. **sah,** *he saw* (§ **68**).

**e** > **eo,** as **meolcan,** OHG. **melkan,** *to milk*; **sceolh,** OHG. **scelh,** *wry, oblique* (§ **84**); **eorþe,** OHG. **erda,** *earth*; **heorte,** OHG. **herza,** *heart* (§ **85**); **cneoht,** OHG. **kneht,** *boy*; **seox,** OHG. **sehs,** *six*; **seoh,** *see thou* (§ **86**).

**i** > **io** (later **eo**), as **liornian, leornian,** from ***lirnōjan,** *to learn*; **miox, meox,** from ***mihst,** *manure* (§ **98**).

**ǣ** > **ēa** in WS. before **h,** as **nēah,** Goth. **nēƕ,** *near*; **nēar** from ***nēahur,** older ***nǣhur,** *nearer* (§ **123**).

**ī** > **īo** (later **ēo**) in WS. before **h** and **ht,** as **lēoht,** Goth. **leihts,** adj. *light*; **wēoh,** *idol,* Goth. **weihs,** *holy* (§ **127**).

### 3. Influence of Nasals.

§ **50.** **a** became a low-back-wide vowel, written **a, o,** before nasals, as **camb, comb,** *comb*; **nama, noma,** *name*; **land, lond,** *land*; **lang, long,** *long* (§ **59**).

**e** > **i** before Germanic **m** (§ **81**), and in early Latin loanwords before nasal + consonant (§ **82**), as **niman,** OHG. **neman,** *to take*; **gimm,** Lat. **gemma,** *gem*; **pinsian,** Lat. **pensāre,** *to weigh, ponder, consider.*

**o** > **u** before nasals, as **guma,** OHG **gomo,** *man*; **numen,** OHG. **ginoman,** *taken*; **hunig,** OHG. **honag,** *honey*; **þunor,** OHG. **donar,** *thunder* (§ **109**).

Before nasals Germanic **ǣ** > **ō** (§ **121**) through the intermediate stage **ā,** as **mōna,** Goth. **mēna,** *moon*; **nōmon,** Goth. **nēmun,** *they took.*

Nasals disappeared before the voiceless spirants **f, þ,** and **s** with lengthening of the preceding vowel, as **fīf,** OHG. **fimf,** *five*; **ōsle,** OHG. **amsala,** *ousel* (§ **283**); **cūþ,** Goth. **kunþs,** *known*; **gōs,** OHG. **gans,** *goose*; **ōþer,** Goth. **anþar,** *other* (§ **286**).

### 4. Influence of Initial Palatal Consonants.

§ **51.** Between initial palatal **c** (§ **309**), **g** (= Germanic **ʒ**, § **313**), **g** (= Germanic **j**, § **268**), **sc** (§ **312**), and the following palatal vowel, a glide was developed in prim. OE., which combined with the vowel to form a rising diphthong, and then at a later period the rising diphthong became a falling diphthong through the shifting of the stress from the second to the first element of the diphthong. The examples given below are chiefly WS.; for the corresponding forms in the other dialects, the student should consult the paragraphs within brackets.

**æ** > **ea** (older **eǽ**), as **ceaster,** Lat. **castra,** *city, fortress*; **ceaf,** *chaff*; **geaf,** Goth. **gaf,** *he gave*; **sceaft,** OHG. **scaft,** *shaft*; **sceal,** Goth. **skal,** *shall* (§ **72**).

e > ie (older ié), as **cieres,** Lat. acc. **cerasum,** *cherry-tree*; **giefan,** OHG. **geban,** *to give*; **scieran,** OHG. **sceran,** *to shear* (§ **91**).

**ǣ** > **ēa** (older **eǽ**), as **cēace,** prim. Germanic ***kǣkōn,** *jaw*; **gēafon,** Goth. **gēbun,** *they gave*; **gēar,** Goth. **jēr,** *year*; **scēap,** Goth. ***skēp,** *sheep* (§ **124**).

Note.—In forms like **gioc, geoc** (OHG. **joh**), *yoke* (§ **110**); **giong, geong** (OHG. **jung**), *young* (§ **116**); **geōmor** (OHG. **jāmar**), *sad* (§ **121,** Note), the **io, eo, eō** may have been rising diphthongs, but it is difficult to determine how far they were diphthongs at all, and how far the **i, e** were merely inserted to indicate the palatal nature of the **g** = Germanic **j** (§ **268**). It is highly probable that in forms like **sceacan,** *to shake,* **sceadu,** *shadow,* beside **scacan, scadu** (§ **57,** Note), **sceolde,** OHG. **scolta,** *should* (§ **110**), **sceādan** beside **scādan,** *to divide* (§ **133,** Note 2), the **e** was merely inserted to indicate the palatal nature of the **sc** (§ **312**).

### 5. Influence of w.

§ **52.** **e** and **ē** (= Germanic **ǣ**) were often rounded to **œ** and **œ̄** after **w** in Nth., as **cuœþa,** WS. **cweþan,** *to say* (§ **80,** Note 1); **cuœlla,** WS. **cwellan,** *to kill*; **tuœlf,** WS. **twelf,** *twelve* (§ **55,** Note 1). **huœ̄r,** *where,* **wœ̄ron,** *were* = WS. **hwǣr, wǣron** (§ **119,** Note 3).

**e** became **eo** before **w** + a following vowel, as gen. **cneowes, treowes,** beside nom **cnēo,** *knee,* **trēo,** *tree* (§ **89**); **eowestre** (cp. Goth. **awistr**), *sheepfold*; **meowle** (Goth. **mawilō**), *maiden* (§ **77**).

**ǣ** became **ā** before **w,** as **blāwan** from ***blǣwan,** *to blow*; **cnāwan,** *to know*; **sāwon,** *they saw* (§ **120**).

Initial **weo-** became **wu-** (rarely **wo-**) in late WS., as **swurd,** *sword,* **swuster,** *sister,* **worold, woruld,** *world,* beside older **sweord** (OHG. **swert**), **sweostor** (OHG. **swester**), **weorold** (OHG. **weralt**), see § **94.**

Initial **wio-** became **wu-** in WS. and Anglian, but

remained in Ken., as **wudu,** *wood,* beside Ken. **wiodu** (§ **103**).

**y,** of whatever origin, became **u** in late WS. in the initial combination **wyr**+consonant, as **wurm** from older **wyrm,** *worm*; **wursa** from older **wyrsa,** still older **wiersa,** *worse.* And then **wyr**+consonant sometimes came to be written for older **wur**+consonant, as **cwyrn,** older **cwiorn, cweorn,** *hand-mill*; **swyrd,** *sword*; **swyster,** *sister.*

§ **53.** The following was the chronological order in which the sound-laws stated in §§ **47–52** took place: (1) The influence of nasals. (2) Breaking. (3) The influence of initial palatal consonants. (4) **i**-umlaut. (5) **u**-, **o/a**-umlaut. (6) Influence of **w.**

Note.—In the case of words where diphthongization by preceding palatals and **u**-, **o/a**-umlaut concur, the latter has the predominance, as **geolo,** *yellow*; **geoloca,** *yolk*; **ceole** (acc. **ceolan,** § **403**), *throat.* This does not however prove that **u**-, **o/a**-umlaut chronologically precedes diphthongization by preceding palatals. Either **geolo,** &c., are not pure WS. forms (see § **92**) or else the **ie** became **eo** by umlaut, in which case forms like **giefu** (§ **365**) would have **ie** from the oblique cases.

## A. The Short Vowels of Accented Syllables.

### a

§ **54.** Apart from the influence of neighbouring sounds the normal development of Germanic **a** (= Goth. O.Icel. OS. OHG. **a**) is **æ** in OE.

Examples in closed syllables are: **dæg,** Goth. **dags,** O.Icel. **dagr,** OS. **dag,** OHG. **tag,** *day*; **þæt,** Goth. **þata,** O.Icel. **þat,** OS. **that,** OHG. **daʒ,** *the*; and similarly **bæc,** *back*; **bæþ,** *bath*; **blæc,** *black*; **bræs,** *brass*; **cræft,** *skill*; **dæl,** *dale*; **æfter,** *after*; **æt** (unstressed **ot**), *at*; **fæst,** *fast, firm*; **fæt,** *vat, vessel*; **glæd,** *glad*; **glæs,** *glass*; **græs** (**gærs**), *grass*; **hæfde,** *he had*; **hwæl,** *whale*; **hwæt,** *what,*

**pæþ**, *path*; **sægde**, *he said*; **smæl**, *small*; **stæf**, *staff*; in the pret. sing. of strong verbs belonging to classes IV (§ **503**) and V (§ **505**), as **bær** (Goth. O.Icel. OS. OHG. **bar**), *bore*; **bræc**, *broke*; **cwæþ**, *said*; **sæt**, *sat*; **wæs**, *was*. On forms like **æppel**, *apple*, beside pl. **appla**, see § **57**.

Examples in open syllables when followed by a palatal vowel, or a vocalic nasal or liquid in the next syllable, are: **æcer** (Goth. **akrs**), *field*, *acre*; **æcern**, *acorn*; **fæder**, *father*; **fæger** (Goth. **fagrs**), *fair*, *beautiful*; **hlædel**, *ladle*; **hræfen**, **hræfn**, *raven*; **hwæþer**, *whether*; **mægen** (Goth. ***magn**), *power*; **nægel**, **nægl** (Goth. ***nagls**), *nail*; **wæter**, *water*; **fæþm** (Goth. ***faþms**), *embrace*, *fathom*; **hægl**, *hail*; **snægl**, *snail*; **tægl**, *tail*; **wægn**, *wagon*; sing. gen. **dæges**, **fætes**, dat. **dæge**, **fæte**, beside nom. **dæg**, *day*; **fæt**, *vat*.

NOTE.—1. **æ** became **e** in Ken. and partly also in Mercian, as **deg**, **feder**, **fet**, **hefde**, **set**, **wes**, **weter** = WS. **dæg**, **fæder**, &c. This **e** is still a characteristic feature of the modern Ken. dialects.

2. **æ** became **ǣ** by loss of **g** (§ **321**), as **brǣd**, *he brandished*; **mǣden**, *maiden*; **sǣde**, *he said*; **wǣn**, *wagon*, beside **brægd**, **mægden** (§ **58**), **sægde**, **wægn** of the non-WS. dialects.

3. **a** often occurs where we should expect **æ**. In such cases the **a** is due to levelling and new formations, as sing. gen. **paþes**, dat. **paþe**, beside **pæþes**, **pæþe**, due to the plural forms **paþas**, **paþa**, **paþum** (§ **336**); fem. gen. dat. acc. singular **sace**, **swaþe**, beside **sæce**, **swæþe**, due to nom. singular **sacu**, *strife*, *quarrel*; **swaþu**, *track*; and plural **saca**, **swaþa**, &c. (§ **366**); masc. gen. sing. **glades**, beside nom. **glæd**, *glad*, due to forms like dat. sing. and plural **gladum** (§ **424**); imperative of strong verbs belonging to class VI (§ **508**), as **far**, **sac**, due to the influence of the infinitive **faran**, *to go*, *travel*; **sacan**, *to quarrel*; and similarly in the pp. **faren**; **grafen**, *dug*; **hladen**, *loaded*, beside **græfen**, **hlæden** (cp. § **508**). On the analogy of such past participles was formed **slagen** beside **slægen**, *slain*.

§ **55**. **æ** became **e** by i-umlaut, as **bedd**, Goth. **badi**, OHG. **betti**, *bed*; **bet(e)ra**, Goth. **batiza**, *better*; **hebban**,

Goth. **hafjan**, OS. **heffian**, *to raise*; **here**, Goth. **harjis**, OS. OHG. **heri**, *army*; **lecgan**, Goth. **lagjan**, OS. **leggian**, *to lay*; and similarly **bere**, *barley*; **bet** from ***batiz**, *better*; **cwellan** (wv.), *to kill*; **ege**, *awe, fear*; **elles**, *else*; **hege**, *hedge*; **hell** (Goth. **halja**), *hell*; **herian**, *to praise*; **hete**, *hate*; **mere**, *lake*; **mete**, *meat, food*; **nerian**, *to save*; **nett**, *net*; **secgan**, *to say*; **sellan**, *to sell*; **settan**, *to set*; **stede**, *place*; **swerian**, *to swear*; **tellan**, *to count*; **twelf** (Goth. **twalif**), *twelve*; **webb**, *web*; **weccan**, *to awake*. But **stæpe** beside **stepe**, *step*.

NOTE.—1. In Nth. **e** was often rounded to **œ** after **w**, as **cuœlla**, *to kill*; **tuœlf**, *twelve*.

2. The regular forms of the second and third pers. singular of the pres. indicative of strong verbs belonging to class VI (§ **508**) would have **e**, as in OHG. **feris**, *thou goest*; **ferit**, *he goes*, but in OE. the **a** of the other forms of the present was extended to the second and third pers. singular, and then **a** became **æ** by **i**-umlaut, as **færest**, **færeþ**.

3. It is difficult to account satisfactorily for the absence of umlaut in **læccan**, *to seize*; **pæþþan**, *to traverse*; **sæcc**, *strife*; **wæcce**, *vigil*; and for **gemæcca**, *mate*; **hæcc**, *gate, hatch*; **mæcg**, *man, warrior*; **stæppan**, *to step*; **wræcca** (OS. **wrekkio**), *exile*, beside the umlauted forms **gemecca**, **mecg**, **steppan**, **wrecca**. For an attempt to explain such forms see Bülbring, *Altenglisches Elementarbuch*, § 177.

§ **56**. Umlaut generally did not take place before Germanic consonant combinations, as **dwæscan**, *to extinguish*; **æsc** from ***askiz**, *ash-tree*; **æspe**, *aspen*; **fæsten**, *to fasten*; **hæftan**, *to hold captive*; **mæstan**, *to fatten*; **næglan**, *to nail*; **ræscan**, *to coruscate*. But umlaut occurs in **eft**, *again*; **esne**, *servant*; **rest**, *rest*; **restan**, *to rest*; and in **efnan**, *to perform*; **stefnan**, *to regulate*, beside **æfnan**, **stæfnan**.

§ **57**. Germanic **a** remained in open syllables when originally followed by a guttural vowel (**ă**, **ŏ**, **ŭ**) in the next syllable, as pl. nom. acc. **dagas**, gen. **daga**, dat.

**dagum,** beside sing. nom. **dæg,** *day,* gen. **dæges,** dat. **dæge;** neut. nom. acc. plural **baþu,** *baths*; **bladu,** *leaves*; **fatu,** *vats,* beside singular **bæþ, blæd, fæt;** OE. Goth. OS. OHG. **faran,** O.Icel. **fara,** *to go, travel*; **nacod,** Goth. **naqaþs,** OHG. **nackot,** *naked*; and similarly **alan,** *to nourish*; **apa,** *ape*; **bacan,** *to bake*; **calan,** *to be cold*; **caru,** *care*; **cradol,** *cradle*; **dragan,** *to draw*; pres. subj. **fare** (Goth. **farái**), *he may travel*; **gaderian** from ***ʒađu·rōjan,** *to gather*; **galan,** *to sing*; **gnagan,** *to gnaw*; **grafan,** *to dig*; **hafoc,** *hawk*; **hafola, hafela,** *head*; **hagol,** *hail*; **hagu,** *enclosure*; **hara,** *hare*; **hladan,** *to load*; **hraþor,** *more quickly*; **lagu,** *law*; **latost,** *latest, slowest*; **laþaþ,** *he invites*; **laþode,** *he invited*; **macaþ,** *he makes*; **macode,** *he made*; **magu,** *boy*; **nafula, nafela,** *navel*; **racu,** *narrative*; **sacan,** *to quarrel*; **sacu,** *strife*; **sadol,** *saddle*; **stapol,** *pillar*; **staþelian** from ***staþulōjan,** *to establish*; **talu,** *statement*; **wadan,** *to go, wade.* **macian** from ***makōjan,** *to make*; and similarly in the inf. of other weak verbs belonging to class II (§ **535**), as **baþian,** *to bathe*; **dagian,** *to dawn*; **gladian,** *to be glad*; **hatian,** *to hate*; **laþian,** *to invite.*

It also remained in closed syllables before double consonants (except **hh, ll, rr**), **sc,** and **st,** when the next syllable originally contained a guttural vowel, as **abbod** (Lat. acc. **abbātem**), *abbot*; **assa,** *donkey*; **catte** (OHG. **kazza**), *cat*; **cassuc,** *sedge*; **gaffetung,** *scoffing*; **habban** (§ **538**), *to have*; **hassuc,** *coarse grass*; **maffa,** *caul*; **mattoc,** *mattock*; **sacc,** *sack*; **þaccian,** *to flap, pat*; **flasce** (**flaxe**), *flask*; **masc** (**max**), *net*; **wascan** (**waxan**), *to wash*; **brastlian,** *to crackle.* But a few words have **æ** beside **a,** as **æsce,** *ash, cinders*; **æppel,** *apple*; **hnæppian,** *to doze*; **læppa,** *lappet,* beside **asce** (**axe**), **appla,** *apples,* **hnappian, lappa.**

Note.—**sca·** was often written **scea·** with **e** to denote the palatal pronunciation of the **sc,** as **sceacan,** *to shake*; **sceadu,** *shadow*; **sceafan,** *to shave*; **scealu,** *scale* (*balance*); **sceamu** (**sceomu,** § 59), *shame*, beside **scacan, scadu, scafan, scalu, scamu** (**scomu**). See § 51, Note.

§ 58. **a** became **æ** when followed by an umlauted vowel in the next syllable, as **æces** (**æx**) from ***akysi,** older ***akusi-,** *axe*; and similarly **æþele** from ***aþali** (OS. **ađali**), *noble*; **æþeling** from ***aþuling,** *nobleman*; **æt-, tō-gædere** from ***-ȝađuri,** *together*; **fæsten** (OS. **fastunnia,** *fasting*), *fortress*; **gædeling** (OS. **gaduling**), *companion*; **hæleþ** from ***χaluþi-,** *hero*; **hærfest** from ***χarubist,** *harvest*; **mægden** from ***maȝađīn** (OHG. **magatīn**), *maiden*. The **æ** in the above examples is sometimes called the secondary umlaut of **a.**

Note.—The **a** in the stem-syllable of the present participle and gerund of strong verbs belonging to class VI (§ 508) is due to the **a** of the infinitive, as **farende** for ***færende** from ***farandi, farenne** for ***færenne** from ***farannjai.**

§ 59. Germanic **a** was probably a mid-back-wide vowel like the **a** in German **Mann.** In OE. it became a low-back-wide vowel before nasals like the **â** in French **pâte,** and the **a** as pronounced in many Scotch dialects in such words as **ant, man, pass,** which English people often mistake for **o** especially when lengthened. In the oldest OE. it was nearly always written **a,** in the ninth century it was mostly written **o,** and in late OE. mostly **a** again, but in some parts of Mercia it seems to have become **o** which has been preserved in many of the Midland dialects down to the present day. Examples are: **gangan, gongan,** Goth. **gaggan,** O.Icel. **ganga,** OS. OHG. **gangan,** *to go*; **hana, hona,** Goth. **hana,** O.Icel. **hane,** OS. OHG. **hano,** *cock*; **lang, long,** Goth. **laggs,** O.Icel. **langr,** OS. OHG. **lang,** *long*; **nama, noma,** Goth. **namō,** OS. OHG. **namo,** *name*; and similarly **ancor** (Lat. **ancora**), *anchor*; **bana,** *slayer*; **brand,** *firebrand*; **camb,** *comb*; **camp,** *battle*; **candel** (Lat. **candēla**), *candle*; **cann,** *he can*; **fana,** *banner*;

**gandra,** *gander*; **gesamnian,** *to collect*; **hamor,** *hammer*; **hand,** *hand*; **lama,** *lame*; **lamb,** *lamb*; **land,** *land*; **manig** (Goth. **manags**), *many*; **mann,** *man*; **ramm,** *ram*; **spannan,** *to clasp, fasten*; **standan,** *to stand*; **strang,** *strong*; **þanc,** *thought*; **þwang,** *thong*; in the pret. singular of many strong verbs of class III (§ **498**), as **begann,** *began*; **dranc,** *drank*; **fand,** *found*; **sang,** *sang*; **swamm,** *swam*; with metathesis of **r** in **born** from older **bronn, brann** (Goth. **brann**), *burned*; **orn** from older **ronn, rann** (Goth. **rann**), *ran.*

Note.—The **a** became **o** in unstressed adverbial and pronominal forms, as **hwonne,** *when*; **on,** *on*; **þonne,** *then*; masc. acc. singular **hwone,** *whom*; **þone,** *the.*

§ **60.** **a** (**o**) became **e** (but **æ** in the oldest period) by **i**-umlaut, as **ende,** Goth. **andeis,** O.Icel. **ende,** OS. **endi,** OHG. **enti,** stem **andja-,** *end*; **lengra,** OS. **lengira,** OHG. **lengiro,** *longer*; **sendan,** Goth. **sandjan,** OS. **sendian,** *to send*; and similarly **benc** from ***baŋkiz,** *bench*; **cemban,** *to comb*; **cempa,** *warrior*; **drencan,** *to give to drink*; **ened,** *duck*; **enge,** *narrow*; **englisc,** *English*; **fremman,** *to perform*; **henn,** *hen*; **lengþ,** *length*; **menn,** *men*; **mengan,** *to mix*; **mennisc,** *human*; **nemnan,** *to name*; **pening,** *penny*; **strengra,** *stronger*; **þencan,** *to think*; **wendan,** *to turn.* **bærnan** (Goth. **brannjan**), *to burn*; **ærnan** (Goth. **rannjan**), *to run, gallop,* with metathesis of **r** and preservation of the older stage of umlaut.

§ **61.** Nasals disappeared before the voiceless spirants, **f, þ, s,** and the preceding **a** (**o**) became **ō** through the intermediate stage of a long nasalized vowel (cp. § **40**), as **hōs,** Goth. OHG. **hansa,** *band, escort, multitude*; **ōþer,** Goth. **anþar,** *second, other*; **sōfte,** OHG. **samfto,** *gently, softly*; and similarly **gōs,** *goose*; **ōs-,** *god*; **ōsle** (OHG. **amsala**), *blackbird*; **smōþe,** *smoothly*; **sōþ,** *true*; **tōþ,** *tooth*; **þrōstle,** *thrush, throstle*; **wōs,** *moisture.*

§ **62.** **ō** became **ē** (older **œ̄**) by **i**-umlaut, as **ēst.** Goth.

**ansts,** stem-form **ansti-,** *favour*; **nēþan,** Goth. **ana-nanþjan,** *to venture on*; **tēþ** from ***tanþiz,** *teeth*; and similarly **fēþe,** *walking, movement*; **gēs,** *geese*; **gesēþan,** *to testify, declare*; **sēfte,** *soft*; **smēþe,** *smooth.*

§ **63.** **a** was broken to **ea** before **l, r,** and **h** + consonant, and before simple **h.** Forms without breaking often occur in the oldest period of the language. Breaking did not take place in Anglian before **l** + consonant, and frequently not before **r** + consonant. See **l, r** (§ 7).

§ **64.** 1. Before **l** + consonant.

**eall,** Goth. **alls,** O.Icel. **allr,** OS. OHG. **al,** *all*; **ceald,** Goth. **kalds,** O.Icel. **kaldr,** OS. **kald,** OHG. **kalt,** *cold*; **healdan,** Goth. OS. **haldan,** O.Icel. **halda,** OHG. **haltan,** *to hold*; and similarly **cealc,** *chalk*; **cealf,** *calf*; **dealf,** *he dug*; **eald,** *old*; **ealh,** *temple*; **fealdan,** *to fold*; **feallan,** *to fall*; **gealga,** *gallows*; **healf,** *half*; **heall,** *hall*; **healp,** *he helped*; **heals,** *neck*; **mealt,** *malt*; **sealf,** *salve, ointment*; **sealfian,** *to anoint*; **sealh,** *willow*; **sealt,** *salt*; **tealde,** *he told*; **wealdan,** *to wield*; **wealh,** *foreigner, Welshman*; **weall,** *wall*; **weallan,** *to boil.* Forms like **bealu,** *bale, evil*; **fealu,** *fallow*; **sealu,** *dark, dusky,* beside **balu, falu, salu,** have the **ea** from the inflected stem-form, as gen. **bealwes, fealwes, sealwes** (see § **265**).

NOTE.—1. **ea** became **ēa** by loss of **h** (§ **329,** 3) before a following vowel, as gen. singular **sēales, wēales,** nom. pl. **sēalas, wēalas,** beside nom. singular **sealh, wealh. ēa** became **īe** by i-umlaut, as **wīelisc,** *foreign, Welsh.*

2. **a** remained unbroken in late Latin loanwords, as **albe** (Lat. **alba**), *alb*; **alter** (Lat. **altāre**), *altar*; **fals** (Lat. **falsus**), *false*; **palm** (Lat. **palma**), *palm-tree.*

§ **65.** **ea** became **ie** (later **i, y**) by **i**-umlaut, as **fiellan** from ***fealljan,** older ***falljan,** *to fell*; **fielst** from ***feallis(t),** *thou fallest*; **fielþ** from ***fealliþ,** *he falls*; **ieldra** (Goth. **alþiza**), *older*; **ieldesta,** *oldest*; **ieldu,** *old age*; **mieltan** (wv.), *to melt.*

NOTE.—The corresponding vowel in Anglian is **æ** (also **e**), as **ældra, eldra, ældu, fælla**(n), **fella**(n); and also in Ken. **æ** (later **e**), as **ældra, ældu** later **eldra, eldu**.

§ **66.** 2. Before **r** + consonant.

**bearn,** Goth. O.Icel. OS. OHG. **barn,** *child*; **heard,** Goth. **hardus,** O. Icel. **harðr,** OS. **hard,** OHG. **hart,** *hard*; and similarly **beard,** *beard*; **bearg,** *pig*; **bearm,** *bosom*; **cearf,** *he carved*; **dearr,** *I dare*; **earc** (Lat. **arca**), *ark*; **earm,** *arm*; **earm,** *poor*; **eart,** *thou art*; **fearh,** *boar, pig*; **geard,** *yard*; **gearn,** *yarn*; **gearwian,** *to prepare*; **ge-mearcian,** *to mark*; **hearg,** *heathen temple*; **hearm,** *harm*; **mearc,** *boundary*; **mearg,** *marrow*; **mearh,** *horse*; **pearroc,** *park*; **scearp,** *sharp*; **swearm,** *swarm*; **wearm,** *warm*; **wearp,** *he threw*; **wearþ,** *he became.* Forms like **bearu,** *grove*; **gearu,** *ready*; **mearu,** *tender*; **nearu,** *narrow*; **searu,** *plot, device,* have **ea** from the inflected stem-form, as gen. **bearwes, gearwes, mearwes,** &c. (see § **265**).

NOTE.—1. In Anglian **ea** became **æ** (later **e**) before **r** + guttural, as **berg, erc, færh** (**ferh**), **mærc** (**merc**), &c.

2. **eo** was often written for **ea** in Nth., especially in S. Nth., as **eorm, heord** = WS. **earm, heard.**

3. **a** remained unbroken in late Latin loanwords, as **carcern,** *prison*; **martyr,** *martyr.*

4. **ea** became **ēa** by loss of **h** (§ **329,** 3) before a following vowel, as gen. singular **fēares, mēares,** nom. pl. **fēaras, mēaras,** beside nom. singular **fearh, mearh.**

5. Forms like **ærn** (Goth. **razn**), *house*; pret. sing. **arn** (Goth. **rann**), *ran*; **barn** (Goth. **brann**), *burned*; **bærst** (OHG. **brast**), *burst*; **gærs** (Goth. **gras**), *grass*; **hærn,** *wave,* are due to a late metathesis of the **r.**

§ **67.** **ea** became **ie** (later **i, y**) by **i**-umlaut, as **dierne,** OS. **derni,** OHG. **tarni,** *secret*; **ierfe,** Goth. **arbi,** OS. OHG. **erbi,** *inheritance*; and similarly **cierran,** *to turn*; **gierd,** *rod, twig*; **gierwan** from ***gearwjan,** *to prepare*;

**ierming,** *pauper*; **iermþu** (OHG. **armida**), *poverty*; **wierman,** *to warm*.

Note.—The corresponding vowel in the non-WS. dialects is **e**, as **derne, erfe, ermþu,** &c.

§ **68.** 3. Before **h** + consonant (also **x** = **hs**) and simple **h. eahta,** Goth. **ahtau,** OS. OHG. **ahto,** *eight*; **seah,** Goth. **saƕ,** OS. OHG. **sah,** *he saw*; **weaxan,** Goth. **wahsjan,** O.Icel. **vaxa,** OS. OHG. **wahsan,** *to grow*; and similarly **eax,** *axle-tree*; **eaxl,** *shoulder*; **feaht,** *he fought*; **feax,** *hair*; **fleax,** *flax*; **gefeah,** *he rejoiced*; **geneahhe,** *enough, often*; **hleahtor,** *laughter*; **meaht** (later **miht**), *power, might*; **meaht,** *thou mayest*; **meahte,** *he might, could*; **neaht** (later **niht**), *night*; **seax,** *knife*; **sleah** (imperative), *slay thou*; **weax,** *wax*.

Note.—1. **ea** became **æ** in Anglian, as **æhta, fæx, hlæhtor, sæh, wæx,** &c.

2. It became **e** in late WS., as **ehta, exl, fex, seh, sex, sleh, wexan.**

§ **69. ea** became **ie** (later **i, y**) by **i**-umlaut, as **hliehhan** (Goth. **hlahjan**), *to laugh*; **mieht** (Goth. **mahts,** stem-form **mahti-**), *power, might*; **miehtig,** *mighty*; **nieht,** *night*; **sliehst** (Goth. **slahis**), *thou slayest*; **sliehþ** (Goth. **slahit**), *he slays*; **slieht,** stem-form **slahti-,** *slaughter*; **wiexþ** (OHG. **wahsit**), *it grows*.

Note.—The corresponding vowel in Anglian is **æ** (also **e**), as **hlæhha(n), mæht** (**meht**), **mæhtig** (**mehtig**); and in Ken. **æ** (later **e**), as **mæht,** later **meht.**

§ **70. ea** became **ēa** by loss of intervocalic **h** (§ **329,** 4), as **ēa,** Goth. **aƕa,** OS. OHG. **aha,** *water, river*; **slēan** from ***sleahan,** Goth. OS. OHG. **slahan,** *to slay, strike*; and similarly **flēan,** *to flay*; **lēa** from ***leahu,** *I blame*; **lēan,** *to blame*; **slēa,** *I slay*; **slēaþ** from ***sleahaþ,** *they slay*; **þwēan,** *to wash*; **ēar** (Nth. **æhher**) from ***eahur,** older ***ahur**, OHG. **ahir**, *ear of corn*; **tēar** (Nth. **tæhher**) from ***teahur**, older ***tahur**, OHG. **zahar**, *tear*.

§ **71**. **ēa** became **īe** (later **ī, ȳ**) by **i**-umlaut, as **stīele** from ***stēali** (cp. § **329**, 2), older ***steahli**, Germanic stem-form ***staχlja-**, *steel*.

§ **72**. **æ** (older **a**) became **ea** (older **eǽ**) after initial palatal **c, g,** and **sc**, as **ceaf**, *chaff*; **ceafor**, *cockchafer*; **ceaster** (Lat. **castra**), *city, fortress*; **forgeat** (OS. **forgat**), *he forgot*; **geaf** (Goth. **gaf**), *he gave*; **geat** (O.Icel. OS. **gat**), *gate, opening, hole*; **sceaft** (OHG. **scaft**), *shaft*; **sceal** (Goth. **skal**), *I shall*; **sceatt** (Goth. **skatts**), *money, property*.

Note.—1. Anglian has **æ** beside **ea**, and Ken. **e** (**æ**), as Anglian **cæster** (**ceaster**), **gæt** (**geat**), **scæl** (**sceal**) = Ken. **cester, get, scel**. **e** also occurs occasionally in Mercian.

2. Forms like **ceald**, *cold*; **cealf**, *calf*; **geard**, *yard*; **gearn**, *yarn*; **scealt**, *thou shalt*; **scearp**, *sharp*, are due to breaking (§§ **64**, **66**), which took place earlier than the influence of palatals upon a following **æ**. In both cases the **ea** became **e** in late WS., as **celf, gef, get**, &c.

§ **73**. **ea** became **ie** (later **i, y**) by **i**-umlaut, as **ciefes** from ***kaƀisō**, *concubine*; **ciele** from ***kaliz**, *cold*; **cietel** (Lat. **catillus**), *kettle*; **giest** (Goth. **gasts**, stem-form **gasti-**), *guest*; **scieppan** (Goth. **skapjan**), *to create*.

Note.—The corresponding vowel in the non-WS. dialects is **e**, as **cefes, cele, gest, sceppan**, &c.

§ **74**. Germanic **a** generally remained before the **w** which was regularly preserved in OE., as gen. dat. singular **clawe** beside nom. **clēa**, *claw*; **awul, awel**, *awl*; **þawian**, *to thaw*.

§ **75**. **a** + **u** (which arose from **wu** or vocalized **w** (§ **265**)) became **ēa** (cp. § **135**), as **clēa** from ***kla(w)u**, *claw*; nom. acc. pl. neuter **fēa** from ***fa(w)u**, *few*; dat. **fēam** from ***fa(w)um**; whence pl. masc. **fēawe** for ***fawe** formed from **fēa, fēam**; **hrēa** from ***hraw-**, *raw*; **strēa** from ***straw-**, *straw*; **þrēa** from ***þra(w)u**, *threat*.

§ **76.** Prim. Germanic **aww** (= Goth. **aggw**) became **auw** in West Germanic, which regularly became **ēaw** in OE. (cp. § **135**), as **dēaw** (Goth. ***daggwa-**, OHG. **tou**, gen. **touwes**), *dew*; **glēaw** (Goth. **glaggwu-ba**, *diligently*), *wise*; **hēawan** (Goth. ***haggwan**, OHG. **houwan**), *to hew*; **scēawian** (Goth. ***skaggwōn**, OHG. **scouwōn**), *to examine, view.*

§ **77.** **a** became **e** by **i**-umlaut, then at a later period the **e** became **eo** before **w**, as **ewe** beside **eowe, eowu** (cp. Lat. **ovis**), *ewe*; **eowde**, *flock, herd*; **eowestre** (cp. Goth. **awistr**), *sheepfold*; **meowle** (Goth. **mawilō**), *girl*; **strewede** beside **streowede** (Goth. **strawida**), *he strewed.*

§ **78.** In Mercian **a** became **ea** before single consonants by **u**- and **o/a**-umlaut, as **ealu**, *ale*; **beadu**, *battle*; **eafora**, *son*; **featu**, *vats*; **heafuc**, *hawk*; **heafola**, *head*; **heaþu**, *war*; **steapul**, *pillar*; **steaþul**, *foundation.* **fearan**, *to go, travel*; **fearaþ**, *they travel*; gen. pl. **feata**, *of vats*; **geata**, *of gates*; **gleadian**, *to rejoice*; **hleadan**, *to load*; **leatian**, *to be slow.* For the corresponding non-Mercian forms, see § **57.**

NOTE.—1. The **ea** became **æ** before gutturals, as **dægas** (= WS. **dagas**), *days*; **dræca**, *dragon*; **mægun**, *they can.*

2. Umlaut rarely took place before double consonants, as **eappultūn** (WS. **æppeltūn**), *orchard*; **hneappian** (WS. **hnappian**), *to doze.*

3. WS. **ealu**, and forms like **eafora**, **heafoc**, &c., which are common in poetry, are all originally from the Mercian dialect.

§ **79.** Final **a** was lengthened to **ā** in monosyllables, as **hwā** (Goth. **ƕas**), *who*; **swā** (Goth. **swa**), *so.*

### e

§ **80.** Germanic **e** (= Goth. **i**, but **aí** before **r**, **h**, and **ƕ**, O.Icel. OS. OHG. **e**) often remained in OE., as OE. OS. OHG. **feld**, *field*; **feþer**, OS. **fethara**, OHG. **fedara**, *feather*; **weg**, Goth. **wigs**, O.Icel. **vegr**, OS. OHG. **weg**, *way*; and similarly **bes(e)ma**, *besom*; **cwene** (Goth. **qinō**, OHG. **quena**), *woman*; **denu**, *valley*; **ef(e)n**, *even*; **fela**, *much*; **fell**, *skin*; **fetor**, *fetter*; **helm**, *helmet*; **leþer**, *leather*; **nefa**, *nephew*; **nest**, *nest*; **reg(e)n**, *rain*; **segl**, *sail*; **seldan**, *seldom*; **senep**, *mustard*; **setl**, *seat*; **snegl**, *snail*; **snell**, *quick*; **þegn**, *thane*; **weder**, *weather*; **wel** (adv.), *well*; **wer**, *man*; **west**, *west*; in the present of strong verbs belonging to classes III (§ **499**), IV (§ **503**), and V (§ **505**), as **helpan**, Goth. **hilpan**, OS. **helpan**, OHG. **helfan**, *to help*; and similarly **belgan**, *to swell with anger*; **bellan**, *to bellow*; **delfan**, *to dig*; **meltan**, *to melt*; **swellan**, *to swell*; **sweltan**, *to die*; **beran**, *to bear*; **brecan**, *to break*; **helan**, *to conceal*; **stelan**, *to steal*; **teran**, *to tear*; **cnedan**, *to knead*; **cweþan**, *to say*; **etan**, *to eat*; **fretan**, *to devour*; **lesan**, *to collect*; **metan**, *to measure*; **sprecan**, *to speak*; **tredan**, *to tread*; **wefan**, *to weave*; **wesan**, *to be*.

Note.—1. In Nth. **e** was often rounded to **œ** after **w**, as **cuœþa**, **wœl**, **wœg** = WS. **cweþan**, **wel**, **weg**.

2. **e** became **ē** by loss of **g** (§ **321**), as **brēdan**, *to brandish*; **rēn**, *rain*; **strēdan**, *to strew*; **þēn**, *thane*, beside **bregdan**, **regn**, **stregdan**, **þegn** of the non-WS. dialects.

§ **81**. **e** became **i** before Germanic **m**, as **niman** (OHG. **neman**), *to take*; **rima**, *rim*. This sound-change did not take place when the **m** arose from **f** by assimilation with **n**, as **emn**, *even*; **stemn**, *voice*, beside older **ef(e)n**, **stefn** (§ **293**, Note).

§ **82**. **e** became **i** before nasal + consonant in early Latin loanwords, but remained in later loanwords, as **gimm** (Lat. **gemma**), *gem*; **minte** (Lat. **mentha**), *mint*; **pinsian** (Lat. **pensāre**), *to consider*; but **templ** (Lat. **templum**), *temple*.

§ **83**. **e** was broken to **eo** before **lc**, **lh**, before **r** and **h** + consonant, and before simple **h**. Breaking did not take place in Anglian before **lc**, **lh**.

§ **84.** 1. Before **lc, lh.**

**āseolcan,** *to become languid*; **eolh** (OHG. **elaho**), *elk*; **meolcan** (OHG. **melkan**), *to milk*; **seolh** (OHG. **selah**), *seal*; **sceolh** (OHG. **scelh, scelah**), *wry, oblique*. But Anglian **elh, melca(n), selh,** &c.

NOTE.—1. **eo** became **ēo** by loss of **h** (§ **329,** 3) before a following vowel, as **fēolan** from ***feolhan** (= Goth. **filhan,** OHG. **bifelhan**), *to hide*; gen. **ēoles, sēoles,** beside nom. **eolh, seolh.**

2. It is difficult to account for the breaking in Angl. and early Ken. **seolf,** *self*, beside early WS. and late Ken. **self,** late WS. **sylf, silf.**

§ **85.** 2. Before **r** + consonant.

**eorþe,** Goth. **aírþa,** OS. **erđa,** OHG. **erda,** *earth*; **heorte,** Goth. **haírtō,** OS. **herta,** OHG. **herza,** *heart*; **weorþan,** Goth. **waírþan,** O.Icel. **verða,** OS. **werđan,** OHG. **werdan,** *to become*; and similarly **beorcan,** *to bark*; **beorg,** *hill*; **beorgan,** *to shelter*; **beorht,** *bright*; **ceorfan,** *to cut, carve*; **ceorl,** *churl*; **deorc,** *dark*; **dweorg,** *dwarf*; **eorl,** *nobleman, earl*; **feorh,** *life*; **feorr,** *far*; **georn,** *eager*; **heord,** *herd, flock*; **heorþ,** *hearth*; **steorfan,** *to die*; **steorra,** *star*; **sweord,** *sword*; **weorc,** *work*; **weorpan,** *to throw*; **weorþ,** *worth.*

NOTE.—1. Breaking is older than the metathesis of **r** in forms like **berstan** (OHG. **brestan**), *to burst*; **fersc,** *fresh*; **þerscan,** *to thrash.*

2. The **eo** became **e** in Anglian before **r** + guttural, as **berga(n), berht, derc, dwerg, ferh, werc** = WS. **beorgan, beorht,** &c.

3. **ea** was often written for **eo** in Nth., especially in n. Nth., and the **eo** became **io** in Ken. (cp. § **137**), as Nth. **earþe, hearte, stearra** = Ken. **iorþe, hiorte, stiorra** = WS. and Mercian **eorþe, heorte, steorra.**

4. **eo** became **ēo** by loss of **h** (§ **329,** 3) before a following vowel, as gen. **fēores, þwēores,** beside nom. **feorh,** *life*; **þweorh,** *perverse, across.*

§ **86.** 3. Before **h** + consonant (also **x** = **hs**) and simple **h**. **cneoht** (OHG. **kneht**), *boy*; **eoh,** *horse*; **feoh,** *cattle*; **feohtan** (OHG. **fehtan**), *to fight*; **Peohtas,** *Picts*; **pleoh,** *danger*; **reoht** (Goth. **raíhts,** OS. OHG. **reht**), *right*; **seox** (Goth. **saíhs,** OS. OHG. **sehs**), *six*; imperative sing. **seoh,** *see thou*. The **eo,** before **h** + dental and **x** (= **hs**), when not followed by a guttural vowel, became **ie** at an earlier period in WS. and Ken.—before the time of Alfred —and then later the **ie** became **i** (rarely **y**), as **cneoht, cnieht, cniht,** *boy*; **reoht, rieht, riht** (**ryht**), *right*; **seox, siex, six,** *six*; **Pihtisc,** *Pictish*; but regularly **cneohtas,** *boys*; **Peohtas,** *Picts*; **feohtan,** *to fight*. Then levelling out often took place in both directions, whence **cnihtas, Pihtas** beside the regular forms **cneohtas, Peohtas**; and **cneoht,** beside the regular form **cniht.**

NOTE.—**eo** became **e** in Anglian, as **cneht, feh, fehta(n), reht, sex** = early WS. **cneoht, feoh,** &c.

§ **87.** **eo** became **ēo** (**īo**) by loss of intervocalic **h** (§ **329,** 4), as **sēon** (**sīon**) from ***seohan,** older ***sehan** = Goth. **saíƕan,** OS. OHG. **sehan,** *to see*; **swēor** from ***sweohur,** older ***swehur** = OHG. **swehur,** *father-in-law*; and similarly **gefēon,** *to rejoice*; **gefēo** from ***gefeohu,** *I rejoice*; **plēon,** *to risk*; **sēo** from ***seohu,** *I see*; gen. singular **fēos, plēos,** beside nom. **feoh,** *cattle*; **pleoh,** *danger*.

§ **88.** Final **ew** became **eu,** and then **eu** became **ēo** at the same time as Germanic **eu** became **ēo** (see § **137**), as sing. nom. **cnēo,** Germanic stem-form ***knewa-,** *knee*; **trēo,** *tree*; **þēo,** *slave, servant*. See § **265.**

§ **89.** Antevocalic **ew** became **eow,** as sing. gen. **cneowes, treowes, þeowes,** dat. **cneowe, treowe, þeowe**; **þeowian** (**þiowian**), *to serve*. Forms like nom. **cnēow, trēow, þēow** had the **w** from the inflected forms. And conversely forms like gen. **cnēowes, trēowes, þēowes** had **ēo** from the uninflected forms.

§ **90.** Prim. Germanic **eww** (= Goth. **iggw**) became **euw** in West Germanic, and then **euw** became **ēow** in OE. (cp. § **137**), as **trēow** (OS. **treuwa,** OHG. **triuwa**), *trust, faith,* cp. Goth. **triggwa,** *covenant.*

Prim. Germanic **ewwj** became **īowj** through the intermediate stages **iwwj, iuwj** (cp. § **138**), and then **īowj** became **īew(e)** in WS. and **īow(e), ēow(e)** in non-WS., as WS. **getrīewe,** non-WS. **getrīowe, getrēowe** (OHG. **gitriuwi**), prim. Germanic ***-trewwjaz,** cp. Goth. **triggws,** *true, faithful*; WS. **getrīewan,** non-WS. **getrīowan, getrēowan,** prim. Germanic ***-trewwjan,** *to trust.* And similarly West Germanic **iwwj** (§ **254**) from prim. Germanic **ewj,** as WS. **hīew, hīw,** non-WS. **hīow, hēow,** prim. Germanic stem-form ***χewja-,** *shape, colour*; WS. **nīewe, nīwe,** non-WS. **nīowe, nēowe,** prim. Germanic stem-form ***newja-,** *new.*

§ **91. e** became **ie** (later **i, y**) after palatal **c, g,** and **sc** in WS., but remained **e** in Anglian and Ken., as **cieres, cires** (Lat. acc. **cerasum**), *cherry-tree*; **forgietan** (OS. **forgetan**), *to forget*; **giefan** (O.Icel. **gefa,** OS. **geƀan,** OHG. **geban**), *to give*; **giefu,** *gift*; **gieldan,** *to yield*; **giellan,** *to yell*; **gielpan,** *to boast*; **giest** (cp. OHG. **jesan,** *to ferment*), *yeast*; **scield,** *shield*; **scieran** (OHG. **sceran**), *to shear.* But Anglian and Ken. **gefa(n), gelda(n), sceld,** &c.

Note.—The above sound-change took place later than breaking, cp. **ceorfan, ceorl, georn,** § **85.**

§ **92. e** became **eo** by **u**-umlaut in Ken. before all single consonants, in Anglian before all single consonants except gutturals (**c, g**), and in WS. before single labials and liquids, as **beofor,** *beaver*; **eofor** (OHG. **ebur**), *boar*; **geoloca,** *yolk*; **geolo** (OS. OHG. **gelo,** gen. **gelwes**), *yellow*; **heofon,** *heaven*; **heolor,** *scales, balance*; **heolfor** from ***heolofr, *helufr,** *blood*; **heolstor** from older **helustr,** *hiding place*; **heorut,** *hart*; Anglian **leolc** from ***leoluc,** *he played*; **meolu** (OHG. **melo,** gen. **mel(a)wes**), *meal, flour*; **seofon,** *seven*; **smeoru,** *grease, fat*; **teoru,** *tar*; **weorod,** *troop*. Non-WS. **eodor**, *enclosure*; **eosol**, *donkey*; **feotor**, *fetter*; **meodu**, *mead* (*drink*); **meotod**, *creator* = WS. **edor**, **esol**, **fetor**, **medu**, **metod**. Ken. **breogo**, *prince*; **reogol** (Lat. **regula**), *rule* = WS. and Anglian **brego**, **regol**.

NOTE.—1. **u**-umlaut took place in WS. in the combination **we**, as **hweogol**, *wheel*; **sweotol**, *plain*, *clear*; **weotuma**, *dowry*, and probably also before two consonants in **sweostor**, *sister*.

2. The regular forms due to **u**-umlaut were often obliterated in WS. by levelling, as **melu**, *meal*, *flour*, with **mel-** from the gen. **melwes**, dat. **melwe**; pl. nom. **speru**, *spears*; dat. **sperum**, due to the forms of the singular, as **spere**, gen. **speres**, gen. pl. **spera**; and similarly for many other forms.

§ **93**. **e** became **eo** by **o**/**u**-umlaut in Ken. before all single consonants, and in Anglian (but Nth. generally **ea**) before all single consonants except gutturals (**c**, **g**), as **beoran**, *to bear*; **eotan**, *to eat*; **feola**, *many*; **meotan**, *to measure*; **seofa**, *heart*; **steolan**, *to steal*; **treodan**, *to tread*; **weofan**, *to weave* = WS. **beran**, **etan**, **fela**, **metan**, **sefa**, **stelan**, **tredan**, **wefan**. But Ken. **weogas**, *ways*; **spreocan**, *to speak* = WS. and Anglian **wegas**, **sprecan**. Nth. **beara**, **eata**, **treada** = WS. **beran**, **etan**, **tredan**.

§ **94**. The combination **weo-** which arose from breaking (§§ **84-6**), or from **u-**, **o**/**a**-umlaut (§§ **92-3**), became **wu-** (rarely **wo-**) in late WS., and **wo-** in late Nth., but remained in Mercian and Ken., as late WS. **swurd** (later **swyrd**, see § **52**), *sword*; **swuster** (later **swyster**, see § **52**), *sister*; **swutol**, *plain*, *clear*; **wurpan** beside **worpan**, *to throw*; **wurþ**, *worth*, *price*; **wurþan**, *to become*; but **worc**, *work*; **woruld**, **worold**, *world*. Late Nth. **sword**, *sword*; **worþ**, *worth*; **worþa**, *to become*; **worold**, *world*; **wosa** from older **weosa** = WS. **wesan**, *to be*.

§ **95**. Final **e** was lengthened to **ē** in monosyllables, as **hē**, *he*; **mē**, *me*; **sē** (masc. nom. sing.), *the*; **wē**, *we*; **þē**, relative particle (§ **468**).

i

§ **96.** Germanic **i** (= Goth. O.Icel. OS. OHG. **i**) generally remained in OE., as **biddan,** Goth. **bidjan,** O.Icel. **biðja,** OS. **biddian,** OHG. **bitten,** *to pray, beg, entreat*; **fisc,** Goth. **fisks,** O.Icel. **fiskr,** OS. **fisk,** OHG. **fisc,** *fish*; **witan,** Goth. OS. **witan,** O.Icel. **vita,** OHG. **wiȝȝan,** *to know*; and similarly **bit(t)er,** *bitter*; **blind,** *blind*; **bridd,** *young bird*; **bringan,** *to bring*; **cild,** *child*; **cinn,** *chin*; **clif,** *cliff*; **cribb,** *crib*; **cwide,** *saying*; **disc,** *dish*; **finger,** *finger*; **gefilde** (sb.), *plain*; **gift,** *price of wife*; **hider,** *hither*; **hild,** *battle, war*; **hind** (sb.), *hind*; **hlid,** *lid*; **hring,** *ring*; **licgan,** *to lie down*; **libban,** *to live*; **lifer,** *liver*; **lim,** *limb*; **list,** *cunning*; **midd,** *middle*; **nift,** *niece*; **niþer,** *downwards*; **pic,** *pitch*; **ribb,** *rib*; **scilling,** *shilling*; **scip,** *ship*; **sibb,** *relationship*; **sife,** *sieve*; **sige,** *victory*; **sittan,** *to sit*; **smiþ,** *smith*; **spinel,** *spindle*; **twig,** *twig*; **þicce,** *thick*; **þider,** *thither*; **þing,** *thing*; **þridda,** *third*; **wilde,** *wild*; **wind,** *wind*; **winter,** *winter*; in the second and third pers. sing. pres. indicative of strong verbs belonging to classes III (§ **499**), IV (§ **503**), and V (§ **505**), as **hilpest, hilpeþ, birest, bireþ, itest, iteþ,** beside inf. **helpan,** *to help*; **beran,** *to bear*; **etan,** *to eat*; in the pret. plural and pp. of strong verbs belonging to class I, as **biton, biten, ridon, riden, stigon, stigen,** beside inf. **bītan,** *to bite*; **rīdan,** *to ride*; **stīgan,** *to ascend*; in the inf. and present of strong verbs belonging to class III (§ **498**), as **bindan,** *to bind*; **drincan,** *to drink*; **findan,** *to find*; **sincan,** *to sink*; **singan,** *to sing*; **spinnan,** *to spin*; **swimman,** *to swim*.

Note.—1. **i** became **ī** by loss of **g** (§ **321**), as **brīdel,** *bridle*; **frīnan,** *to ask*; **līþ,** *he lies down*; **rīnan,** *to rain*; **sīþe,** *scythe*; **tīle** (Lat. **tēgula**), *tile*, beside **brigdel, frignan, ligeþ, sigþe, tigele** of the non-WS. dialects.

2. **i** appears as **e** in the Latin loanwords, **peru** (Lat. **pirum**), *pear*; **segn** (Lat. **signum**), *sign*.

§ **97.** **i** became **ī** by loss of nasal before a voiceless spirant, as **fīf**, Goth. OHG. **fimf**, *five*; **fīfel**, *sea-monster*; **gesīþ** (OHG. **gisindo**), *companion*; **hrīþer** (OHG. **rind**), *ox*; **līþe** (OHG. **lindi**), *gentle*; **sīþ** (Goth. **sinþs**), *way*; **swīþ** (Goth. **swinþs**), *strong*. But **in** remained when it came to stand before a voiceless spirant at a later period, as **pinsian** from Lat. **pensāre**, *to weigh, consider*; **winster** beside **winester** (OHG. **winister**), *left* (*hand*).

§ **98.** **i** was broken to **io** before **r** and **h**+consonant, and simple **h**, but already in early WS. the **io** became **eo** and thus fell together with the **eo** from **e** (§§ **85–6**), as **liornian**, **leornian** from ***lirnōjan**, *to learn*; **miox**, **meox** from ***mihst**, *manure*, cp. Goth. **maíhstus**, *dunghill*; **tiohhian**, **teohhian** from ***tihhōjan**, *to arrange, think, consider*.

The **io** became **īo** (**ēo**) by loss of intervocalic **h** (cp. § **329**, 4), as **twīogan**, **twēogan** from ***twiohian**, older ***twiχōjan**, *to doubt*.

Note.—1. **eo** then became **ie**, later **i**, in WS. before **h**+consonant, as **stihtan**, *to arrange, regulate*; **wriexl**, **wrixl**, *exchange*.

2. In Anglian **io** became **i** before gutturals, as **getihhian**, *to arrange, think, consider*.

3. In the two verbs corresponding to Goth. **brinnan**, *to burn*; and **rinnan**, *to run*, the metathesis of the **r** took place earlier than breaking, whence Anglian **biorna(n)**, **beorna(n)**, **iorna(n)**, **eorna(n)**. In WS. we have **biernan** (later **birnan**, **byrnan**), **iernan** (later **irnan**, **yrnan**) for ***biornan**, ***beornan**, ***iornan**, ***eornan**, with **ie** from the third pers. singular **biern(e)þ** (= Goth. **brinniþ**), **iern(e)þ** (= Goth. **rinniþ**). The new formation in WS. was doubtless due to the fact that the two verbs were mostly used impersonally, cp. the similar new formations in NHG. **ziemen**, *to beseem*; and **wiegen**, *to weigh*.

§ **99.** **io** became **ie** (later **i**, **y**) by **i**-umlaut in WS., as **āfierran** (OHG. **arfirren**), from ***-firrjan**, *to remove*; **bierce**, *birch*; **fiehst** (OHG. **fihtis**), *thou fightest*; **fieht**, *he fights*; **gebierhtan**, *to make bright*; **gesiehþ**, *vision*; **giernan** (OS. **girnian**), *to desire*; **hierde** (OHG. **hirti**), *shepherd*; **ierre** (OS. OHG. **irri**), *angry*; **rihtan**, **ryhtan**

(OS. **rihtian**), *to set straight*; **siehst** (OHG. **sihis**), *thou seest*; **siehþ** (OHG. **sihit**), *he sees*; **smierwan** (OHG. **smirwen**), *to anoint*; **wierresta, wiersta** (OHG. **wirsisto**), *worst*; **wiersa** (OHG. **wirsiro**), *worse*; **wierþe** (OHG. **wirdi**), *worthy*.

Note.—1. The i-umlaut of **io** generally did not take place in the non-WS. dialects, hence we have **io** in Nth. and Ken., and **io** (**eo**) in Mercian, as Nth. Ken. **giorna(n), hiorde, iorre** = Mercian **geornan, heorde, iorre,** WS. **giernan, hierde, ierre.** Forms like **afirra(n)**, *to remove*; **smirwan,** *to smear*, are not pure Anglian forms.

2. **io** became **i** in Anglian before a following guttural or **r** + guttural, as **birce, gebirhta(n), gesihþ; mixen** (mod. northern dialects **mixen**), *dunghill*; **rihtan; wircan** (OS. **wirkian**), *to work*. The **i** then became **ī** by loss of intervocalic **h** and contraction in Nth., as **sīs(t)** from ***sihis,** WS. **siehst,** *thou seest*; **sīþ** from ***sihiþ,** WS. **siehþ,** *he sees* (§ **141**).

3. **io** in the combination **wio** became **u** at an early period in Anglian, and then **u** became **y** by **i**-umlaut, as **wyrresta,** *worst*; **wyrsa,** *worse*; **wyrsian,** *to worsen*; **wyrþe,** *worthy*.

§ **100.** **i** became **io** by **u-, o/a**-umlaut in Ken. before all single consonants, in Anglian before all single consonants except gutturals (**c, g**), and in WS. before single labials and liquids. But already at an early period (ninth century) the **io** became **eo** in WS. and Mercian.

§ **101.** 1. **u**-umlaut.

Pret. **cliopude, -ode,** beside inf. **clipian,** *to call*; **cliopung,** *calling*; **mioluc, miolc** (later **milc**), *milk*; **sioluc,** *silk*; **siolufr, siolfor,** *silver*; pret. **tiolude, -ode,** beside inf. **tilian,** *to aim at*; **tiolung,** *produce, labour*. Anglian and Ken. **liomu, leomu,** *limbs*; **nioþor** (WS. **niþor**), *lower*; **siodu** (WS. **sidu**), *custom*; **sionu** (WS. **sinu**), *sinew*. Ken. **siocol,** *sickle*; **stiogol,** *stile* = WS. and Anglian **sicol, stigol.** Forms like **liomu, nioþor,** which are occasionally found in WS. prose, are not pure WS.

Note.—1. **u**-umlaut was mostly obliterated in WS. by levelling and new formations, as plural **clifu**, *cliffs*; **scipu**, *ships* (Anglian **cliofu**, **sciopu**), due to levelling out the stem-forms of those cases which had no **u** in the ending. Pret. plural **drifun**, **-on**, *they drove*; **gripun**, **-on**, *they seized*, due to preterites like **biton**, *they bit*; **stigon**, *they ascended*. Pret. **tilode** beside **tiolode**, *he aimed at*, formed direct from the inf. **tilian**. And conversely forms like inf. **cliopian** (**cleopian**), **tiolian** (**teolian**), were formed from the pret. **cliopode**, **tiolode**.

2. io became i in Anglian before **l**+guttural, as **milc** from **miolc**, older **mioluc**, *milk*.

§ **102**. 2. o/a-umlaut.

**hiora**, **heora**, *their*, *of them*; **liofast**, *thou livest*. Anglian and Ken. **behionan**, *on this side of*; **glioda**, *kite*, *vulture*; **hionan**, **heonan**, *hence*; **nioma(n)**, *to take*; **niomaþ**, *they take*; **piosan** (WS. **pisan**), *peas*; **wiota**, *sage*, *wise man*; **wiotan**, *to know*. Ken. **stiocian**, WS. and Anglian **stician**, *to prick*.

Note.—Forms like **behionan**, **wiotan**, &c., which occasionally occur in WS. prose, are not pure WS.

§ **103**. The combination **wio-** which arose from breaking (§ **98**) or from **u-**, **o/a-**umlaut (§§ **101–2**), generally became **wu-** in WS. and Anglian, but remained in Ken., as **betwuh** (**betuh**), *between*; **betwux** (**betux**), *betwixt*; **c(w)ucu**, *alive*; **c(w)udu**, *cud*; **wucu** (Goth. **wikō**, OS. **wika**), *week*; **wudu** (OS. **widu**, Ken. **wiodu**), *wood*; **wuduwe** (Goth. **widuwō**, OS. **widuwa**), *widow*; **wuht** (OS. OHG. **wiht**), *creature*, *thing*; **wuton** (**uton**), *let us!* But before gutturals we have **wi-** in Anglian, as **betwih**, **betwix**, **cwic(u)**; **cwician** (WS. **cwucian**), *to revive*, *bring to life*; **wicu**, **wiht**.

§ **104**. **i** or **ij** by contraction with a following guttural vowel became **īo** (**ēo**), as **bīo**, **bēo** (OHG. **bīa**, Germanic stem-form ***bijōn-**), *bee*; **dīofol**, **dēofol** (Lat. **diabolus**), *devil*; **fīond**, **fēond** (Goth. **fijands**), *enemy*, *fiend*; **frīo**, **frēo** from ***frija-**, *free*; **frīond**, **frēond** (Goth. **frijōnds**), *friend*;

**hīo, hēo** from ***hi + u**, *she*; fem. nom. sing. **sīo, sēo** from ***si + u**, *the*; nom. acc. neuter **þrīo, þrēo** from ***þriju** = Goth. **þrija**, *three*.

§ **105**. **īo** (**ēo**) became **īe** by **i**-umlaut, as plural **fīend** from ***fijandiz**, *enemies*; **frīend** from ***frijōndiz**, *friends*.

### o

§ **106**. Germanic **o**, which arose from older **u** (§ **43**), generally remained in OE. as also in the other Germanic languages except Gothic. In Gothic it became **u** which was broken to **o** (written **aú**) before **r, h,** and **ƕ**. Examples are: **dohtor**, Goth. **daúhtar**, OS. **dohtar**, OHG. **tohter**, *daughter*; **folc**, O.Icel. OS. OHG. **folk**, *folk*; **hord**, Goth. **huzd**, OS. **hord**, OHG. **hort**, *treasure*; **oxa**, Goth. **aúhsa**, O.Icel. **oxe**, OHG. **ohso**, *ox*; and similarly **boda**, *messenger*; **bodig**, *body*; **boga**, *bow*; **bohte**, *he bought*; **bold**, *house*; **bolt**, *bolt*; **bord**, *board*; **botm**, *bottom*; **broþ**, *broth*; **cnotta**, *knot*; **cocc**, *cock*; **col**, *coal*; **colt**, *colt*; **corn**, *corn*; **coss**, *kiss*; **dogga**, *dog*; **dor** (OS. **dor**, OHG. **tor**), *door, gate*; **dropa**, *drop*; **fola**, *foal*; **folgian**, *to follow*; **forst**, *frost*; **fox**, *fox*; **frogga**, *frog*; **god**, *God*; **gold**, *gold*; **hlot**, *lot*; **hof**, *enclosure*; **hol**, *hole*; **hold**, *loyal, gracious*; **hopian**, *to hope*; **horn**, *horn*; **hors**, *horse*; **loc**, *lock*; **lof**, *praise*; **molde**, *earth*; **morgen**, *morning*; **morþ, morþor**, *murder*; **norþ**, *north*; **nosu**, *nose*; **ofen**, *oven*; **ofer**, *over*; **open**, *open*; **smocc**, *smock*; **storm**, *storm*; **toll**, *toll*; **þorn**, *thorn*; **þorp**, *village*; **word**, *word*; **worhte**, *he worked*; in the pp. of strong verbs belonging to classes II (§ **493**), III (§ **499**), and IV (§ **503**), as **boden**, Goth. **budans**, O.Icel. **boðenn**, OS. **gibodan**, OHG. **gibotan**, *offered, commanded*; and similarly **coren**, *chosen*; **froren**, *frozen*; **soden**, *cooked, sodden*; **togen**, *drawn*; **fohten**, *fought*; **holpen**, *helped*; **worden**, *become*; **worpen**, *thrown*; **boren**, *borne*; **brocen**, *broken*; **stolen**, *stolen*; **toren**, *torn*.

NOTE.—**o** became **ō** by loss of consonant, as gen. **hōles** beside nom. **holh,** *hole*; **brōden** beside **brogden,** *brandished, woven.*

§ **107.** **o** became **e** (older **œ**) by **i**-umlaut. All native words containing this umlaut are really new formations due to levelling or analogy, because prim. Germanic **u** (cp. § **43**) did not become **o** in OE. when followed by an **i** or **j** in the next syllable. Examples are: dat. sing. **dehter,** *to a daughter*, from ***dohtri** with **o** levelled out from the other cases, the regular form would be ***dyhter** from older ***duhtri**; **efes** (OHG. **obasa**) beside **yfes,** *eaves*, cp. Goth. **ubizwa,** *porch*; pl. nom. acc. **exen,** beside nom. sing. **oxa,** *ox*; **mergen** (Goth. **maurgins**), beside **morgen,** *morning*; **ele** (Lat. **oleum**), *oil*.

§ **108.** In a certain number of words **o** became **u** in OE., especially before and after labials, as **bucc** (OHG. **boc**), *buck*; **bucca,** *he-goat*; **fugol** (OHG. **fogal**), *bird, fowl*; **full** (OHG. **fol**), *full*; **furþor,** *further*; **furþum,** *even*; **lufian,** *to love*; **lufu,** *love*; **murcnian,** *to murmur, grumble*; **murnan,** *to mourn*; **spura** beside **spora,** *spur*; **spurnan** beside **spornan,** *to kick*; **ufan** (OHG. **obana,** *from above*), *above*; **ufer(r)a,** *upper, higher*; **ufor,** *higher*; **wulf** (OHG. **wolf**), *wolf*; **wulle** (OHG. **wolla**), *wool*; **cnucian** beside **cnocian,** *to knock*; **scurf,** *scurf*; **turf,** *turf*.

§ **109.** **o** became **u** in OE. before nasals, as pp. **cumen** (OHG. **quoman**), *come*; **guma** (OHG. **gomo**), *man*; **hunig** (OHG. **honag**), *honey*; and similarly **numen,** *taken*; **scunian,** *to shun*; **sumor,** *summer*; **þunor,** *thunder*; **wunian,** *to dwell.* Also in early Latin loanwords, as **munuc** (Lat. **monachus**), *monk*; **munt** (Lat. acc. **montem**), *mountain*; **nunne** (Lat. **nonna**), *nun*; **pund** (Lat. **pondō**), *pound.*

This **u** became **y** by **i**-umlaut, as **mynster** (Lat. **monasterium**), *minster, monastery*; **mynet** (Lat. **monēta**), *coin, money.*

§ **110.** **o** may have become the rising diphthong **ió (eó)** after **g** = Germanic **j** (§ **268**), and also occasionally after sc, as **gioc** (**geoc**), OHG. **joh,** *yoke*; **geon,** *yon, that*; **sceofl,** *shovel*; **sceolde,** *should*; **sceop,** *poet, singer*; **sceort,** *short*; **sceoten** (pp.), *shot,* beside **scofl, scolde, scop, scort, scoten.** But see § **51,** Note.

Note.—The **e** in the combination **sceo-** probably merely indicated the palatal pronunciation of the **sc-**.

**u**

§ **111.** Germanic **u** (§ **21**) generally remained in OE. as also in the other Germanic languages, as **dumb,** Goth. **dumbs,** O.Icel. **dumbr,** OS. **dumb,** OHG. **tumb,** *dumb*; **hund,** Goth. **hunds,** O.Icel. **hundr,** OS. **hund,** OHG. **hunt,** *dog, hound*; and similarly **burg,** *city*; **duru,** *door*; **grund,** *ground*; **hnutu,** *nut*; **hund,** *hundred*; **hungor,** *hunger*; **lust,** *desire*; **sugu,** *sow*; **sulh,** *plough*; **sunne,** *sun*; **sunu,** *son*; **tunge,** *tongue*; **tungol,** *star*; **þurst,** *thirst*; **under,** *under*; **wund,** *wound*; **wundor,** *wonder*; in the pret. plural of strong verbs belonging to classes II (§ **493**) and III (§ **497**), as **budon,** Goth. **budum,** O.Icel. **buðum,** OS. **budun,** OHG. **butum,** *we offered, commanded*; and similarly **curon,** *chose*; **flugon,** *flew*; **gruton,** *wept*; **tugon,** *drew*; **bundon,** Goth. O.Icel. **bundum,** OS. **bundun,** OHG. **buntum,** *we bound*; and similarly **druncon,** *drank*; **dulfon,** *dug*; **fundon,** *found*; **fuhton,** *fought*; **hulpon,** *helped*; **spunnon,** *spun*; **suncon,** *sank*; **sungon,** *sung*; **wurdon,** *became*; **wurpon,** *threw*; in the pp. of strong verbs belonging to class III, as **bunden,** *bound*; **druncen,** *drunk*; **funden,** *found*; **spunnen,** *spun*; **suncen,** *sunk*; **sungen,** *sung*.

Note.—**u** became **o** in the prefix **or-** ( = Goth. **us-**, OHG. **ur-**, *out*), as **orsorg,** *without anxiety*; **orþanc,** *skill*; **orwēne,** *despairing*. And in the Latin loanwords **box** (Lat. **buxus**), *boxtree*; **copor** (Lat. **cuprum**), *copper*.

§ **112.** **u** became **y** by **i**-umlaut, as **cyning,** OS. OHG. **kuning,** *king*; **cynn,** Goth. **kuni,** OS. OHG. **kunni,** *race, generation*; **þyncan,** Goth. **þugkjan,** OS. **thunkian,** *to seem*; and similarly **blyscan,** *to blush*; **bryce,** *brittle*; **brycg,** *bridge*; **bycgan** (Goth. **bugjan**), *to buy*; **byrd,** *birth*; **clyppan,** *to embrace*; **cnyttan,** *to bind*; **crycc,** *crutch*; **cyme,** *advent*; **cyre,** *choice*; **cyrnel,** *kernel*; **cyssan,** *to kiss*; **cyst,** *choice*; **drync,** *potion*; **dyppan,** *to dip*; **dysig,** *foolish*; **flyht,** *flight*; **fyllan,** *to fill*; **fyrhtan,** *to fear*; **fyxen,** *vixen*; **gemynd,** *remembrance*; **gesynto,** *health*; **gyden** (OHG. **gutin**), *goddess*; **gylden** (OHG. **guldīn**), *golden*; **hrycg,** *back, ridge*; **hycgan** (Goth. **hugjan**), *to think*; **hyge,** *thought*; **hyldu,** *grace, favour*; **hyll,** *hill*; **hyngran,** *to hunger*; **hype,** *hip*; **hyrdel,** *hurdle*; **hyrnen,** *of horn*; **lyge,** *falsehood*; **mycel,** *much*; **mycg,** *midge*; **myrþran,** *to murder*; **nytt,** *use*; **scyld,** *guilt*; **scyldig,** *guilty*; **scyrtra,** *shorter*; **stycce,** *piece*; **synn,** *sin*; **trymman,** *to make strong*; **þynne,** *thin*; **þyrstan,** *to thirst*; **yfel,** *evil*; **ymb(e),** *about*; **yppan,** *to open*; **wyllen** (OHG. **wullīn**), *woollen*; **wynn,** *joy*; **wyrcan,** *to work*; **wyrhta** (OS. **wurhtio**), *workman*; **wyrm** from ***wurmiz,** *snake, dragon, worm*; **wyrt,** *herb*. See § **52.**

Also in early Latin loanwords, as **cycene** (late Lat. **coquīna, cucīna**), *kitchen*; **cylen** (Lat. **culīna**), *kiln*; **mylen** (late Lat. **molīna**), *mill*; **pyle** (Lat. acc. **pulvīnum**), *pillow*; **pytt** (Lat. acc. **puteum**), *pit*.

Note.—1. **y** became **e** in Ken. in the ninth century, as **besig, efel, gelden, senn** = WS. **bysig,** *busy*, **yfel, gylden, synn.** The **e** from OE. **y** in the modern dialects of East Sussex and East Anglia shows however that this change of **y** to **e** was not confined to Kent in the OE. period, cf. also § **3**, Note.

2. **i** for **y** occurs occasionally in early WS., as **cining,** *king*, **disig,** *foolish*, **scildig,** *guilty*, beside **cyning, dysig, scyldig**; and in late WS. and Anglian **y** was often unrounded to **i**, especially before and after **c, g, h,** (and then **y** often came to be written for original **i**) as **cinn, cining, fliht, hricg, hige, scildig, þincan,** &c.

§ **113.** **u** became **ū** by loss of **n** before **s** and **þ**, as **cūþ** (Goth. **kunþs**), *known, familiar*; **cūþe** (Goth. **kunþa**), *he could*; **dūst** (OHG. **tunst**, *storm*), *dust*; **fūs** (OHG. **funs**), *ready, eager for*; **gūþ** (OHG. **gundia**), *war, battle*; **hūsl** (Goth. **hunsl**), *Eucharist*; **mūþ** (Goth. **munþs**), *mouth*; **ūs** (Goth. OHG. **uns**), *us*; **tūsc** from ***tunsk**, *tusk*; **sūþ** (OHG. **sund**), *south*.

§ **114.** **ū** became **ȳ** by **i**-umlaut, as **cȳþan** (Goth. **gaswi-kunþjan**), *to make known*; **dȳstig** (OHG. **tunstig**, *stormy*), *dusty*; **fȳsan** from ***funsjan**, *to send forth, hasten*; **wȳscan** from ***wunskjan**, OHG. **wunsken**, *to wish*; **ȳst** (OHG. **unst**), *storm, tempest*; **ȳþ** (OHG. **undea**), prim. Germanic ***unþjō**, *wave*.

§ **115.** **u** became **ū** by loss of **h** after **l**, **r**, before a following vowel, as gen. sing. **fūre**, pl. gen. **fūra**, dat. **fūrum**, beside nom. sing. **furh**, *furrow*; pl. gen. **sūla**, dat. **sūlum**, beside nom. sing. **sulh**, *plough* (cp. § **329**, 3).

§ **116.** **u** may have become the rising diphthong **iú**, later **ió** (**eó**), after **g** = Germanic **j** (§ **268**), and also occasionally after **sc**, as **giung**, **giong**, **geong**, older **iung** (**gung**) = Goth. **juggs**, OHG. **jung**, *young*; **gioguþ**, **geoguþ**, older **iuguþ** (**guguþ**), *youth*; inf. **sceolan**, *shall*; pl. indicative **sceolon**, beside **sculan**, **sculon**. The i-umlaut of which was **ie** (later **i**, **y**), as **giengra** (OHG. **jungiro**), **gingra**, **gyngra**, *younger*; **giengesta** (OHG. **jungisto**), **gingesta**, **gyngesta**, *youngest*. But see § **51**, Note.

Note.—The **e** in the combination **sceo-** probably merely indicated the palatal pronunciation of the **sc-**.

## B. The Long Vowels of Accented Syllables.

### ā

§ **117.** Germanic nasalized **ā**, which arose from **a** according to § **40**, became **ō** in OE, as **brōhte**, Goth. OS. OHG. **brāhta**, *I brought*; **fōn** from ***fōhan**, Goth. OS. OHG.

**fāhan,** *to grasp, seize*; and similarly **hōh,** *heel*; **hōn,** *to hang*; **ōht,** *persecution*; **tōh,** *tough*; **þō** (Goth. **þāhō**), *clay*; **þōhte,** *I thought*; **wōh,** *crooked, wry.*

§ **118.** **ō** became **ē** (older **œ̄**) by **i**-umlaut, as **ēhtan** (OS. **āhtian**), *to persecute*; **fēhþ** (OS. **fāhid**), *he seizes*; **hēla** from older ***hōhila,** *heel.*

**ǣ**

§ **119.** Germanic **ǣ** (Goth. **ē,** OS. OHG. **ā**) generally remained in WS., but became **ē** in Anglian and Ken., as WS. **dǣd,** non-WS. **dēd,** Goth. **ga-dēþs,** OS. **dād,** OHG. **tāt,** *deed*; WS. **sǣd,** non-WS. **sēd,** OS. **sād,** OHG. **sāt,** *seed*; WS. **rǣdan,** non-WS. **rēdan,** OS. **rādan,** OHG. **rātan,** *to advise*; and similarly **bǣr,** *bier*; **blǣdre,** *bladder*; **blǣtan,** *to bleat*; **brǣr,** *briar*; **ǣfen,** *evening*; **ǣl,** *eel*; **ǣs,** *carrion*; **ǣþm,** *breath*; **hǣr,** *hair*; **lǣce,** *physician*; **lǣtan,** *to leave*; **mǣg,** *kinsman*; **mǣl,** *meal-time*; Anglian **mēce** (OS. **māki**), *sword*; **mǣre,** *renowned*; **nǣdl,** *needle*; **nǣdre,** *snake*; **rǣd,** *advice*; **swǣs,** *pleasant*; **þǣr,** *there*; **wǣg,** *wave*; **wǣpen,** *weapon*; in the pret. plural of strong verbs belonging to classes IV (§ **503**) and V (§ **505**), as **bǣron,** *bore*; **cwǣdon,** *said*; **ǣton,** *ate*; **stǣlon,** *stole*; **sǣton,** *sat.*

Note.—1. Some scholars assume that Germanic **ǣ** became **ā** in prim. West Germanic and that the **ā** then became **ǣ** again in prim. OE. in the above and similar examples.

2. It is difficult to account satisfactorily for the **ā** beside **ǣ** in a few words, such as **lācnian,** *to cure*; **slāpan,** *to sleep*; **swār,** *heavy*; **tāl,** *blame,* **wāt,** *wet*; beside **lǣcnain, slǣpan, swǣr, tǣl, wǣt.** In forms like **wāg** beside **wǣg,** *wave,* the **ā** is due to the stem-form of the plural, see § **120** (2). For a possible explanation of the **ā** for older **ǣ**, see *EOE. Gr.* § 45.

3. The **ē** from older **ǣ** was often rounded to **œ̄** after **w** in Nth., as **huœ̄r,** *where*; **wœ̄pen,** *weapon*; **wœ̄ron,** *they were* = WS. **hwǣr, wǣpen, wǣron.**

4. The **ā** in early Latin loanwords had the same development in OE. as Germanic **ǣ**, as **nǣp** (Lat. **nāpus**), *turnip*; **strǣt** (Lat. **strāta**), *street.*

§ **120**. Germanic **ǣ** became **ā** in OE. (1) before **w**, as **blāwan** (OHG. **blāen**), *to blow*; **cnāwan** (OHG. **knāen**), *to know*; **crāwan** (OHG. **krāen**), *to crow*; **māwan** (OHG. **māen**), *to mow*; **sāwan** (OHG. **sāen**), *to sow*; **sāwon** (OS. **sāwun**), *they saw*; **tāwian**, *to prepare*; **þrāwan**, *to twist*; **wāwan** (OHG. **wāen**), *to blow*.

This **ā** became **ǣ** by **i**-umlaut, as **lǣwan** from ***lāwjan**, older ***lǣwjan** = Goth. **lēwjan**, *to betray*.

(2) In the combination **ǣg** followed by a guttural vowel in the next syllable, as plural nom. **māgas**, gen. **māga**, dat. **māgum**, beside nom. singular **mǣg**, *kinsman*; pret. plural **lāgon**, *lay*; **þāgon**, *received*; **wāgon**, *carried* (§§ **505**, **507**).

Note.—Forms like **mǣgas**; **wǣgas**, *waves*, were new formations from the singular **mǣg**, **wǣg**. And **lǣgon**, **þǣgon**, **wǣgon** were due to the analogy of such preterites as **bǣron**, **stǣlon** which regularly have **ǣ**.

§ **121**. Before nasals Germanic **ǣ** became **ō** through the intermediate stage **ā**, as **mōna**, Goth. **mēna**, OS OHG. **māno**, *moon*; **nōmon**, Goth. **nēmun**, OS. OHG. **nāmun**, *they took*; and similarly **brōm**, *broom*; **c(w)ōmon**, *they came*; **gedōn**, *done*; **mōnaþ**, *month*; **ōm**, *rust*; **sōna**, *soon*; **spōn**, *chip*; **wōma**, *tumult*.

Note.—The **ō** may have become the rising diphthong **eṓ** after **g** = Germanic **j** (§ **268**), as **geōmor** (OS. OHG. **jāmar**), *sad*; **geōmrian**, *to mourn*. But see § **51**, Note.

§ **122**. **ō** became **ē** (older **ǣ**) by **i**-umlaut, as **wēnan** from ***wōnjan** = Goth. **wēnjan**, OS. **wānian**, OHG. **wānen**, *to hope*; and similarly **brēmel**, *bramble*; **cwēman**, *to please*; **cwēn**, *queen*; **gecwēme**, *agreeable*; **wēn**, *hope*.

§ **123**. In WS. **ǣ** was broken to **ēa** before **h**, as **nēah**, Goth. **nēƕ**, OS. OHG. **nāh**, *near*; **nēar** from ***nēahur**, older ***nǣhur**, *nearer*. By **i**-umlaut **ēa** became **īe** (later **ī**, **ȳ**), as **nīehsta** from ***nēahista**, but Anglian **nēsta** from ***nēhista** (OHG. **nāhisto**), *nearest*.

§ **124.** In WS. it became **ēa** (older **eá́**) through the intermediate stage **eǽ** after palatal **c, g,** and **sc,** as **gēar,** Goth. **jēr,** OS. OHG. **jār,** *year*; and similarly **cēace,** *jaw*; **forgēaton,** *they forgot*; **gēa,** *yes*; **gēafon,** *they gave*; **scēap,** *sheep*; **scēaron,** *they sheared.* **ēa** became **īe** by **i**-umlaut, as **cīese** from ***cēasi** (Lat. **cāseus**), *cheese.*

Note.—The **ē** (§ **119**), which arose from **ǣ**, remained uninfluenced by palatals in the non-WS. dialects, as **gēr, gēfon, scēp** = WS. **gēar, gēafon, scēap.** This **ēa** also became **ē** in late WS.

**ē**

§ **125.** Besides **ǣ** (= long open Indg. **ē,** § **24**) prim. Germanic had also a long close **ē** which arose from various sources, see § **38,** Note. In Gothic the two sounds fell together in **ē,** but in the other Germanic languages they were kept quite apart, thus Indg. **ē** = OE. **ǣ** (§ **119**), Goth. **ē,** O.Icel. OS. OHG. **ā,** but Germanic **ē** = OE. Goth. O.Icel. OS. **ē,** OHG. **ia** (**ie**).

Germanic **ē** remained in OE., as **cēn** (OHG. **kian**), *torch*; OE. Goth. O.Icel. OS. **hēr,** OHG. **hiar,** *here*; OE. **mēd,** OS. **mēda,** OHG. **miata,** *pay, reward*; in the preterite of the old reduplicated verbs (§§ **512–14**), as OE. OS. **hēt,** OHG. **hiaʒ,** inf. OE. **hātan,** *to call*; and similarly the preterites **fēng, rēd, slēp,** beside inf. **fōn,** *to seize*; **rǣdan,** *to advise*; **slǣpan,** *to sleep.*

Note.—Latin **ē** became **ī** in early loanwords, as **cīpe,** Lat. **cēpa,** *onion*; **pīn** (OHG. **pīna**), Lat. **pœna,** late Lat. **pēna,** *torture*; **sīde** (OHG. **sīda**), late Lat. **sēta,** *silk*; but **ē** remained in later loanwords, as **bēte,** Lat. **bēta,** *beetroot*; **crēda,** *creed,* Lat. **crēdō,** *I believe.*

**ī**

§ **126.** Germanic **ī** generally remained in OE., as also in the oldest periods of the other Germanic languages, as OE. OS. OHG. **sīn,** Goth. **seins,** *his*; OE. OS. OHG. **swīn,** Goth. **swein,** O.Icel. **svīn,** *pig, swine*; and similarly **blīþe,** *blithe*; **hwīl,** *space of time*; **hwīt,** *white*; **īdel,** *empty*;

**īfig,** *ivy*; **īs,** *ice*; **īsen, īren,** *iron*; **līf,** *life*; **mīn,** *mine*; **rīce,** *kingdom*; **rīm,** *number*; **sīde,** *side*; **slīm,** *slime*; **tīd, tīma,** *time*; **þīn,** *thine*; **wīd,** *wide*; **wīf,** *wife*; **wīs,** *wise*; in the present of strong verbs belonging to class I (§ **490**), as OE. OS. **bītan,** Goth. **beitan,** O.Icel. **bīta,** OHG. **bīȥan,** *to bite*; and similarly **bīdan,** *to remain*; **drīfan,** *to drive*; **glīdan,** *to glide*; **grīpan,** *to seize*; **līþan,** *to go*; **rīdan,** *to ride*; **scīnan,** *to shine*; **slīdan,** *to slide*; **smītan,** *to smite*; **snīþan,** *to cut*; **stīgan,** *to ascend*; **strīdan,** *to stride*; **wrītan,** *to write.*

§ **127.** **ī** was broken to **īo** before **h** and **ht** in WS. But already at an early period the **īo** mostly became **ēo** (= Anglian **ī**), as **betwēoh,** *between,* cp. Goth. **tweihnái,** *two each*; **lēoht,** Goth. **leihts,** OHG. **līhti,** adj. *light*; **wēoh** (Anglian **wīh**), *idol,* Goth. **weihs,** OHG. **wīh,** *holy,* OS. **wīh,** *temple*; imperative singular **lēoh** (Anglian **līh**), Goth. **leiƕ,** OS. OHG. **līh,** *lend thou*; and similarly **tēoh,** *accuse*; **þēoh,** *thrive*; **wrēoh,** *cover.* With loss of medial **h** after breaking had taken place, as **betwēonum,** *between*; **fēol** (Anglian **fīl,** OHG. **fīhala**), *file*; infinitives **līon, lēon** (Goth. **leiƕan,** OS. OHG. **līhan**), *to lend*; and similarly **sīon, sēon,** *to strain*; **þīon, þēon,** *to thrive*; **wrīon, wrēon,** *to cover.*

The **i**-umlaut of this **īo** (**ēo**) is **īe,** as **līehtan** from ***līoht-jan,** *to lighten, make easier*, Anglian **gelīhtan**; **līehst** from ***līohis** (OHG. **līhis**), *thou lendest*; **līehþ** from ***līohiþ** (OHG **līhit**), *he lends.*

### ō

§ **128.** Germanic **ō** (= Goth. O.Icel. OS. **ō,** OHG. **uo**) generally remained in OE., as **brōþor,** Goth. **brōþar,** O.Icel. **brōðer,** OS. **brōđer,** OHG. **bruoder,** *brother*; OE. OS. **fōt,** Goth. **fōtus,** O.Icel. **fōtr,** OHG. **fuoȥ,** *foot*; and similarly **blōd,** *blood*; **blōwan,** *to bloom*; **bōc,** *book*; **bōsm,** *bosom*; **brōc,** *brook*; **brōd,** *brood*; **cōl,** *cool*; **dōm,** *judgment, doom*; **dōn,** *to do*; **flōd,** *flood*; **flōwan,** *to flow*;

**fōda**, *food*; **genōg**, *enough*; **glōf**, *glove*; **glōm**, *gloom*; **glōwan**, *to glow*; **gōd**, *good*; **grōwan**, *to grow*; **hōc**, *hook*; **hōd**, *hood*; **hōf**, *hoof*; **hrōc**, *rook*; **hrōf**, *roof*; **hrōpan**, *to shout*; **mōd**, *mood, mind*; **mōdor**, *mother*; **rōwan**, *to row*; **sōhte**, *he sought*; **sōt**, *soot*; **stōl**, *stool*; in the preterite of strong verbs belonging to class VI (§ **508**), as OE. Goth. O.Icel. OS. **fōr**, OHG. **fuor**, *he went, travelled*; and similarly **bōc**, *baked*; **hōf**, *raised*; **slōg**, *struck, slew*; **swōr**, *swore*.

Note.—The combination **scō-** was often written **sceō-** with **e** to denote the palatal pronunciation of the **sc-**, as preterite **sceōc**, *shook*; **sceōp**, *created*, beside **scōc**, **scōp**; **sceōh** beside **scōh**, *shoe*.

§ **129.** **ō** became **ē** (older **œ̄**, preserved in Nth.) by **i**-umlaut, as **fēt**, OS. **fōti**, OHG. **fuoȥi**, from ***fōtiz**, older ***fōtez**, *feet*; **sēcan**, Goth. **sōkjan**, OS. **sōkian**, *to seek*; and similarly **bēc**, *books*; **bētan**, *to improve*; **blēdan**, *to bleed*; **brēþer**, dat. sing. of **brōþor**, *brother*; **cēlan**, *to cool*; **dēman**, *to judge*; **drēfan**, *to make turbid*; **fēdan**, *to feed*; **fēlan**, *to feel*; **glēd**, *live coal*; **grēne**, *green*; **grētan**, *to greet*; **hēdan**, *to heed*; **mēder**, dat. sing. of **mōdor**, *mother*; **mētan**, *to meet*; **spēd**, *success*; **swēte**, *sweet*; **wēpan**, *to weep*.

§ **130.** Final **wō** became **ū** in monosyllables, as **cū**, OS. **kō**, OHG. **kuo**, *cow*, from an original acc. form ***gʷōm** (cp. Gr. Dor. *βῶν*) = prim. Germanic ***kwōn**, older ***kwōm**; **hū** (OS. **hwō**), *how*; **tū** (neut.) from ***twō**, *two*. The neuter **bū** for older ***bō**, *both*, is due to association with **tū** in the combination **bū tū**, *both*, literally *both two*.

**ū** became **ȳ** by **i**-umlaut, as **cȳ** from older ***kū-i**, prim. Germanic ***kwō-iz**, *cows*.

### ū

§ **131.** Germanic **ū** generally remained in OE., as also in the oldest periods of the other Germanic languages, as OE. O.Icel. OS. OHG. **hūs**, *house*, cp. Goth. **gud-hūs**, *temple*; OE. O.Icel. OS. OHG. **rūm**, Goth. **rūms**, *room*; **þūhte**, Goth. **þūhta**, OS. **thūhta**, OHG. **dūhta**, *it seemed*, inf. OE. **þyncan**, *to seem*; and similarly **brū**, *eyebrow*; **brūcan**, *to enjoy*; **brūn**, *brown*; **būan**, *to dwell*; **būgan**, *to bow down*; **clūd**, *rock*; **clūt**, *clout*; **fūl**, *foul*; **hlūd**, *loud*; **hlūtor**, *clear, pure*; **lūcan**, *to close*; **lūs**, *louse*; **mūs**, *mouse*; **nū**, *now*; **prūt**, *proud*; **rūst**, *rust*; **scrūd**, *garment*; **scūfan**, *to push*; **slūpan**, *to glide*; **sūcan**, *to suck*; **scūr**, *shower*; **sūpan**, *to sup, drink*; **sūr**, *sour*; **tūn**, *enclosure*; **trūwian** (pret. **trūde**), *to trust*; **ūder**, *udder*; **ūhta**, *early dawn*; **ūt**, *out*; **þūma**, *thumb*; **þūsend**, *thousand*.

NOTE.—OE. **ū** has generally been preserved in the modern dialects of Scotland and of the northern counties of England, whereas OE. **ī** has not been preserved in any of the dialects.

§ **132.** **ū** became **ȳ** by **i**-umlaut, as **brȳd**, from prim. Germanic ***brūđiz**, *bride*; **mȳs**, from prim. Germanic ***mūsiz**, *mice*; **rȳman**, Goth. ***rūmjan**, OS. **rūmian**, *to make room*; and similarly **fȳr**, *fire*; **fȳst**, *fist*; **hlȳdan**, *to make a sound*; **hȳd**, *hide*; **hȳdan**, *to hide, conceal*; **hȳf**, *hive*; **lȳs**, *lice*; **lȳtel**, *little*; **ontȳnan**, *to open*; **scrȳdan**, *to dress*; **þȳmel**, *thumbstall*; in the second and third pers. sing. pres. indicative of strong verbs which have **ū** in the infinitive (§ **496**), as **brȳcst**, **brȳcþ**, from older ***brūkis**, ***brūkiþ**, inf. **brūcan**, *to enjoy*.

NOTE.—**ȳ** became **ē** in Ken. in the ninth century, as Ken. **hēf**, **mēs**, **ontēnan** = WS. **hȳf**, **mȳs**, **ontȳnan**. See § **3**, Note.

## C. THE DIPHTHONGS OF ACCENTED SYLLABLES.

### ai

§ **133.** Germanic **ai** (= Goth. **ái**, O.Icel. **ei**, OS. **ē**, OHG. **ei** (**ē**)) became **ā** in OE., as **ān**, Goth. **áins**, O.Icel. **einn**, OS. **ēn**, OHG. **ein**, *one*; **hāl**, Goth. **háils**, O.Icel. **heill**, OS. **hēl**, OHG. **heil**, *whole, sound, hale*; **hātan**, Goth.

**háitan,** O.Icel. **heita,** OS. **hētan,** OHG. **heiʒan,** *to name, call*; and similarly **āc,** *oak*; **ād,** *heap, funeral pile*; **āgan,** *to possess*; **āgen,** *own*; **ār,** *oar*; **āscian,** *to ask*; **ātor,** *poison*; **āþ,** *oath*; **bā,** *both*; **bān,** *bone*; **bār,** *boar*; **bāt,** *boat*; **brād,** *broad*; **clāþ,** *cloth*; **dā,** *doe*; **dāg,** *dough*; **gāst,** *spirit*; **gāt,** *goat*; **grāpian,** *to grope*; **hād,** *rank, order*; **hām,** *home*; **hāt,** *hot*; **hlāf,** *loaf*; **hlāford,** *lord*; **hlāw,** *grave, mound*; **hrāw,** *corpse*; **lār,** *lore, learning*; **māþm,** *treasure*; **rā** (OHG. **rēho**), *roe*; **rād,** *raid*; **rāp,** *rope*; **sāl,** *rope*; **sār,** *sore*; **sāwol,** *soul*; **slā** (OHG. **slēha**), *sloe*; **snāw,** *snow*; **stān,** *stone*; **swāpan,** *to sweep*; **tā** (OHG. **zēha**), *toe*; **tācen,** *token*; **twā,** *two*; **þās,** *those*; **wā,** *woe*; **wāt,** *he knows*; in the pret. singular of strong verbs belonging to class I (§ **490**), as **bād,** Goth. **báiþ,** O.Icel. **beið,** OS. **bād,** OHG. **beit,** *he awaited*; and similarly **bāt,** *bit*; **lāþ,** *went*; **drāf,** *drove*; **lāh,** *lent*; **rād,** *rode*; **stāg,** *ascended.*

NOTE.—1. The **ā** in the above and similar words has generally fallen together with Germanic **a** in open syllables in the modern dialects north of the Humber, whereas they are still kept apart in the other dialects. On the other hand the dialects north of the Humber still preserve the distinction between the OE. **ā** from Germanic **ai** and Germanic **o** in open syllables, whereas in the other dialects they have generally fallen together just as in the standard language.

2. Unaccented **ā** became **ō** when originally followed by **w**, as **ō** (Goth. **áiw**), *ever*, beside accented **ā**; and similarly in compounds **ōwþer,** *one of two*; **nōwþer,** *neither of two*; **ōwiht,** *anything*; **nōwiht,** *nothing*; beside **āwþer,** &c.

3. The combination **scā-** was often written **sceā-** with **e** to denote the palatal pronunciation of **sc-**, as **sceādan,** *to divide*; pret. singular **sceān,** *shone*, beside **scādan, scān.** See § **51**, Note.

§ **134.** **ā** became **ǣ** (late Ken. **ē**) by **i**-umlaut, as **hǣþ,** Goth. **háiþi,** *heath*; **hǣlan,** Goth. **háiljan,** OS. **hēlian,** *to heal*; **ǣ, ǣw** from ***āwi-**, prim. Germanic ***aiwiz,** *divine* *law*; and similarly **ǣht**, *possession*; **ǣnig**, *any*; **ǣr**, *formerly, before*; **blǣcan**, *to bleach*; **brǣdan**, *to broaden*; **clǣne**, *clean*; **dǣl**, *part, portion*; **dǣlan**, *to deal*; **drǣfan**, *to drive*; **flǣsc**, *flesh*; **gǣt**, *goats*; **hǣtan**, *to heat*; **hlǣder**, *ladder*; **hlǣw**, *grave, mound*; **hrǣw**, *corpse*; **hwǣte**, *wheat*; **lǣdan**, *to lead*; **lǣfan**, *to leave*; **lǣran**, *to teach*; **lǣstan**, *to follow*; **mǣnan**, *to mean*; **rǣcan**, *to reach*; **rǣran**, *to raise*; **sǣ**, *sea*; **sprǣdan**, *to spread*; **stǣnen**, *of stone*.

Note.—Many of the modern northern dialects still preserve the distinction between Anglian **ē** from Germanic **ǣ** (§ **119**) and the **ǣ** from the **i**-umlaut of **ā**.

### au

§ **135**. Germanic **au** (= Goth. **áu**, O.Icel. **au**, OS. **ō**, OHG. **ou** (**ō**)) became **ēa** in OE., as **dēaþ**, Goth. **dáuþus**, O.Icel. **dauðe**, OS. **dōđ**, OHG. **tōd**, *death*; **ēage**, Goth. **áugō**, O.Icel. **auga**, OS. **ōga**, OHG. **ouga**, *eye*; **rēad**, Goth. **ráuþs**, O.Icel. **rauðr**, OS. **rōd**, OHG. **rōt**, *red*; and similarly **bēacen**, *beacon*; **bēag**, *ring, bracelet*; **bēan**, *bean*; **brēad**, *bread*; **cēap**, *cheap*; **cēapian**, *to buy*; **dēad**, *dead*; **dēaf**, *deaf*; **drēam**, *joy*; **ēac**, *also*; **ēadig** (Goth. **áudags**), *blessed*; **ēare**, *ear*; **ēast**, *east*; **flēa(h)**, *flea*; **ġelēafa**, *belief*; **grēat**, *great*; **hēafod**, *head*; **hēah**, *high*; **hēap**, *troop*; **hlēapan**, *to leap*; **lēac**, *leek*; **lēaf**, *leaf*; **lēad**, *lead*; **lēan**, *reward*; **scēaf**, *sheaf*; **stēap**, *steep*; **strēam**, *stream*; **tēag**, *rope*; in the pret. singular of strong verbs belonging to class II (§ **493**), as **cēas**, Goth. **káus**, O.Icel. **kaus**, OS. OHG. **kōs**, *he chose*, inf. OE. **cēosan**, *to choose*; and similarly **bēad**, *offered*; **brēac**, *enjoyed*; **clēaf**, *cleft*; **frēas**, *froze*; **gēat**, *poured out*; **lēag**, *lied*; **scēat**, *shot*; **tēah**, *drew*.

Note.—1. **ēa** became **ē** in late WS. before **c, g, h**, and after **c, g, sc**, as **bēcen, lēc, bēg, ēge, hēh, tēh**; **cēpian, cēs, gēt, scēf, scēt**.

2. In Anglian it became **ǣ** (later **ē**) before **c, g, h,** as **ǣc, lǣc, flǣh, hǣh, tǣg,** later **ēc, lēc, flēh, hēh, tēg.**

§ **136.** **ēa** became **īe** (= non-WS. **ē**) by **i**-umlaut in the oldest period of WS. **īe** then became **ī, ȳ** already in early WS. (see § **174,** Note), as **gelīefan,** early WS. **gelīfan, gelȳfan,** non-WS. **gelēfan,** Goth. **galáubjan,** OS. **gilōƀian,** *to believe*; **hīeran,** early WS. **hīran, hȳran,** non-WS. **hēran,** Goth. **háusjan,** OS. **hōrian,** *to hear*; **nīed,** early WS. **nīd, nȳd,** non-WS. **nēd,** Goth. **náuþs,** prim. Germanic ***nauđiz,** *need*; and similarly **bīecnan,** *to beckon*; **bīegan** (Goth. ***báugjan**), *to bend*; **cīepan,** *to buy*; **drīeman,** *to rejoice*; **drīepan,** *to let drop*; **īecan,** *to increase*; **īeþe,** *easy*; **gīeman,** *to take notice of*; **hīehra,** *higher*; **hīehsta** (Goth. **háuhista**), *highest*; **hīenan,** *to humiliate*; **nīedan,** *to compel*; **scīete,** *sheet*; **slīefe,** *sleeve*; **stīepel,** *steeple.*

### eu

§ **137.** Germanic **eu** (= Goth. **iu,** O.Icel. **jō** (**jū**), OS. OHG. **eo** (**io**)) became **ēo** in OE. The **ēo** remained in WS. and Mercian, but was often written **īo** in early WS. and Mercian. In Nth., especially in n. Nth., it generally became **ēa** which fell together with the **ēa** from Germanic **au** (§ **135**). In Ken. it became **īo** (also written **īa**), and thus fell together with **īo** from Germanic **iu** (§ **138**). Examples are: **dēop,** Goth. **diups,** O.Icel. **djūpr,** OS. **diop,** OHG. **tiof,** *deep*; WS. and Mercian **lēof, līof,** Nth. **lēaf,** Ken. **līof,** Goth. **liufs,** O.Icel. **ljūfr,** OS. **liof,** OHG. **liob,** *dear*; WS. and Mercian **dēor, dīor,** Nth. **dēar,** Ken. **dīor,** *deer*; and similarly **bēod,** *table*; **bēor,** *beer*; **flēos,** *fleece*; **lēoht,** *a light*; **sēoc,** *sick*; **stēor,** *rudder*; **þēod,** *nation, race*; **þēof,** *thief*; **þēoh,** *thigh*; in the present of strong verbs belonging to class II (§ **493**), as **bēodan,** Goth. **biudan,** O.Icel. **bjōđa,** OS. **biodan,** OHG. **biotan,** *to offer*; **cēosan,** Goth. **kiusan** (*to test*), O.Icel **kjōsa,** OS. OHG. **kiosan,** *to choose*; and similarly **clēofan,** *to cleave*; **crēopan,** *to* *creep*; **drēosan,** *to fall*; **flēogan,** *to fly*; **frēosan,** *to freeze*; **gēotan,** *to pour out*; **lēogan,** *to lie*; **rēocan,** *to smoke*; **scēotan,** *to shoot*; **sēoþan,** *to boil, cook*; **tēon** (Goth. **tiuhan**), *to draw, lead.*

NOTE.—1. The old diphthong **eu** was occasionally preserved in the oldest monuments, as **steupfaedaer,** later **stēopfæder,** *stepfather,* see § **32.**

2. **ēo** (**ēa**) became **ē** in Anglian before **c, g, h,** as **rēça(n), sēc, flēga(n), lēga(n), lēht** = WS. **rēocan, sēoc,** &c.

**iu**

§ **138.** The normal development of Germanic **iu,** which arose from older **eu** when the next syllable contained an **i, ī,** or **j** (§ **44**), is **īo** in OE. (= Goth. **iu,** O.Icel. **jū** (**ȳ**), OS. OHG. **iu**). In WS. **īo** generally became **īe** (later **ī, ȳ**) by **i**-umlaut. But when no umlaut took place, early WS. had **īo** beside **ēo,** and later generally **ēo** only. It is difficult to account for the non-umlauted forms, unless we may suppose that they are not pure WS. Examples are: **cīesþ,** Goth. **kiusiþ,** O.Icel. **kȳs(s),** OS. **kiusid,** OHG. **kiusit,** *he chooses, tests,* inf. OE. **cēosan**; **tīehþ,** Goth. **tiuhiþ,** OS. **tiuhid,** OHG. **ziuhit,** *he draws, leads,* inf. OE. **tēon**; **līehtan,** Goth. **liuhtjan,** OS. **liuhtian,** OHG. **liuhten,** *to give light.* **dīere** beside **dēore,** OS. **diuri,** OHG. **tiuri,** *dear, beloved*; **dīerling** beside **dēorling,** *darling*; **geþīedan** beside **geþīodan, geþēodan,** *to join, associate*; **stīeran** (O.Icel. **stȳra** OHG. **stiuren**) beside **stēoran,** *to steer*; **þīefþ, þīestre** (OS. **thiustri**), beside **þēofþ,** *theft*; **þīostre, þēostre,** *dark.* **geþīode, geþēode,** *language*; **līode, lēode** (OS. **liudi,** OHG. **liuti**), *people*; and a few other words.

The **i**-umlaut of **īo** did not take place in the other dialects, so that we have in Nth. and Ken. **īo** (also written **īa** in the latter dialect), and in Mercian **īo** beside **ēo** (later mostly **ēo**), as Nth. Ken. **dīore, līode, þīostre, stīora(n),** but in Mercian **īo** beside **ēo.**

NOTE.—In Anglian **īo** became **ī** before **c** and **h**, as **cīcen**, older ***kīoken** from ***kiukīn**, *chicken*; **līhta(n)**, **tīþ** from ***tīhiþ** = WS. **līehtan**, **tīehþ**.

## VOWEL CONTRACTION.

§ **139**. Vowel contraction took place in OE. when intervocalic **h**, **w**, or **j** had disappeared.

A long vowel or a long diphthong absorbed a following short vowel, as **rā** beside older **rāha**, *roe* (§ **133**); pl. **tān** from ***tāhan**, *toes*; **tā** older ***tāhæ**, *toe*; gen. **sǣs** from ***sǣes** older ***sāwis** (§ **134**) beside nom. **sǣ**, *sea*; Anglian **nēsta** from ***nēhista** beside WS. **nīehsta**, *nearest* (§ **123**); Anglian **tīþ** from ***tīhiþ**, older ***tiuχiþ**, *he draws* (§ **138**, Note); **fōn** from ***fōhan**, *to seize*; **fō** from ***fōhu**, *I seize* (§ **117**); pl. **scōs** from ***scōhas**, beside sing. **scōh**, *shoe* (§ **128**, Note); **sēon** from ***sēo(h)an** older ***seohan**, *to see*; **sēo** from ***sēo(h)u** older ***seohu**, *I see*; gen. **fēos** from ***fēo(h)es** older ***feohes**, beside nom. **feoh**, *cattle* (§ **87**); **slēan** from ***slēa(h)an** older ***sleahan**, *to slay*; **slēa** from ***slēa(h)u** older ***sleahu**, *I slay*; **ēar** from ***ēa(h)ur** older ***eahur**, *ear of corn* (§ **70**); **nēar** from ***nēa(h)ur**, *nearer* (§ **123**); **līon**, **lēon** from ***līo(h)an**, older ***līhan**, *to lend*; **lēo** from ***līo(h)u**, *I lend* (§ **127**); **tēon** from ***tēo(h)an**, *to draw, lead*; dat. pl. **þrūm** from ***þrū(h)um** beside nom. sing. **þrūh**, *trough*.

§ **140**. **a + u** (from older **wu** or vocalized **w**) became **ēa**, as **clēa** from ***cla(w)u**, *claw*; neut. pl. **fēa** from ***fa(w)u**, *few*; **strēa** from ***straw-**, *straw* (§ **75**).

**e + u** (from **w**) became **ēo**, as **cnēo** from ***cnewa-**, *knee*, **trēo** from ***trewa-**, *tree* (§ **88**).

**i** or **ij** + guttural vowel became **īo** (**ēo**), as **bīo**, **bēo** from ***bijōn-**, *bee*; **fīond**, **fēond**, Goth. **fijands**, *enemy*; **frīond**, **frēond**, Goth. **frijōnds**, *friend*; nom. acc. neut. **þrīo**, **þrēo**, from ***þri(j)u** = Goth. **þrija**, *three* (§ **104**).

§ **141**. **i + i** became **ī**, as Nth. **sīs(t)** from ***sihis**, *thou seest*; **sīþ** from ***sihiþ**, *he sees* (§ **329**, 4).

§ **142**. Long palatal vowels absorbed a following short palatal vowel, as **gǣst** from ***ʒǣis** older ***ʒāis,** *thou goest*; **gǣþ** from ***ʒǣiþ,** *he goes*; **dēst** from ***dōis,** *thou doest*; **dēþ** from ***dōiþ,** *he does*; gen. **drȳs** from ***drȳes,** beside nom. **drȳ,** *magician.*

Note.—Special Anglian contractions are:—

**æ + æ > ǣ,** as **slǣ** from ***slæhæ** older ***sleahæ,** *I may slay.*

**e + æ > ē,** as **gesē** from ***-sehæ** older ***-seohæ,** *I may see.*

**ē + i > ē,** as **nēst(a)** from ***nēhist(a)** = WS. **nīehst(a),** *nearest.*

**ī̆ + i > ī,** as **sīs(t)** from ***sihis** = WS. **siehst,** *thou seest*; **sīþ** from ***sihiþ** = WS. **siehþ,** *he sees*; **tīþ** from ***tīhiþ** = WS. **tīehþ,** *he draws, leads.*

Nth. **a + a > ā,** as **slā** from ***slaha(n),** *to slay*; **þwā** from ***þwaha(n),** *to wash.*

## The Lengthening of Short Vowels.

§ **143.** From our knowledge of ME. phonology it is clear that short vowels must have been lengthened some time during the OE. period before certain consonant combinations, especially before a liquid or nasal + another voiced consonant. But it is impossible to ascertain the date at which these lengthenings took place, and whether they took place in all the dialects at the same time.

§ **144.** Final short vowels were lengthened in monosyllables, as **hwā,** *who?*, **swā,** *so* (§ **79**); **hē,** *he*, **mē,** *me*, **wē,** *we* (§ **95**).

§ **145.** There was a tendency to lengthen short vowels in monosyllables ending in a single consonant, as **wēl** (mod. northern dial. **wīl** from older **wēl**) beside **wel,** *well.* **lōf,** *praise*, **wēg,** *way*, but in words of this kind the short vowel was restored again through the influence of the inflected forms, **lofes, weges,** &c.

§ **146.** Short vowels were lengthened through the loss of **g** before a following consonant, as **mǣden,** *maiden*, **sǣde,** *he said*, beside older **mægden, sægde** (§ **54,** Note 2);

**brēdan,** *to brandish,* **strēdan,** *to strew,* beside older **bregdan, stregdan** (§ **80,** Note 2); **brīdel,** *bridle,* **tīle,** *tile,* beside older **brigdel, tigele** (§ **96,** Note 1).

§ **147.** By the loss of a nasal before a following voiceless spirant, as **ōþer,** Goth. **anþar,** *other*; **gōs,** OHG. **gans,** *goose*; **sōfte,** OHG. **samfto,** *softly* (§ **61**); **swīþ,** Goth. **swinþs,** *strong*; **fīf,** Goth. **fimf,** *five* (§ **97**); **cūþ,** Goth. **kunþs,** *known*; **ūs,** Goth. **uns,** *us* (§ **113**).

§ **148.** Short diphthongs were lengthened by the loss of intervocalic **h,** as **slēan** from ***sleahan,** Goth. **slahan,** *to strike, slay* (§ **70**); **sēon** from ***seohan,** OHG. **sehan,** *to see* (§ **87**).

§ **149.** By the loss of antevocalic **h** after **l** and **r,** as gen. **sēales** beside nom. **sealh,** *seal* (§ **64,** Note 1); gen. **mēares** beside nom. **mearh,** *horse* (§ **66,** Note 3); gen. **ēoles** beside nom. **eolh,** *elk* (§ **84,** Note 1); gen. **fēores** beside nom. **feorh,** *life* (§ **85,** Note 4); gen. **hōles** beside nom. **holh,** *hole* (§ **106,** Note).

## THE SHORTENING OF LONG VOWELS.

§ **150.** Long vowels were shortened during the OE. period before two consonants in polysyllabic forms, before combinations of three consonants, and before double consonants, as **enlefan** from older ***ǣnlefan,** *eleven*; **samcucu** (from ***sāmi-,** older **sǣmi-** = OHG. **sāmi-**), *half-dead*; **bledsian, bletsian** from ***blōdisōjan,** *to bless.* Pl. **bremblas** beside sing. **brēm(b)el,** *bramble.* **bliss,** *joy,* **hlammæsse,** *Lammas,* **wimman,** *woman,* beside older **blīþs, hlāfmæsse, wīfman**; **blæddre,** *bladder,* **deoppra,** *deeper,* beside older **blǣdre, dēopra,** see § **260.**

§ **151.** In the first or second elements of compounds which were no longer felt as such, as **enlefan,** prim. Germanic ***ainliƀan-,** cp. Goth. dat. **áinlibim,** *eleven*; **siþþan, sioþþan** from **sīþ + þan,** *since.* **ēorod** from **eoh + rād,** *troop of cavalry.* Adjectives ending in -lic, as **dēadlic,** *deadly,* see § **634.**

§ **152.** From what has been said in §§ **54–151** it will be seen that the Germanic vowel-system (§ **45**) assumed the following shape in OE. :—

| | |
|---|---|
| Short vowels | **a, æ, e, i, o, u, œ, y** |
| Long „ | **ā, ǣ, ē, ī, ō, ū, œ̄, ȳ** |
| Short diphthongs | **ea, eo, ie, io** |
| Long „ | **ēa, ēo, īe, īo** |

# CHAPTER V

## THE PRIM. GERMANIC EQUIVALENTS OF THE OE. VOWELS OF ACCENTED SYLLABLES

### A. The Short Vowels.

§ **153. a** = (1) Germanic **a** in open syllables when originally followed by an **ă, ŏ, ŭ** in the next syllable, as **faran,** *to go*; **nacod,** *naked*; pl. **dagas,** *days,* gen. **daga,** dat. **dagum** (§ **57**); gen. **clawe,** *of a claw*; **þawian** from ***þawōjan,** *to thaw* (§ **74**).

= (2) Germanic **a** in closed syllables before double consonants (except **hh, ll, rr**), **sc,** and **st,** when the next syllable originally contained a guttural vowel, as **abbod,** *abbot*; **catte,** *cat*; **sacc,** *sack*; **wascan,** *to wash*; **brastlian,** *to crackle* (§ **57**).

§ **154. a (o)** = Germanic **a** before nasals, as **lang, long,** *long*; **lamb, lomb,** *lamb*; **mann, monn,** *man*; **nama, noma,** *name* (§ **59**).

§ **155. æ** = (1) Germanic **a** in closed syllables, as **dæg,** *day*; **bær,** *he bore*; **sæt,** *he sat* (§ **54**).

= (2) Germanic **a** in open syllables when followed by a palatal vowel or vocalic nasal or liquid in the next syllable, as **æcer,** *field*; **fæder,** *father*; gen. **dæges,** *of a day*, dat. **dæge; fæþm,** *embrace, fathom*; **hægl,** *hail* (§ **54**).

= (3) Germanic **a** by semi-umlaut, as **æþele** from ***aþali,** *noble*; **æþeling,** from ***aþuling,** *nobleman*; **gædeling** from ***ȝaduling,** OS. **gaduling,** *companion* (§ **58**).

§ **156.** **e** = (1) Germanic **e,** as **beran,** *to bear*; **cwene,** *woman*; **weg,** *way* (§ **80**).

= (2) **i**-umlaut of **æ,** as **bedd** (Goth. **badi**), *bed*; **here,** *army*; **lecgan,** *to lay* (§ **55**).

= (3) **i**-umlaut of **a** (**o**), as **ende,** *end*; **benc,** *bench*; **sendan,** *to send* (§ **60**).

= (4) **i**-umlaut of **o,** as dat. **dehter,** beside nom. **dohtor,** *daughter*; **ele,** *oil*; **exen,** *oxen* (§ **107**).

§ **157.** **i** = (1) Germanic **i,** as **biddan,** *to pray*; **bireþ,** *he bears*; **bindan,** *to bind*; **ridon,** *we rode*; **riden,** *ridden* (§ **96**).

= (2) Germanic **e** before **m,** as **niman** (OHG. **neman**), *to take* (§ **81**).

= (3) Latin **e** before nasal + consonant in early loanwords, as **gimm** (Lat. **gemma**), *gem*; **pinsian** (Lat. **pensāre**), *to weigh, ponder* (§ **82**).

= (4) older **eo** (**ie**) before **hs** and **ht,** as **cniht,** *boy*; **six,** *six* (§ **86**).

= (5) older **ie,** see § **170.**

= (6) the unrounding of **y** before and after **c, g, h** in late WS. and Anglian, as **cinn,** *race, generation*; **cining,** *king*; **þincan,** *to seem*; **fliht,** *flight* (§ **112,** Note 2).

§ 158. o = (1) Germanic **o**, as **dohtor**, *daughter*; **coren**, *chosen*; **hord**, *treasure*; **oxa**, *ox* (§ 106).
= (2) **a** (**o**), see § 154.

§ 159. u = (1) Germanic **u**, as **curon**, *they chose*; **dumb**, *dumb*; **hund**, *dog*; **hungor**, *hunger* (§ 111).
= (2) Germanic **o** before or after labials, as **bucc** (OHG. **boc**), *buck*; **full** (OHG. **fol**), *full*; **fugol** (OHG. **fogal**), *bird*; **wulf** (OHG. **wolf**), *wolf* (§ 108).
= (3) Germanic **o** before nasals, as **guma**, *man*; **hunig**, *honey*; **þunor**, *thunder* (§ 109).
= (4) older **eo** in the combination **weo-**, as **swurd**, *sword*; **swuster**, *sister* (§ 94).
= (5) older **io** in the combination **wio-**, as **wucu**, *week*; **wuduwe**, *widow* (§ 103).

§ 160. y = (1) i-umlaut of **u**, as **bycgan** (Goth. **bugjan**), *to buy*; **cyning**, *king*; **gylden**, *golden*; **wyllen**, *woollen* (§ 112).
= (2) older **ie**, see § 170.

B. The Long Vowels.

§ 161. ā = (1) Germanic **ai**, as **ān**, *one*; **bāt**, *he bit*; **hāl**, *whole*; **hātan**, *to call* (§ 133).
= (2) Germanic **ǣ** before **w**, as **blāwan**, *to blow*; **cnāwan**, *to know*; **sāwon**, *they saw* (§ 120).
= (3) Germanic **ǣ** in the combination **ǣg** followed by a guttural vowel, as pl. **māgas**, beside sing. **mǣg**, *kinsman*; pret. **lāgon**, *they lay* (§ 120).
= (4) lengthening of final **a** in monosyllables, as **hwā**, *who?*; **swā**, *so* (§ 79).

§ 162. ǣ = (1) Germanic **ǣ** (non-WS. **ē**), as **bǣron**, *they* *bore*; **cwǣdon,** *they said*; **dǣd,** *deed*; **rǣdan,** *to advise* (§ **119**).

= (2) i-umlaut of **ā** = Germanic **ai,** as **dǣlan,** *to divide*; **hǣlan,** *to heal*; **hǣþ,** *heath* (§ **134**).

= (3) i-umlaut of **ā** = Germanic **ǣ** before **w,** as **cnǣwþ,** *he knows*; **lǣwan,** *to betray* (§ **120**).

= (4) OE. **æg,** as **mǣden,** *maiden,* **sǣde,** *he said,* beside **mægden, sægde** (§ **54,** Note 2).

= (5) Latin **ā** in early loanwords, as **nǣp** (Lat. **nāpus**), *turnip*; **strǣt** (Lat. **strāta**), *street* (§ **119,** Note 3).

§ **163.** **ē** = (1) Germanic **ē,** as **hēr,** *here*; **mēd,** *pay, reward* (§ **125**).

= (2) i-umlaut of Germanic **ō,** as **bēc,** *books*; **fēt,** *feet*; **dēman,** *to judge*; **sēcan,** *to seek* (§ **129**).

= (3) i-umlaut of **ō** = Germanic nasalized **ā**, as **ēhtan,** *to persecute*; **fēhþ,** *he seizes* (§ **118**).

= (4) i-umlaut of **ō** = Germanic **ǣ** before nasals, as **cwēn,** *queen, wife*; **wēnan,** *to hope* (§ **122**).

= (5) i-umlaut of **ō** = Germanic **am, an** before **f, þ, s,** as **sēfte,** *soft*; **tēþ,** *teeth*; **gēs,** *geese* (§ **62**).

= (6) OE. **eg,** as **brēdan,** *to brandish,* **rēn,** *rain,* beside **bregdan, regn** (§ **80,** Note 2).

= (7) lengthening of final **e** in monosyllables, as **hē,** *he*; **mē,** *me*; **þē,** *thee* (§ **95**).

= (8) early WS. **ēa** = Germanic **au,** before **c, g, h** and after **c, g, sc,** as **bēcen,** *beacon*; **ēge**, *eye*; **hēh**, *high*; **cēpian**, *to buy*; **gēt**, *he poured out*; **scēf**, *he pushed* (§ **135**, Note 1).

§ **164**. **ī** = (1) Germanic **ī**, as **bītan**, *to bite*; **īs**, *ice*; **mīn**, *mine*; **rīdan**, *to ride* (§ **126**).

= (2) Germanic **im**, **in** before **f**, **þ**, as **fīf** (Goth. **fimf**), *five*; **līþe**, *gentle*; **swīþ**, *strong* (§ **97**).

= (3) OE. **ig**, as **brīdel**, *bridle*, **sīþe**, *scythe*, beside **brigdel**, **sigþe** (§ **96**, Note 1).

= (4) older **īe**, see § **174**.

= (5) Latin **ē** (**œ**) in early loanwords, as **cīpe** (Lat. **cēpa**), *onion*; **pīn** (Lat. **pœna**, late Lat. **pēna**), *torture* (§ **125**, Note).

§ **165**. **ō** = (1) Germanic **ō**, as **bōc**, *book*; **brōþor**, *brother*; **grōwan**, *to grow*; **fōr**, *he went* (§ **128**).

= (2) Germanic nasalized **ā**, as **brōhte**, *he brought*; **fōn** from ***fōhan**, older ***fāhan**, *to seize*; **þōhte**, *he thought* (§ **117**).

= (3) Germanic **ǣ** before nasals, as **mōna**, *moon*; **nōmon**, *they took*; **sōna**, *soon* (§ **121**).

= (4) Germanic **am**, **an** before **f**, **þ**, **s**, as **sōfte**, *softly*; **gōs**, *goose*; **tōþ**, *tooth* (§ **61**).

= (5) from Germanic **o** by loss of **h**, as gen. **hōles** beside nom. **holh**, *hole* (§ **106**, Note).

§ **166**. **ū** = (1) Germanic **ū**, as **hūs**, *house*; **mūs**, *mouse*; **scūfan**, *to push*; **þūsend**, *thousand* (§ **131**).

= (2) Germanic final **wō**, as **cū**, *cow*; **hū**, *how* (§ **130**).

= (3) Germanic **un** before **þ**, **s**, as **cūþ**, *known*; **mūþ**, *mouth*; **ūs**, *us* (§ **113**).

= (4) Germanic **u** by loss of **h**, as gen. pl. **sūla** beside nom. sing. **sulh**, *plough* (§ **114**).

§ **167**. **ȳ** = (1) i-umlaut of Germanic **ū**, as **brȳd**, *bride*; **mȳs**, *mice*; **brȳcþ**, *he enjoys* (§ **132**).
= (2) i-umlaut of **ū** = Germanic **un** before **þ**, **s**, as **cȳþan**, *to make known*; **ȳst**, *storm* (§ **114**).
= (3) older **īe**, see § **174**.

C. The Short Diphthongs.

§ **168**. **ea** = (1) Germanic **a** by breaking, as **eall**, *all*; **ceald**, *cold* (§ **64**); **heard**, *hard*; **wearþ**, *he became* (§ **66**); **eahta**, *eight*; **weaxan**, *to grow*; **seah**, *he saw* (§ **68**).
= (2) older **æ** = Germanic **a**, after palatal **c**, **g**, **sc**, as **ceaster**, *city*, *fortress*; **geaf**, *he gave*; **sceal**, *shall* (§ **72**).

§ **169**. **eo** = (1) Germanic **e** by breaking, as **meolcan**, *to milk*; **sceolh**, *wry*, *oblique* (§ **84**); **eorþe**, *earth*; **heorte**, *heart* (§ **85**); **cneoht**, *boy*; **feohtan**, *to fight* (§ **86**).
= (2) i-umlaut of Germanic **a** before **w**, as **eowestre**, *sheepfold*; **meowle**, *maiden* (§ **77**).
= (3) Germanic **e** before **w**+vowel, as gen. **cneowes**, **treowes**, beside nom. **cnēo**, *knee*, **trēo**, *tree* (§ **89**).
= (4) Germanic **e** by **u**-umlaut, as **eofor**, *boar*; **meolu**, *meal*, *flour*; **seofon**, *seven* (§ **92**).

§ **170**. **ie** (later **i**, **y**) = (1) i-umlaut of **ea** = Germanic **a** by breaking, as **fiellan**, *to fell*; **ieldra**, *elder*, *older* (§ **65**); **ierfe**, *inheritance*; **dierne**, *secret* (§ **67**); **hliehhan**, *to laugh*; **sliehþ**, *he slays* (§ **69**).
= (2) i-umlaut of **io** = Germanic **i** by breaking, as **fiehst**, *thou fightest*; **ierre**, *angry*; **siehþ**, *he sees* (§ **99**).

= (3) Germanic **e** after palatal **c, g, sc,** as **cieres,** *cherry-tree*; **giefan,** *to give*; **scieran.** *to shear* (§ **91**).

= (4) **i**-umlaut of **ea,** after palatal **c, g,** as **ciele,** *cold*; **giest,** *guest* (§ **73**).

NOTE.—**ie** only occurs in WS. and is therefore a special characteristic of this dialect. It became **y** in the ninth century in some parts of the WS. area and in other parts it became **i,** although the **ie** was often retained in writing. In the ninth century **ie** was often written **i,** and conversely old **i** was often written **ie,** which shows that the two sounds had fallen together in **i.**

§ **171.** **io** (later **eo**) = (1) Germanic **i** by breaking, as **liornian,** *to learn*; **miox,** *manure* (§ **98**).

= (2) Germanic **i** by **u-, o/a**-umlaut, as **cliopung,** *calling*; **mioluc,** *milk* (§ **101**); **liofast,** *thou livest* (§ **102**).

### D. THE LONG DIPHTHONGS.

§ **172.** **ēa** = (1) Germanic **au,** as **cēas,** *he chose*; **dēaþ,** *death*; **ēage,** *eye*; **hēafod,** *head*; **rēad,** *red* (§ **135**).

= (2) Germanic **ǣ** after palatal **c, g, sc,** as **cēace,** *jaw*; **gēafon,** *they gave*; **gēar,** *year*; **scēap,** *sheep* (§ **124**).

= (3) Germanic **ǣ** by breaking before **h,** as **nēah,** *near*; **nēar,** older ***nēahur,** *nearer* (§ **123**).

= (4) Germanic **aw** which became final in prim. OE., as **hrēa,** *raw*; **strēa,** *straw* (§ **75**).

= (5) from **au** after the loss of intervocalic **w,** as **clēa** from ***cla(w)u,** *claw*; **þrēa** from ***þra(w)u,** *threat* (§ **75**).

= (6) Germanic **aw** in the combination **ēaw** = Germanic **aww**, as **dēaw** (Goth. ***daggwa-**), *dew*; **hēawan,** *to hew* (§ **76**).

= (7) OE. **ea,** Germanic **a,** by loss of antevocalic **h** after **l** and **r,** as gen. **sēales, wēales,** beside nom. **sealh,** *willow,* **wealh,** *foreign* (§ **64,** Note 1); gen. **fēares, mēares,** beside nom. **fearh,** *pig,* **mearh,** *horse* (§ **66,** Note 3).

= (8) OE. **ea,** by loss of intervocalic **h,** as **ēa,** *river*; **slēan,** *to slay*; **tēar,** *tear* (§ **70**).

§ **173.** **ēo** = (1) Germanic **eu,** as **cēosan,** *to choose*; **dēop,** *deep*; **lēof,** *dear*; **þēof,** *thief* (§ **137**).

= (2) Germanic **ew** which became final in prim. OE., as **cnēo,** *knee*; **trēo,** *tree* (§ **88**).

= (3) Germanic **ew** in the combination **ēow** = Germanic **eww,** as **trēow,** *trust, faith* (§ **90**).

= (4) OE. **eo,** Germanic **e,** by loss of antevocalic **h** after **l** and **r,** as **fēolan,** *to hide*; gen. **ēoles,** beside nom. **eolh,** *elk* (§ **84,** Note 1); gen. **fēores,** beside nom. **feorh,** *life* (§ **85,** Note 4).

= (5) OE. **eo** by loss of intervocalic **h,** as **sēon,** *to see*; **swēor,** *father-in-law*; gen. **fēos,** beside nom. **feoh,** *cattle* (§ **87**).

§ **174.** **īe** (later **ī, ȳ**) = (1) i-umlaut of **ēa,** Germanic **au,** as **gelīefan,** *to believe*; **hīeran,** *to hear*; **hīehsta,** *highest* (§ **136**).

= (2) i-umlaut of **īo,** Germanic **iu,** as **cīesþ,** *he chooses*; **dīerling,** *darling*; **līehtan,** *to give light*; **tīehþ,** *he draws, leads* (§ **138**).

= (3) i-umlaut of **īo,** Germanic **ī** before **h, ht**

by breaking, as **līehst**, *thou lendest*; **līehtan**, *to lighten, make easier* (§ **127**).

= (4) **i-umlaut of īo (ēo)**, Germanic **ij** + guttural vowel, as **fīend** from ***fijandiz**, *fiends*; **frīend** from ***frijōndiz**, *friends* (§ **105**).

= (5) Germanic **ew** in the combination **īew(e)** = Germanic **ewwj**, as **getrīewe**, *true, faithful* (§ **90**).

= (6) Germanic **ew** in the combination **īew(e)** = Germanic **ewj**, as **nīewe**, *new* (§ **90**).

NOTE.—**īe** only occurs in WS. and is therefore a special characteristic of this dialect. It became **ȳ** in the ninth century in some parts of the WS. area, and in other parts it became **ī**, although the **īe** was often retained in writing. In the ninth century **īe** was sometimes written for old **ī**, which shows that the two sounds had fallen together in **ī**.

§ **175**. **īo (ēo)** = (1) Germanic **iu**, as **geþīode**, **geþēode**, *language*; **līode**, **lēode**, *people*; **þīostre**, **þēostre**, *dark* (§ **138**).

= (2) Germanic **i** or **ij** + guttural vowel, as **fīond**, **fēond**, Goth. **fijands**, *fiend, enemy*; **frīond**, **frēond**, Goth. **frijōnds**, *friend*; neut. pl. **þrīo**, **þrēo** from ***þriju**, Goth. **þrija**, *three* (§ **104**).

= (3) Germanic **ī** by breaking before **h** and **ht**, as **þīon**, **þēon**, OHG. **dīhan**, *to thrive*; **līoh**, **lēoh**, OHG. **līh**, *lend thou*; **betwēoh**, *between*; **lēoht**, OHG. **līhti**, adj. *light* (§ **127**).

## THE CHIEF DEVIATIONS OF THE OTHER DIALECTS FROM WEST SAXON.

§ **176**. **a** (Anglian) = WS. **ea** before **l** + consonant, as **cald**, *cold*, **fallan**, *to fall*, **haldan**, *to hold*, WS. **ceald**, **feallan**, **healdan** (§ **63**).

§ **177**. **æ** (Anglian) = (1) WS. **ea** before **h** and **h**+consonant, as **sæh**, *he saw*, **fæx**, *hair*, **æhta**, *eight*, WS. **seah**, **feax**, **eahta** (§ **68**, Note 1).

= (2) WS. **ie**, **i**-umlaut of **ea**, before **h**+consonant, as **hlæhha(n)**, *to laugh*, **mæhtig**, *mighty*, WS. **hliehhan**, **miehtig** (§ **69**, Note).

§ **178**. **æ** (later **e**) = (1) WS. **ea** before **r**+guttural, as **berg**, *pig*, **erc**, *ark*, **færh**, **ferh**, *boar*, *pig*, **mærc**, **merc**, *boundary*, WS. **bearg**, **earc**, **fearh**, **mearc** (§ **66**, Note 1).

= (2) WS. **ie**, **i**-umlaut of **ea**, before **l**+consonant, as **ældra**, **eldra**, *older*, **fælla**(n), **fella**(n), *to fell*, WS. **ieldra**, **fiellan** (§ **65**, Note).

§ **179**. **æ** beside **ea** (Anglian) = WS. **ea** after palatal **c**, **g**, **sc**, as **cæster**, *city*, *fortress*, **gæt**, *gate*, **scæl**, *shall*, beside **ceaster**, **geat**, **sceal** (§ **72**, Note 1).

§ **180**. **æ** (Merċian for older **ea** by **o**/**a**-umlaut) = WS. **a** before gutturals, as **dræca**, *dragon*, **dægas**, *days*, WS. **draca**, **dagas** (§ **78**, Note 1).

§ **181**. **e** (Anglian and Ken.) = (1) WS. **ie** after palatal **c**, **g**, **sc**, as **gefa(n)**, *to give*, **gelda(n)**, *to pay*, **sceld**, *shield*, WS. **giefan**, **gieldan**, **scield** (§ **91**).

= (2) WS. **ie**, **i**-umlaut of **ea**, before **r**+consonant, as **derne**, *secret*, **erfe**, *inheritance*, WS. **dierne**, **ierfe** (§ **67**, Note).

= (3) WS. **ie**, **i**-umlaut of **ea**, after palatal **c**, **g**, **sc**, as **cele**, *cold*, **gest**, *guest*, **sceppan**, *to create*, WS. **ciele**, **giest**, **scieppan** (§ **73**, Note).

§ **182**. **e** (Anglian) = (1) WS. **eo** before **lc**, **lh**, as **elh**, *elk*,

**melca(n)**, *to milk*, WS. **eolh, meolcan** (§ **84**).

= (2) WS. **eo** before **h, hs, ht,** as **feh,** *cattle*, **sex,** *six*, **cneht,** *boy*, early WS. **feoh, seox, cneoht** (§ **86**, Note).

= (3) WS. **eo** before **r** + guttural, as **derc,** *dark*, **werc,** *work*, **dwerg,** *dwarf*, **ferh,** *life*, WS. **deorc, weorc, dweorg, feorh** (§ **85**, Note 2).

§ **183**. **e** (Ken.) = (1) WS. **æ**, as **deg,** *day*, **feder,** *father*, **hefde,** *he had*, WS. **dæg, fæder, hæfde** (§ **54**, Note 1).

= (2) WS. **ea** after palatal **c, g, sc,** as **cester,** *city, fortress*, **get,** *gate*, **scel,** *shall*, WS. **ceaster, geat, sceal** (§ **72**, Note 1).

= (3) WS. **y**, **i**-umlaut of **u**, as **besig,** *busy*, **efel,** *evil*, **senn,** *sin*, WS. **bysig, yfel, synn** (§ **112**, Note 1).

= (4) WS. **ie**, **i**-umlaut of **ea**, as **eldra,** *older*, **eldu,** *old age*, WS. **ieldra, ieldu** (§ **65**, Note).

§ **184**. **i** (Anglian) = (1) WS. **ie** before a guttural or **r** + guttural, as **birce,** *birch*, **gebirhta(n)**, *to make bright*, **gesihþ,** *vision*, WS. **bierce, gebierhtan, gesiehþ** (§ **99**, Note 2).

= (2) WS. **io** (**u**-umlaut) before **l** + guttural, as **milc,** *milk*, WS. **mioluc, miolc** (§ **101**, Note 2).

= (3) WS. **io** (**eo**) before gutturals, as **getih-hia(n)**, WS. **tiohhian, teohhian,** *to arrange, think, consider* (§ **98**, Note 2).

= (4) WS. **u** in the combination **wu-** before gutturals, as **betwih,** *between*, **cwic(u)**, *quick, alive*, **wicu,** *week*, WS. **betwuh, c(w)ucu, wucu** (§ **103**).

§ **185**. **o** (late Nth.) = late WS. **u** in the combination

**wu·**, as **sword**, *sword*, **worþa**, *to become*, late WS. **swurd**, **wurþan** (§ **94**).

§ **186**. **œ** (Nth.) = (1) WS. **e**, **i**-umlaut of **o**, as dat. **dœhter**, *to a daughter*, **œle**, *oil*, WS. **dehter**, **ele** (§ **107**).

(2) WS. **e** after **w**, as **cuœþa**, *to say*, **wœg**, *way*, WS. **cweþan**, **weg** (§ **80**, Note 1); **cuœlla**, *to kill*, WS. **cwellan** (§ **55**, Note 1).

§ **187**. **ǣ** (Anglian) later **ē** = WS. **ēa**, Germanic **au**, before **c**, **g**, **h**, as **ǣc**, *also*, **hǣh**, *high*, **tǣg**, *rope*, later **ēc**, **hēh**, **tēg**, WS. **ēac**, **hēah**, **tēag** (§ **135**, Note 2).

§ **188**. **ē** (Anglian and Ken.) = (1) WS. **ǣ**, Germanic **ǣ**, as **bēron**, *they bore*, **dēd**, *deed*, **sēton**, *they sat*, **slēpan**, *to sleep*, WS. **bǣron**, **dǣd**, **sǣton**, **slǣpon** (§ **119**).

= (2) WS. **ēa** after palatal **c**, **g**, **sc**, as **cēce**, *jaw*, **gēr**, *year*, **gēfon**, *they gave*, **scēp**, *sheep*, WS. **cēace**, **gēar**, **gēafon**, **scēap** (§ **124**, Note).

= (3) WS. **īe**, **i**-umlaut of **ēa**, Germanic **au**, as **gelēfan**, *to believe*, **hēran**, *to hear*, **nēd**, *need*, WS. **gelīefan**, **hīeran**, **nīed** (§ **136**).

§ **189**. **ē** (Anglian) = (1) WS. **ēo**, Germanic **eu**, before **c**, **g**, **h**, as **rēca(n)**, *to smoke*, **sēc**, *sick*, **flēga(n)**, *to fly*, **lēht**, *light*, WS. **rēocan**, **sēoc**, **flēogan**, **lēoht** (§ **137**, Note 2).

= (2) WS. **īe**, **i**·umlaut of **ēa** from older **ǣ** by breaking, as **nēsta** from ***nēhista**, WS. **nīehsta**, *nearest*, *next* (§ **123**).

= (3) older **ǣ**, see § **187**.

§ **190**. **ē** (Ken.) = Anglian and WS. **ȳ**, **i**·umlaut of **ū**, as **hēf**, *hive*, **mēs**, *mice*, **ontēnan**, *to open*, Anglian and WS. **hȳf**, **mȳs**, **ontȳnan** (§ **132**, Note).

§ **191.** **ē** (late Ken.) = Anglian and WS. **ǣ**, i-umlaut of **ā**, as **clēne**, *clean*, **hēlan**, *to heal*, **hētan**, *to heat*, Anglian and WS. **clǣne**, **hǣlan**, **hǣtan** (§ **134**).

§ **192.** **ī** (Anglian) = (1) WS. **īo** (**ēo**), Germanic **ī**, before **h** and **ht**, as **wīh**, *idol*, **līh**, *lend thou*, **līht**, adj. *light*, WS. **wēoh**, **lēoh**, **lēoht** (§ **127**).

= (2) WS. **īe**, i-umlaut of **īo** = Germanic **iu**, before **c** and **ht**, as **cīcen**, *chicken*, **līhtan**, *to give light*, WS. **cīecen**, **līehtan** (§ **138**, Note).

= (3) WS. **īe**, i-umlaut of **īo**, Germanic **ī**, before **ht**, as **līhtan**, *to lighten*, *make easier* (§ **127**).

§ **193.** **ī** (Nth.) = WS. **ieh**, as **sīs(t)** from ***sihis**, *thou seest*, **sīþ** from ***sihiþ**, *he sees*, WS. **siehst**, **siehþ** (§ **99**, Note 2).

§ **194.** **œ̄** (Nth.) = (1) WS. **ē**, i-umlaut of **ō** of whatever origin, as **bœ̄c**, *books*, **fœ̄t**, *feet*, **grœ̄ne**, *green*, WS. **bēc**, **fēt**, **grēne** (§ **129**); **gœ̄s**, WS. **gēs**, *geese* (§ **62**); **fœ̄þ**, WS. **fēhþ**, *he seizes* (§ **118**).

= (2) WS. **ǣ**, Germanic **ǣ**, after **w**, as **huœ̄r**, *where*, **wœ̄ron**, *they were*, WS. **hwǣr**, **wǣron** (§ **119**, Note 2).

§ **195.** **ea** (Anglian) beside **æ**, see § **179**.

§ **196.** **ea** (Nth.) = (1) WS. **eo** before **r** + consonant, as **earþe**, *earth*, **hearte**, *heart*, **stearra**, *star*, WS. **eorþe**, **heorte**, **steorra** (§ **85**, Note 3).

= (2) WS. **e**, Mercian **eo** by **o/a**-umlaut, **beara**, *to bear*, **eata**, *to eat*, **treada**, *to tread*, WS. **beran**, **etan**, **tredan** (§ **93**).

§ **197.** **ea** (Mercian) by **u-**, **o/a**-umlaut = WS. **a**, as **featu**, *vats*, **heafuc**, *hawk*, **fearan**, *to go* WS. **fatu**, **hafuc**, **faran** (§ **78**).

§ **198.** **eo** (Mercian and Ken.) by **u**-umlaut = WS. **e** (before all single consonants except labials and liquids), as **eodor**, *enclosure*, **eosol**, *donkey*, WS. **edor, esol** (§ **92**).

§ **199.** **eo** (Ken.) by **u**-umlaut = Anglian and WS. **e** before gutturals, as **breogo**, *prince*, **reogol**, *rule*, Anglian and WS. **brego, regol** (§ **92**).

§ **200.** **eo** (Mercian and Ken.) by **o**/**a**-umlaut = WS. **e**, as **beoran**, *to bear*, **eotan**, *to eat*, **feola**, *many*, WS. **beran, etan, fela** (§ **93**).

§ **201.** **eo** (Mercian and Ken.) = late WS. **u** in the combination **wu**, as **sweord**, *sword*, **sweostor**, *sister*, late WS. **swurd, swuster** (§ **94**).

§ **202.** **io** (Anglian and Ken.) by **u**-umlaut = WS. **i** (before all single consonants except labials and liquids), as **liomu**, *limbs*, **nioþor**, *lower*, **siodu**, *custom*, **sionu**, *sinew*, WS. **limu, niþor, sidu, sinu** (§ **101**).

§ **203.** **io** (Anglian and Ken.) by **o**/**a**-umlaut = WS. **i**, as **nioman**, *to take*, **niomaþ**, *they take*, WS. **niman, nimaþ** (§ **102**).

§ **204.** **io** (Nth. and Ken.) = WS. **ie**, **i**-umlaut of **io**, Germanic **i**, as **hiorde**, *shepherd*, **iorre**, *angry*, WS. **hierde, ierre** (§ **99**, Note 1).

§ **205.** **io** (Ken.) = WS. **eo** by breaking before **r** + consonant, as **hiorte**, *heart*, **iorþe**, *earth*, **stiorra**, *star*, WS. **heorte, eorþe, steorra** (§ **85**, Note 3).

§ **206.** **io** (Ken.) by **o**/**a**-umlaut = Anglian and WS. **i** before gutturals, as **stiocian**, Anglian and WS. **stician**, *to prick* (§ **102**).

§ **207.** **io** (Mercian) beside **eo** = WS. **ie**, **i**-umlaut of **io**, as **iorre, eorre**, *angry*, **hiorde, heorde**, *shepherd*, WS. **ierre, hierde** (§ **99**, Note 1).

§ **208.** **ēa** (Nth.) = Mercian and WS. **ēo,** Germanic **eu,** as **dēap,** *deep,* **dēar,** *deer,* **lēaf,** *dear,* Mercian and WS. **dēop, dēor, lēof** (§ **137**).

§ **209.** **īo** (Ken.) beside **īa** = (1) Mercian and WS. **ēo,** Germanic **eu,** as **dīop** (**dīap**), **dīor, līof** = Mercian and WS. **dēop, dēor, lēof** (§ **137**).
= (2) WS. **īe,** i-umlaut of **īo,** Germanic **iu,** as **dīore** (**dīare**), *dear,* **līohtan,** *to give light,* WS. **dīere, līehtan** (§ **138**).

§ **210.** **īo** (Mercian) beside **ēo** = WS. **īe,** i-umlaut of **īo,** as **dīore** (**dēore**), **līohtan** (**lēohtan**), WS. **dīere, līehtan** (§ **138**).

## CHAPTER VI

## THE OLD ENGLISH DEVELOPMENT OF THE PRIMITIVE GERMANIC VOWELS OF UNACCENTED SYLLABLES

§ **211.** In the Germanic languages as in all the other languages which had predominantly stress accent, the Indg. vowels underwent far more changes in unaccented than in accented syllables. In final syllables there was a great tendency in all these languages for short vowels to disappear, for long vowels to become shortened, and then partly to disappear, and for diphthongs, whether originally short or long, to become monophthongs, and then to become shortened. These changes took place partly in prim. Germanic, and partly in the prehistoric and historic periods of the separate languages.

Before beginning, however, with the history of the Indg. vowels in final syllables, it is necessary to state what became of the Indg. consonants in final syllables, because the vowels which were originally final, and those which became final in prim. Germanic through the loss of final consonants, generally had the same fate :—

(1) Indg. final **-m** became **-n** in prim. Germanic. This **-n** remained after a short accented vowel, and when protected by a particle, as Goth. **ƕan,** OS. **hwan** = Lat. **quom,** *when* ; OE. **þan, þon,** Goth. **þan** = Lat. **tum,** *then* ; masc. acc. sing. OE. **þon-e,** late OE. **þæn-, þan-e,** Goth. **þan-a,** *the, that* = Skr. **tám,** Gr. *τόν,* Lat. **tum** in **is-tum,** but in all other forms it, as also Indg. final **-n,** disappeared in prim. Germanic with nasalization of the preceding vowel. And then during the prim. Germanic period, the short nasalized vowels became oral again, but the long nasalized vowels remained, and only became oral again in the separate languages. The oldest Norse runic inscriptions preserved the short vowels which became final through the loss of a final nasal, but in Goth. O.Icel. and the West Germanic languages they underwent the same treatment as the short vowels which were originally final, as acc. sing. **staina** = OE. **stān,** Goth. **stáin,** O.Icel. OHG. **stein,** OS. **stēn,** *stone* ; OE. **geoc,** Goth. **juk** = Lat. **jugum,** Gr. *ζυγόν,* Indg. ***jugóm,** *yoke* ; acc. sing. OE. Goth. OS. **wulf,** O.Icel. **ūlf,** OHG. **wolf** = Lat. **lupum,** Gr. *λύκον, wolf* ; OE. **giest,** Goth. **gast,** from ***ʒastin,** *guest,* cp. Lat. **turrim,** *tower* ; OE. **fōt,** Goth. **fōtu,** from ***fōtun,** cp. Lat. **pedem,** Gr. *πόδα* (§ **34**), *foot* ; acc. sing. of **ō**-stems, as OE. **giefe,** Goth. **giba,** OS. OHG. **geba,** *gift,* prim. Germanic ***ʒeƀō** (with nasalized **ō**), older **-ōn, -ōm** = Indg. **-ām** ; gen. pl. OE. O.Icel. **daga,** OS. **dago,** OHG. **tago,** *of days,* prim. Germanic ***đaʒō̃** (with nasalized **-ō̃**), older **-ō̃n, -ō̃m** = Indg. **-ō̃m** ; and similarly in the genitive plural of all nouns, adjectives, and pronouns ; nom. sing. of feminine and neuter **n**-stems, as **tunge,** *tongue,* **ēage,** *eye,* original ending **-ōn** ; pret. sing. **nerede,** Goth. **nasida,** prim. Germanic ***naziđōn,** older **-ōm,** *I saved.*

(2) The Indg. final explosives (**t, d**) disappeared in

prim. Germanic, except after a short accented vowel in monosyllables, and then the vowels which became final underwent the same treatment as original final vowels, as OE. **wile,** Goth. OS. OHG. **wili** from ***welīt,** *he will* = O.Lat. **velīt**; OE. O.Icel. OS. OHG. **bere,** Goth. **baíráі**= Skr. **bhárēt,** *he may bear*; **bǣrun,** Goth. **bērun** from an original ***bhērnt** with vocalic **n** (§ **35**), *they bore*; but OE. **hwæt,** O.Icel. **hvat,** OS. **hwat** = Lat. **quod,** *what*; OE. **æt,** Goth. O.Icel. OS. **at** = Lat. **ad,** *at*.

(3) Prim. Germanic final **-z,** which arose from Indg. **-s** by Verner's law (§ **252**), disappeared in the West Germanic languages, but became **-r** in O.Icel., and **-s** again in Goth., as OE. **dæg,** OS. **đag,** OHG. **tag,** O.Icel. **dagr,** Goth. **dags,** from prim. Germanic ***đaȝaz,** *day*; and similarly in the nom. sing. of masculine and feminine **i-** and **u-**stems; in the gen. singular of **ō-**, and consonantal stems; in the nom. plural of masculine and feminine nouns. Prim. Germanic final **nz** disappeared in prim. ON. and West Germanic, as acc. pl. O.Icel. **daga,** OHG. **taga** = Goth. **dagans,** *days*; O.Icel. **geste,** OS. OHG. **gesti** = Goth. **gastins,** *guests*. In the dat. plural of all nouns, adjectives, and pronouns it disappeared already in prim. Germanic.

Note.—It is difficult to account satisfactorily for the **-s** in the nom. plural of **a-**stems in OE. and OS., as **dagas,** OS. **dagos,** see § **334**.

(4) Indg. final **-r** remained in prim. Germanic and also in the separate languages, as OE. **fæder,** Goth. **fadar,** O.Icel. **faðer,** OS. **fadar,** OHG. **fater** = Lat. **pater,** Gr. *πατήρ*, *father*.

Note.—The treatment of the Indg. final consonants in prim. Germanic may be stated in general terms thus:—With the exception of **-s** and **-r** all Indg. final consonants disappeared in prim. Germanic. In the case of the explosives it cannot be determined whether they had or had not undergone the first sound-shifting (§ **239**).

§ **212.** (1) **a** (= Indg. **a** and **o**), which was originally final or became final in prim. Germanic through the loss of a following consonant, disappeared in dissyllabic and polysyllabic forms already in primitive OE., as **wāt,** Goth. **wáit,** Gr. *οἶδα, I know*; **wāst,** Goth. **wáist,** Gr. *οἶσθα, thou knowest*; pret. first pers. singular of strong verbs, as **band,** *I bound*; **bær,** *I bore,* **sæt,** *I sat,* prim. Germanic ***ƀanđa,** ***ƀara,** ***sata,** from older ***bhondha,** ***bhora,** ***soda**; nom. sing. **wulf** from ***wulfaz** = Gr. *λύκος, wolf*; acc. **wulf** from ***wulfan** = Gr. *λύκον*; nom. acc. neut. **geoc** from ***jukan** = Gr. *ζυγόν,* Lat. **jugum,** *yoke*; gen. sing. **dæges** from ***đaȝasa,** older **-o,** *of a day*; **beran** from ***ƀeranan** = Indg. ***bheronom,** *to bear*; pp. **boren** from ***ƀurenaz,** *borne*; pp. **genered** from ***-naziđaz,** *saved*; **cyning** from ***kuniŋȝaz,** *king.*

§ **213.** (2) Original final **e** disappeared in primitive OE. without leaving any trace, but when the **e** was originally followed by a consonant it became **i** in prim. Germanic, and then underwent the same further development in OE. as original **i** (see below), as **wāt,** Goth. **wáit** = Gr. *οἶδε, he knows*; pret. third pers. singular of strong verbs, as **band,** *he bound*; **bær,** *he bore*; **sat,** *he sat,* prim. Germanic ***ƀanđe,** ***ƀare,** ***sate,** from older ***bhondhe,** ***bhore,** ***sode**; imperative **ber** from ***ƀere** = Gr. *φέρε, bear thou*; **nim** from ***neme,** *take thou* = Gr. *νέμε, distribute thou*; voc. singular **wulf** from ***wulfe** = Gr. *λύκε,* Lat. **lupe,** *wolf*; **fīf,** Goth. **fimf** = Gr. *πέντε,* Indg. ***peŋqʷe,** *five*; **mec,** Goth. **mik,** cp. Gr. *ἐμέγε, me.* But pl. nom. **fœ̄t, fēt** from ***fōtiz,** older **-ez,** cp. Gr. *πόδες, feet*; **guman** from ***ȝumaniz,** *men,* cp. Gr. *ποιμένες, shepherds*; **hnyte** from ***χnutiz,** *nuts.*

§ **214.** (3) Final long vowels, inherited from prim. Germanic, became shortened already in prim. OE. :—

**-ō** (= Indg. **ō** and **ā**) became **u,** as **beru** from ***ƀerō** = Lat. **ferō,** Gr. *φέρω, I bear*; nom. singular **giefu** from ***ȝeƀō,** Indg. ***ghebhā,** *gift,* cp. Gr. *χώρᾱ, land*; nom. acc.

neut. plural **geocu** from ***jukō**, older ***jukā** = O.Lat. **jugā**, Indg. ***jugā**, *yokes*.

Prim. Germanic **-ǣ** (= Indg. **-ē**) became **-æ**, as pret. sing. **nerede**, Goth. **nasida**, prim. Germanic ***naziđǣ(t)**, *he saved*.

**-ī** became **-i**, later **-e**, as pres. subj. third pers. singular **wile**, *he will* = O.Lat. **velīt**; imper. second pers. singular **nere**, Goth. **nasei**, OHG. **neri**, from ***nazī**, older ***nazij(i)**, Indg. ***noséje**, *save thou*.

§ **215**. (4) Short **u** and **i**, which were originally final or became final through the loss of a consonant, disappeared in trisyllabic and polysyllabic forms. They, as well as the **u** and **i**, which arose from the shortening of **ō** and **ī**, disappeared also in dissyllabic forms when the first syllable was long, but remained when the first syllable was short. The regular operation of this law was often disturbed by analogical formations.

Regular forms were: nom. sing. **giest** = Goth. **gasts**, from ***ʒastiz**, *guest* = Lat. **hostis**, *stranger*, *enemy*; acc. **giest** = Goth. **gast**, from ***ʒastin** = Lat. ***hostim**; dat. sing. of consonantal stems, as **fœ̄t, fēt** (nom. **fōt**, *foot*) from ***fōti**, cp. Gr. **ποδί**; dat. plural of nouns, as **dagum** (nom. **dæg**, *day*) from ***đaʒomiz**; **giefum** (nom. **giefu**, *gift*) from ***ʒeƀōmiz**; **hīer** = Goth. **háusei**, from ***χauzī**, *hear thou*; **sēc** = Goth. **sōkei**, *seek thou*; **bend** = Goth. **bandi**, from ***ƀanđī**, *band*; in the second and third pers. singular and third pers. plural of the pres. indicative, as prim. Germanic ***nimiz**, *thou takest*; ***nimiđ**, *he takes*; ***nemanđ**, *they take*, from older ***nemesi**, ***nemeti**, ***nemonti** (on the OE. endings of these forms, see § **476**); sing. nom. **hand** = Goth. **handus**, *hand*; acc. **hand** = Goth. **handu**; acc. singular of consonantal stems, as **fōt** = Goth. **fōtu**, *foot*; **fæder** from ***fađerun**, *father*; **guman** from ***ʒumanun**, *man*; nom. **lār** from ***lāru**, older ***laizō**, *lore, teaching*; neut. pl. **word** from ***wordu**, older ***wurđō**, *words*; nom. acc. pl. neuter **yfel** from ***uƀilu**, older ***uƀilō**, *evil*; nom. acc. singular

**wini, wine** (OHG. **wini**), from ***winiz, *winin,** *friend*; **mere** (OHG. **meri**), from ***mari,** *lake*; nom. plural **wine** (OHG. **wini**), from ***winīz,** older **-ij(i)z, -ejes,** *friends*; imperative **sete** from ***satī,** Indg. ***sodeje,** *set thou*; pres. subj. **scyle** from older ***skulī,** *shall*; sing. nom. **sunu** = Goth. **sunus,** *son*; acc. **sunu** = Goth. **sunu**; **feola (fela)** = Goth. **filu,** *much*; neut. pl. **fatu,** from ***fatō,** *vats*; **beru (beoru)** from ***ƀerō,** *I bear*. Then after the analogy of these and similar forms were made **feoh** for ***feohu,** *money* = Goth. **faíhu,** OHG. **fihu,** Lat. **pecu,** *cattle*; **bindu,** *I bind*, **helpu,** *I help*, **cēosu,** *I choose*, for ***bind, *help, *cēos.** The final **-u** from older **-w** (§ 265) also disappeared after long stem-syllables, as **gād,** Goth. **gáidw,** *want, lack*; **ā,** Goth. **áiw,** *ever*; **hrā,** Goth. **hráiw,** *corpse*; but remained after short stem-syllables, as **bealu,** *evil, calamity*, **bearu,** *grove*, beside gen. **bealwes, bearwes.**

Note.—Final **i,** which remained in the oldest period of the language, regularly became **e** in the seventh century. And final **u** became **o** at an early period, and then in late OE. **a,** whence forms like nom. acc. **sunu, suno, suna,** *son*; pl. **fatu, fato, fata,** *vats*.

§ **216.** In trisyllabic forms final **-u,** which arose from prim. Germanic **-ō,** disappeared after a long medial syllable. It also disappeared when the stem and medial syllable were short, but remained when the stem-syllable was long and the medial syllable short, as **leornung** from ***lirnungu,** *learning*; **byden** from ***budinu,** older **ƀuđīnō,** *tub*; pl. **reced** from ***rakidu,** older ***rakiđō,** *halls, palaces*; neut. pl. **yfel** from ***uƀilu,** older ***uƀilō,** *evil*; but fem. nom. sing. **hāligu,** *holy*, **hēafodu,** *heads*, **nīetenu,** *animals*.

§ **217.** (5) The Indg. long diphthongs **-āi (-ā̃i), -ōi (-ō̃i), -ōu** became shortened to **-ai, -au** in prim. Germanic, and then underwent the same further changes as old **-ai, -au,** that is, they became **-ǣ, -ō** in West Germanic.

Later than the shortening mentioned in § **214** occurred the shortening which was undergone in dissyllabic and polysyllabic words by the long vowel, after which an **-n** or **-z** had disappeared, and by the **-ǣ** and **-ō** from older **-ai** and **-au**, which were either already final in prim. Germanic, or had become so after the loss of **-z.** In this case a distinction must be made according as the long vowel originally had the 'slurred' (circumflex) or 'broken' (acute) accent (§ **9**). **-ō̃** with the circumflex accent became **-e** (older **-æ**) after the loss of **-z,** but **-a** after the loss of **-n.** **-ō** with the acute accent became **-e** (older **-æ**) after the loss of **-n.** The **-ǣ** and **-ō** from older **-ai** and **-au** became **-e** (older **-æ**) and **-a.** All these shortenings took place in prehistoric Old English. Examples are :—gen. sing. and nom. plural **gefe** (Anglian) from ***ʒeƀō̃z** = Goth. **gibōs,** nom. sing. **giefu** (WS.), *gift*; gen. plural **daga** from ***đaʒō̃n,** older **-ō̃m,** *of days*; **fōta** from ***fōtō̃n,** *of feet,* cp. Gr. θεῶν, *of gods*; and similarly in the gen. plural of other vocalic and consonantal stems; acc. singular **giefe** from ***ʒeƀōn,** older **-ōm** (Indg. **-ām**), *gift,* cp. Gr. χώρᾱν; nom. singular of feminine and neuter **n**-stems (see below), as **tunge** from ***tuŋʒōn,** *tongue*; **ēage** from ***auʒōn,** *eye*; pret. singular **nerede** from ***naziđōn,** older **-ōm,** *I saved*; **fore,** *before* = Gr. παραί, *near*; dat. sing. **dæge** from ***đaʒai,** older **-oi** or **-ō̃i,** cp. Gr. locative οἴκοι, *at home,* dat. θεῷ (Indg. **-ō̃i**), *to a god*; dat. sing. **giefe** = Goth. **gibái,** Indg. ***ghebhā̃i,** *to a gift,* cp. Gr. dat. θεᾷ, *to a goddess*; fem. dat. sing. **blindre** from ***ƀlinđizai,** *blind*; masc. nom. plural **blinde** = Goth. **blindái,** *blind*; **bere** = Goth. **baírái,** Gr. φέροι, *he may bear*; **eahta** = Goth. **ahtáu,** from an original form ***oktōu,** *eight*; **eþþa** = Goth. **aíþþáu,** *or*; gen. singular **suna** = Goth. **sunáus,** *of a son.*

In the parent Indg. language the nom. singular of **n**-stems ended partly in **-ōn, -ēn,** and partly in **-ō̃, -ē̃.** The reason for this difference in the kind of accent in the ending is uncertain, but it was probably due to the loss of the final nasal under conditions which have not yet been ascertained. The various Indg. languages generalized one or other of the two forms in prehistoric times, as in Gr. nom. ἡγεμών, *leader*; ποιμήν, *shepherd*; acc. ἡγεμόνα, ποιμένα, beside nom. Skr. **rā́jā**, *king*; Lat. **sermo,** *discourse*; **homo,** *man*; acc. **rā́jānam, sermōnem, hominem.** In prim. Germanic the two types existed side by side, but **-ōn** (= OE. **-e,** OHG. OS. Goth. **-a**) became restricted to the feminine and neuter in the West Germanic languages and to the masculine in Gothic, whereas **-ō̃** (= OE. **-a,** OHG. OS. **-o,** Goth. **-ō**) became restricted to the masculine in the West Germanic languages and to the feminine and neuter in Gothic, as fem. OE. **tunge,** OHG. **zunga,** OS. **tunga** beside Goth. **tuggō,** *tongue*; neut. OE. **ēage,** OHG. **ouga,** OS. **ōga** beside Goth. **áugō,** *eye*; masc. OE. **guma,** OHG. **gomo,** OS. **gumo** beside Goth. **guma,** *man*. See §§ **400, 403.**

## Summary.

Now that we have traced the history of the Indg. vowels in final syllables in prim. Germanic, Gothic, and Old English, the result may be briefly summarized in the table on p. 98. The sign —, followed by a blank, denotes that the vowel regularly disappeared. From the table it will be seen that all the Indg. endings **-i, -is, -im, -es, -ī, -īt, -ei** became —, **-i(e)** in OE.; that **-u, -us, -um, -m̥, -ā, -ō** became —, **-u**; that **-ō̃, -ō̃d, -ō̃m, -ēu, -ōu, -oũs** became **-a**; and that **-ēt, -ām, -ōm, -ōn, -ā̃s, -ō̃s, -ai, -oi, -ā̃i, -ō̃i, -oĩs** became **-e.**

§ **218.** After the operation of the sound-laws described in §§ **212–17,** many vowels, which originally stood in medial syllables, came to stand in final syllables in prehistoric OE. These vowels underwent various changes.

1. Indg. **o** remained longer in unaccented syllables than in accented syllables in prim. Germanic. It became **a**

| Indg. | P.G. | Goth. | OE. | Goth. | OE. |
|---|---|---|---|---|---|
| ·a, ·e, ·o | — | — | — | wáit, baír, ƕis | wāt, ber, hwæs |
| ·i | —, ·i | — | —, ·i(e) | baíriþ, gast, staþ | bir(e)þ, giest, stede |
| ·u | ·u | ·u | —, ·u | handu, sunu | hand, sunu |
| ·os | ·az | ·s | — | dags, gen. gumins | dæg, gen. guman |
| ·is | ·iz | ·s | —, ·i(e) | gasts, staþs | giest, stede |
| ·us | ·uz | ·us | —, ·u | handus, sunus | hand, sunu |
| ·om | ·a(n) | — | — | dag | dæg |
| ·im | i(n) | — | —, ·i(e) | anst, staþ | ēst, stede |
| ·m̥, ·um | —, ·u(n) | —, u | —, ·u | hanan, handu, sunu | hanan, hand, sunu |
| ·es | ·iz | ·s | —, ·i(e) | pl. hanans, baúrgs | hanan, byrg, hnyte |
| ·ā, ·ō | ·ō | ·a | —, ·u | waúrda, giba | word, giefu |
| ·ēt | ·ǣ | ·a | ·e | nasida | nerede |
| ·ī, ·īt | ·ī | ·i | —, ·i(e) | bandi, wili | bend, wile |
| ·ām, ·ōm | ·ō(n) | ·a | ·e | giba, nasida | giefu, nerede |
| ·ōn | ·ō(n) | ·a | ·e | guma | tunge, ēage |
| ·ō̃, ·ō̃d | ·ō̃ | ·ō | ·a | tuggō, unwēniggō | guma, unwēnunga |
| ·ō̃m | ·ō̃(n) | ·ō | ·a | gibō | giefa |
| ·ā̃s, ·ō̃s | ·ō̃z | ·ōs | ·e | gibōs, dagōs | giefe |
| ·oi | ·ai | ·ai | ·e | blindái, baírái | blinde, bere, dæge |
| ·ei | ·ī | | —, ·i(e) | | stede |
| ·ēu | ·au | ·áu | ·a | sunáu | suna |
| ·ōu | ·au | ·áu | ·a | ahtáu | eahta |
| ·ā̃i, ·ō̃i | ·ai | ·ái | ·e | gibái | giefe, dæge |
| ·oīs | ·aiz | ·áis | ·e | anstáis | ēste |
| ·oūs | ·auz | ·áus | ·a | sunáus | suna |

during the prim. Germanic period except (1) when followed by an **m** which remained in historic times, and (2) when the following syllable originally contained a **u**. In these cases the **o** became **u** in OE., as dat. plural **dagum** beside Goth. **dagam**, prim. Germanic ***đaȝomiz**, *to days*; acc. sing. **brōþur** (later **-or**, **-ar**), from ***ƀrōþorun**, *brother* = Gr. φρᾱ́τορα (§ **34**), *member of a clan*. Prim. Germanic **a** remained before **n**, but became **e** (older **æ**) in other cases, as inf. **beran** from ***ƀeranan**, Indg. ***bheronom**, *to bear*; acc. sing. of masc. and feminine **n**-stems, as **guman**, *man*; **tungan**, *tongue*, from **-anun**, older **-onm** (with vocalic **m**); nom. plural **guman**, **tungan**, from **-aniz**, older **-ones**; but gen. sing. **dæges** older **dægæs**, from prim. Germanic ***đaȝas(a)**, *of a day*; **huneg**, older **hunæg** (OHG. **honag**), *honey*.

2. Indg. **e** remained in OE. when originally not followed by a palatal vowel in the next syllable, as **hwæþer** = Gk. πότερος, *whether, which of two*; pp. **bunden** from ***ƀunđenaz**, Indg. ***bhndhenos**, *bound*; **ōþer** from ***anþeraz**, *other*. But when **e** was originally followed by a palatal vowel it became **i** already in prim. Germanic, see below.

3. Prim. Germanic **i** remained in OE. before palatal consonants, as **englisc**, *English*; **hefig**, *heavy*; **ūsic**, *us*. It also remained in other cases in the oldest period of the language, but became **e** in the seventh century (see § **215**, Note), as pp. **genered** from ***-naziđaz**, *saved*; **nimes(t)**, OHG. **nimis**, *thou takest*, Indg. ***nemesi**; **nimeþ**, OHG. **nimit**, *he takes*, Indg. ***nemeti**. The **e** in the second and third pers. singular was mostly syncopated in WS. and Ken., but generally remained in Anglian (see § **476**).

4. Prim. Germanic **u** always remained before a following **m**, but in other cases it became **o** already at an early period, and in late OE. also **a** (see § **215**, Note), as dat. plural **sunum**, *to sons*; **fōtum**, *to feet*, prim. Germanic **-umiz**; pret. pl. indicative **bǣrun**, **-on**, *they bore*; **neredun**, **-on**, *they saved*.

5. All long vowels underwent shortening already in prehistoric Old English:—

**ǣ** > **e**, as **fæder**, cp. Gr. πατήρ, *father*; **neredes** (older **-dæs**) from ***naziđǣs**, cp. Goth. **nasidēs**, *thou didst save*.

**ī** > **i**, later **e**, except before palatal consonants, as **gylden** (OHG. **guldīn**) from ***ȝulþīnaz**; **mægden** = OHG. **magatīn**, *maiden*; subj. pret. plural **bǣren** = Goth. **bēreina**, OHG. **bārīn**, *they might bear*; but **mihtig** = Goth. **mahteigs**, OHG. **mahtīg**, *mighty*; **gōdlic**, *goodly*, beside the stressed form **gelīc**, *like*.

**ō** > **u**, later **o**, **a** (cp. § **215**, Note), but **u** always remained before a following **m**, as **huntoþ**, **-aþ**, from ***χuntōþuz**, *hunting*; **heardost**, *hardest*, **lēofost**, *dearest*, prim. Germanic superlative suffix **-ōst-**; **sealfas(t)** = Goth. **salbōs**, *thou anointest*; **sealfaþ** = Goth. **salbōþ**, *he anoints*; pret. sing. **sealfude**, **-ode**, **-ade** = Goth. **salbōda**, *I anointed*; pp. **gesealfud**, **-od**, **-ad** = Goth. **salbōþs**; but always **u** in the dat. pl. **giefum** = Goth. **gibōm**, *to gifts*; **tungum** = Goth. **tuggōm**, *to tongues*. The combination **-ōj-** was weakened to **-i-** (through the intermediate stages **-ēj-**, **-ej-**, **-ij-**), as in the inf. of the second class of weak verbs: **lufian**, *to love*; **macian**, *to make*; **sealfian**, *to anoint*. The prim. OE. ending **-ōþ** from older **-onþ** (see § **61**), **-anþ**, **-anþi**, Indg. **-onti**, was regularly weakened to **-aþ**, as **beraþ** = Gr. Dor. φέροντι, *they bear* (cp. end of § **476**).

**ū** > **u** (later **o**, **a**). In this case the **ū** arose in prim. OE. from the loss of **n** before a voiceless spirant (§ **286**). Examples are: **fracuþ**, **-oþ**, from ***frakunþaz**, *wicked* = Goth. **frakunþs**, *despised*; **duguþ** from ***đuȝunþ-** = OHG. **tugunt**, *valour*, *strength*; **geoguþ** from ***juȝunþ-** = OHG. **jugunt**, *youth*.

§ **219.** If a nasal or a liquid, preceded by a mute consonant, came to stand finally after the loss of a vowel (§ **212**), it became vocalic, and then a new vowel was generated before it in prehistoric OE. just as was the case in prehistoric OS. and OHG The vowel thus generated was generally **e** when the preceding vowel was palatal, but **o** (**u**), later also **e**, when the preceding vowel was guttural, as nom. **efen** from ***eƀnaz,** cp. Goth. **ibns,** *even*; nom. acc. **æcer** from ***akr,** older ***akraz, *akran,** cp. Goth. **akrs, akr,** *field*; nom. acc. **fugul, -ol,** from ***fugl,** older ***foȝlaz, *foȝlan,** cp. Goth. **fugls, fugl,** *bird, fowl*; nom. acc. **māþum** from ***maiþm,** older ***maiþmaz, *maiþman,** cp. Goth. **máiþms, máiþm,** *gift.* In the oldest period of the language forms with and without the new vowel often existed side by side. The new vowel occurred most frequently before **r**. Vocalic **l** was common especially after dentals, and vocalic **m** and **n** generally occurred after a short syllable. The forms with vocalic **l, m, n, r** in the nom. acc. singular were due to levelling out the stem-form of the inflected cases. Thus regular forms were: nom. **segel,** *sail*; **māþum,** *gift*; **bēacen,** *sign, beacon*; **efen,** *even*; **æcer,** *field*; **þunor,** *thunder*; gen. **segles, māþmes, bēacnes, efnes, æcres, þunres.** Then from the latter were formed new nominatives **segl, māþm, bēacn, efn**; and from the former new genitives **æceres, þunores.** Examples are: **æppel, æpl,** *apple*; **hūsul, hūsel, hūsl,** *Eucharist,* cp. Goth. **hunsl,** *sacrifice*; **nǣdl** (Goth. **nēþla**), *needle*; **nægl,** *nail*; **setl** (Goth. **sitls**), *seat*; **tempel, templ** (Lat. **templum**), *temple*; **tungul, -ol, -el,** *star.* **bōsm,** *bosom*; **botm,** *bottom*; **ǣþm,** *breath*; **þrosm,** *smoke*; **wæstum, -em, wæstm,** *growth.* **hræfn,** *raven*; **regn** (Goth. **rign**), *rain*; **stefn,** *voice*; **tācen, tācn** (Goth. **táikns**), *token*; **þegen, þegn,** *retainer*; **wægn,** *wagon.* **ātr, ātor,** *poison*; **fæger** (Goth. **fagrs**), *fair, beautiful*; **finger** (Goth. **figgrs**), *finger*; **hlūtor** (Goth. **hlūtrs**), *pure, clear*; **snotor,** *wise*; **winter** (Goth. **wintrus**), *winter*; **wundor,** *wonder.*

§ **220.** In OE., especially in the later period, a svarabhakti vowel was often developed between **r** or **l** + **c, g,** or

**h**; and between **r, l, d,** or **t** + **w**. In the former case the quality of the vowel thus developed regulated itself after the quality of the stem-vowel. In the latter case it fluctuated between **u** (**o**) and **e**, rarely **a**. The development of a similar vowel in these consonant combinations also took place in OS. and OHG. Examples are: nom. sing. **burug, buruh** (OS. OHG. **burug**) beside **burg, burh** (OS. OHG. **burg**), *city*; but dat. sing. and nom. plural **byrig** beside **byrg**; **byriga** beside **byrga**, *bail, surety*; **fyligan** beside **fylgan**, *to follow*; **myrigþ** beside **myrgþ**, *mirth*; **styric** beside **styrc**, *calf*, cp. modern northern dial. **stərək** beside **stǝ̄k**; **woruhte, worohte** (OHG. **worahta**) beside **worhte** (OHG. **worhta**), *he worked*. **beadu, -o**, *battle*, gen. dat. **beaduwe, -owe** beside **beadwe**; **bealu**, *evil*, gen. **bealuwes, -owes** beside **bealwes**; **bearu**, *grove*; **bearuwes, -owes** beside **bearwes**; **frætuwe, -ewe** beside **frætwe**, *trappings*; **gearu**, *ready*, gen. **gearuwes** (OHG. **garawes**), **-owes, -ewes** beside **gearwes**; **gearuwe** (OHG. **garawa**), **-ewe** beside **gearwe** (OHG. **garwa**), *yarrow*; **geolu**, *yellow*, gen. **geoluwes, -owes** beside **geolwes**; **melu, meolu**, *meal, flour*, gen. **meluwes** (OHG. **melawes**), **-owes, ewes** beside **melwes** (OHG. **melwes**); **nearu**, *narrow*, gen. **nearuwes, -owes, -ewes** beside **nearwes**; and similarly with several other words.

§ **221.** Original short medial vowels in open syllables regularly remained in trisyllabic forms when the stem-syllable was short, as **æþele**, *noble*; gen. sing. **heofones, metodes, nacodes, rodores, stapoles, wæteres**, beside nom. **heofon**, *heaven*; **metod**, *creator*; **nacod**, *naked*; **rodor**, *sky*; **stapol**, *pillar*; **wæter**, *water*; gen. dat. sing. **idese** beside nom. **ides**, *woman*; pret. **fremedest** from ***framiđǣs**, *thou didst perform*; **neredest** from ***naziđǣs**, *thou didst save*; pp. gen. sing. **gefremedes, generedes**, nom. pl. **gefremede, generede**: nom. sing. **gefremed, genered** from prim. Germanic ***-framiđás, *-naziđás** (cp.

§§ **442, 523**). On the syncope of **i** after prim. Germanic short stems in the preterite and past participle of weak verbs, see § **534.**

They also remained in closed syllables irrespectively as to whether the stem-syllable was long or short, as gen. sing. **cyninges, fǣtelses, hengestes, wēstennes,** beside nom. **cyning,** *king*; **fǣtels,** *tub*; **hengest,** *stallion*; **wēsten,** *desert*; **fāgettan,** *to change colour*; pres. participle **nime de,** *taking*; superlatives **ieldesta,** *oldest*; **lengesta,** *longest.* It is difficult to account for the syncope in **hīehsta,** *highest*; and **nīehsta,** *nearest.*

They also remained after consonant combinations, when preceded by a closed stem-syllable, or a stem-syllable containing a long diphthong or vowel, as pret. **hyngrede, timbrede, dīeglede, frēfrede,** pp. gen. sing. **gehyngredes, getimbredes, gedīegledes, gefrēfredes,** beside inf. **hyngran,** *to hunger,* **timbran,** *to build,* **dīeglan,** *to conceal,* **frēfran,** *to comfort*; dat. pl. **syndrigum** beside nom. sing. **syndrig,** *separate.*

They regularly disappeared in open syllables when the stem-syllable was long, as gen. sing. **dīegles, engles, hālges, hēafdes, ōþres,** beside nom. **dīegol,** *secret*; **engel,** *angel*; **hālig,** *holy*; **hēafod,** *head*; **ōþer,** *other*; **hālgian,** *to make holy*; **strengþu** from ***straŋʒiþō** (OHG. **strengida**), *strength*; **ieldra** (Goth. **alþiza**), *older*; gen. dat. sing. **frōfre, mōnþe, sāwle,** beside nom. **frōfor,** *consolation*; **mōnaþ,** *month*; **sāwol,** *soul*; **dǣldest** (Goth. **dáilidēs**), *thou didst divide*; **hīerdest** (Goth. **háusidēs**), *thou heardest*; pp. gen. sing. **gedǣldes, gehīerdes,** nom. pl. **gedǣlde, gehīerde**: nom. sing. **gedǣled, gehīered** from prim. Germanic ***-đailiđás, *-χauziđás.**

§ **222.** Short medial guttural vowels, followed by a guttural vowel in the next syllable, often became palatal by dissimilation, as **hafela,** *head,* beside **hafola**; **nafela,** *navel,* beside **nafola**; **gaderian** from ***ʒađurōjan,** *to gather*;

pl. nom. **heofenas,** gen. **heofena,** dat. **heofenum,** beside sing. gen. **heofones,** dat. **heofone,** nom. **heofon,** *heaven*; pl. nom. **roderas,** gen. **rodera,** dat. **roderum,** beside sing. gen. **rodores,** dat. **rodore,** nom. **rodor,** *firmament*; pl. nom. **stapelas,** gen. **stapela,** dat. **stapelum,** beside sing. gen. **stapoles,** dat. **stapole,** nom. **stapol,** *pillar*. The interchange between e and **o** in forms like **sealfedon** (OHG. **salbōtun**), *they anointed*, beside **sealfode** (OHG. **salbōta**), *he anointed*, is probably due to the same cause, and may be the reason why some verbs of sub-division (*b*) of the first class of weak verbs often went over into the second class (see §§ **528, 532**).

§ **223.** In prim. OE. polysyllabic forms the second medial short vowel disappeared when it stood in an open syllable, but remained when it stood in a closed syllable, as pp. acc. sing. masc. **generedne,** *saved*, from ***-nazidanō**(n); **gedēmedne,** *judged*, from ***-dōmidanō**(n); acc. sing. masc. **ōþerne** from ***anþeranō(n),** *other*; and similarly **hāligne,** *holy*; &c.; dat. fem. singular **ōþerre** from ***anþerizai;** and similarly **hāligre;** gen. plural **ōþerra,** prim. Germanic ***anþeraizō̃**(n), older **-ō̃m;** and similarly **hāligra.** But having a secondary accent in a closed syllable, the vowel regularly remained, as nom. plural **gædelingas,** *companions*; dat. singular **gaderunge,** *to an assembly*; **innemesta,** *inmost*.

Note.—1. There are many exceptions to the above sound-laws, which are due to analogical formations. Thus forms like masc. and neut. gen. singular **micles,** dat. **miclum,** *great*; **yfles, yflum,** beside **yfeles, yfelum,** *evil*; gen. pl. **glædra,** *glad*, were made on analogy with forms having a long stem-syllable. And forms like gen. singular **dēofoles** (nom. **dēofol,** *devil*), **ēþeles** (nom. **ēþel,** *native land*), **hāliges,** *holy*, beside older **dēofles, ēþles, hālges,** were made on analogy with forms having a short stem-syllable.

2. In late OE. syncope often took place after short stems, and sometimes in closed syllables, as **betra,** *better*; **circe,**

*church*; **fægnian,** *to rejoice*, **gadrian,** *to gather*, beside older **betera, cirice, fægenian, gaderian**; **betsta,** *best*; **winstre,** *left* (*hand*), beside older **betesta, winestre.**

3. Original medial long vowels, which were shortened at an early period, were syncopated in trisyllabic forms in OE., but remained when the shortening took place at a later period, as dat. singular **mōnþe** beside **mōnaþ** (Goth. **mēnōþs**), *month*; but **lōcodest** from ***lōkōđæs,** *thou didst look.*

# CHAPTER VII

## ABLAUT (VOWEL GRADATION)

§ **224.** By ablaut is meant the gradation of vowels both in stem and suffix, which was chiefly caused by the primitive Indo-Germanic system of accentuation. See § **9**.

The vowels vary within certain series of related vowels, called ablaut-series. In OE., to which this chapter will be chiefly confined, there are six such series, which appear most clearly in the stem-forms of strong verbs. Four stem-forms are to be distinguished in an OE. strong verb which has vowel gradation as the characteristic mark of its different stems:—(1) The present stem, to which belong all the forms of the present, (2) the stem of the first or third person singular of the preterite indicative, (3) the stem of the preterite plural, to which belong the second pers. pret. singular, and the whole of the pret. subjunctive, (4) the stem of the past participle.

By arranging the vowels according to these four stems we arrive at the following system:—

| | i. | ii. | iii. | iv. |
|---|---|---|---|---|
| I. | ī | ā | i | i |
| II. | ēo | ēa | u | o |
| III. | i, e | a | u | u, o |
| IV. | e | æ | ǣ | o |
| V. | e | æ | ǣ | e |
| VI. | a | ō | ō | æ (a) |

Three grades of ablaut are to be distinguished—strong, weak, and lengthened. The strong grade occurs in i and ii of I to VI; the weak grade in iii of I to III, and in iv of I to VI; and the lengthened grade in iii of IV to VI. i and ii are sometimes further distinguished as strong grade 1 (sg. 1) and strong grade 2 (sg. 2); and similarly iv of V and VI, and iv of I to IV are distinguished as weak grade 1 (wg. 1) and weak grade 2 (wg. 2). The preterite-present verbs have weak grade in iii of IV, whereas the ordinary strong verbs have lengthened grade.

NOTE.—1. The six series as given above represent the simple vowels and diphthongs when uninfluenced by neighbouring sounds. For the changes caused by umlaut and the influence of consonants. see the phonology, especially §§ **47–52**, and the various classes of strong verbs, §§ **490–519**.

2. On the difference in Series III between **i** and **e**, see § **41**; and between **u** and **o**, § **43**.

3. It should be noted that the **u, o** in Series II are not of the same origin as the **u, o** in Series III and the **o** in Series IV. In Series II the **u, o** arose from Indg. **u** (cp. §§ **21, 43**), whereas the **u, o** in Series III and the **o** in Series IV arose from Indg. vocalic **l, m, n, r** (cp. §§ **34–7** and Note).

4. For the **ǣ** in Series IV we have **u** from Indg. vocalic **l, m** in the preterite presents, as **sculon**, *shall*, **munon**, *think* (§ **543**). The **ǣ** (= Indg. ē, § **24**) in Series IV and V represents a lengthening of **e** which took place in the parent Indg. language, and is called the lengthened grade of ablaut. It is the same grade of ablaut which occurs in forms like Lat. pf. **lēgī, vēxī**: pres. **legō**, *I gather*, **vehō**, *I carry*; OE. **bǣr**, *bier*: **beran**, *to bear*; OE. **sprǣc**, *speech*: **sprecan**, *to speak*; Goth. **us-mēt** with **ē** from older **ǣ** (§ **119**), *manner of life*: OE. **metan**, *to measure*. It is important to remember that the **ǣ** did not arise from the contraction of the stem-vowel with a reduplicated syllable. That this is not the origin of the **ǣ** is clearly seen by the fact that it often occurs in other than verbal forms where there can be no question of a reduplicated syllable, as in OE. **bǣr, sprǣc**: **beran, sprecan**; Goth. **qēns** from ***qǣniz**, *wife, woman*: **qinō**

from ***qenō** (§ **80**), *woman*; Gr. nom. **πατήρ** : acc. **πατέρα**, *father*; Lat. nom. **pēs** (Indg. ***pḗts**) : acc. **pedem** (Indg. ***pédm**), *foot*.

5. On the **a**, **ō** in Series VI, see § **228**. In many verbs belonging to this series the **ō** is of similar origin to the **ǣ** in Series IV and V, that is it represents a lengthening of **o** which took place in the parent Indg. language, and is called the lengthened grade of ablaut. The verbs which have the **ō** of this origin in the preterite had originally **e** in the present, but already in prim. Germanic the **e** was supplanted by **a** after the analogy of those verbs which regularly had **a** in the present and **ō** in the preterite, as in OE. **scafan**, *to scrape*: pret. **scōf** = Lat. **scabō**, *I scrape*: pf. **scābī** (cp. § **23**), and then the new **a** of the present was extended analogically to the past participle; see Brugmann, *Indogermanische Forschungen*, vol. xxxii, pp. 179–95.

6. Strong verbs belonging to Series II have **īe** from older **iu** (§ **138**) in the second and third pers. singular of the pres. indicative; and strong verbs belonging to Series III–V with **e** in the infinitive have **i** in the second and third pers. singular of the pres. indicative (§ **41**).

§ **225.** But although the series of vowels is seen most clearly in the stem-forms of strong verbs, the learner must not assume that ablaut occurs in strong verbs only. Every *syllable* of every word of whatever part of speech contains some form of ablaut. As for example the sonantal elements in the following stem-syllables stand in ablaut relation to each other:—

**līþan**, *to go*, **līþend**, *sailor*: **lād**, *way*, *course*: **lida**, *sailor*; **lār**, *learning*: **liornung** (**leornung**), *learning*; **snīþan**, *to cut*: **snǣd** from ***snādi-**, *morsel*, *slice*: **snide**, *incision*; **wītega**, *prophet*: **wāt**, *he knows*: **witan**, *to know*, **wita**, *wise man*, **gewit**, *intelligence*.

**bēodan**, *to command*, *order*: **gebod**, *command*, *precept*, **bydel** from ***budil**, *messenger*; **flēon**, *to flee*: **flēam**, *flight*: **flyht** from ***fluhti-**, *flight*; **nēotan**, *to use*: **genēat**, *companion*: **notu**, *use*, **nytt** (Germanic stem-form ***nutja-**), *useful*; **tēon**, *to draw*, *lead*: **tēam**, *progeny*: **here-toga**, *army leader*, *general*.

**bindan**, *to bind*: **bend** from ***bandi-**, *band*; **drincan**, *to drink*: **drenc** from ***dranki-**, *drink*: **druncen**, *drunk*; **sweltan**, *to die*: **swylt** from ***swulti-**, *death*; **weorþan** from ***werþan**, *to become*: **wyrd** from ***wurdi-**, *fate*.

**beran**, *to bear*: **bǣr**, *bier*: **ge-byrd** from ***ʒi-burdi-**, *birth*, **byre** from ***buri-**, *son*; **cwelan**, *to die*: **cwalu**, *killing*; **stelan**, *to steal*: **stalu**, *theft*: **stulor**, *stealthy*.

**giefan**, *to give*, **giefa** from ***ʒeƀa**, *giver*, **gift** from ***ʒefti-**, *price of wife*: **gafol**, *tribute*; **cweþan**, *to say*: **cwide**, prim. Germanic ***kweđi-**, *speech*; **sprecan**, *to speak*: **sprǣc**, *speech*.

**calan**, *to be cold*: **cōl**, *cool*; **faran**, *to go, travel*, **fierd** from ***fardi-**, *army*: **fōr**, *journey*, **gefēra**, prim. Germanic ***-fōrjō̃**, *companion*; **stede** from ***stađi**, *place*: **stōd**, *herd of horses*. See § **562**.

Examples of ablaut relation in other than stem-syllables are:—

Goth. gen. sing. **dagi-s**: acc. pl. **daga-ns**, *days*; Goth. nom. pl. **anstei-s**, *favours*: gen. sing. **anstái-s**: acc. pl. **ansti-ns**; Goth. nom. pl. **sunju-s** from an original form ***suneu-es**, *sons*: gen. sing. **sunáu-s**: acc. pl. **sunu-ns**; Goth. nom. sing. **brō-þar**, *brother*: dat. sing. **brō-þr**; Gr. nom. pl. *πα-τέρ-ες*: *εὐ-πά-τορ-ες*: nom. sing. *πα-τήρ*, *father*: *εὐ-πά-τωρ*, *born of a noble sire*: gen. sing. *πα-τρ-ός*; Gr. *φέρο-μεν*, *we bear*: *φέρε-τε*, *ye bear* = Goth. **baíra-m**, **baíri-þ**.

§ **226**. In this paragraph will be given the prim. Germanic and Gothic equivalents of the above six ablaut-series, with one or two illustrations from OE. For further examples see the various classes of strong verbs, §§ **490–510**.

I.

| | | | | |
|---|---|---|---|---|
| Prim. Germ. | **ī** | **ai** | **i** | **i** |
| Gothic | **ei** | **ái** | **i** | **i** |
| OE. | **bītan**, *to bite* | **bāt** | **biton** | **biten** |
| | **līþan**, *to go* | **lāþ** | **lidon** | **liden** |

NOTE.—Cp. the parallel Greek series **πείθω**: **πέποιθα**: **ἔπιθον**.

II.

| | | | | |
|---|---|---|---|---|
| Prim. Germ. | eu | au | u | o |
| Gothic | iu | áu | u | u |
| OE. | **bēodan,** *to offer* | **bēad** | **budon** | **boden** |
| | **cēosan,** *to choose* | **cēas** | **curon** | **coren** |

NOTE.—Cp. the parallel Greek series ἐλεύ(θ)σομαι (fut.): εἰλήλουθα : ἤλυθον.

III.

| | | | | |
|---|---|---|---|---|
| Prim. Germ. | e, i | a | u | u, o |
| Gothic | i | a | u | u |
| OE. | **helpan,** *to help* | **healp** | **hulpon** | **holpen** |
| | **weorþan,** *to become* | **wearþ** | **wurdon** | **worden** |
| | **bindan,** *to bind* | **band** | **bundon** | **bunden** |

NOTE.—1. To this series belong all strong verbs having a medial nasal or liquid + consonant, and a few others in which the vowel is followed by two consonants other than a nasal or liquid + consonant.

2. On the forms **healp, wearþ** see §§ **64, 66,** and on **weorþan** see § **85.**

3. Cp. the parallel Greek series δέρκομαι : δέδορκα : ἔδρακον; πέμπω : πέπομφα.

IV.

| | | | | |
|---|---|---|---|---|
| Prim. Germ. | e | a | ǣ | o |
| Gothic | i | a | ē | u |
| OE. | **beran,** *to bear* | **bær** | **bǣron** | **boren** |
| | **stelan,** *to steal* | **stæl** | **stǣlon** | **stolen** |

NOTE.—1. To this series belong all strong verbs whose stems end in a single liquid or nasal.

2. Cp. the parallel Greek series μένω : μονή : μί-μνω; δέρω : δορά : δε-δαρ-μένος.

V.

| | | | | |
|---|---|---|---|---|
| Prim. Germ. | e | a | ǣ | e |
| Gothic | i | a | ē | i |
| OE. | **metan,** *to measure* | **mæt** | **mǣton** | **meten** |
| | **cweþan,** *to say* | **cwæþ** | **cwǣdon** | **cweden** |

NOTE.—1. To this series belong all strong verbs whose stems end in a single consonant other than a liquid or a nasal.

2. Cp. the parallel Greek series **πέτομαι : πότμος : ἐ-πτ-όμην ; τρέπω : τέ-τροφα : τραπέσθαι.**

VI.

| | | | | |
|---|---|---|---|---|
| Prim. Germ. | **a** | **ō** | **ō** | **a** |
| Gothic | **a** | **ō** | **ō** | **a** |
| OE. | **faran,** *to go* | **fōr** | **fōron** | **færen, faren** |

§ **227.** Class VII of strong verbs embracing the old reduplicated verbs (§§ **511–19**) has been omitted from the ablaut-series, because the exact relation in which the vowel of the present stands to that of the preterite has not yet been satisfactorily explained. The old phases of ablaut have been preserved in the present and preterite of a few Gothic verbs, as **lētan,** *to let,* **laílōt, laílōtum, lētans; saian,** *to sow,* **saí-sō, saí-sō-um, saians.**

§ **228.** The ablaut-series as given in § **226** have for practical reasons been limited to the phases of ablaut as they appear in the various classes of strong verbs. From an Indo-Germanic point of view, the series I–V belong to one and the same series, generally called the **e**-series, which underwent in primitive Germanic various modifications upon clearly defined lines. What is called the sixth ablaut-series in the Germanic languages is really a mixture of several original series, owing to several Indg. vowel-sounds having fallen together in prim. Germanic; thus the **a,** which occurs in the present and past participle, corresponds to three Indg. vowels, viz. **a** (§ **17**), **o** (§ **20**), and **ə** (§ **22**); and the **ō** in the preterite corresponds to Indg. **ā** (§ **23**), and Indg. **ō** (§ **26**); see also § **224,** Note 5. For the phases of ablaut which do not occur in the various parts of strong verbs, and for traces of ablaut-series other than those given above, the student should consult Brugmann's

*Kurze vergleichende Grammatik der indogermanischen Sprachen*, pp. 138–50; Streitberg's *Urgermanische Grammatik*, pp. 79–95; Wright's *Comparative Grammar of the Greek Language*, pp. 49–61.

## CHAPTER VIII

## THE FIRST SOUND-SHIFTING, VERNER'S LAW, AND OTHER CONSONANT CHANGES WHICH TOOK PLACE IN THE PRIMITIVE GERMANIC LANGUAGE.

§ **229.** The first sound-shifting, popularly called Grimm's Law, is rightly regarded as one of the most characteristic features of the Germanic languages. With the exception of Armenian, in which the Indg. mediae became tenues, there is no similar sound-shifting in any of the other branches of the parent Indg. language. The first sound-shifting is so called in order to distinguish it from the special sound-shifting which only took place in Old High German. It relates to the changes which the Indg. explosives underwent in the period of the Germanic primitive community, i. e. before the Germanic parent language became differentiated into the separate Germanic languages:—Gothic, O.Norse, O.English, O.Frisian, O. Saxon (= O. Low German), O. Low Franconian (O. Dutch), and O. High German. The approximate date at which these changes took place cannot be ascertained, but they must have taken place some hundreds of years before the beginning of the Christian era, as is proved by the forms of Germanic words—chiefly proper names—found in ancient classical writers. See § **236**.

The Indo-Germanic parent language had the following system of consonants:—

| | | Labial. | Dental. | Palatal. | Velar. |
|---|---|---|---|---|---|
| *Explosives* | tenues | **p** | **t** | **k** | **q, qʷ** |
| | mediae | **b** | **d** | **g** | **g, gʷ** |
| | tenues aspiratae | **ph** | **th** | **kh** | **qh, qʷh** |
| | mediae aspiratae | **bh** | **dh** | **gh** | **gh, gʷh** |
| *Spirants* | voiceless | | **s** | | |
| | voiced | | **z** | | |
| *Nasals* | | **m** | **n** | **ń** | **ŋ** |
| *Liquids* | | | **l, r** | | |
| *Semivowels* | | **w (u̯)** | | **j (i̯)** | |

Note.—1. Explosives are consonants which are formed with complete closure of the mouth passage, and may be pronounced with or without voice, i. e. with or without the vocal chords being set in action; in the former case they are said to be voiced (e. g. the mediae), and in the latter voiceless (e. g. the tenues). The aspirates are pronounced like the simple tenues and mediae followed by an **h**, like the Anglo-Irish pronunciation of **t** in **tell**.

The palatal explosives are formed by the front or middle of the tongue and the roof of the mouth (hard palate); whereas the velars are formed by the root of the tongue and the soft palate (velum). In the parent Indo-Germanic language there were two kinds of velars, viz. pure velars and velars with lip rounding. In philological works the former are often written **q**, **g**, **qh**, **gh**, and the latter **qʷ**, **gʷ**, **qʷh**, **gʷh** in order to distinguish the two series of velars. The pure velars fell together with the Indg. palatals in Germanic, Latin, Greek, and Keltic, but were kept apart in the Aryan and Baltic-Slavonic languages. The velars with lip rounding appear in the Germanic languages partly with and partly without labialization, see § **237**. The palatal and velar nasals only occurred before their corresponding explosives, **ńk**, **ńg**; **ŋq**, **ŋg**, &c.

2. Spirants are consonants formed by the mouth passage being narrowed at one spot in such a manner that the outgoing breath gives rise to a frictional sound at the narrowed part.

**z** only occurred before voiced explosives, e. g. ***nizdos** = Lat. **nīdus**, English **nest**; ***ozdos** = Gr. **ὄζος**, Germ. **ast**, *twig, bough*.

From the above system of consonants have been excluded certain rare sounds which only existed in the parent language in combination with other sounds, viz. **sh** and **zh, þ** and **đ, þh** and **đh.** The spirants **sh, zh** only occurred in combination with tenues and mediae and arose in prim. Indo-Germanic from the combinations tenues aspiratae and mediae aspiratae + **s**, as **tsh, psh, ksh, qsh; dzh, bzh, gzh, gzh** from older **ths, phs, khs, qhs; dhs, bhs, ghs, ghs.** These combinations had in Greek, Latin and prim. Germanic the same development as the original tenues + **s**, see § **240. þ** and **đ** only occurred after palatals and velars which were originally unaspirated, as **kþ, qþ, gđ, gđ. þh** and **đh** only occurred after palatals and velars which were originally aspirated, as **kþh, qþh, gđh, gđh** from older **khþ, qhþ, ghđ, ghđ.** In the present state of our knowledge it is impossible to determine how the four spirants **þ** and **đ, þh** and **đh** were pronounced in the parent language. In Sanskrit, Latin, Germanic and Baltic-Slavonic they became **s**-sounds, and in Greek **t**-sounds.

3. The semivowels, nasals and liquids had the functions both of vowels and consonants. When a vowel disappeared through loss of accent in the combinations vowel + semivowel, liquid or nasal, the semivowel, liquid or nasal became vocalic or remained consonantal according as it was followed by a consonant or a vowel in the next syllable. Cp. also § **16**, Note 1.

4. The essential difference between the so-called semivowels and full vowels is that the latter always bear the stress (accent) of the syllable in which they occur, e.g. in English **ców, stáin** the first element of the diphthong is a vowel, the second a consonant; but in words like French **rwá** (written **roi**), **bjér** (written **bière**), the first element of the diphthong is a consonant, the second a vowel. In consequence of this twofold function, a diphthong may be defined as the combination of a sonantal with a consonantal vowel. And it is called a falling or rising diphthong according as the stress is upon the first or second element. In this book the second element of diphthongs is written **i, u** when the first element is the bearer of the stress, thus **ái, áu,** &c., but when the second element has the stress, the first element is written **j, w,** thus **já, wá,** &c.

5. In the writing down of prim. Germanic forms the signs

**þ** (= **th** in Engl. **thin**), **đ** (= **th** in Engl. **then**), **ƀ** (= a bilabial spirant, which may be pronounced like the **v** in Engl. **vine**), **ʒ** (= **g** often heard in German **sagen**), **χ** (= NHG. **ch** and the **ch** in Scotch **loch**).

§ **230.** In the following tables of the normal equivalents of the Indg. explosives in Latin, Greek, and the Germanic languages, Table I contains the Indg. tenues **p, t, k,** the mediae **b, d, g** and the pure velars **q, g**. Table II contains the Indg. mediae aspiratae and the velars **q**ʷ, **g**ʷ with labialization. The equivalents in the Germanic languages do not contain the changes caused by Verner's Law, &c. The East Franconian dialect is taken as the normal for OHG.

The following points should be noticed :—

(1) The Indg. tenues **p, t, k** and the mediae **b, d, g** generally remained unchanged in Latin and Greek.

(2) The pure velars (**q, g**) fell together with the palatals **k, g** in Latin and Greek. They became **χ, k** in prim. Germanic, and thus fell together with the **χ, k** from Indg. **k, g.**

(3) The pure velar **gh** fell together with the original palatal **gh** in Latin and Greek.

(4) The Indg. mediae aspiratae became in prehistoric Latin and Greek tenues aspiratae, and thus fell together with the original tenues aspiratae.

(5) The Indg. tenues aspiratae became voiceless spirants in prim. Germanic, and thus fell together with the voiceless spirants from the Indg. tenues. See § **233.**

(6) In Latin Indg. **q**ʷ with labialization became **qu,** rarely **c.** **g**ʷ with labialization became **v** (but **gu** after **n,** and **g** when the labialized element had been lost, as **gravis** = Gr. *βαρύς, heavy*).

Indg. **ph, bh** became **f** initially and **b** medially.

Indg. **th, dh** became **f** initially, **b** medially before and after **r,** before **l** and after **u (w)**, in other cases **d.**

Indg. **kh, gh** became **h** initially before and medially between vowels; **g** before and after consonants, and **f** before **u** (**w**).

Indg. **qʷh, gʷh** with labialization became **f** initially, **v** medially except that after **n** they became **gu.**

(7) In Greek Indg. **qʷ, gʷ** with labialization became π, β before non-palatal vowels (except **u**) and before consonants (except Indg. **j**); τ, δ before palatal vowels; and κ, γ before and after **u.**

Indg. **ph, bh** became φ; **th, dh** became θ; and **kh, gh** became χ.

Indg. **qʷh, gʷh** with labialization became φ before non-palatal vowels (except **u**) and before consonants (except Indg. **j**); θ before palatal vowels; and χ before and after **u.**

(8) When two consecutive syllables would begin with aspirates, the first was de-aspirated in prehistoric times in Sanskrit and Greek, as Skr. **bándhanam,** *a binding,* Goth. OE. **bindan,** OHG. **bintan,** *to bind,* root ***bhendh-**; Skr. **bṓdhati,** *he learns, is awake,* Gr. πεύθεται, *he asks, inquires,* Goth. **anabiudan,** OE. **bēodan,** *to bid,* OHG. **biotan,** *to offer,* root ***bheudh-**; Gr. κανθύλη, *a swelling,* OE. **gund,** OHG. **gunt,** *matter, pus*; Gr. θρίξ, *hair,* gen. τριχός; ἔχω, *I have,* fut. ἕξω.

(9) In OHG. the prim. Germanic explosives **p, t** became the affricatae **pf, tz** (generally written **zz, z**), initially, as also medially after consonants, and when doubled. But prim. Germanic **p, t, k** became the double spirants **ff, ʒʒ, hh** (also written **ch**) medially between vowels and finally after vowels. The double spirants were simplified to **f, ʒ, h** when they became final or came to stand before other consonants, and also generally medially when preceded by a long vowel or diphthong.

TABLE I.

| Indg. | Latin | Greek | P. Germanic | Gothic | OE. | OHG. |
| --- | --- | --- | --- | --- | --- | --- |
| p | p | π | f | f | f | f |
| t | t | τ | þ | þ | þ | d |
| k, q | c | κ | χ | h, χ | h, χ | h, χ |
| b | b | β | p | p | p | pf, ff |
| d | d | δ | t | t | t | z, ʒʒ |
| g, g | g | γ | k | k | c | k, hh |

TABLE II.

| Indg. | Latin | Greek | P. Germanic | Gothic | OE. | OHG. |
| --- | --- | --- | --- | --- | --- | --- |
| $q^w$ | qu, c | π, τ, κ | χw, χ | ƕ, h | hw, h | (h)w, h |
| $g^w$ | v, gu, g | β, δ, γ | kw, k | q, k | cw, c | qu; k, hh |
| bh | f, b | φ | b, ƀ | b, ƀ | b, ƀ, (f) | b |
| dh | f, b, d | θ | d, đ | d, đ | d | t |
| gh | h, g, f | χ | g, ʒ | g, ʒ | g, ʒ | g |
| $g^wh$ | f, v, gu | φ, θ, χ | ʒw, ʒ, w | ʒ, w | g, ʒ, w | g, w |

§ **231.** The Indg. tenues **p, t, k, q, q**[w] became in prim. Germanic the voiceless spirants **f, þ, χ, χ, χ**[w].

**p** > **f.** Lat. **pēs,** Gr. πούς, OE. OS. **fōt,** Goth. **fōtus,** O.Icel. **fōtr,** OHG. **fuoʒ,** *foot*; Lat. **piscis,** OE. **fisc,** Goth. **fisks,** O.Icel. **fiskr,** OS. OHG. **fisk,** *fish*; Gr. πλωτός, *floating, swimming,* OE. OS. **flōd,** Goth. **flōdus,** O.Icel. **flōð,** OHG. **fluot,** *flood, tide*; Lat. **pecu,** OE. **feoh,** Goth. **faíhu,** O.Icel. **fē,** OS. **fehu,** OHG. **fihu,** *cattle*; Lat. **nepos,** OE. **nefa,** O.Icel. **nefe,** OHG. **nefo,** *nephew.*

**t** > **þ.** Lat. **tū,** Gr. Doric τύ, OE. O.Icel. OS. **þū,** Goth. **þu,** OHG. **dū,** *thou*; Lat. **trēs,** Gr. τρεῖς, OE. **þrī,** OS. **thria,** O.Icel. **þrīr,** OHG. **drī,** *three*; Lat. **tenuis,** OE. **þynne,** O.Icel. **þunnr,** OHG. **dunni,** *thin*; O.Lat. **tongēre,** *to know,* OE. **þencan,** Goth. **þagkjan,** OS. **þenkian,** OHG. **denchen,** *to think*; Lat. **frāter,** OE. **brōþor,** Goth. **brōþar,** O.Icel. **brōðer,** OS. **brōđar,** OHG. **bruoder,** *brother*; Lat. **vertō,** *I turn,* OE. **weorþan,** Goth. **waírþan,** O.Icel. **verða,** OS. **werđan,** OHG. **werdan,** to become.

**k** > **χ.** Lat. **canis,** Gr. κύων, OE. OS. **hund,** Goth. **hunds,** O.Icel. **hundr,** OHG. **hunt,** *hound, dog*; Lat. **cor** (gen. **cordis**), Gr. καρδίᾱ, OE. **heorte,** Goth. **haírtō,** O.Icel. **hjarta,** OS. **herta,** OHG. **herza,** *heart*; Lat. **centum,** Gr. ἑ-κατόν, OE. Goth. OS. **hund,** OHG. **hunt,** *hundred*; Lat. **pecu,** OE. **feoh,** Goth. **faíhu,** O.Icel. **fē,** OS. **fehu,** OHG. **fihu,** *cattle*; Lat. **decem,** Gr. δέκα, OE. **tīen** from ***teohuni-**, older ***teχuni-** (cp. §§ **87, 447**), Goth. **taíhun,** OS. **tehan,** OHG. **zehan,** *ten*; Lat. **dūcō,** *I lead,* OE. **tēon** from ***tēohan,** older ***teuχan** (§ **137**), Goth. **tiuhan,** OS. **tiohan,** OHG. **ziohan,** *to draw, lead.*

**q** > **χ.** Lat. **capiō,** *I take, seize,* OE. **hebban,** Goth. **hafjan,** O.Icel. **hefja.** OS. **hebbian,** OHG. **heffen,** *to raise*; Lat. **canō,** *I sing,* OE. **hana, hona,** Goth. **hana,** O.Icel. **hane,** OS. OHG. **hano,** *cock,* lit. *singer*; Lat. **vincō** (perf. **vīcī**), *I conquer,* Goth. **weihan,** OHG. **wīhan,** *to fight.*

qʷ > χw. Lat. **quis**, Gr. τίς, OE. **hwā**, Goth. **ƕas**, OS. **hwē**, OHG. **hwer**, *who?*; Lat. **linquō**, Gr. λείπω, *I leave*, OE. **līon**, **lēon** from ***līohan**, older ***līχwan** (see §§ **127**, **246**), OS. OHG. **līhan**, *to lend*.

NOTE.—1. The Indg. tenues remained unshifted in the combination **s** + tenuis.

**sp**. Lat. **spuere**, OE. OS. OHG. **spīwan**, Goth. **speiwan**, *to vomit, spit*; Lat. **con-spiciō**, *I look at*, OHG. **spehōn**, *to spy*.

**st**. Gr. στείχω, *I go*, Lat. **vestīgium**, *footstep*, OE. OS. OHG. **stīgan**, Goth. **steigan**, O.Icel. **stīga**, *to ascend*; Lat. **hostis**, *stranger, enemy*, OE. **giest**, Goth. **gasts**, O.Icel. **gestr**, OS. OHG. **gast**, *guest*.

**sk**. Gr. σκιά, *shadow*, OE. OS. OHG. **scīnan**, Goth. **skeinan**, O.Icel. **skīna**, *to shine*; Lat. **piscis**, OE. **fisc**, Goth. **fisks**, O.Icel. **fiskr**, OS. OHG. **fisk**, *fish*.

**sq**. Gr. θυο-σκόος, *sacrificing priest*, OE. **scēawian**, Goth. ***skaggwōn**, OS. **scauwōn**, OHG. **scouwōn**, *to look, view*.

2. The **t** also remained unshifted in the Indg. combinations **pt**, **kt**, **qt**.

**pt** > **ft**. Lat. **neptis**, OE. OHG. **nift**, *niece, granddaughter*; Lat. **captus**, *a taking, seizing*, OE. **hæft**, OHG. **haft**, *one seized* or *taken, a captive*.

**kt** > **χt**. Lat. **octō**, Gr. ὀκτώ, OE. **eahta**, Goth. **ahtáu**, OS. OHG. **ahto**, *eight*; Gr. ὀ-ρεκτός, *stretched out*, Lat. **rēctus**, OE. **riht**, Goth. **raíhts**, OS. OHG. **reht**, *right, straight*.

**qt** > **χt**. Gen. sing. Lat. **noctis**, Gr. νυκτός, nom. OE. **neaht**, **niht**, Goth. **nahts**, OS. OHG. **naht**, *night*.

§ **232**. The Indg. mediae **b**, **d**, **g**, **g**, **gʷ** became the tenues **p**, **t**, **k**, **k**, **kw**.

**b** > **p**. Gr. βαίτη, *a shepherd's goatskin coat*, OE. **pād**, Goth. **páida**, OS. **pēda**, *coat, cloak*; Lithuanian **dubùs**, OE. **dēop**, Goth. **diups**, O.Icel. **djūpr**, OS. **diop**, OHG. **tiof**, *deep*; Lithuanian **trobà**, *house*, OE. **þorp**, OS. **thorp**, OHG. **dorf**, *village*, Goth. **þaúrp**, *field*; O.Bulgarian **slabŭ**, *slack, weak*, OE. **slǣpan**, Goth. **slēpan**, OS. **slāpan**, OHG. **slāfan**, *to sleep*, originally, *to be slack*. **b** was a rare sound in the parent language.

**d** > **t**. Lat. **decem**, Gr. δέκα, OE. **tīen**, Goth. **taíhun**, O.Icel. **tīo**, OS. **tehan**, OHG. **zehan**, *ten*; Lat. **dens** (gen. **dentis**), OE. **tōþ**, Goth. **tunþus**, OS. **tand**, OHG. **zand**, *tooth*; Lat. **vidēre**, *to see*, OE. Goth. OS. **witan**, O.Icel. **vita**, OHG. **wiȥȥan**, *to know*; Lat. **edō**, Gr. ἔδω, *I eat*, OE. OS. **etan**, Goth. **itan**, O.Icel. **eta**, OHG. **eȥȥan**, *to eat*; gen. Lat. **pedis**, Gr. ποδός, nom. OE. OS. **fōt**, Goth. **fōtus**, O.Icel. **fōtr**, OHG. **fuoȥ**, *foot*.

**g** > **k**. Lat. **genu**, Gr. γόνυ, OE. **cnēo**, Goth. **kniu**, O.Icel. **knē**, OS. OHG. **knio**, *knee*; Lat. **gustō**, *I taste*, Gr. γεύω, *I let taste*, OE. **cēosan**, Goth. **kiusan**, O.Icel. **kjōsa**, OS. OHG. **kiosan**, *to test, choose*; Lat. **ager**, Gr. ἀγρός, OE. **æcer**, Goth. **akrs**, O.Icel. **akr**, *field, acre*; Lat. **ego**, Gr. ἐγώ, OE. **ic**, Goth. OS. **ik**, O.Icel. **ek**, OHG. **ih**, *I*.

**ɡ** > **k**. Lat. **gelu**, *frost*, OE. **ceald**, Goth. **kalds**, O.Icel. **kaldr**, OS. **kald**, OHG. **kalt**, *cold*; Lat. **augēre**, Goth. **áukan**, O.Icel. **auka**, OS. **ōkian**, OHG. **ouhhōn**, *to add, increase*, OE. participial adj. **ēacen**, *great*; Lat. **jugum**, Gr. ζυγόν, OE. **geoc**, Goth. **juk**, OHG. **joh**, *yoke*.

**ɡ$^{w}$** > **kw**. Gr. Bœotian βανά, OE. **cwene**, Goth. **qinō**, OS. **quena**, *woman, wife*; Gr. βίος from ***ɡ$^{w}$ī̆wos**, *life*, Lat. **vīvos** from ***gwīwos**, OE. **cwicu**, Goth. **qius**, O.Icel. **kvikr**, OS. **quik**, OHG. **quec**, *quick, alive*; Lat. **veniō** from ***gwemjō**, *I come*, Gr. βαίνω from *βανjω, older *βαμjω = Indg. ***ɡ$^{w}$mjō**, *I go*, OE. OS. **cuman**, Goth. **qiman**, O.Icel. **koma**, OHG. **queman**, *to come*.

§ **233**. The Indg. tenues aspiratae became voiceless spirants in prim. Germanic, and thus fell together with and underwent all further changes in common with the voiceless spirants which arose from the Indg. tenues (§ **231**), the latter having also passed through the intermediate stage of tenues aspiratae before they became spirants. The tenues aspiratae were, however, of so rare occurrence in the prim. Indg. language that two or three examples must suffice for the purposes of this book; for further examples and details, the learner should consult Brugmann's *Grundriss der vergleichenden Grammatik der indogermanischen Sprachen*, vol. I:—Skr. root **sphal-**, *run violently against*, OE. **feallan**, O.Icel. **falla**, OS. OHG. **fallan**, *to fall*; Gr. ἀ-σκηθής, *unhurt*, OE. **sceþþan**, Goth. **skaþjan**, OHG. **skadōn**, *to injure*; Gr. σχίζω, *I split*, OE. **scādan**, Goth. **skáidan**, OHG. **sceidan**, *to divide, separate*; Gr. φάλλη, OE. **hwæl**, O.Icel. **hvalr**, OHG. **(h)wal**, *whale*.

§ **234**. The Indg. mediae aspiratae **bh**, **dh**, **gh**, **ǥh**, **gʷh** became first of all the voiced spirants **ƀ**, **đ**, **ʒ**, **ʒ**, **ʒw**. These sounds underwent the following changes during the prim. Germanic period:—**ƀ**, **đ** initially, and **ƀ**, **đ**, **ʒ**, **ʒw** medially after their corresponding nasals, became the voiced explosives **b**, **d**, **g**, **gw**, as

**b**. OE. OS. OHG. **beran**, Goth. **baíran**, O.Icel. **bera**, *to bear*, Skr. **bhárāmi**, Gr. φέρω, Lat. **ferō**, *I bear*; OE. OS. **bītan**, Goth. **beitan**, O.Icel. **bīta**, OHG. **bīʒʒan**, *to bite*, Skr. **bhḗdāmi**, Lat. **findō**, *I cleave*; OE. **brōþor**, Goth. **brōþar**, O.Icel. **brōðer**, OS. **brōđar**, OHG. **bruoder**, Skr. **bhrā́tar-**, Lat. **frāter**, *brother*, Gr. φρᾱ́τηρ, *member of a clan*.

OE. **ymbe**, OS. OHG. **umbi**, Gr. ἀμφί, *around*; OE. **camb**, **comb**, O.Icel. **kambr**, OHG. **kamb**, *comb*, Skr. **jámbhas**, *tooth*, Gr. γόμφος, *bolt, nail*, prim. form ***gombhos**.

**d**. OE. **dæg**, Goth. **dags**, O.Icel. **dagr**, OS. **đag**, OHG. **tag**, *day*, Skr. **ni-dāghás**, older ***ni-dhāghás**, *hot season, summer*, Indg. form ***dhoǥhos**; OE. **dǣd**, OS. **đād**, OHG. **tāt**, *deed*, related to Gr. θή-σω, *I shall place*, Skr. **dhā́ma**, *law, dwelling-place*, root ***dhē-**, *put, place*; OE. **dohtor**, Goth. **daúhtar**, O.Icel. **dōtter**, OS. **dohter**, OHG. **tohter**, Gr. θυγάτηρ, *daughter*; OE. **duru**, OS. **duri**, OHG. **turi**, Gr. θύρᾱ, *door*.

OE. Goth. OS. **bindan**, O.Icel. **binda**, OHG. **bintan**, *to* *bind*, Skr. **bándhanam**, *a binding*, cp. *πενθερός*, *father-in-law*, Lat. **of-fendimentum**, *chin-cloth*, root ***bhendh-**.

**g.** OE. **enge**, Goth. **aggwus**, OS. OHG. **engi**, *narrow*, cp. Lat. **angō**, Gr. *ἄγχω*, *I press tight*, root ***angh-**; OE. **lang, long**, Goth. **laggs**, O.Icel. **langr**, OS. OHG. **lang**, Lat. **longus**, *long*.

**gw.** Goth. **siggwiþ**, *he sings*, cp. Gr. *ὀμφή*, *divine voice*, Indg. ***soŋgʷhá**.

§ **235.** **ƀ, đ, ʒ, ʒw** remained in other positions, and their further development belongs to the history of the separate Germanic languages. In Goth. **ƀ, đ** (written **b, d**) remained medially after vowels, but became explosives (**b, d**) after consonants. They became **f, þ** finally after vowels and before final **-s**. **ʒ** (written **g**) remained medially between vowels, and medially after vowels before voiced consonants, but probably became **χ** (written **g**) finally after vowels and before final **-s**. It became **g** initially, and also medially after voiced consonants. In O.Icel. **ƀ** (written **f**) remained medially between and finally after voiced sounds, but became **f** before voiceless sounds. **đ** (written **ð**) generally remained medially and finally. **ʒ** (written **g**) remained medially after vowels and liquids, but became **χ** and then disappeared finally. It became **g** initially. **đ** became **d** in all the West Germanic languages and then **d** became **t** in OHG. In OS. **ƀ** (written **ƀ, b**) generally remained between voiced sounds. It became **f** medially before **l** and **n**, and before voiceless consonants, and also finally. **ʒ** (written **g**) remained initially and medially, but became **χ** finally, although it was generally written **g**. In OHG. **ƀ, ʒ** became **b, g**. On the history of **ƀ, ʒ** in OE. see §§ **293–4, 313–24.** Geminated **ƀƀ, đđ, ʒʒ**, of whatever origin, became **bb, dd, gg** in the prehistoric period of all the Germanic languages. Examples are:—Goth. ***nibls**, OS. **neƀal**, OHG. **nebul**, Lat. **nebula**, Gr. *νεφέλη*, *mist, cloud*, cp. Skr. **nábhas**, Gr. *νέφος*, *cloud*; OE. **lēof**, Goth.

**liufs,** O.Icel. **ljūfr,** OS. **liof,** OHG. **liob,** *dear,* original form ***leubhos,** cp. Skr. **lúbhyāmi,** *I feel a strong desire,* Lat. **lubet (libet),** *it pleases*; OE. OS. **ūder,** OHG. **ūter,** Skr. **ū́dhar,** Gr. *οὖθαρ, udder*; OE. **rēad,** Goth. **ráuþs,** O.Icel. **rauðr,** OS. **rōd,** OHG. **rōt,** prim. form ***roudhos,** cp. Skr. **rudhirás,** Gr. *ἐ-ρυθρός,* prim. form ***rudhros,** *red*; OE. Goth. **guma,** O.Icel. **gume,** OS. **gumo,** OHG. **gomo,** Lat. **homō,** prim. Germanic stem-form ***guman-, -in-,** *man*; OE. **gōs,** O.Icel. **gās,** OHG. **gans,** Gr. *χήν, goose*; OE. OS. OHG. **wegan,** Goth. **gawigan,** O.Icel. **vega,** *to move, carry,* Lat. **vehō,** prim. form ***weghō,** *I carry*; OE. **giest,** Goth. **gasts,** O.Icel. **gestr,** OS. OHG. **gast,** *guest,* Lat. **hostis,** *stranger, enemy,* prim. form ***ǵhostis**; OE. OS. OHG. **stīgan,** Goth. **steigan,** O.Icel. **stīga,** *to ascend,* Gr. *στείχω,* prim. form ***steiǵhō,** *I go,* cp. Lat. **vestīgium,** *footstep.*

§ **236.** It is impossible to state the precise chronological order in which the first sound-shifting took place. The most commonly accepted theory is that the changes took place in the following order:—1. The tenues became tenues aspiratae and thus fell together with the original tenues aspiratae. 2. The new and the original tenues aspiratae became voiceless spirants. 3. The mediae aspiratae became voiced spirants. 4. And lastly the mediae became tenues. But only so much is certain: that at the time when the Indg. mediae became tenues, the Indg. tenues must have been on the way to becoming voiceless spirants, otherwise the two sets of scunds would have fallen together.

§ **237.** We have already seen (§ **229,** Note 1) that the parent Indg. language contained two series of velars: (1) pure velars which never had labialization. These velars fell together with the palatals in the Germanic, Latin, Greek, and Keltic languages, but were kept apart in the Aryan and Baltic-Slavonic languages. (2) Velars with labialization. These velars appear in the Germanic languages partly with and partly without labialization; in the latter case they fell together with prim. Germanic χ, **k, ʒ** which arose from Indg. **k, g, gh.** The **w** in prim. Germanic **χw, kw, ʒw** from Indg. **qʷ, gʷ, gʷh,** and in prim. Germanic **ʒw** from Indg. **qʷ** by Verner's law (§ **238**) regularly remained before Indg. **ĕ, ĭ, ə, a, ā** (= prim. Germanic **ō,** § **23**), and also in the combinations vowel + **ʒw** + liquid or **n,** but regularly disappeared before Indg. **ŭ, ō, o** (= prim. Germanic **a,** § **20**), and also in the initial combinations **kw-** or **ʒw-** + liquid, in the medial combinations **-ʒwj-, -ŋʒwr-, -χwt-,** and when final. These sound-laws became greatly obscured during the prim. Germanic period through form-transference and levelling out in various directions:—

1. Prim. Germanic **χw** from Indg. **qʷ.** Regular forms were: OE. **hwīl,** Goth. **ƕeila,** *time*; Goth. **saíƕit,** *he sees,* Indg. ***séqʷeti**; Goth. **ƕis,** Indg. ***qʷeso,** *whose*; and with regular loss of **w** OE. **heals,** Goth. **hals,** *neck,* Indg. ***qʷolsos**; OS. OHG. **gi-siht,** *sight, look*; OE. **seah,** OS. OHG. **sah,** *he saw.* After the analogy of forms like Goth. **ƕis** were formed Goth. **ƕas,** OE. **hwă** for ***has, *hă,** Indg. ***qʷos,** *who.* From forms like Goth. **saíƕit,** the **ƕ** was levelled out into all forms of the verb; and conversely from forms like OE. **sēon** from ***seohan,** older ***sehan** = OS. OHG. **sehan,** *to see,* Indg. ***séqʷonom,** the **h** (= χ) was levelled out into all forms of the present.

2. Prim. Germanic **kw** from Indg. **gʷ.** Regular forms were: OE. **cwicu,** Goth. **qius,** Lat. **vīvus** from ***gwīwos,** *quick, alive*; Goth. **qima,** OHG. **quimu** beside OE. **cume,** *I come*; pret. pl. Goth. **qēmun,** OE. **cwōmon** from ***cwǣmun,** *they came*; OE. **cū,** OS. **kō,** Indg. acc. ***gʷōm,** *cow.* After the analogy of forms like Goth. **qima,** OHG. **quimu,** Indg. ***gʷémō,** the **q, qu** were levelled out into all forms of these verbs, as pret. **qam, quam** for ***kam,** Indg. ***gʷóma.**

From forms like Goth. **sigqiþ**, *he sinks*, the **q** (= **kw**) was levelled out into all forms, and conversely from forms like OE. **sincan**, Indg. ***seŋgʷonom** the **c** was levelled out into all forms.

3. Prim. Germanic **ʒw** from Indg. **gʷh**, and the **ʒw** from Indg. **qʷ** by Verner's law (§ **238**) became **gw** in the medial combination **-ŋʒw-** before palatal vowels, as Goth. **siggwiþ**, *he sings*. But in all other cases either the **ʒ** or the **w** regularly disappeared according to the sound-laws stated above.

4. Prim. Germanic **ʒw** from Indg. **gʷh**. Regular forms were: Goth. **mawi**, *maiden*, beside **magus**, OE. **magu**, *boy, son*; OE. **snīweþ**, OHG. **snīwit**, *it snows*, OHG. pp. **versnigan**; Goth. **siggwiþ**, *he sings*, beside OE. inf. **singan**; Goth. **hneiwiþ**, *he bows, declines*, beside OE. inf. **hnīgan**. And then through levelling out in different directions the **w**, **gw** or **g** became generalized in the verbs, as OE. **snīwan**, **singeþ**, **hnīgeþ** for ***snīgan**, ***singweþ**, ***hnīweþ**; Goth. **siggwan**, **hneiwan** for ***siggan**, ***hneigan**.

5. Prim. Germanic medial **-ʒw-** from Indg. **-qʷ-** by Verner's law. Regular forms were: Goth. **siuns**, OE. **sīen** (**sīon**, **sēon**), from ***se(ʒ)wn̥ís**, *a seeing, face*; Goth. **saíƕiþ**, *he sees*; OE. **hwēol**, **hweowol** from ***χwe(ʒ)wlo-**, *wheel*; OE. gen. **holwes**, **horwes** beside nom. **holh**, *hollow*, **horh**, *dirt*; pret. pl. subj. **sāwen** (OS. **sāwin**) beside pret. pl. indic. **sǣgon** (Anglian **sēgon**), *we saw*; pp. **sewen** from ***se(ʒ)wenós**, *seen*.

Analogical formations were: WS **sāwon** with **w** from the pret. subj. **sāwe**, pl. **sāwen**, and the pp. **sewen**; Anglian pp. **segen** with **g** from **sēgon**; and similarly pp. **sigen** beside the regular form **siwen**, *strained*; and **ligen** for ***liwen**, *lent*.

NOTE.—In several words the Indg. velars, when preceded or followed by a **w** or another labial in the same word, appear in the Germanic languages as labials by assimilation. The most important examples are:—OE. OS. **wulf**, Goth. **wulfs**, OHG. **wolf** = Gr. **λύκος**, for ***ϝλύκος**, prim. form ***wl̥qos**, cp. Skr. **vr̥kas**, *wolf*; OE. **fēower** (but **fyþer-fēte**, *four-footed*), Goth. **fidwōr**, OS. OHG. **fior**, prim. form ***qʷetwóres**, cp. Lithuanian **keturì**, Lat. **quattuor**, Gr. **τέσσαρες**, Skr. **catvā́ras**, *four*; OE. OS. **fīf**, Goth. **fimf**, OHG. **fimf**, **finf**, prim. form ***peŋqʷe**, cp. Skr. **páñca**, Gr. **πέντε**, Lat. **quīnque** (for ***pīnque**), *five*; OE. **weorpan**, Goth. **waírpan**, O.Icel. **verpa**, OS. **werpan**, OHG. **werfan**, *to throw*, cp. O. Bulgarian **vrĭgą**, *I throw*; OE. **swāpan**, OHG. **sweifan**, *to swing*, cp. Lithuanian **swaikstù**, *I become dizzy*.

## Verner's Law.

§ **238.** After the completion of the first sound-shifting, and while the principal accent was not yet confined to the root-syllable (see § **9**), a uniform interchange took place between the voiceless and voiced spirants, which may be thus stated:—

The medial spirants **f**, **þ**, **χ**, **χw**, **s** and the final spirant **-s** (see § **211**, Note) regularly became **ƀ**, **đ**, **ʒ**, **ʒw**, **z** when the vowel next preceding them did not, according to the original Indg. system of accentuation, bear the principal accent of the word.

The **ƀ**, **đ**, **ʒ**, **ʒw** which thus arose from Indg. **p**, **t**, **k**, **qʷ** underwent in the Germanic languages all further changes in common with the **ƀ**, **đ**, **ʒ**, **ʒw** from Indg. **bh**, **dh**, **gh**, **gʷh**.

Verner's law manifests itself most clearly in the various parts of strong verbs, where the infinitive, present participle, present tense, and preterite (properly perfect) singular had the principal accent on the root-syllable, but the indicative pret. plural, the pret. subjunctive (properly optative), and past participle had the principal accent on the ending, as prim. Germanic ***wérþō** > OE. **weorþe**, *I become* = Skr. **vártā-mi**, *I turn*; pret. indic. 3. sing. ***wárþi** > OE. **wearþ**, *he became* = Skr. **va-várta**, *has turned*; pret.

1. pers. pl. ***wurđumí** > OE. ***wurdum** (**wurdon** is the 3. pers. pl. used for all persons) = Skr. **va-vrtimá**, *we have turned*; past participle ***wurđaná-** > OE. **worden** = Skr. **va-vrtānā́-**; OS. **birid**, OHG. **birit** = Skr. **bhárati**, *he bears*; Goth. 2. sing. indic. passive **baíraza** = Skr. **bhárasē**; Goth. **baírand**, OHG. **berant** = Skr. **bháranti**, *they bear*; present participle OE. **berende**, Goth. **baírands**, O.Icel. **berande**, OS. **berandi**, OHG. **beranti**, Gr. gen. φέροντος. Or to take examples from noun-forms, &c., we have e. g. Skr. **pitár-**, Gr. πατέρ- = prim. Germanic ***fađér-**, OE. **fæder**, Goth. **fadar**, O.Icel. **faðer**, OS. **fader**, OHG. **fater**, *father*; Gr. πλωτός, *floating, swimming*, OE. OS. **flōd**, Goth. **flōdus**, O.Icel. **floð**, OHG. **fluot**, *flood, tide*; Skr. **çatám**, Gr. ἑ-κατόν, Lat. **centum** = prim. Germanic ***χunđóm**, older ***χumđóm**, OE. Goth. OS. **hund**, OHG. **hunt**, *hundred*; Indg. ***swékuros**, Goth. **swaíhra**, OHG. **swehur**, OE. **swēor** (§ **329**), *father-in-law*, beside Gr. ἑκυρᾱ́, OE. **sweger**, OHG. **swigar**, *mother-in-law*; Gr. δέκα, Goth. **taíhun**, OS. **tehan**, OHG. **zehan**, *ten*, beside Gr. δεκάς, OE. OS. **-tig**, OHG. **-zug**, Goth. pl. **tigjus**, *decade*; Skr. **saptá**, Gr. ἑπτά, OE. **seofon**, Goth. **sibun**, OS. **siƀun**, OHG. **sibun**, *seven*; Gr. νυός from *σνυσός, OE. **snoru**, OHG. **snura**, *daughter-in-law*; OHG. **haso** beside OE. **hara**, *hare*; Goth. **áusō** beside OE. **ēare**, *ear*.

The combinations **sp, st, sk, ss, ft, fs, hs,** and **ht** were not subject to this law.

Note.—The prim. Germanic system of accentuation was like that of Sanskrit, Greek, &c., i. e. the principal accent could fall on any syllable; it was not until a later period of the prim. Germanic language that the principal accent was confined to the root-syllable. See § **9**.

§ **239**. From what has been said above it follows that the interchanging pairs of consonants due to Verner's law were in prim. Germanic: **f—ƀ, þ—đ, s—z, χ—ȝ, χw—ȝw.** They underwent various changes partly in prim. Germanic, partly in West Germanic, and partly in Old English. Already in prim. Germanic **ʒw** became **ʒ** before **u**, but **w** in other cases (§§ **237, 241**); **ŋ** disappeared before χ (§ **245**), and **ŋʒ** became **ŋg** (§ **234**), whence the interchange of χ—**ŋg**; **ƀ, đ** became **b, d** after their corresponding nasals (§ **234**). In West Germanic **đ** became **d** (§ **253**); **z** became **r** medially and was dropped finally (§ **252**); χ**w** became χ (§ **246**). In OE. the two sounds **f—ƀ** fell together in **ƀ** (written **f**) medially, and in **f** finally, see §§ **293–4, 296**, so that the original interchange between **f—ƀ** became entirely obliterated; χ disappeared between vowels (§ **329**, 4), when preserved it was written **h**; and **þ, s** became voiced between vowels, although the **þ, s** were preserved in writing. So that in OE. we have the following interchanging pairs of consonants:—

**þ—d** **s—r**
**h** or loss of **h** (= prim. Germ. χ)—**g** (§ **320**)
**h** or loss of **h** (= prim. Germ. χ**w**)—**g, w** (= prim. Germ. **ʒw**)
**h** or loss of **h** (= prim. Germ. **ŋ**χ, § **245**)—**ng**.

**þ—d.** **cweþan,** *to say,* **līþan,** *to go,* **snīþan,** *to cut*; pret. sing. **cwæþ, lāþ, snāþ**; pret. pl. **cwǣdon, lidon, snidon**; pp. **cweden, liden, sniden**; **cwide,** *saying, proverb*; **snide,** *incision*; **dēaþ,** *death,* beside **dēad,** *dead.*

**s—r.** **cēosan,** *to choose,* **drēosan,** *to fall,* **forlēosan,** *to ose*; pret. sing. **cēas, drēas, forlēas**; pret. pl. **curon, druron, forluron**; pp. **coren, droren, forloren**; **cyre,** *choice*; **dryre,** *fall*; **lyre,** *loss.*

**h—g.** **flēon** (OHG. **fliohan**), *to flee,* **slēan** (Goth. **slahan**), *to strike, slay,* **tēon** (Goth. **tiuhan**), *to draw, lead*; pret. sing. **flēah, slōh, tēah**; pret. pl. **flugon, slōgon, tugon**; pp. **flogen, slægen, togen**; **slaga,** *homicide*; **slege,** *stroke, blow*; **here-toga,** *leader of an army, duke.*

**h—g, w.** **sēon** (Goth. **saíƕan**), *to see*; pret. sing. **seah**;

pret. pl. WS. **sāwon,** Anglian **sēgon**; pp. WS. **sewen,** Anglian **segen**; **sīon, sēon** (Goth. ***seihvan,** OHG. **sīhan**), *to strain*; pret. sing. **sāh**; pp. **siwen, sigen**; **horh,** *dirt*, gen. **horwes.** See Note 1 below.

**h—ng. fōn** (Goth. **fāhan,** prim. Germ. ***faŋχanan,** § **245**), *to seize*, **hōn** (Goth. **hāhan,** prim. Germ. ***χaŋχanan**), *to hang*; pret. pl. **fēngon, hēngon**; pp. **fangen, hangen**; **feng,** *grasp, booty*; **hangian,** *to hang*; **þīon, þēon** (Goth. **þeihan,** prim. Germ. ***þiŋχanan**), *to thrive*; pret. pl. **þungon**; pp. **þungen**; the usual pret. pl. **þigon,** pp. **þigen,** were new formations, see § **492.**

Note.—1. The results of the operation of Verner's law were often disturbed in OE. through the influence of analogy and levelling, e.g. the **þ, s** of the present and pret. singular were extended to the pret. plural and pp. in **ābrēoþan,** *to fail*; **mīþan,** *to avoid*; **wrīþan,** *to twist*; **ārīsan,** *to arise*; **genesan,** *to recover*; **lesan,** *to collect*; pret. pl. **ābruþon, miþon, wriþon, ārison, genǣson, lǣson**; pp. **ābroþen, miþen, wriþen, ārisen, genesen, lesen.** The **g** of the pret. plural was levelled out into the singular in **flōg,** *he flayed*; **hlōg,** *he laughed*; **lōg,** *he blamed*; **slōg,** *he slew*; **þwōg,** *he washed*, see §§ **509–10.** The **nd** of the pret. plural and pp. was extended to the present and pret. singular in **findan,** pret. sing. **fand.** The regular forms of this verb would be ***fīþan** ( = Goth. **finþan,** OS. **fīþan**), *to find*; pret. sing. ***fōþ** (see § **61**), pret. pl. **fundon,** pp. **funden.** The WS. pret. pl. **sāwon,** *they saw*, had its **w** from the pp. **sewen,** and conversely the Anglian pp. **segen,** *seen*, had its **g** from the pret. plural **sēgon,** see § **241.**

2. Causative verbs (cp. § **521**) had originally suffix accentuation, and therefore also exhibit the change of consonants given above, as **weorþan,** *to become*: **ā-wierdan,** *to destroy, injure*, cp. Skr. **vártāmi,** *I turn*: **vartáyāmi,** *I cause to turn*; **līþan,** *to go*: **lǣdan,** *to lead*; **ā-rīsan,** *to arise*: **rǣran,** *to raise*; **genesan,** *to recover*: **nerian,** *to save*.

## OTHER CONSONANT CHANGES.

§ **240.** Most of the sound-changes comprised under this paragraph might have been disposed of in the paragraphs dealing with the shifting of the Indg. mediae and mediae aspiratae, but to prevent any possible misunderstanding or confusion, it was thought advisable to reserve them for a special paragraph.

1. The mediae + **t** or **s** became tenues + **t** or **s** in Indo-Germanic.

2. The Indg. mediae aspiratae + **t** became tenues + **t** in early prim. Germanic.

3. The Indg. tenues aspiratae and mediae aspiratae + **s** had in prim. Germanic the same development as the original tenues + **s**.

Examples are: Lat. **nūptum, nūpsī,** beside **nūbere,** *to marry*; Skr. loc. pl. **patsú,** beside loc. sing. **padí,** *on foot*; Lat. **rēxī, rēctum,** beside **regere,** *to rule*; Lat. **vēxī, vectum,** beside **vehere,** *to carry*, root ***wegh-**; Lat. **lectus,** Gr. λέχος, *bed*, OE. **licgan,** Goth. **ligan,** *to lie down*; Skr. **yuktá-,** Gr. ζευκτός, Lat. **jūnctus,** *yoked*, root ***jeuǵ-,** cp. Skr. **yugám,** Gr. ζυγόν, Lat. **jugum,** OE. **geoc,** Goth. **juk,** *yoke*; &c.

Then **pt, kt, qt**; **ps, ks, qs** (cp. § **229,** Note 2) were shifted to **ft, χt**; **fs, χs** at the same time as the original Indg. tenues became voiceless spirants (§ **231**). And **tt** (through the intermediate stage of **tˢt**), **ts** became **ss. ss** then became simplified to **s** after long syllables, and before and after consonants. So that for purely practical purposes the above sound-laws may be thus formulated:—Every labial + **t** or **s** became **ft, fs**; every guttural + **t** or **s** became **χt, χs**; every dental + **t** or **s** became **ss, s.**

This explains the frequent interchange between **p, ƀ (b),** and **f**; between **k, ʒ (g),** and **h** (i. e. χ); and between **t, þ, đ (d),** and **ss, s** in forms which are etymologically related.

**p, ƀ** (b)—**f.** OE. **scieppan,** Goth. **skapjan,** *to create*, beside OE. **ge·sceaft,** OHG. **gi·skaft,** *creature,* Goth. **ga·skafts,** *creation*; Goth. **giban,** OHG. **geban,** *to give,* beside Goth. **fra·gifts,** *a giving, espousal,* OE. OHG. **gift,** *gift*; OHG. **weban,** *to weave,* beside English **weft.**

**k, ʒ** (g)—**h.** OE. **wyrcan,** Goth. **waúrkjan,** OHG. **wurken,** *to work,* beside pret. and pp. OE. **worhte, worht,** Goth. **waúrhta, waúrhts,** OHG. **worhta, giworht**; OE. **þyncan,** Goth. **þugkjan,** OHG. **dunken,** *to seem,* beside pret. and pp. OE. **þūhte, þūht,** Goth. **þūhta, *þūhts,** OHG. **dūhta, gidūht**; OE. **magon,** Goth. ***magun,** OHG. **magun,** *they may, can,* beside pret. OE. **meahta,** Goth. OHG. **mahta,** pp. Goth. **mahts,** cp. also OE. **meaht,** Goth. **mahts,** OHG. **maht,** *might, power*; OE. **bycgan,** Goth. **bugjan,** *to buy,* beside pret. and pp. OE. **bohte, boht,** Goth. **baúhta, baúhts**; OE. OHG. **bringan,** Goth. **briggan,** *to bring,* pret. and pp. OE. **brōhte, brōht,** OHG. **brāhta, gibrāht,** Goth. **brāhta, *brāhts.**

**t, þ, đ** (d)—**ss, s.** OE. Goth. OS. **witan,** O.Icel. **vita,** *to know,* beside pret. OE. **wisse,** Goth. OS. OHG. **wissa,** O.Icel. **vissa,** participial adj. OE. **gewiss,** O.Icel. **viss,** OS. **wis(s),** OHG. **giwis(s),** *sure, certain*; OE. **sittan,** O.Icel. **sitja,** OS. **sittian,** *to sit,* beside OE. O.Icel. OS. **sess,** *seat*; OE. **cweþan,** Goth. **qiþan,** *to say,* beside Goth. **ga-qiss,** *consent*; Goth. **ana·biudan,** *to command,* beside **ana·busns,** *commandment,* pre-Germanic **·*bhŭtsni·,** root ***bheudh·.**

**ss** became **s** after long syllables, and before and after consonants, as OE. **hātan,** Goth. **háitan,** *to call,* beside OE. **hǣs** from ***haissi·,** *command*; OE. Goth. OS. **witan,** *to know,* beside OE. OS. OHG. **wīs,** *wise,* Goth. **unweis,** *unknowing*; OE. **etan,** Goth. **itan,** *to eat,* beside OE. **ǣs,** OHG. **ās,** *carrion*; OE. **hȳdan,** *to hide,* beside **hūs** from ***χūtso·,** *house*; OE. **mōt,** *I may,* beside OHG. pret. **muosa.**

Instead of **ss** (s) we often meet with **st.** In such cases the **st** is due to the analogy of forms where **t** was quite regular, e. g. regular forms were Goth. **last,** *thou didst gather,* inf. **lisan;** Goth. **slōht,** *thou didst strike,* inf. **slahan;** OE. **meaht,** OHG. **maht,** *thou canst,* inf. **magan;** then after the analogy of such forms were made OE. **wāst** for ***wās,** Goth. **wáist** for ***wáis,** OHG. **weist** for ***weis,** *thou knowest*; OE. **mōst** for ***mōs,** *thou art allowed*; regular forms were pret. sing. OE. **worhte,** Goth. **waúrhta,** OHG. **worhta,** beside inf. OE. **wyrcan,** Goth. **waúrkjan,** OHG. **wurken,** *to work*; then after the analogy of such forms were made OE. **wiste** beside **wisse,** OHG. **wista** beside **wissa,** *I knew*; OE. **mōste** for ***mōse** (= OHG. **muosa**), *I was allowed.*

§ **241.** Prim. Germanic **ʒw,** which arose from Indg. **gʷh** (§ **237**) and from Indg. **qʷ** (§ **238**) by Verner's law, became **ʒ** before **u,** in other cases it became **w,** as Goth. **magus,** *boy,* beside **mawi** from ***ma(ʒ)wí,** *girl*; pret. pl. Anglian **sēgon** from ***sǣʒ(w)un,** *they saw,* beside pp. **sewen** from ***se(ʒ)wenós;** OE. **sīen** (**sīon, sēon,** cp. § **138**), Goth. **siuns,** from ***se(ʒ)wnís,** *a seeing, face*; OE. **snāw** (with **-w** from the oblique cases), Goth. **snáiws,** from ***snai(ʒ)waz,** prim. form ***snóigʷhos,** *snow*; OE. OHG. **snīwan** for ***snīgan,** formed from the third pers. sing. OE. **snīweþ,** OHG. **snīwit,** *it snows.* See § **239**, Note 1, § **249**.

§ **242.** Assimilation:—**-nw-** > **-nn-,** as OE. Goth. OHG. **rinnan** from ***rinwan,** *to run*; OE. **cinn,** Goth. **kinnus,** OHG. **kinni,** from ***genw-,** Gr. γένυ-ς, *chin, cheek*; Goth. **minniza,** OS. **minnira,** OHG. **minniro,** from ***minwizō,** *less,* cp. Lat. **minuō,** Gr. μινύθω, *I lessen*; OE. **þynne,** O.Icel. **þunnr,** OHG. **dunni,** *thin,* cp. Skr. fem. **tanvī́,** *thin.*

**-md-** > **-nd-,** as OE. Goth. OS. **hund,** OHG. **hunt,** prim. form ***kmtóm,** *hundred*; OE. **scamian,** Goth. **skaman,** OHG. **scamēn,** *to be ashamed,* beside OE. **scand,** Goth. **skanda,** OHG. **scanta,** *shame, disgrace*; OE. **sund,** *a swimming,* beside **swimman,** *to swim.*

**-ln-** > **-ll-**, as OE. **full**, Goth. **fulls**, Lithuanian **pìlnas**, prim. form ***plnós**, *full*; OE. **wulle**, Goth. **wulla**, OHG. **wolla**, Lithuanian **vìlna**, *wool*.

§ **243**. Prim. Germanic **ƀn**, **đn**, **ʒn** = Indg. **pń**, **tń**, **kń**, **qń** (by Verner's law), and **bhń**, **dhń**, **ghń**, **ghń**, became **ƀƀ**, **đđ**, **ʒʒ** before the principal accent, then later they became **bb**, **dd**, **gg**; and in like manner Indg. **bń**, **dń**, **gń**, **gń** became **bb**, **dd**, **gg**. And these mediae were shifted to **pp**, **tt**, **kk** at the same time as the original Indg. mediae became tenues (§ **232**). These geminated consonants were simplified to **p**, **t**, **k** after long syllables. Examples are: OE. **hnæpp**, OHG. **napf**, from ***χnaƀń** or ***χnabń**, *basin, bowl*; OE. **hoppian**, O.Icel. **hoppa**, MHG. **hopfen**, from ***χoƀń**, *to hop*; OE. OS. **topp**, O.Icel. **toppr**, from ***toƀń**, *top, summit*; OE. **hēap**, OS. **hōp**, OHG. **houf**, from ***χauƀń**; OE. **cnotta**, from ***knođń**, beside OHG. **chnodo**, **chnoto**, *knot*; OE. OS. **hwīt**, Goth. **ƕeits**, from ***χwīđń**, *white*; OE. **bucc**, O.Icel. **bokkr**, OHG. **boc** (gen. **bockes**), prim. form ***bhugnós**, *buck*; and similarly OE. **bucca**, *he-goat*; OE. **liccian**, OS. **leccōn**, OHG. **lecchōn**, from ***leʒń**, *to lick*; OE. **locc**, O.Icel. **lokkr**, prim. form ***lugnós**, *lock*; OE. **smocc**, O.Icel. **smokkr**, from ***smoʒń**, *smock*; OE. **lōcian**, OS. **lōkōn**, from ***lōgń** or ***lōʒń**, *to look*.

§ **244**. Indg. **z**+media became **s**+tenuis, as Goth. **asts**, OHG. **ast** = Gr. *ὄζος*, from ***ozdos**, *branch, twig*; OE. OHG. **nest**, Lat. **nīdus**, from ***ni-zdos**, *nest*, related to root ***sed-**, *sit*; OE. **masc**, OHG. **masca**, *mesh, net*, cp. Lithuanian **mezgù**, *I tie in knots*.

Indg. **z**+media aspirata became **z**+voiced spirant, as OE. **meord**, Goth. **mizdō**, *pay, reward*, cp. O. Bulgarian **mĭzda**, Gr. *μισθός*, *pay*; OE. **mearg**, OHG. **marg**, O. Bulgarian **mozgŭ**, *marrow*, root ***mezgh-**.

§ **245**. Guttural **n** (ŋ) disappeared before χ, as Goth. OS. OHG. **fāhan**, OE. **fōn**, from ***faŋχanan**, *to seize*; Goth. OS. OHG. **hāhan**, OE. **hōn**, from ***χaŋχanan**, *to hang*;

Goth. **þeihan,** OS. **thīhan,** OHG. **dīhan,** OE. **þīon, þēon,** from ***þiŋχanan,** *to thrive*; pret. OE. **þōhte,** Goth. **þāhta,** OS. **thāhta,** OHG. **dāhta,** from ***þaŋχtō-,** *I thought,* beside inf. OE. **þencan.** See §§ **40-1.**

§ **246.** χ became an aspirate (written **h**) initially before vowels, as OE. Goth. OS. **hund,** OHG. **hunt,** from ***χunđan,** prim. form ***kmtóm,** *hundred*; OE. OS. **hund,** Goth. **hunds,** O.Icel. **hundr,** OHG. **hunt,** from ***χunđaz,** *dog, hound.* Some scholars assume that it also became an aspirate medially between vowels. Upon this assumption it would be difficult to account for the breaking in OE., as OE. **slēan,** from ***sleahan,** older ***slaχan-,** Goth. **slahan,** *to strike, slay*; OE. **swēor,** from ***sweohur,** older ***sweχur,** OHG. **swehur,** *father-in-law.* See §§ **87, 329,** 4.

Medial and final **χw** became χ in Old Norse and the West Germanic languages, as OS. OHG. **sehan,** OE. **sēon,** O.Icel. **sjā,** from ***seχ(w)an-,** beside Goth. **saíƕan,** *to see*; OS. OHG. **līhan,** OE. **līon, lēon,** O.Icel. **ljā,** from ***līχ(w)an-,** beside Goth. **leiƕan,** *to lend*; OS. OHG. **aha,** OE. **ēa** from ***eahu,** beside Goth. **aƕa,** *water, river*; OE. **seah,** OS. OHG. **sah,** beside Goth. **saƕ,** *he saw*; OE. **nēah,** OS. OHG. **nāh,** beside Goth. **nēƕ,** *near.* Cp. § 237.

§ **247.** The consonants, which arose from the Indg. final explosives (**t, d**), were dropped in prim. Germanic, except after a short accented vowel, as OE. OHG. **bere,** Goth. **baírái,** from an original form ***bheroīt,** *he may bear.* See § **211.**

§ **248.** Original final **-m** became **-n,** and then it, as also Indg. final **-n,** disappeared in dissyllabic and polysyllabic words during the prim. Germanic period. For examples, see § **211.**

§ **249.** Postconsonantal **w** disappeared before **u,** as Goth. **kaúrus** from ***kwuruz,** Gr. *βαρύς, heavy*; OE. **æces,** OHG. **ackus,** from ***ak(w)usi-,** beside Goth. **aqizi,** *axe*; OE. **ancod,** older ***nakud,** OHG. **nackut,** from ***nak(w)uđ-,** beside Goth. **naqaþs,** *naked*; OE. **sund,** *a swimming*, from ***swumda-**, beside inf. **swimman**; OE. pp. **sungen,** beside inf. **swingan,** *to swing*. In verbal forms the **w** was mostly reintroduced in the pret. plural and pp. after the analogy of forms which regularly had **w**, e.g. pret. pl. **swummon, swungon, swullon,** pp. **swummen, swungen** (beside regular form **sungen**), **swollen,** beside inf. **swimman,** *to swim*, **swingan,** *to swing*, **swellan,** *to swell*. For levelling out in the opposite direction, cp. OE. OS. OHG. **singan,** beside Goth. **siggwan** (regular form), *to sing*; OE. **sincan,** OS. OHG. **sinkan,** beside Goth. **sigqan,** *to sink*. Cp. § **241.**

§ **250.** Initial and medial **sr** became **str,** as OE. **strēam,** O.Icel. **straumr,** OS. OHG. **strōm,** *stream*, cp Skr. **srávati,** *it flows*; pl. OE. **ēastron,** OHG. **ōstarūn,** *Easter*, cp. Skr. **usrā́,** *dawn*; OE. **sweostor,** Goth. **swistar,** OHG. **swester,** *sister*, with **t** from the weak stem-form, as in the locative singular Goth. **swistr** = prim. Germanic ***swesri,** cp. Skr. dat. **svásrē**; OE. **fōstor,** O.Icel. **fōstr,** *food, sustenance*, cp. Goth. **fōdjan,** OE. **fēdan,** *to feed*.

§ **251.** The remaining Indg. consonants suffered no further material changes which need be mentioned here. Summing up the results of §§ **231–50,** we arrive at the following system of consonants for the close of the prim. Germanic period :—

| | | Labial. | Inter-dental. | Dental. | Palatal and Guttural. |
|---|---|---|---|---|---|
| *Explosives* | voiceless | **p** | | **t** | **k** |
| | voiced | **b** | | **d** | **g** |
| *Spirants* | voiceless | **f** | **þ** | **s** | **χ** |
| | voiced | **ƀ** | **đ** | **z** | **ʒ** |
| *Nasals* | | **m** | | **n** | **ŋ** |
| *Liquids* | | | | **l, r** | |
| *Semivowels* | | **w** | | | **j** (palatal) |

To these must be added the aspirate **h.**

# CHAPTER IX

## SPECIAL WEST GERMANIC MODIFICATIONS OF THE GENERAL GERMANIC CONSONANT-SYSTEM

§ **252.** Prim. Germanic **z**, which arose from **s** (§ **238**), became **r** medially, and was dropped finally, as OE. **māra**, OHG. **mēro** = Goth. **máiza**, *greater*; pp. OE. **coren**, OHG. **gikoran**, beside inf. OE. **cēosan**, OHG. **kiosan**, *to choose*; OE. **herian**, Goth. **hazjan**, *to praise*; and similarly **hīeran**, *to hear*, **lǣran**, *to teach*; **leornian** from ***liznōjan-**, *to learn*; **nerian**, *to save*; OE. **bet(e)ra**, OS. **betera**, OHG. **beȥȥiro**, Goth. **batiza**, *better*; OE. OS. **hord**, OHG. **hort**, Goth. **huzd**, *hoard, treasure*; OE. **dēor**, OS. **dior**, OHG. **tior**, Goth. **dius** (gen. **diuzis**), prim. Germanic ***đeuzan**, from an original form ***dheusóm**, *deer, wild animal*; OE. **dæg**, OS. **dag**, OHG. **tag** = Goth. **dags**, from ***đaʒaz**, *day*; OE. **giest**, OS. OHG. **gast** = Goth. **gasts**, from ***ʒastiz**, *guest*; OE. OS. OHG. **sunu** = Goth. **sunus**, from ***sunuz**, *son*; pl. OE. **giefa**, OS. **geba**, OHG. **gebā** = Goth. **gibōs**, from ***ʒeƀõz**, *gifts*; OE. **guman** = Goth. **gumans**, from ***ʒomaniz**, cp. Gr. ποιμένες, *shepherds*; OE. **men(n)** = Goth. **mans**, from ***maniz**, *men*; adv. OE. OS. **bet**, O.Icel. **betr**, from ***batiz**, *better*; OE. OS. **leng**, O.Icel. **lengr**, from ***laŋgiz**, *longer*. The following OE. pronouns are developed from original unstressed forms where **-s** became **-z** and then disappeared: **gē**, OS. **gĭ**, Goth. **jus**, *ye*; **hwā**, OS. **hwē**, Goth. **ƕas**, *who?*; dat. **mē**, OS. **mĭ**, Goth. **mis**, *me*; dat. **þē**, OS. **thĭ**, Goth. **þus**, *thee*; **wē**, OS. **wĭ**, Goth. **weis**, *we*.

§ **253.** Prim. Germanic **đ** (§§ **235**, **238**) became **d**, which was shifted to **t** in OHG., as OE. **bēodan**, OS. **biođan**, OHG. **biotan**, beside O.Icel. **bjōđa**, *to offer*; OE. **fæder**,

OS. **fadar**, OHG. **fater**, beside O.Icel. **faðer**, *father*; OE. **mōdor**, OS. **mōdar**, OHG. **muoter**, beside O.Icel. **mōðer**, *mother*; pp. OE. **worden**, OS. **wordan**, OHG. **wortan**, beside inf. OE. **weorþan**, *to become*; OE. OS. **god**, OHG. **got**, beside O.Icel. **goð**, *God*; OE. OS. **word**, OHG. **wort**, beside O.Icel. **orð**, *word*.

§ **254**. All single consonants, except **r**, were doubled after a short vowel before a following **j**. This **j** was mostly retained in Old Saxon, but was generally dropped in OE. and OHG. **ƀj, đj, ȝj** became **bb, dd, gg** (generally written **cg** in OE.). Examples are: OE. **hliehhan**, OS. ***hlahhian**, OHG. **hlahhen** = Goth. **hlahjan**, *to laugh*; OE. **lecgan**, OS. **leggian**, OHG. **leggen** = Goth. **lagjan**, *to lay*; OE. **settan**, OS. **settian**, OHG. **setzen** = Goth. **satjan**, *to set*; OE. **scieppan**, OS. **skeppian**, OHG. **skephen** = Goth. **skapjan**, *to create*; and similarly OE. **biddan**, *to pray*; **fremman**, *to perform*; **licgan**, *to lie down*; **sceþþan**, *to injure*; **sellan**, *to sell, give*; **sittan**, *to sit*; **swebban**, *to lull to sleep*; **þennan**, *to stretch*; **þridda** (Goth. **þridja**), *third*; **hell** (Goth. **halja**), *hell*; **sibb** (Goth. **sibja**), *relationship*; gen. **cynnes** (Goth. **kunjis**), *of a race, generation*; and similarly **brycg**, *bridge*; **cribb**, *crib, stall*; **crycc**, *crutch*; **henn**, *hen*. But OE. OS. **nerian**, OHG. **nerien** = Goth. **nasjan**, *to save*; OE. **herian** = Goth. **hazjan**, *to praise*. For examples of West Germanic **ww** from **wj**, see § **90**.

NOTE.—1. The **j** in the combination **ji** had disappeared before the West Germanic doubling of consonants took place, e.g. in the 2. and 3. pers. sing. of the pres. indicative, as OE. **legest**, **legeþ**, OS. **legis**, **legid**, OHG. **legis**, **legit** = Goth. **lagjis**, **lagjiþ**, beside inf. OE. **lecgan**, OS. **leggian**, OHG. **leggen**, Goth. **lagjan**, *to lay*. See § **272**, Note.

2. The sing. nom. and acc. of neuter nouns like **bedd** (Goth. nom. **badi**, gen. **badjis**), *bed*; **cynn** (Goth. **kuni**), *race, generation*; **nett** (Goth. **nati**), *net*, had their double consonants from the inflected forms, see § **274**.

§ **255.** **p, t, k,** and **h** (= χ) were also doubled in West Germanic before a following **r** or **l**. The doubling regularly took place in the inflected forms (as gen. OE. OS. OHG. **bittres,** OE. **æpples,** OS. **apples,** OHG. **aphles**), and was then generally extended to the uninflected forms by levelling, as OE. **bitter** (**biter**), OS. OHG. **bittar,** cp. Goth. **báitrs,** *bitter*; OE. **hlŭttor** (**hlūtor**), OS. **hluttar,** OHG. **hlūttar,** cp. Goth. **hlūtrs,** *clear, pure*; OHG. **kupfar,** beside OE. **copor,** Lat. **cuprum,** *copper*; OE. **snottor** (**snotor**), OS. OHG. **snottar,** cp. Goth. **snutrs,** *wise*; OE. **wæccer** (**wæcer, wacor**), OHG. **wackar,** *watchful*; OS. **akkar,** OHG. **ackar,** beside OE. **æcer,** cp. Goth. **akrs,** *field*; OE. **æppel** (**æpl**), OS. **appul,** OHG. **aphul,** cp. O.Icel. **epli,** *apple*; OS. **luttil,** OHG. **lutzil,** beside OE. **lȳtel,** *little*. In some words double forms arose through levelling out in different directions; thus regular forms were nom. sing. **tēar** (= OHG. **zahar**) from ***teahur,** older ***taχur,** *tear*, gen. ***teahhres** (Nth. **tæhhres**), nom. pl. ***teahhras** (Nth. **tæhhras**). From **tæhhres, tæhhras,** &c., was formed a new nom. sing. **tæhher** in Nth., whereas the other dialects generalized **tēar,** whence gen. sing. **tēares,** nom. pl. **tēaras.** In like manner arose **ēar** beside Nth. **æhher,** *ear of corn*; **gēol** beside **geohhol,** *Yule, Christmas*. See §§ **219, 260.**

§ **256.** Doubling of consonants by the assimilation of postconsonantal **n** to the preceding consonant also regularly took place in the weak declension of nouns, as sing. nom. ***lapō̃,** *lappet*, acc. ***lapan(un),** beside gen. pl. ***lapnō̃(n)** > ***lappō̃(n),** cp. § **401.** This interchange between the single and double consonants gave rise to levelling in a twofold direction, so that one or other of the forms was extended to all cases; thus in OE. the forms with double consonants were generalized in words like **ēarwicga,** *earwig*; **ebba,** *ebb*; **frogga,** *frog*; **lappa** (**læppa**), *lappet*; **scucca,** *demon*; **stagga,** *stag*; **sugga,** *water wagtail*; and the forms with single consonant in words like **boga,** *bow*; **cnafa** beside OHG. **knabo, knappo,** *boy, youth*; **draca** (Lat. **dracō**) beside OHG. **trahho, traccho,** *dragon*; **dropa** beside OHG. **troffo, tropfo,** *drop*; **nama,** *name*; **nefa,** *nephew* **wita,** *wise man.*

# CHAPTER X

## THE OE. DEVELOPMENT OF THE GENERAL GERMANIC CONSONANT-SYSTEM

§ **257.** Before entering upon the history of the individual consonants, it will be well to treat here several points concerning the OE. consonants in general.

§ **258.** In OE. as in the oldest period of the other Germanic languages, intervocalic double consonants were really long, and were pronounced long as in Modern Italian and Swedish, thus OE. **buc-ca,** *he-goat*; **set-tan,** *to set*; and similarly **cyssan,** *to kiss*; **feallan,** *to fall*; **feorran,** *from afar*; **frogga,** *frog*; **hebban,** *to raise*; **lecgan,** *to lay*; **sceþþan,** *to injure*; **scieppan,** *to create*; **þennan,** *to stretch*; **swimman,** *to swim.*

§ **259.** OE. double consonants were simplified in pronunciation, although they were very often retained in writing, especially finally:—

1. Finally, as **buc,** *buck,* **cos,** *kiss,* **eal,** *all,* **feor,** *far,* **man,** *man,* beside **bucc, coss, eall, feorr, mann**; **fæsten,** *fortress,* **gyden,** *goddess,* **sǣwet,** *sowing,* beside gen. **fæstennes, gydenne, sǣwettes.** cg was always preserved in writing in order to show that it was an explosive and not a spirant (cp. § **319**), as **brycg,** *bridge*; **mycg,** *midge*; **secg,** *man.* In this grammar the double consonants are generally retained in writing, as **cinn,** *chin*; **full,** *full*; **hyll,** *hill*; **pytt,** *pit*; **sceatt,** *treasure, money*; **synn,** *sin*; **swamm,** *he swam.*

2. Medially before other consonants, as acc. masc. sing. **ealne,** gen. dat. fem. sing. **ealre,** *all,* beside **eallne, eallre**; pret. sing. **āfierde, cyste, fylde, ypte,** beside inf. **āfierran,** *to remove,* **cyssan,** *to kiss,* **fyllan,** *to fill,* **yppan,** *to reveal*; third pers. sing. pres. indic. **fielþ, gielþ, onginþ, swimþ, winþ,** beside inf. **feallan,** *to fall,* **giellan,** *to yell,* **onginnan,** *to begin,* **swimman,** *to swim,* **winnan,** *to fight.*

3. Medially after consonants, as **geornes** from **georn + nes,** *zeal*; **gesynto** from ***gesynttu,** older ***gisundiþu** (§ **305**), *health*; **þearlic** from **þearl + līc,** *severe*; **wiersa** from ***wierssa,** older ***wiers(i)ra,** *worse*; **wilder, wildēor** from **wild + dēor,** *wild beast*; **wyrtruma** from **wyrt + truma,** *root-stump*; pret. sing. **gewielde** from ***gewield-de, gyrde** from ***gyrd-de, lǣste** from ***lǣst-te, reste** from ***rest-te, sende** from ***send-de, wende** from ***wend-de,** beside inf. **gewieldan,** *to subdue,* **gyrdan,** *to gird,* **lǣstan,** *to perform,* **restan,** *to rest,* **sendan,** *to send,* **wendan,** *to turn.*

4. In late OE. in unstressed syllables, as **bliccetan,** *to glitter,* **līc(c)etan,** *to pretend, feign,* beside **bliccettan, līc(c)ettan**; **atelic,** *terrible,* **singalīce,** *always,* **yfelic,** *bad,* beside **atollic, singallīce, yfellic**; **forgiefenes,** *forgiveness,* **forlorenes,** *destruction,* beside **forgiefennes, forlorennes**; gen. sing. **fæstenes,** *of a fortress,* **sǣwetes,** *of a sowing,* beside **fæstennes, sǣwettes**; gen. pl. **ōþera,** *other,* **snot(t)era,** *prudent, wise,* beside **ōþerra, snot(t)erra**; **fægera** beside **fægerra,** *fairer.*

§ **260.** Consonants were doubled during the OE. period before a following **r** or **l**, with shortening of a preceding long vowel or diphthong, as **ætgæddre,** *together,* **blæddre,** *bladder,* **eddre,** *vein,* **gegaddrode,** *he gathered,* **næddre,** *adder,* beside older **ætgæd(e)re, blǣdre, ǣdre, gegad(e)rode, nǣdre**; comparative **bettra,** *better,* **deoppra,** *deeper,* **geliccra,** *more like,* **hwittra,** *whiter,* **riccra,** *more powerful,* **yttra,** *outer,* beside older **bet(e)ra, dēopra, gelīcra, hwītra, rīcra, ȳtra.** Gen. **miccles** beside older **micles,** nom.

**micel**, *great*. In words like **attor**, *poison*, **foddor**, *food*, **moddor**, *mother*, **tuddor**, *progeny*, beside older **ātor**, **fōdor**, **mōdor**, **tūdor**, the doubling of the consonant went out from the inflected forms, as gen. **ātres**, nom. pl. **mōdru**, which regularly became **attres**, **moddru** and from which a new nom. **attor**, **moddor** was formed. On a similar doubling of consonants in West Germanic, see § **255**.

§ **261**. The Germanic voiceless spirants **f**, **þ**, **s** became the voiced spirants **ƀ**, **đ**, **z** medially between voiced sounds, although the **f**, **þ**, **s** were retained in writing, as **cēafl**, *jaw*; **ofen**, *oven*; **wulfas**, *wolves* (§ **296**); **āþas**, *oaths*; **brōþor**, *brother*; **eorþe**, *earth* (§ **302**); **bōsm**, *bosom*; **nosu**, *nose*; **ōsle**, *ousel* (§ **307**).

Note.—This voicing of **f**, **þ**, **s** only took place in simple words, but not in compounds, such as **āþwēan**, *to wash*; **gefeoht**, *battle*; **gesendan**, *to send*; **wynsum**, *pleasant*.

§ **262**. The Germanic voiced spirants **ƀ**, **ʒ** became the voiceless spirants **f** (§ **294**), **χ** (§§ **320**, Note, **323**) before voiceless sounds and finally, as **geaf**, OHG. **gab**, *he gave*; **healf**, OHG. **halb**, *half*; **wīf**, OHG. **wīb**, *woman, wife*; **burh**, *city*, **sorh**, *sorrow*, **dāh**, *dough*, **bēah**, *ring, bracelet*, beside gen. **burge**, **sorge**, **dāges**, **bēages**; **stīhst** beside older **stīgest**, *thou ascendest*.

## The Semivowels.

### w

§ **263**. Germanic **w** = the **w** in NE. **wet** (written **uu**, **u**, **ƿ** in OE. manuscripts) remained initially before vowels, and generally also initially before and after consonants, as **wæs**, Goth. OS. OHG. **was**, *was*; OE. OS. Goth. **witan**, OHG. **wiʒʒan**, *to know*; and similarly **wadan**, *to go, wade*; **wascan**, *to wash*; **wǣpen**, *weapon*; **wǣron**, *were*; **wæter**, *water*; **wearm**, *warm*; **weder**, *weather*; **wefan**, *to weave*; **weorþan**, *to become*; **wīd**, *wide*; **wilde**, *wild*; **windan**, *to wind*; **winter**, *winter*; **wolcen**, *cloud*; **wundor**, *wonder*; **wyrcan**, *to work*.

**wlanc**, *proud*; **wlite**, OS. **wliti**, *form, beauty*, Goth. **wlits**, *face, countenance*; **wlitig**, *beautiful*; **wracu**, Goth. **wraka**, *revenge, persecution*; **wrāþ**, *angry*; **wrītan**, *to write*.

**cwēn**, Goth. **qēns**, *queen, wife*; **cweþan**, Goth. **qiþan**, *to say*; **hwā**, Goth. **ƕas**, *who?*; **hwǣte**, Goth. **ƕáiteis**, *wheat*; **dwellan**, OHG. **twellen**, *to tarry*; **dweorg**, OHG. **twerg**, *dwarf*; **þwēan**, Goth. **þwahan**, *to wash*; **þweorh**, Goth. **þwaírhs**, *angry, perverse*; **sweltan**, Goth. **swiltan**, *to die*; **sweostor**, Goth. **swistar**, *sister*; **twā**, Goth. **twái**, *two*; **twelf**, Goth. **twalif**, *twelve*.

§ **264**. Medial **w** generally remained before vowels, as OE. OS. OHG. **spīwan**, Goth. **speiwan**, *to vomit, spit*; and similarly **awel**, *awl*; **gesewen**, *seen*; **lāwerce**, *lark*; **sāwol**, Goth. **sáiwala**, *soul*; **snīwan**, *to snow*; **þawian** from ***þawōjan**, *to thaw*. In verbs like **blāwan**, OHG. **blāan** beside **blāian**, *to blow*; **blōwan**, OHG. **bluoan** beside **bluoian**, **bluowen**, *to bloom*; **sāwan**, Goth. **saian**, OHG. **sāan** beside **sāian**, **sāwen**, *to sow*; **wāwan**, Goth. **waian**, OHG. **wāen** beside **wāian**, *to blow* (*of the wind*), it is difficult to determine how far the **w** was etymological and how far it was originally merely a consonantal glide developed between the long and the short vowel; and similarly in **cnāwan**, *to know*; **crāwan**, *to crow*; **flōwan**, *to flow*; **grōwan**, *to grow*; **hlōwan**, *to low*; **māwan**, *to mow*; **rōwan**, *to row*; **þrāwan**, *to twist*.

**eowe**, *ewe*; **eowestre**, Goth. **awistr**, *sheepfold*; **hweowol**, *wheel*; **meowle**, Goth. **mawilō**, *maiden*; **streowede**, Goth. **strawida**, *I strewed*; **þeowian**, *to serve*. See §§ **77**, **89**.

Gen. sing. **bearwes**, **bealwes**, **cneowes**, **gearwes**, **snāwes**, ***strawes**, **treowes**, **þeowes**, beside nom. **bearu**, *grove*, **bealu**, *evil, calamity*, **cnēo**, *knee*, **gearu**, *ready*, **snā**, *snow*, **strēa**, *straw*, **trēo**, *tree*, **þēo**, *servant*; gen. dat. sing.

**lǣswe, mǣdwe, sceadwe,** beside nom. **lǣs,** *pasture,* **mǣd,** *meadow,* **sceadu,** *shade, shadow.* See § **266.**

**frætwan,** *to adorn*; **gearwe,** *completely*; **gearwian,** *to prepare*; **nearwe,** *narrowly*; **nierwan,** *to narrow*; **sierwan,** *to devise*; **smierwan,** *to anoint, smear*; **spearwa,** Goth. **sparwa,** *sparrow*; **wealwian,** *to wallow*; **wielwan,** *to roll.*

**brēowan,** *to brew,* cp. O.Icel. pp. **bruggenn,** *brewed*; **cēowan,** OHG. **kiuwan,** *to chew*; **getrīewe,** *true, faithful*; **getrīewan,** *to trust*; **hēawan,** Goth. ***haggwan,** *to hew*; **nīewe, nīwe,** *new*; **scēawian,** Goth. ***skaggwōn,** *to examine, view.* See §§ **76, 90.**

§ **265.** When **w** came to stand at the end of a word or syllable, it became vocalized to **u** (later **o**). The **u** then combined with a preceding short vowel to form a long diphthong, but disappeared after long stems, long vowels, and diphthongs, as nom. **bealu** (later **bealo**), *evil, calamity,* **bearu,** *grove,* **gearu,** *ready,* **mearu,** *tender,* **nearu,** *narrow,* **searu,** *armour,* beside gen. **bealwes, bearwes, gearwes, mearwes, nearwes, searwes**; masc. acc. sing. **gearone** from ***gearwne,** *ready.* Nom. **cnēo,** *knee,* **strēa,** *straw,* **trēo,** *tree,* **þēo,** *servant,* beside gen. **cneowes, strēawes** with **-ēa-** from the nominative, **treowes, þeowes. gād,** Goth. **gáidw,** *want, lack*; **ā, ō,** Goth. **áiw,** *ever*; **hrā,** Goth. **hráiw,** *corpse*; **hrēa,** *raw*; **snā,** Goth. **snáiws,** *snow.*

But the **w** was mostly reintroduced into the nom. sing. from the inflected forms, especially after long vowels and long diphthongs. Regular forms were: nom. **cnēo, snā, strēa,** gen. **cneowes, snāwes, *strawes,** from the latter of which was formed a new nom. **cnēow, snāw, strēaw**; and similarly **hrāw,** *corpse*; **hrēaw,** *raw*; **trēow,** *tree*; **þēow,** *servant*; **slāw,** *lazy*; **stōw,** *place*; **bēow,** *barley*; **dēaw,** *dew*; **glēaw,** *wise*; **hīew, hīw,** *shape, colour*; **hnēaw,** *stingy*; **hrēow,** *repentance*; **trēow,** *faith.* And conversely from the new nom. was sometimes formed a new gen., as **cnēowes, trēowes,** beside older **cneowes, treowes.**

§ **266. w** disappeared before **u,** and **e** (= older **i**), as nom. **clēa** from ***cla(w)u,** *claw*; **lǣs** from ***lǣs(w)u,** *pasture*; **mǣd** from ***mǣd(w)u,** *meadow*; **sceadu** from ***scad(w)u,** *shade, shadow*; **þrēa** from ***þra(w)u,** *threat,* beside gen. **lǣswe, mǣdwe, sceadwe;** nom. acc. neut. **fēa** from ***fa(w)u,** *few*; dat. **fēam** from ***fa(w)um,** see § **140**; dat. pl. **cnēom** from ***cne(w)um,** beside nom. sing. **cnēo,** *knee.* And similarly at a later period: **betuh,** *between,* **cucu,** *quick, alive,* **cudu,** *cud,* **uton,** *let us,* beside older **betwuh, cwucu, cwudu, wuton.**

**cū** from ***k(w)ū,** older ***kwō,** *cow*; **hū** from ***h(w)ū,** older ***hwō,** *how*; neut. **tū** from ***t(w)ū,** older ***twō,** *two.* See § **130.**

**ǣ** from ***ā(w)i-,** older ***aiwi-** (Goth. **áiws**), *law*; **hrǣ** from ***hrā(w)i-,** older ***hraiwi-,** *corpse*; **sǣ** from ***sā(w)i-,** older ***saiwi-** (Goth. **sáiws**), *sea*; **giereþ,** prim. Germanic ***ȝarwiþ,** *he prepares*; pret. **gierede,** prim. Germanic ***ȝarwiđǣ-,** *he prepared,* beside inf. **gierwan;** and similarly pret. **nierede, sierede, smierede, wielede,** beside inf. **nierwan,** *to narrow*; **sierwan,** *to devise*; **smierwan,** *to anoint*; **wielwan,** *to roll.*

The **w** was often reintroduced after the analogy of forms where **w** was regular, as nom. **clawu, þrawu** (beside the regular nom. **clēa, þrēa**), new formations from the gen. and dat. **clawe, þrawe;** dat. pl. **sǣwum** beside **sǣm,** with **w** from the gen. pl. **sǣwa,** *of seas*; pret. pl. **rēowun** beside **rēon,** with **w** from **rōwan,** *to row*; and similarly **grēowun, -on,** *they grew*; **sēowun,** *they sowed*; &c. On forms like pret. pl. **swulton,** *they died*; **swummon,** *they swam,* see § **249. gierweþ,** *he prepares,* pret. **gierwede,** beside the regular forms **giereþ, gierede,** with **w** from **gierwan;** **cnǣwþ** for ***cnǣþ** from ***cnā(w)iþ,** *he knows,* with **w** from the inf. **cnāwan.**

§ **267.** **w** often disappeared in the second element of compounds, as **ealneg, -ig,** for **ealne weg,** *always*; **fulluht** from ***full wuht,** *baptism*; **hlāford** from **hlāfweard,** *lord*; **hwīlende** from **hwīlwende,** *transitory*; **nāuht** beside older **nā-wuht,** *naught.* And in certain verbal forms with the negative prefix, as **næs = ne wæs,** *was not*; **nǣron = ne wǣron,** *were not*; **nāt = ne wāt,** *knows not*; **nolde = ne wolde,** *would not*; **nyle = ne wile,** *will not*; **nysse = ne wisse,** *he knew not*; **nyton = ne witon,** *they know not.*

## j

§ **268.** Germanic **j** (= consonantal **i**) generally remained initially in Gothic, OS. and OHG., but disappeared in O.Icel. In OE. it had become a palatal spirant like the **y** in NE. **yet, yon** already in the oldest period of the language. It was usually written **g, ge** (also **i, gi** before a following **u**). Examples are: **gēar,** Goth. **jēr,** OS. OHG. **jār,** O.Icel. **ār,** *year*; **geoc, iuc,** Goth. **juk,** OHG. **joh,** O.Icel. **ok,** *yoke*; **geong, giong, giung, iung,** Goth. **juggs,** OS. OHG. **jung,** O.Icel. **ungr,** *young*; and similarly **gē, gīe,** *ye*; **gēo, gīo, iū,** *formerly, of old*; **geogoþ, giogoþ, iugoþ,** *youth*; **geōmor,** *sad, mournful*; **geond,** *through, beyond*; **giest,** *yeast*; **gingra,** *younger.* See § **51.**

§ **269.** Germanic medial **-ij-** became **-ī-** which combined with a following guttural vowel to form a diphthong, as **bīo, bēo,** Germanic stem-form ***bijōn-,** *bee*; **fēond,** Goth. **fijands,** *enemy*; **frēo** from ***frija-,** *free*; **frēond,** Goth. **frijōnds,** *friend*; nom. acc. neut. **þrīo, þrēo,** from ***þriju** = Goth. **þrija,** *three,* see § **104.**

§ **270.** It is generally assumed that Germanic **j** remained in OE. between vowels when the first element was a long vowel or diphthong, but it is, however, more probable that **j** regularly disappeared in this position and that at a later period a consonantal glide (written **g, ge**) was developed between the vowels, as was sometimes the case in OS. and OHG., as **cīegan** from ***kaujan,** *to call*; **frīgea** older **frīegea** = Goth. **fráuja,** *lord, master*; dat. **hīege,** Anglian **hēge** = Goth. **háuja**; **īege** = Goth. ***áujái,** beside nom. **hīeg,** *hay,* **īeg,** *island*; **þrēagean** from ***þrauōjan,** *to threaten*; and similarly **fēog(e)an,** *to hate*; **frēog(e)an,** *to love.* Cp. § **275.**

NOTE.—Forms like nom. **hīeg,** Goth. **hawi,** *hay*; **īeg, īg,** Goth. ***awi,** gen. ***áujōs,** had the final **g** from the inflected forms, as gen. **hīeges,** dat. **hīege,** gen. and dat. **īege.**

§ **271.** Germanic medial **j** (written **i, g; ig, eg,** also **ige** before **a**) remained after **r** in the combination short vowel + **r,** as **herian, hergan, herigan, heregan, herigean,** Goth. **hazjan,** *to praise*; and similarly **nerian,** Goth. **nasjan,** *to save*; **werian,** Goth. **wasjan,** *to clothe, wear*; gen. sing. **heries, herges, heriges,** Goth. **harjis,** nom. pl. **hergas, herigas, herigeas,** Goth. **harjōs,** *armies.* The **i, e** in **ig, eg** represent a vocalic glide which was developed between the **r** and the **j.** And the **e** in **ige** merely indicates the palatal nature of the preceding **g.**

§ **272.** Germanic medial **j** disappeared after original long closed syllables or syllables which became long by the West Germanic gemination of consonants (§ **254**), as **dǣlan,** Goth. **dáiljan,** *to divide*; **dēman,** Goth. **dōmjan,** *to judge*; **fyllan,** Goth. **fulljan,** *to fill*; **gelīefan,** Goth. **galáubjan,** *to believe*; **hīeran,** Goth. **háusjan,** *to hear*; **sēcan,** Goth. **sōkjan,** *to seek.* **gierd** from ***ȝeardju** = Goth. ***gardja,** *rod, twig*; **hild** from ***hildju** = Goth. ***hildja,** *war*; gen. **rīces** from ***rīkjes,** Goth. **reikjis,** *of a kingdom.*

**biddan,** Goth. **bidjan,** *to pray*; **hebban,** Goth. **hafjan,** *to raise*; **hliehhan,** Goth. **hlahjan,** *to laugh*; **lecgan,** Goth. **lagjan,** *to lay*; **scieppan,** Goth. **skapjan,** *to create*; **settan,** Goth. **satjan,** *to set.* Gen. sing. **beddes,** Goth. **badjis,** *of a bed*; **cynnes,** Goth. **kunjis,** *of a race, generation*;

**willa,** Goth. **wilja,** *will*; **henn** from ***hennju,** older ***χannjō** = Goth. ***hanja,** *hen*; and similarly **crycc,** Goth. ***krukja,** *crutch*; **hell,** Goth. **halja,** *hell*; **sibb,** Goth. **sibja,** *relationship*; gen. **helle, sibbe** = Goth. **haljōs, sibjōs.**

NOTE.—**j** disappeared medially before **i** already in West Germanic; hence verbs, which have double consonants in the inf. by the West Germanic gemination of consonants, have only a single consonant in the second and third pers. sing. of the present indicative, as **legest, legeþ** = Goth. **lagjis, lagjiþ,** beside inf. **lecgan** = Goth. **lagjan,** *to lay*. See § **254**, Note.

§ **273.** Germanic final **-ōjan** became **-ian** through the intermediate stages **-ējan, -ejan, -ijan, -īan,** as **lōcian** from ***lōkōjan,** *to look*; **macian** from ***makōjan,** *to make*. The **g** in forms like **lōcig(e)an, macig(e)an** is merely a consonantal glide which was developed between the **i** and the **a.**

The Germanic ending **-ij(i)** from Indg. **-eje** became **-ī** during the prim. Germanic period, then **-ī** became shortened to **-i** (§ **214**). This **-i** regularly disappeared in prehistoric OE. after original long stems, but remained **-i** (later **-e**) after original short stems, as **hīer,** Goth. **háusei,** from ***χauzī,** *hear thou*; **sēc,** Goth. **sōkei,** *seek thou*; but **nere,** Goth. **nasei,** *save thou*; and similarly **bide,** *pray thou*; **freme,** *perform thou*; **lege,** *lay thou*; **sete,** *set thou*.

§ **274.** When **j** came to stand finally after the loss of the case endings **-az, -an** (= Indg. **-os, -om**), it became vocalized to **-i** which became **-e** at a later period, as **hierde,** OS. **hirdi,** OHG. **hirti,** Goth. (acc.) **haírdi,** *shepherd*; and similarly **ende,** *end*; **here,** *army*; **lǣce,** *physician*; **rīce,** OS. **rīki,** OHG. **rīhhi,** Goth. **reiki,** *kingdom*; **wīte,** OS. **wīti,** *punishment*. The regularly developed forms of **hrycg,** *back*, **secg,** *man*, **bedd,** *bed*, **cynn,** *race, generation*, **nett,** *net*, and of similar masculine and neuter nouns with double consonants in the nom. and acc. singular, would be ***hryge,** Goth. (acc.) ***hrugi**; ***sege,** Goth. (acc.) ***sagi**; ***bede,** Goth. **badi**; ***cyne,** Goth. **kuni**; ***nete,** Goth. **nati.**

The nom. and acc. sing. are new formations with double consonants from the inflected stem-forms.

§ **275.** Germanic **jj** became **ddj** in Goth. and **gg(j)** in O.Icel. In OE. **-ijj-** became **-ī-** through the intermediate stage **-īj-**; and **-ajj-** became **-ǣ-** through the intermediate stages **-aij-**, **-āj-**. And then between the **-ī-**, **-ǣ-** and a following vowel a consonantal glide (written **g**) was developed (cp. § **270**), which was often levelled out into the uninflected forms, as **frīgedæg, frīgdæg,** *Friday*, beside **frēo** from ***frīo,** older ***frījō,** OS. **frī,** *woman*; **ēode** from ***īode,** older ***ījō-dǣ-,** Goth. **iddja,** *he went*; gen. **ǣges, cǣge, wǣge,** beside nom. **ǣg** (O.Icel. **egg,** OS. OHG. **ei**), *egg*, **cǣg,** *key*, **wǣg** (Goth. **waddjus,** O.Icel. **veggr**), *wall*; **clǣg,** Goth. (fem.) ***kladdja,** OS. **klei,** *clay*.

## The Liquids.

### l

§ **276.** Germanic **l** generally remained in OE. both initially, medially, and finally, as **lecgan,** Goth. **lagjan,** O.Icel. **leggja,** OS. **leggian,** OHG. **leggen,** *to lay*; **slǣpan,** Goth. **slēpan,** OS. **slāpan,** OHG. **slāfan,** *to sleep*; OE. OS. OHG. **stelan,** Goth. **stilan,** O.Icel. **stela,** *to steal*; OE. OS. **helpan,** Goth. **hilpan,** O.Icel. **hjalpa,** OHG. **helfan,** *to help*; **sellan,** Goth. **saljan,** O.Icel. **selja,** OS. **sellian,** OHG. **sellen,** *to give, sell*; **feallan,** O.Icel. **falla,** OS. OHG. **fallan,** *to fall*; **sceal,** Goth. O.Icel. OS. OHG. **skal,** *shall*; and similarly **lamb,** *lamb*; **land,** *land*; **lang,** *long*; **lǣdan,** *to lead*; **lēof,** *dear*; **leornian,** *to learn*; **līf,** *life*; **lufu,** *love*; **lȳtel,** *little*. **ealu,** *ale*; **meolu,** *meal*; **mioluc,** *milk*; **talu,** *number, tale*. **blōd,** *blood*; **clǣne,** *clean*; **flēon,** *to flee*; **glæd,** *glad*; **hlāford,** *lord*; **wlonc,** *proud*. **feld,** *field*; **folc,** *folk*; **folgian,** *to follow*; **gold,** *gold*; **helm,** *helmet*; **meltan,** *to melt*; **wealdan,** *to wield, govern*. **stille,** *still, silent*; **tellan,** *to tell*; **willa,** *will*. **fyllan,** *to fill*;

**gealla**, *gall*; **weallan**, *to boil*; **wulle**, *wool*. **col**, *coal*; **cōl**, *cool*; **fūl**, *foul*; **fugol**, *fowl, bird*; **smæl**, *slender*; **sadol**, *saddle*; **stæl**, *he stole*. **hyll**, *hill*. **eall**, *all*; **full**, *full*.

On vocalic **l** as in **æpl**, *apple*; **nǣdl**, *needle*; **nægl**, *nail*; **segl**, *sail*; **setl**, *seat*, see § **219**.

On the simplification of medial **ll** to **l**, see § **259**.

§ **277**. **sl** underwent metathesis in unstressed syllables, as **byrgels**, OS. **burgisli**, *tomb*; **rǣdels**, OS. **rādislo**, MHG. **rætsel**, *riddle*; and similarly **brīdels**, *bridle*; **fǣtels**, *tub, vessel*; **gyrdels** older **gyrdisl**, *girdle*; **rīecels**, *incense*. Metathesis of **l** rarely took place in stem-syllables, as Anglian **bold**, *dwelling*, **seld**, *seat*, **spāld**, *saliva*, beside WS. **botl**, **setl**, **spātl**.

### r

§ **278**. Germanic **r** generally remained in OE. both initially, medially, and finally, as **rēad**, Goth. **ráuþs**, O.Icel. **rauðr**, OS. **rōd**, OHG. **rōt**, *red*; OE. OS. OHG. **bringan**, Goth. **briggan**, *to bring*; **here**, Goth. **harjis**, OS. OHG. **heri**, *army*; OE. OS. **word**, Goth. **waúrd**, OHG. **wort**, *word*; **feorran**, *from afar*, Goth. **faírra**, *far off*; **fæder**, Goth. OS. **fadar**, O.Icel. **faðer**, OHG. **fater**, *father*; and similarly **rǣdan**, *to advise*; **rāp**, *rope*; **regn**, *rain*; **rīce**, *kingdom*; **rīdan**, *to ride*; **rīm**, *number*; **rodor**, *sky*; **rūm**, *room*. **crēopan**, *to creep*; **drēam**, *mirth*; **frēo**, *free*; **grēne**, *green*; **hrōf**, *roof*; **strēam**, *stream*; **trēo**, *tree*; **wrītan**, *to write*. **beran**, *to bear*; **cearu**, *care, sorrow*; **duru**, *door*; **faran**, *to go, travel*. **bierce**, *birch*; **burg**, *city*; **earm**, *arm*; **eorþe**, *earth*; **feorh**, *life*; **heard**, *hard*; **scearp**, *sharp*; **spearwa**, *sparrow*; **steorfan**, *to die*; **þorn**, *thorn*; **þurh**, *through*; **weorc**, *work*. **āfierran** (pret. **āfierde**, see § **259**, 2), *to remove*; **steorra**, *star*. **fȳr**, *fire*; **hamor**, *hammer*; **mōdor**, *mother*; **tēar**, *tear*; **wer**, *man*.

NOTE.—**r** disappeared in late OE. in **specan**, *to speak*, **spǣc**, *speech*, beside older **sprecan**, **sprǣc**.

§ **279.** West Germanic medial **r** from older **z** (§ **252**) remained in OE., as **betra**, Goth. **batiza**, *better*; **herian**, Goth. **hazjan**, *to praise*; **hord**, Goth. **huzd**, *treasure*; and similarly **coren**, *chosen*; **dēor** (Goth. **dius**, gen. **diuzis**), *deer, wild animal*; **ēare**, *ear*; **hīeran**, *to hear*; **ieldra**, *elder*; **lǣran**, *to teach*; **leornian**, *to learn*; **māra**, *larger*; **nerian**, *to save*; **wǣron**, *they were*. **ierre**, Goth. **aírzeis**, OS. OHG. **irri**, *angry*; and similarly ***durran**, *to dare*; **mierran**, *to hinder, mar*; **þyrre**, *dry, withered*.

On the simplification of medial **rr** (= Germanic **rz**) to **r** in unstressed syllables, see § **259**, 4.

§ **280.** Antevocalic **r** often became postvocalic by metathesis when a short vowel was followed by **n**, **nn**, **s**, or **s**+consonant, as **ærn**, Goth. **razn**, O.Icel. **rann**, *house*; **forsc**, O.Icel. **froskr**, OHG. **frosk**, *frog*; **forst**, O.Icel. OS. OHG. **frost**, *frost*; **hors**, O.Icel. OS. **hross**, OHG. **ros** (gen. **rosses**), *horse*; **iernan**, Goth. OS. OHG. **rinnan**, O.Icel. **rinna**, *to run*; and similarly **bærnan** (wv.), **biernan** (sv.), *to burn*; **bærs**, *perch* (*a fish*); **berstan**, *to burst*; **cærse**, *cress*; **fersc**, *fresh*; **fierst**, *space of time*; **gærs**, *grass*; **hærn**, *wave*; **þerscan**, *to thresh* (*corn*); **wærna** beside **wrænna**, *wren*.

§ **281.** **s** or **l**+**r** became **ss**, **ll** by assimilation, as **lǣssa** from ***lǣs(i)ra**, *smaller*; fem. gen. dat. sing. **þisse** (OHG. **desera, desero**), from ***þisre**, *of this*; gen. pl. **þissa** (OHG. **desero**), from ***þisra**; gen. sing. **ūsses** from ***ūsres**, *of our*; dat. **ūssum** from ***ūsrum**. **sēlla** beside **sēlra**, *better*.

## The Nasals.

### m

§ **282.** Germanic **m** generally remained in OE. both initially, medially, and finally, as **mōna**, Goth. **mēna**, O.Icel. **māne**, OS. OHG. **māno**, *moon*; OE. Goth. **guma**, O.Icel. **gume**, OS. **gumo**, OHG. **gomo**, *man*; OE. OS.

**dumb**, Goth. **dumbs**, O.Icel. **dumbr**, OHG. **tumb**, *dumb*; OE. O.Icel. OS. OHG. **rūm**, *room*; and similarly **macian**, *to make*; **mann**, *man*; **māwan**, *to mow*; **meltan**, *to melt*; **mīn**, *my*; **mōdor**, *mother*; **mūþ**, *mouth*. **cuman**, *to come*; **nama**, *name*; **niman**, *to take*; **tīma**, *time*; **þūma**, *thumb*. **besma**, *besom*; **climban**, *to climb*; **gelimpan**, *to happen*; **lamb**, *lamb*. **fremman** from ***framjan**, *to perform*; **swimman**, *to swim*. **bēam**, *tree*; **brōm**, *broom*; **hām**, *home*; **helm**, *helmet*; **wyrm**, *snake*. **swamm**, *he swam*.

On vocalic **m** as in **ǣþm**, *breath*; **bōsm**, *bosom*; **botm**, *bottom*; **māþm**, *treasure*, see § **219**.

§ **283**. **m** disappeared in prehistoric OE. before **f**, **s** with lengthening of the preceding vowel, as **fīf**, Goth. OHG. **fimf**, *five*; **ōsle**, OHG. **amsala**, *ousel*; **sōfte**, OHG. **samfto**, *softly*; **sēfte**, *soft*. But **m** remained when it came to stand before **s** at a later period, as **grimsian** from ***grimisian** = OHG. **grimmisōn**, *to rage*; **þrims** beside older **trimes**, **trymesse** (OHG. **drimissa**), *a coin*.

§ **284**. Final **-m**, when an element of inflexion, became **-n** in late OE., as dat. pl. **dagon**, **giefon**, **sunon** beside older **dagum**, **giefum**, **sunum**; dat. sing. and pl. **gōdon** beside older **gōdum**, *good*.

## n

§ **285**. Germanic **n** generally remained in OE. both initially, medially, and finally, as **nama**, Goth. **namō**, OS. OHG. **namo**, *name*; OE. OS. OHG. **sunu**, Goth. **sunus**, O.Icel. **sunr**, *son*; OE. Goth. OHG. **spinnan**, O.Icel. **spinna**, *to spin*; **þennan**, OS. **thennian**, OHG. **dennen**, Goth. **þanjan**, O.Icel. **þenja**, *to stretch*; and similarly **nacod**, *naked*; **nǣdl**, *needle*; **nefa**, *nephew*; **nett**, *net*. **clǣne**, *clean*; **grēne**, *green*; **mōna**, *moon*; **munuc**, *monk*; **wēnan**, *to expect*. **bindan**, *to bind*; **blind**, *blind*; **cnēo**, *knee*; **frēond**, *friend*; **hand**, *hand*; **hnutu**, *nut*; **sendan**, *to send*; **windan**, *to wind*. **spannan**, *to clasp*; **sunne**, *sun*;

**þynn(e)**, *thin*. **bān**, *bone*; **cwēn**, *queen*; **heofon**, *heaven*; **mylen**, *mill*; **stān**, *stone*. **cinn**, *chin*; **henn**, *hen*; **mann**, *man*; **synn**, *sin*.

On vocalic **n** as in **hræfn**, *raven*; **regn**, *rain*; **tācn**, *token*, see § **219**.

On the simplification of medial **nn** to **n**, see § **259**.

§ **286**. **n** disappeared in prehistoric OE. before **þ**, **s** with lengthening of the preceding vowel, as **cūþ**, Goth. **kunþs**, OHG. **kund**, *known*; **ēst**, Goth. **ansts**, OHG. **anst**, stem-form **ansti-**, *favour*; **ōþer**, Goth. **anþar**, OHG. **andar**, *other*; **ūs**, Goth. OHG. **uns**, *us*; and similarly **cȳþan**, *to make known*; **dūst**, *dust*; **fūs**, *ready*; **gesīþ**, *companion*; **gōs**, *goose*; **hōs** (OHG. **hansa**), *band, escort*; **mūþ**, *mouth*; **sīþ**, *journey*; **tōþ**, *tooth*; **wȳscan**, *to wish*; **ȳst**, *storm*. The long vowel became shortened in unstressed syllables, as **fracuþ**, **-oþ**, Goth. **frakunþs**, *despised*; and similarly **duguþ**, *strength, valour*; **geoguþ**, *youth*; **nimaþ** from ***nimōþ**, older ***nemonþ-**, *they take*, see § **218**. But **n** remained when it came to stand before **s** at a later period, as **clǣnsian** from ***clǣnisian**, older ***klainisōjan**, *to cleanse*; **minsian** from ***minnisian**, *to diminish*; **winster** older **winester** (OHG. **winister**), *left, left hand*; also in the Latin loanword **pinsian** (Lat. **pensāre**), *to consider*.

§ **287**. **n** sometimes disappeared between consonants, as **elboga** beside **elnboga**, *elbow*; pret. **nemde** from ***nemnde**, *he named*; **sæterdæg** beside **sæterndæg**, *Saturday*.

§ **288**. Final **-n** generally disappeared in verbal forms before the pronouns **wē**, **wit**; **gē**, **git**, as **binde wē**, *let us bind*; **binde gē**, *bind ye!*; **bunde wē?**, *did we bind?*. See § **477**.

Final **-n** disappeared in Nth. in words of more than one syllable. This law was fairly well preserved in the infinitive, the pres. and pret. pl. subjunctive, the weak declension of nouns and adjectives, numerals, and adverbs, but in strong nouns and adjectives including the pp. of strong verbs, the final -n was generally reintroduced into the nom. singular from the inflected forms. It was also mostly reintroduced into the indic. pret. plural through the influence of the (?)past participle which itself was a new formation. Examples are: **bera,** *to bear*; **gehēra,** *to hear*, **lǣra,** *to teach*, **senda,** *to send* = WS. **beran, gehīeran, lǣran, sendan**; **gihēre,** *they may hear*, **sprece,** *they may speak* = WS. **gehīeren, sprecen**; **bite,** *they might bite* = WS. **biten**; gen. dat. acc. sing. **fola,** *foal*, **heorta,** *heart* = WS. **folan, heortan**; nom. acc. pl. **galga** = WS. **gealgan,** *gallows*; **seofo** beside inflected form **seofona,** *seven*; **befora,** *before*, **binna,** *within*, **fearra,** *from afar*, **norþa,** *from the north*, **westa,** *from the west* = WS. **beforan, binnan, feorran, norþan, westan**; but **dryhten,** *lord*, **heofon,** *heaven*, **hēþen,** *heathen*, **ārisen,** *arisen*, **genumen,** *taken*, with -n from the inflected forms; **bērun,** *they bore*, **cwōmun,** *they came*, **lǣddun,** *they led*.

### ŋ

§ **289.** The Germanic guttural nasal **ŋ** (written **g** in Gothic, and **n** in the other Germanic languages) only occurred medially before **g** and **k** (written c in OE.). It disappeared in the combination **ŋχ** already in prim. Germanic (§ **245**). In OE. it remained guttural or became palatal according as the following **g, c** remained guttural or became palatal, cp. § **309**. Examples are: OE. OHG **bringan,** Goth. **briggan,** *to bring*; **drincan,** Goth. **drigkan** OS. **drinkan,** OHG. **trinkan,** *to drink*; **geong,** Goth. **juggs,** O.Icel. **ungr,** OS. OHG. **jung,** *young*; and similarly **finger,** *finger*; **gangan,** *to go*; **hangian,** *to hang*; **hungor,** *hunger*; **lang,** *long*; **tunge,** *tongue*; **sincan,** *to sink*; **singan,** *to sing*; **swincan,** *to labour*; **tungol,** *star, constellation*.

**benc** from ***baŋkiz,** *bench*; **lengra,** OS. **lengira,** OHG. **lengiro,** *longer*; **þencan,** Goth. **þagkjan,** OS. **thenkian,**

OHG. **denken,** *to think*; and similarly **drencan,** *to give to drink*; **enge,** *narrow*; **engel,** *angel*; **englisc,** *English*; **finc,** *finch*; **mengan,** *to mix*; **sengan,** *to singe*; **strengþ,** prim. Germanic **straŋʒiþō,** *strength*; **þyncan,** *to seem.*

§ **290.** The guttural **ŋ** disappeared in an unstressed syllable when preceded by **n** in a stressed syllable in the course of the OE. period, as **cynig,** *king,* **penig,** *penny,* beside older **cyning, pening; hunig,** O.Icel. **hunang,** OHG. **honang** beside **honag,** *honey.*

## The Labials.

### p

§ **291.** Germanic **p** from Indg. **b** (§ **232**) was of rare occurrence, especially initially. Most of the words beginning with **p** in OE. are Latin or Greek loanwords. **p** remained in OE. both initially, medially, and finally, as **pād** (Goth. **páida**), *cloak*; **pening,** O.Icel. **penningr,** OHG. **pfenning,** *penny*; **open,** O.Icel. **openn,** OS. **opan,** OHG. **offan,** *open*; **slǣpan,** Goth. **slēpan,** OS. **slāpan,** OHG. **slāfan,** *to sleep*; **dēop,** Goth. **diups,** O.Icel. **djūpr,** OS. **diop,** OHG. **tiof,** *deep*; and similarly **pæþ,** *path*; **pott,** *pot.* **plegan,** *to play*; **pliht,** *danger, plight*; **plōg,** *plough*; **prūt,** *proud.* **spere,** *spear*; **sprecan,** *to speak.* **clyppan,** *to embrace*; **grāpian,** *to grope*; **stæppan,** *to step*; **sūpan,** *to drink*; **swāpan,** *to sweep*; **wǣpen,** *weapon*; **wēpan,** *to weep.* **hearpe,** *harp*; **helpan,** *to help*; **weorpan,** *to throw, cast.* **hēap,** *troop, heap*; **rāp,** *rope*; **scēap,** *sheep*; **scearp,** *sharp*; **scip,** *ship*; **ūp,** *up.*

Examples of Lat. loanwords are: **cuppe** (late Lat. **cuppa**), *cup*; **pāwa, pēa** (Lat. **pāvo**), *peacock*; **peru** (Lat. **pirum**), *pear*; **pic** (Lat. acc. **picem**), *pitch*; **pinsian** (Lat. **pensāre**), *to weigh, consider*; **pise** (Lat. **pisum**), *pea*; **pund** (Lat. **pondō**), *pound*; **pyle** (Lat. acc. **pulvīnum**), *pillow*; **pytt** (Lat. acc. **puteum**), *pit.*

### b

§ **292.** We have already seen that prim. Germanic **ƀ** from Indg. **bh** became **b** initially, and also medially after **m** during the prim. Germanic period (§ **234**); that prim. Germanic **ƀj** became **bb** in West Germanic (§ **254**); and that the further development of prim. Germanic **ƀ** belonged to the history of the separate Germanic languages (§ **235**). Germanic **b**, and West Germanic **bb** from **ƀj** (§ **254**) and **ƀn** in the weak declension of nouns (§ **256**), remained in OE., as OE. OS. OHG. **beran,** Goth. **baíran,** O.Icel. **bera,** *to bear*; OE. OS. **blind,** Goth. **blinds,** O.Icel. **blindr,** OHG. **blint,** *blind*; **brecan,** Goth. **brikan,** OHG. **brehhan,** *to break*; and similarly **bæc,** *back*; **bæþ,** *bath*; **bān,** *bone*; **bēam,** *tree*; **bedd** (Goth. gen. **badjis**), *bed*; **bēodan,** *to command*; **bindan,** *to bind*; **bītan,** *to bite*; **blæc,** *black*; **blāwan,** *to blow*; **blōd,** *blood*; **bōc,** *book*; **bodig,** *body*; **brād,** *broad*; **bringan,** *to bring*; **brycg,** *bridge*.

**dumb,** Goth. **dumbs,** O.Icel. **dumbr,** OHG. **tumb,** *dumb*; and similarly **camb,** *comb*; **climban,** *to climb*; **lamb,** *lamb*; **ymb(e),** *about, around*; **wamb,** *stomach*.

**sibb,** Goth. **sibja,** OS. **sibbia,** OHG. **sibba,** *relationship, peace*; and similarly **cribb,** *crib*; **habban,** *to have*; **libban,** *to live*; **nebb,** *beak*; **ribb,** *rib*; **webb,** *web*. **ebba** (§ **256**), *ebb*.

§ **293.** Germanic medial **ƀ** remained in OE. between voiced sounds. In the oldest period of the language it was mostly written **b,** as **gibaen,** *given*; **libr,** *liver*; **ober,** *over*. But owing to the fact that Germanic **f** became **ƀ** medially between voiced sounds, although the **f** was retained in writing (§ **296**), the **f** also came to be used regularly to represent Germanic **ƀ** in OE. On the normal development of **ƀ** in the other Germanic languages, see § **235**. Examples are: **giefan,** Goth. **giban,** O.Icel. **gefa,** OS. **geƀan,** OHG. **geban,** *to give*; **hæfde,** Goth. **habáida,**

OS. **haƀda, habda,** OHG. **habēta,** *he had*; **sealfian,** Goth. OHG. **salbōn,** OS. **salƀon,** *to anoint*; **seofon,** Goth. OHG. **sibun,** OS. **siƀun,** *seven*; and similarly **ǣfen,** *evening*; **beofor,** *beaver*; **cnafa,** *boy*; **delfan,** *to dig*; **drīfan,** *to drive*; **hafast,** *thou hast*; **hafaþ,** *he has*; **heafoc,** *hawk*; **hēafod,** *head*; **hefig,** *heavy*; **heofon,** *heaven*; **hlāford,** *lord, master*; **hræfn,** *raven*; **lǣfan,** *to leave*; **lifde,** *he lived*; **lifer,** *liver*; **lofian,** *to praise*; **lufian,** *to love*; **ofer,** *over*; **scūfan,** *to push*; **siolufr, seolfor,** *silver*; **stefn,** *voice*; **steorfan,** *to die*; **wefan,** *to weave*; **yfel,** *evil*; gen. **wīfes,** OHG. **wībes,** dat. **wīfe,** OHG. **wībe,** beside nom. **wīf,** OHG. **wīb,** *woman*. Also in Lat. loanwords with **b** = late Lat. **v,** as **dēofol** (Lat. **diabolus**), *devil*; **fēfor** (Lat. **fĕbris**), *fever*; **tæfl** (Lat. **tabula**), *chess-board, die*; **trifot** (Lat. **tribūtum**), *tribute*.

Note.—**fn, fm** became **mn, mm** in late OE., as **emn** (Goth. **ibns**), *even*; **stemn** (Goth. **stibna**), *voice*, beside older **ef(e)n, stef(e)n**; **wĭmman** (pl. **wĭmmen**) beside older **wīfman,** *woman*.

§ **294.** Final **ƀ** became the voiceless spirant **f** in OE. Goth. and OS. and thus fell together with Germanic final **f** (§ **295**), as **geaf,** Goth. OS. **gaf,** OHG. **gab,** *he gave*; **healf,** OS. **half,** OHG. **halb,** *half*; **hlāf,** Goth. acc. **hláif,** OHG. **hleib,** *loaf, bread*; and similarly **cealf,** *calf*; **dēaf,** *deaf*; **dealf,** *he dug*; **lēaf,** *leaf*; **lēof,** *dear*; **līf,** *life*; **lof,** *praise*; **scēaf,** *he pushed*; **wīf,** *wife, woman*.

### f

§ **295.** Germanic **f** remained initially, medially before voiceless consonants, and finally, as **fæder,** Goth. **fadar,** O.Icel. **faðer,** OS. **fadar,** OHG. **fater,** *father*; OE. OS. **fīf,** Goth. OHG. **fimf,** *five*; OE. OS. **fōt,** Goth. **fōtus,** O.Icel. **fōtr,** OHG. **fuoȥ,** *foot*; **gesceaft,** Goth. **gaskafts,** *creation*, OS. **giskaft,** *destiny*, OHG. **giscaft,** *creature*; OE. O.Icel. OS. OHG. **hof,** *court, dwelling*; OE. OS. **wulf,** Goth. acc. **wulf,** OHG. **wolf,** *wolf*; and similarly

**fæger,** *fair, beautiful*; **fæst,** *firm*; **fæt,** *vessel, vat*; **fēa,** *few*; **feallan,** *to fall*; **feld,** *field*; **feohtan,** *to fight*; **fēower,** *four*; **feþer,** *feather*; **findan,** *to find*; **flǣsc,** *flesh*; **fleax,** *flax*; **flēogan,** *to fly*; **fōda,** *food*; **folc,** *folk*; **folgian,** *to follow*; **fram,** *from*; **frēo,** *free*; **frēond,** *friend*; **frēosan,** *to freeze*; **fugol,** *bird*; **full,** *full*; **fȳr,** *fire*. **æfter,** *after*; **cræft,** *skill*; **gift,** *marriage gift*; **offrian,** *to offer*; **pyffan,** *to puff*; **ræfsan, refsan,** *to reprove*; **sceaft,** *shaft, pole*. **ceaf,** *chaff*; **hōf,** *he raised*; **hrōf,** *roof*.

§ **296.** Germanic medial **f** became **ƀ** (= the v in NE. **vat**) between voiced sounds and thus fell together with Germanic **ƀ** in this position (§ **293**). In the oldest period of the language the two Germanic sounds were mostly kept apart, the former being written **f**, and the latter **b**. Examples are: **cēafl,** OS. **kāfl,** cp. MHG. **kivel,** *jaw*; **ofen,** O.Icel. **ofn,** OHG. **ofan,** *oven*; **ceafor,** OHG. **kefar,** *cockchafer*; **sceofl,** Goth. ***skufla,** cp. OHG. **scūfala,** *shovel*; sing. gen. **wulfes,** OHG. **wolfes,** dat. **wulfe,** OHG. **wolfe,** beside nom. **wulf,** OHG. **wolf,** *wolf*; and similarly in the inflected forms of words like **ceaf,** *chaff*; **hrōf,** *roof*.

§ **297.** **fj** became **bb** through the intermediate stage **ƀj,** as **hebban,** Goth. **hafjan,** *to raise*.

## The Dentals.

### t

§ **298.** Germanic **t** remained in OE. both initially, medially, and finally, as **tōþ,** Goth. **tunþus,** OS. **tand,** OHG. **zan(d),** *tooth*; **tunge,** Goth. **tuggō,** O.Icel. OS. **tunga,** OHG. **zunga,** *tongue*; **twā,** Goth. **twái,** *two*; OE. OS. **etan,** Goth. **itan,** O.Icel. **eta,** OHG. **ezzan,** *to eat*; OE. Goth. OS. **witan,** O.Icel. **vita,** OHG. **wizzan,** *to know*; **settan,** Goth. **satjan,** O.Icel. **setja,** OS. **settian,** OHG. **setzen,** *to set*; **snottor,** Goth. **snutrs,** O.Icel. **snotr,** OS. OHG. **snottar,** *wise*; **sceatt,** Goth. **skatts,**

O.Icel. **skattr,** *money, tribute*; **neaht,** Goth. **nahts,** OS. OHG. **naht,** *night*; and similarly **tācn,** *token*; **tam,** *tame*; **tēar,** *tear*; **tellan,** *to tell, count*; **tīd, tīma,** *time*; **timber,** *timber*; **tōl,** *tool*; **tredan,** *to tread*; **trēo,** *tree*; **trog,** *trough*; **turf,** *turf*; **twelf,** *twelve*; **twig,** *twig*. **bītan,** *to bite*; **botm,** *bottom*; **feohtan,** *to fight*; **hatian,** *to hate*; **hwǣte,** *wheat*; **meltan,** *to melt*; **mētan,** *to find, meet*; **restan,** *to rest*; **setl,** *seat*; **swēte,** *sweet*; **wæter,** *water*. **cnotta,** *knot*; **hwettan,** *to whet, incite*; **mattoc,** *mattock*; **sittan,** *to sit*. **fōt,** *foot*; **gāst,** *spirit*; **gylt,** *guilt*; **hwæt,** *what*; **hāt,** *hot*; **hwīt,** *white*; **pytt,** *pit*; **strǣt,** *street*.

On the simplification of medial **tt** to **t,** see § **259.**

NOTE.—1. Medial and final **st** was sometimes written **sþ** in early WS., as **dūsþ,** *dust*, **fæsþ,** *fast*, **giefesþ,** *thou givest*, **wæsþm,** *growth*, **wāsþ,** *thou knowest*, for **dūst, fæst, giefest, wæstm, wāst.**

2. Latin medial **t** became **d** in Low Latin, so that words borrowed at an early period have **t,** but those borrowed at a later period have **d,** as **bēte** (Lat. **bēta**), *beetroot*; **strǣt** (Lat. **strāta**), *street, road*; but **abbod** (Lat. acc. **abbātem**), *abbot*; **læden** (Lat. acc. **latīnum**), *Latin* (*language*); **sīde** (Lat. **sēta**), *silk*.

3. **t** often disappeared between consonants, as **fæsnian,** *to fasten*, **rihlīce,** *justly*, **þrīsnes,** *boldness*, beside **fæstnian, rihtlīce, þrīstnes.**

### d

§ **299.** Germanic **d** became **d** initially, and also medially after **n** during the prim. Germanic period (§ **234**). And **đ** in other positions became **d** in West Germanic (§ **253**). On the normal development of Germanic **đ** in Goth. and O.Icel., see § **235.** **d** generally remained in OE. both initially, medially, and finally, as **dæg,** Goth. **dags,** O.Icel. **dagr,** OS. **dag,** OHG. **tag,** *day*; **dohtor,** Goth. **daúhtar,** O.Icel. **dōtter,** OS. **dohtar,** OHG. **tohter,** *daughter*; **fæder,** Goth. **fadar,** O.Icel. **faðer,** OS. **fadar,** OHG. **fater,** *father*; OE. Goth. OS. **bindan,** O.Icel. **binda,** OHG. **bintan,** *to bind*; **biddan**, Goth. **bidjan**, O.Icel. **biðja**, OS. **biddian**, OHG. **bitten**, *to pray*; OE. OS. **blōd**, Goth. **blōþ**, O.Icel. **blōð**, OHG. **bluot**, *blood*; **ceald**, Goth. **kalds**, O.Icel. **kaldr**, OS. **kald**, OHG. **kalt**, *cold*; and similarly **dāg**, *dough*; **dēad**, *dead*; **dēaf**, *deaf*; **dēaþ**, *death*; **dēman**, *to judge*; **dēofol**, *devil*; **dēop**, *deep*; **deorc**, *dark*; **dōn**, *to do*; **dragan**, *to drag*; **drīfan**, *to drive*; **drincan**, *to drink*; **dūfan**, *to dive*; **dumb**, *dumb*; **duru**, *door*; **dwellan**, *to lead astray*. **bodig**, *body*; **cwǣdon**, *they said*; **fōdor**, *fodder, food*; **healdan**, *to hold*; **hīerde**, *he heard*; **hider**, *hither*; **lǣdan**, *to lead*; **lǣdde**, *he led*; **mōdor**, *mother*; **nǣdre**, *adder*; **sadol**, *saddle*; **sendan**, *to send*; **slīdan**, *to slide*; **þridda**, *third*; **weder**, *weather*; pp. **worden**, *become*; **wudu**, *wood*. **brȳd**, *bride*; **dǣd**, *deed*; **frēond**, *friend*; pp. **gemacod**, *made*; **god**, *God*; **gōd**, *good*; **hand**, *hand*; **hēafod**, *head*; **heard**, *hard*; **hlūd**, *loud*; **midd**, *middle*; **nacod**, *naked*; **rēad**, *red*; **word**, *word*.

On the simplification of medial **dd** to **d**, see § **259**, 3.

NOTE.—**d** disappeared in the combination **ldl**, as **sellic** beside **seldlic** (OS. **seldlīk**, Goth. **sildaleiks**), *strange, wonderful*.

§ **300**. **d** became **t** before and after voiceless consonants. When two dentals thus came together, they became **tt** which was simplified to **t** finally and after consonants. And interconsonantal **t** generally disappeared before **s**. Examples are: **blētsian**, older **blœdsian** from ***blōdisōjan**, *to bless*; **bitst** beside **bidest**, *thou prayest*; **bint** from ***bindþ**, older **bindeþ**, *he binds*; **bit**, **bitt** from ***bidþ**, older **bideþ**, *he prays* (cp. § **305**); **cyste** (see § **259**, 2) from ***cyssde**, *he kissed*; **gesynto** from ***gesundiþu**, *health*; **grētte** from ***grētde** (= Goth. ***grōtida**), *he greeted*; **īecte**, Goth. ***áukida**, *he increased*; **lǣtst** beside **lǣdest**, *thou leadest*. **bin(t)st**, older **bindest**, *thou bindest*; and similarly **fin(t)st**, *thou findest*; **giel(t)st**, *thou yieldest*; **sten(t)st**, *thou standest*; **mils**, *mercy*, **milsian**, *to pity*, beside **milts**, **milt-**

**sian.** The **d** was often restored from forms where it was regular, as **findst : findan** **milds, mildsian : milde,** *merciful.*

### þ

§ **301.** Germanic **þ** generally remained in OE. initially, medially when doubled, and finally, as **þencan,** Goth. **þagkjan,** OS. **thenkian,** OHG. **denken,** *to think* ; **þūsend,** Goth. **þūsundi,** OHG. **dūsunt,** *thousand* ; **sceþþan,** Goth. **skaþjan,** *to injure* ; **oþþe, eþþa,** Goth. **aíþþáu,** OS. **eđđo, ođđo,** OHG. **eddo,** *or* ; **āþ,** Goth. acc. **áiþ,** OS. **ēđ,** OHG. **eid,** *oath* ; pret. **wearþ,** Goth. **warþ,** OS. **warđ,** OHG. **ward,** *he became* ; and similarly **þancian,** *to thank* ; **þeccan,** *to cover* ; **þēof,** *thief* ; **þing,** *thing* ; **þorn,** *thorn* ; **þrǣd,** *thread* ; **þringan,** *to press* ; **þūma,** *thumb* ; **þunor,** *thunder* ; **þwang,** *thong* ; **þyncan,** *to seem.* **moþþe,** *moth* ; **siþþan,** *since, afterwards* ; **smiþþe,** *smithy.* **bæþ,** *bath* ; **beraþ,** *they bear* ; **bireþ,** *he bears* ; **broþ,** *broth* ; **clāþ,** *cloth* ; **cūþ,** *known* ; **cwæþ,** *he said* ; **dēaþ,** *death* ; **hæleþ,** *hero, man* ; **hǣþ,** *heath* ; **mōnaþ,** *month* ; **mūþ,** *mouth* ; **norþ,** *north* ; **tōþ,** *tooth.*

NOTE.—In late Nth. final **þ** appears as **-s** in the personal endings of verbs, as **bindes,** *he binds,* **bindas,** *they bind,* beside **bindeþ, bindaþ.** See the end of § **476.**

§ **302.** Germanic medial **þ** became **đ** between voiced sounds in OE., although the **þ** was retained in writing. In the oldest period of the language it was often written **d.** Examples are : **baþian,** *to bathe* ; **brōþor,** *brother* ; **byrþen,** *burden* ; **eorþe,** *earth* ; **fæþm,** *embrace, fathom* ; **feþer,** *feather* ; **hǣþen,** *heathen* ; **morþor,** *murder* ; **ōþer,** *other* ; **weorþan,** *to become.* Gen. **āþes, bæþes,** beside nom. **āþ,** *oath,* **bæþ,** *bath* ; inf. **cweþan,** *to say,* beside pret. sing. **cwæþ.**

§ **303.** Germanic medial **lþ** became **ld** in OE. The **ld** then became extended to the final position by levelling.

Examples are: **feaḍan**, Goth. **falþan**, *to fold*; **wilde**. Goth. **wilþeis**, *wild*; **wuldor**, Goth. **wulþus**, *glory*. Gen. **goldes** (= Goth. ***gulþis**), dat. **golde** (= Goth. **gulþa**), from which a new nom. **gold** for ***golþ** (= Goth. **gulþ**) was formed; and similarly **beald**, *bold*; **eald**, *old*; **feld**, *field*; **hold**, *gracious*; **weald**, *forest*. But the **lþ**, which arose from vowel syncope, remained, as **sǣlþ**, OHG. **sālida**, *happiness*; **fielþ** from older ***fielleþ**, *he falls*.

§ **304**. Germanic **þl** generally remained in Anglian, but became **dl** after long vowels in WS., as **ādl** (Anglian **āþl**, **ādl**, **āld**), *disease*; **nǣdl** (Anglian **nēþl**, Goth. **nēþla**), *needle*; **wǣdl** (Anglian **wēþl**), *poverty*; **wǣdla**, *pauper*; **wīdlian**, *to defile*.

§ **305**. The combinations **tþ**, **dþ** became **tt** which was simplified to **t** finally and after consonants, as **bīt(t)** from ***bītþ**, older **bīteþ**, *he bites*; **it(t)** from ***itþ**, older **iteþ**, *he eats*; **þætte** from **þæt þe**, *that which*. **bit(t)** from ***bidþ**, older **bideþ**, *he prays*; **bīt(t)** from ***bīdþ**, older **bīdeþ**, *he awaits*; **bint** from ***bindþ**, older **bindeþ**, *he binds*; **gesynto** from ***gesundiþu**, *health*; **lātteōw** (also **lādteōw**, **lātþeōw** due to the influence of the uncompounded forms) from older **lādþeōw**, *leader*; **mittȳ** from **mid þȳ**, *when, while*; **ofermētto** from ***ofermōdiþu**, *pride*. Cp. § **300**.

The combinations **s**, **ss** + **þ** became **st**, as **cīest** from **cīesþ**, older **cīeseþ**, *he chooses*; and similarly **forlīest**, *he loses*; **wiext**, *it grows*; **hafastu** = **hafas** + **þŭ**, *hast thou*. **cyst** (cp. § **259**, 2) from older **cysseþ**, *he kisses*.

**þs** became assimilated to **ss**, as **bliss**, *bliss*, **blissian**, *to rejoice*, **liss**, *favour*, beside **blīþs**, **blīþsian**, **līþs**. In late OE. **þd** became assimilated to **dd**, as **cȳdde** beside older **cȳþde**, *he made known*.

**þ** disappeared before **st**, as **cwist**, older **cwiþest**, *thou sayest*; **wierst**, older **wierþest**, *thou becomest*, cp. § **476**.

On forms like **cwiþ**, **wierþ** from **cwiþeþ**, *he says*, **wierþeþ**, *he becomes*, cp. § **259**, I.

## The Sibilant s.

§ **306.** Germanic **s** remained in OE. initially, medially in combination with voiceless consonants, and finally, as **sǣ**, Goth. **sáiws**, OS. OHG. **sēo**, *sea*; **slǣpan**, Goth. **slēpan**, OS. **slāpan**, OHG. **slāfan**, *to sleep*; OE. OS. OHG. **sunu**, Goth. **sunus**, O.Icel. **sunr**, *son*; **gāst**, OS. **gēst**, OHG. **geist**, *spirit*; OE. Goth. O.Icel. OS. OHG. **hūs**, *house*; and similarly **sadol**, *saddle*; **sǣd**, *seed*; **sealt**, *salt*; **sēcan**, *to seek*; **sēon**, *to see*; **sittan**, *to sit*; **slīdan**, *to slide*; **smæl**, *small, slender*; **snaca**, *snake*; **sōna**, *soon*; **sōt**, *soot*; **spearwa**, *sparrow*; **sprecan**, *to speak*; **standan**, *to stand*; **strēam**, *stream*; **sūþ**, *south*; **sweostor**, *sister*. **assa**, *ass, donkey*; **cyssan**, *to kiss*; **restan**, *to rest*; **þyrstan**, *to thirst*; **cēas**, *he chose*; **gærs**, *grass*; **gōs**, *goose*; **heals**, *neck*; **hors**, *horse*; **īs**, *ice*; **mūs**, *mouse*; **wæs**, *was*. It is difficult to account for the loss of the final **-s** in the OE. adv. **mā**, *more*, beside Goth. **máis** = prim. Germanic ***mais**, Oscan **mais**.

For the Germanic combinations **sk** and **hs**, see §§ **312**, **327**.

Note.—**s** sometimes underwent metathesis with **p**, especially in late OE.; as **æps**, *aspen*, **cops**, *fetter, bond*, **wlips**, *lisping*, **wæsp**, *wasp*, beside **æsp**, **cosp**, **wlisp**, **wæps** (**wæfs**).

§ **307.** Germanic **s** became **z** between voiced sounds in OE., but the **s** was retained in writing, as **bōsm**, *bosom*; **cēosan**, *to choose*; **grasian**, *to graze*; **hæsl**, *hazel shrub*; **lesan**, *to collect*; **nosu**, *nose*; **ōsle**, *ousel*; **wesole**, **wesle**, *weasel*; **wesan**, *to be*, beside **wæs**, *was*; gen. **hūses**, dat. **hūse**, beside nom. **hūs**, *house*.

§ **308.** We have already seen that prim. Germanic **z** from Indg. **s** became **r** medially and was dropped finally in West Germanic (§ **252**). Examples of medial **r** have been given in § **279**; and of the loss of final **-z** in § **252**.

## The Gutturals.

### k

§ **309.** Germanic **k**, generally written **c** in OE., remained a guttural initially before consonants and before the guttural vowels **a, ā, o, ō, u, ū**, and their umlauts **æ** (e), **ǣ, e, ē** (œ̄), **y, ȳ**, but became a palatal before the palatal vowels, **æ, ǣ** (ē) = Germanic **ǣ, e** (= Germanic **e**), **ē** (= Germanic **ē**); **ea, eo, io** from Germanic **a, e, i** by breaking (§ **49**), **ēa, ēo, īo, i, ī**, and their umlauts **e, ie** (= **i**-umlaut of **ea, io**), **īe** (= **i**-umlaut of **ēa, īo**), see § **47**.

Germanic medial **k** and **kk** remained guttural when originally followed by a guttural vowel, as **bucca,** *he-goat*; **macian** from ***makōjan,** *to make*; **sacu,** *strife*; **geoc,** prim. Germanic ***jukan,** *yoke*; but became palatal when originally followed by an **i** or **j**, as **bryce** from ***brukiz,** *breach*; **sēcan** = Goth. **sōkjan,** *to seek*; **þeccan** from ***þakjan,** *to cover*.

The guttural and palatal **c** often existed side by side in different forms of the same word, as pret. pl. **curon,** pp. **coren,** beside inf. **cēosan,** *to choose*; **brecan,** *to break*, beside **bricþ** from ***brikiþ,** *he breaks*.

Some scholars assume that palatal **c** and **nc** became **tʃ** (= **ch** in NE. **chin**), **ntʃ** in Mercian, WS. and Ken. in the earliest period of the language, but this is an assumption which cannot be proved. All that we know for certain is that OE. had a guttural and a palatal **k**, that the former was sometimes written **k** and the latter always **c**, and that the two **k**-sounds had separate characters in the OE. runic alphabet. Both the guttural and the palatal **k** were generally written **c** in OE. When **c** was palatal it was often written **ce, ci** medially before a following guttural vowel, with **e, i** to indicate the palatal nature of the **c**, as **sēcean,** *to seek*; **þeccean,** *to cover*; **þencean,** *to think*, cp. § **319,** Note.

NOTE.—OE. **fecc(e)an** beside **fetian** (of unknown etymology), *to fetch*, and OE. **orceard** beside **ortgeard** (Goth. **aúrti-gards**), *orchard, garden*, are not sufficient proof that palatal **c, cc** became **tʃ** in the oldest periods of the above dialects. All that can be said for certain is that the change had already taken place by the beginning of the Middle English period.

§ **310.** 1. Guttural c.

**cēlan** from ***kōljan,** *to cool*; **cemban** from ***kambjan,** *to comb*; **corn,** Goth. **kaúrn,** *corn*; **cūþ,** Goth. **kunþs,** *known*; **cynn,** Goth. **kuni,** *race, generation*; **cnēo,** Goth. **kniu,** *knee*; and similarly **camb, comb,** *comb*; **cēne,** *keen, bold*; **cennan,** *to give birth*; **cēpan,** *to keep*; **cōl,** *cool*; **coss,** *kiss*; **cū,** *cow*; **cuman,** *to come*; **cyning,** *king*; **cyssan,** *to kiss*; **cȳþan,** *to make known*. **clǣne,** *clean*; **climban,** *to climb*; **cnotta,** *knot*; **cræft,** *skill*; **cwēn,** *queen*. Also in Lat. loanwords, as **candel** (Lat. **candēla**), *candle*; **copor** (Lat. **cuprum**), *copper*; **cycene** (late Lat. **coquīna, cucīna**), *kitchen*; and similarly **camp,** *fight, battle*; **cempa,** *warrior*; **cōc,** *cook*; **cuppe,** *cup*.

**æcer,** Goth. **akrs,** prim. Germanic ***akraz,** *field*; **nacod,** Goth. **naqaþs,** OHG. **nakot,** *naked*; **wracu,** Goth. **wraka,** *persecution*; and similarly **bacan,** *to bake*; **bucca,** *he-goat*; **draca,** *dragon*; **ficol,** *cunning*; **hnecca,** *neck*; **sprecan,** *to speak*; **sticca,** *stick*. **macian** from ***makōjan,** *to make*; and similarly **liccian,** *to lick*; **lōcian,** *to look*; **prician,** *to prick*. **drincan,** *to drink*; **þancian,** *to thank*.

**bucc,** O.Icel. **bokkr,** Indg. ***bhugnós,** *buck*; **blæc,** prim. Germanic ***blakaz,** *black*; **geoc,** Goth. **juk,** prim. Germanic ***jukan,** *yoke*; and similarly **āc,** *oak*; **bæc,** *back*; **bōc,** *book*; **brocc,** *badger*; **flocc,** *flock*; **folc,** *folk*; **mioluc,** *milk*; **sēoc,** *sick*; **weorc,** *work*; **þanc,** *thought*.

§ **311.** 2. Palatal c.

**cēapian,** Goth. **káupōn,** *to trade, traffic*; **cēosan,** Goth. **kiusan,** *to choose*; **cinn,** *chin*, Goth. **kinnus,** *cheek*; and similarly **ceaf,** *chaff*; **ceafor,** *cockchafer*; **cealc,** *chalk*;

**ceald,** *cold*; **cealf,** *calf*; **ceorfan,** *to carve, cut*; **ceorl,** *churl, man*; **cēowan,** *to chew*; **cīdan,** *to chide*; **cīese,** *cheese*; **cierran,** *to turn*; **cild,** *child*; **cirice,** *church.*

**bēc** from ***bōkiz,** *books*; **lǣce,** Goth. **lēkeis,** *physician*; **smīec** from ***smaukiz,** *smoke*; **weccan,** Goth. **us-wakjan,** *to arouse*; **benc** from ***baŋkiz,** *bench*; **þenc(e)an,** Goth. **þagkjan,** *to think*; and similarly **birce,** *birch*; **crycc,** *crutch*; **flicce,** *flitch*; **mēce,** *sword*; **mycel,** *great*; **sēc(e)an,** *to seek*; **strecc(e)an,** *to stretch*; **stycce,** *piece*; **tǣc(e)an,** *to teach*; **wicce,** *witch*; **drenc(e)an,** *to submerge*; **þync(e)an,** *to seem*; **stenc,** *smell, odour.*

NOTE.—1. **cs** was generally written **x** in OE., as **æx** beside older **æces,** *axe*; **rīxian** beside **rīcsian** from ***rīkisōjan,** *to rule.*

2. OE. final **c** became palatal when preceded by **i** or **ī**, as **ic,** *I*; **hwelc** from ***hwa-līk,** *which*; **līc,** *body*; **pic,** *pitch*; **swelc** from ***swa-līk,** *such.*

3. In Anglian final c became χ (written **h**) in unstressed words, as **ah** beside late WS. **ac,** *but*; **īowih** (**īwih**), *you*, **ūsih,** *us*, beside WS. **ēowic, ūsic**; **ih,** *I*, **meh,** *me*, **þeh,** *thee*, beside the stressed forms **ic, mec, þec.**

§ **312.** In the oldest period of the language **sc,** like **c** (§ **309**), was guttural or palatal, but some time during the OE. period the guttural **sc** became palatal, except in loanwords. It was often written **sce, sci** before a following guttural vowel with **e, i** to indicate the palatal nature of the **sc.** There is no definite proof that **sc** became ʃ (= the **sh** in NE. **ship, shape**) in early OE. as is assumed by some scholars. Examples are: **sc(e)acan,** *to shake*; **scand,** *disgrace*; **sc(e)adu,** *shadow*; **sceaft,** *shaft*; **sceal,** *shall*; **scēap,** *sheep*; **scearp,** *sharp*; **sc(e)ort,** *short*; **scēotan,** *to shoot*; **scield,** *shield*; **scieppan,** *to create*; **scieran,** *to shear*; **scilling,** *shilling*; **scip,** *ship*; **scōh,** *shoe*; **scrūd,** *dress, garment*; **sculdor,** *shoulder*; **scūr,** *shower*; **scyldig,** *guilty.* **blyscan,** *to blush*; **þerscan,** *to thresh*; **wascan,** *to wash*;

**wȳscan,** *to wish.* **englisc,** *English*; **fisc,** *fish*; **flǣsc,** *flesh.* But **scōl** (Lat. **schola**), *school*; **scinn** (O.Icel. **skinn**), *skin.*

Note.—Medial **sc** often underwent metathesis to **cs** (written **x**), especially in late WS., as **axe,** *ashes,* **āxian,** *to ask,* **fixas,** *fishes,* **waxan,** *to wash,* beside **asce, āscian** (OHG. **eiskōn**), **fiscas, wascan.**

### g

§ **313.** Germanic **ʒ** became **g** after **ŋ** during the prim. Germanic period (§ **234**). **ʒj** (§ **254**) and **ʒn** (§ **256**) became **gg** in West Germanic. Germanic **ʒ** remained a spirant in all other positions in the oldest period of OE. On the normal development of Germanic **ʒ** in the other Germanic languages, see § **235.**

Germanic initial and medial **ʒ** became differentiated in prehistoric OE. into a guttural and a palatal voiced spirant under the same conditions as those by which Germanic **k** became differentiated into a guttural and a palatal explosive (§ **309**).

§ **314.** Initial guttural **ʒ** remained in the oldest period of the language, but had become the voiced explosive **g** before the end of the OE. period. Initial palatal **ʒ** (written **g**) remained a spirant (= the **y** in NE. **yet, yon**) and fell together with Germanic initial **j** (§ **268**). This explains why Germanic initial **j** was written **g** in OE.

§ **315.** 1. Guttural **ʒ.**

**gāst,** OS. **gēst,** OHG. **geist,** *spirit*; OE. OS. **gōd,** Goth. **gōþs,** O.Icel. **gōðr,** OHG. **guot,** *good*; OE. OS. OHG. **gold,** Goth. **gulþ,** *gold*; OE. Goth. **guma,** O.Icel. **gume,** OS. **gumo,** OHG. **gomo,** *man*; **græs,** Goth. OS. OHG. **gras,** *grass*; and similarly **gād,** *goad*; **gaderian,** *to gather*; **galan,** *to sing*; **gamen,** *game, amusement*; **gār,** *spear, javelin*; **gāt,** *goat*; pl. **gatu,** *gates*; **gēs,** *geese*; **god,** *God*; **gōs,** *goose*; pret. pl. **guton,** *they poured out*; pp. **goten,**

*poured out*; **gūþ**, *war*; **gylden**, *golden*. **glæd**, *glad*; **glōf**, *glove*; **gnætt**, *gnat*; **grēne**, *green*; **grund**, *ground*.

§ **316.** 2. Palatal **ᵹ**.

**geaf**, Goth. O.Icel. OS. **gaf**, OHG. **gab**, *he gave*; **gealga**, OS. OHG. **galgo**, *gallows*, Goth. **galga**, *cross*; **gēotan**, Goth. **giutan**, OS. **giotan**, OHG. **giozan**, *to pour out*; **giefan**, Goth. **giban**, O.Icel. **gefa**, OS. **geƀan**, OHG. **geban**, *to give*; and similarly **gēafon**, *they gave*; **geard**, *courtyard*; **gearn**, *yarn*; **geat** (NE. dial. **yet**), *gate*; **geolu**, *yellow*; **gewiss**, *certain*; **giefu**, *gift*; **gieldan**, *to repay, yield*; **giellan**, *to yell*; **gielpan**, *to boast*; **gīeman**, *to take notice of*; **giernan**, *to yearn for*; **giest**, *guest*; **gierwan**, *to prepare*; **gift**, *marriage gift*.

NOTE.—The guttural and palatal **ᵹ** often existed side by side in different forms of the same word, as pl. **gatu** beside sing. **geat**; pret. pl. **guton**, pp. **goten**, beside inf. **gēotan**, pret. sing. **gēat**.

§ **317.** The **g** in the combination **ŋg** remained guttural or became palatal according as it was originally followed by a guttural or a palatal vowel or **j**. It also remained guttural before consonants.

1. Guttural **ŋg**: OE. OS. OHG. **bringan**, Goth. **briggan**, *to bring*; **cyning** from ***kuniŋgaz**, *king*; **lang** from ***laŋgaz**, *long*; **tunge**, Goth. **tuggō**, OS. **tunga**, OHG. **zunga**, *tongue*; and similarly **englisc**, *English*; **finger** (Goth. **figgrs**), *finger*; **hring**, *ring*; **hungor**, *hunger*; **singan**, *to sing*; **springan**, *to leap*; **stingan**, *to sting*; **þing**, *thing*.

2. Palatal **ŋg**, often written **ge** medially before guttural vowels with **e** to denote the palatal nature of the **g**:

**seng(e)an** from ***saŋgjan**, *to singe*; **streng** from ***straŋgiz**, *string*; and similarly **feng**, *grasp*; **gemeng(e)an**, *to mix*; **lengra** (OHG. **lengiro**), *longer*; **steng**, *pole*.

§ **318.** **ŋg** became **ŋc** before voiceless consonants, but the **g** was generally restored through association with forms where **g** was regular, as **brincst**, *thou bringest*, **brincþ**, *he brings*, beside **bringst**, **bringþ**, with **g** restored from the other forms of the verb; **strencþ** from ***strangiþu**, beside **strengþ**, *strength*, with **g** restored from **strang**, *strong*; and similarly **ancsum**, *narrow*, **lencten**, *spring*, **sprincþ**, *he leaps*, beside **angsum**, **lengten**, **springþ**.

§ **319**. West Germanic **gg** from prim. Germanic **ʒn** (§ **256**) remained guttural in OE. and was generally written **gg**, as **dogga**, *dog*; **ēarwicga**, *earwig*; **frogga**, *frog*; **stagga**, *stag*; **sugga**, *water wagtail*.

West Germanic **gg** from prim. Germanic **ʒj** (§ **254**) became palatal **gg** in OE. and was generally written **cg**, and before a medial guttural vowel also **cge**, **cgi** (especially before **u**), as **brycg**, Goth. ***brugja**, *bridge*; **bycg(e)an**, Goth. **bugjan**, *to buy*; **secg**, Goth. ***sagjis**, *man*; **secg**, *sedge*; **lecg(e)an**, Goth. **lagjan**, *to lay*; and similarly **cycgel**, *dart*; **hrycg**, *back, ridge*; **licg(e)an**, *to lie down*; **mycg**, *midge*; **secgan**, *to say*; **wecg**, *wedge*.

Note.—Some scholars assume that palatal **ŋg** and **gg** became **ndž**, **dž** (= the **g** in NE. **gem**) in Mercian, WS. and Ken. in early OE., but there is no definite proof that this sound-change took place in OE., cp. § **309**. It is worthy of note that the voiced explosive in OE. **brycg**, **hrycg**, **secg** (*sedge*), **licg(e)an** and late OE. **un-fligge** (*implumes*) has been preserved in the dialects of the northern, midland, and eastern counties down to the present day, as **brig**, **rig**, **seg**, **lig**, **fligd** (**flegd**), *fledged*. See Wright's *English Dialect Grammar*, §§ 353–4.

§ **320**. Medial **ʒ** remained a guttural spirant before original guttural vowels, but became a palatal spirant when originally followed by a palatal vowel or **j**. It also became palatal between OE. palatal vowels.

1. Guttural **ʒ**.

OE. Goth. OS. **dragan**, O.Icel. **draga**, OHG. **tragan**, *to draw*; **ēage**, Goth. **áugō**, O.Icel. **auga**, OS. **ōga**, OHG. **ouga**, *eye*; OE. OS. OHG. **stīgan**, Goth. **steigan**, O.Icel. **stīga**, *to ascend*; and similarly **āgan**, *to possess*; **dagian** from ***daʒōjan**, *to dawn*; **duguþ**, *strength, virtue*; **belgan** *to become angry*; **beorgan,** *to protect, shelter*; **boga,** *bow*; **būgan,** *to bow down*; **flēogan,** *to fly*; **flēoge,** *fly*; **folgian,** *to follow*; **fugol,** *bird, fowl*; **lagu,** *law*; **lēogan,** *to lie*; **maga,** *stomach*; **slōgon,** *they slew*; **sugu,** *sow*; **swelgan,** *to swallow*; pl. **dagas,** *days*; **wegas,** *ways.*

2. Palatal **ʒ**, often written **ge** before a following guttural vowel:

**bīegan** from ***bauʒjan,** *to bend*; **ege,** Goth. **agis,** *fear*; **sige,** Goth. **sigis,** *victory*; **wǣg** from ***wǣʒiz,** *wave*; and similarly **byge,** *traffic*; **eglan,** *to molest*; **hyge,** *mind*; **lyge,** *falsehood*; **myrg(i)þ,** *mirth.* **fægen,** *glad*; **fæger,** *fair*; **mægen,** *strength*; **nægel,** *nail*; **slægen,** *slain*; **tæg(e)l,** *tail*; gen. sing. **dæges, weges.**

Note.—**ʒ** became **h** (= χ) before voiceless consonants, but the **ʒ** was often restored from forms where **ʒ** was regular, as **stīhst,** *thou ascendest*, **stīhþ,** *he ascends*, beside older **stīgest, stīgeþ**; and similarly **flīehst, flīehþ,** beside inf. **flēogan,** *to fly.*

§ **321.** **ʒ** often disappeared after palatal vowels before a following dental or consonantal **n** with lengthening of the preceding vowel, as **brēdan,** *to brandish*, **brīdel, brīdels,** *bridle*, **frīnan,** *to ask*, **lēde,** *he laid*, **mǣden,** *maiden*, **ongēan** (**ongēn**), *against*, **rīnan,** *to rain*, **sǣde,** *he said*, **strēdan,** *to strew*, **tīþian,** *to grant*, **þēnian,** *to serve*, beside **bregdan, brigdel, brigdels, frignan, legde, mægden, ongeagn, rignan, sægde, stregdan, tigþian, þegnian.** Gen. **rēnes** beside **regnes,** from which a new nom. **rēn** beside **regn,** *rain*, was formed; and similarly **þēn,** *servant*, **wǣn,** *wagon*, beside **þegn, wægn.** See §§ **54,** Note 1; **80,** Note 2; **96,** Note 1.

§ **322.** Medial **-igi-, -ige-** were contracted to **-ī-** as in MHG., as **gelīre** beside **geligere,** *fornication*; **īl** beside **igil,** *hedgehog*; **sīþe** from ***sigiþe,** *scythe*; **tīle** beside **tigele,** *tile*; **līþ** (MHG. **līt**) beside **ligeþ** (MHG. **liget**), *he lies*; **līst** beside **ligest,** *thou liest.*

§ **323.** When Germanic ʒ came to stand finally in OE., it is probable that it became a voiceless spirant (χ) just as in Goth. OS., and prehistoric O.Icel., but that the **g** (= ʒ) was mostly restored again owing to the influence of the inflected forms. After liquids and guttural vowels the restoration of the **g** was merely orthographical, but the further history of the sound in OE. shows that after palatal vowels it was mostly restored in pronunciation as well, because -**h** rarely occurs after palatal vowels, as in **sextih** beside **sextig,** *sixty*; **weh** beside **weg,** *weigh thou.* The **h** (= χ) seldom occurs in early OE., but is common in late OE. especially after liquids and long vowels, as **mearh,** *marrow,* **bealh,** *he became angry,* beside **mearg, bealg;** and similarly **beorh,** *hill*; **burh,** *city*; **sorh,** *sorrow*; **swealh,** *he swallowed.* **dāh,** *dough,* **plōh,** *plough,* **stāh,** *he ascended,* beside **dāg, plōg, stāg;** and similarly **bēah,** *ring, bracelet*; **bōh,** *bough*; **flēah,** *he flew*; **genōh,** *enough*; **stīh,** *path*; **troh** beside **trog,** *trough.*

§ **324.** Final ʒ bceame palatal after palatal vowels, as **dæg,** *day*; **mæg,** *may*; **weg,** *way*; **ǣnig,** *any*; **bodig,** *body*; **dysig,** *foolish*; **hālig,** *holy*; **hefig,** *heavy*; **manig,** *many.* Then at a later period (earliest in Ken.) **g** became **i** consonant which combined with a preceding **æ, e** to form a diphthong, as **dæi** (Ken. **dei**), **mæi, wei,** late WS. also **dæig, mæig, weig.** And -**ig** became -**i** through the intermediate stage -**ī**, as **ǣni, dysi, hefi,** &c.

Note.—The above **æi, ei** from older **æg, eg** have fallen together in all the modern dialects just as in the standard language.

## h

§ **325.** Initial χ had become an aspirate before vowels already in prim. Germanic (§ **246**). In OE. it also became an aspirate initially before consonants except in the combination χ**w**. The spirant remained in the combination χ**w** and has been preserved in many Scottish dialects down to the present day. Examples are: OE. Goth. O.Icel. OS. OHG. **hūs,** *house*; **habban,** Goth. **haban,** O.Icel. **hafa,** OHG. **habēn,** *to have*; and similarly **hamor,** *hammer*; **hand,** *hand*; **hǣlan,** *to heal*; **hēafod,** *head*; **heard,** *hard*; **heorte,** *heart*; **hīeran,** *to hear*; **hold,** *gracious*; **hungor,** *hunger*.

**hlāf,** Goth. **hláifs,** OHG. **hleib,** *loaf, bread*; OE. OS. OHG. **hnīgan,** *to bend down*; OE. OS. OHG. **hring,** O.Icel. **hringr,** *ring*; and similarly **hladan,** *to load*; **hlēapan,** *to leap*; **hlid,** *lid*; **hlot,** *lot*; **hnutu,** *nut*; **hræfn,** *raven*; **hrēod,** *reed*; **hrīmig,** *rimy*.

**hwā,** Goth. **ƕas,** OS. **hwē,** OHG. **hwer,** *who*; **hwīl,** Goth. **ƕeila,** O.Icel. **hvīl,** OS. OHG. **hwīla,** *space of time*; and similarly **hwæl,** *whale*; **hwǣte,** *wheat*; **hwæþer,** *which of two*; **hwelp,** *whelp*; **hwīt,** *white*.

NOTE.—**h** often disappeared with **ne** and **habban,** as **nabban,** *not to have*; **næbbe,** *I have not*; **næfde,** *I had not*. It also disappeared in the second element of compounds which were no longer felt as such in OE., as **bēot** from ***bi-hāt,** *boast*; **frēols** from ***frī-hals,** *freedom*; **eofot** from ***ef-hāt,** *debt*; **līcuma** beside older **līc-hama,** *body*; **ōnettan** from ***on-hātjan,** *to hasten*; **ōret** (OHG. **urheiȥ**) from ***or-hāt,** *battle*; **wælrēow** beside older **wæl-hrēow,** *fierce, cruel*.

§ **326.** Medial χ remained in OE. before voiceless consonants, and when doubled. It was guttural or palatal according as it was originally followed by a guttural or palatal vowel or **j**, as **brōhte,** Goth. OS. OHG. **brāhta,** *he brought*; **dohtor,** Goth. **daúhtar,** OS. **dohtar,** OHG. **tohter,** *daughter*; **eahta,** Goth. **ahtáu,** OS. OHG. **ahto,** *eight*; and similarly **bohte,** *he bought*; **cnieht, cniht,** *boy*; **feohtan,** *to fight*; **hleahtor,** *laughter*; **lēoht,** *a light*; pret. **meahte,** *he might*; **reoht, rieht, ryht,** *right*; **sōhte,** *he sought*; **þōhte,** *he thought*; **ūhta,** *dawn*. **crohha,** *crock, pot*; **geneahhe,** *sufficiently*; **pohha,** *pocket*; **tiohhian,** *to think, consider*.

Dat. **dehter** from ***dohtri,** beside nom. **dohtor,** *daughter*; **flyht** from ***fluχtiz,** *flight*; **hīehsta** from ***χauχist-,** *highest*; **hliehhan,** Goth. **hlahjan,** *to laugh*; **līehtan,** Goth. **liuhtjan,** *to give light*; **siehst,** OHG. **sihis,** *thou seest*; **siehþ,** OHG. **sihit,** *he sees*; and similarly **fēhst,** *thou seizest*; **fēhþ,** *he seizes*; **nīehsta,** *nearest*; **tyht,** *training, habit.*

§ **327.** **χs** became **ks** (written **x**) in OE., as **oxa,** Goth. **aúhsa,** OS. OHG. **ohso,** *ox*; **siex,** Goth. **saíhs,** OS. OHG. **sehs,** *six*; **weaxan,** OS. OHG. **wahsan,** *to grow*; and similarly **feax,** *hair*; **fleax,** *flax*; **fox,** *fox*; **fyxen,** *vixen*; **miox,** *dung*; **wrixlan,** *to exchange.*

§ **328.** Final **χ** remained, as **hēah,** OS. OHG. **hōh,** *high*; **nēah,** OS. OHG. **nāh,** *near*; **seah,** OS. OHG. **sah,** *he saw*; **sealh,** OHG. **salaha,** *willow*; **þurh,** Goth. **þaírh,** OS. **thurh,** OHG. **duruh, durh,** *through*; and similarly **feoh,** *cattle, property*; **rūh,** *rough*; **scōh,** *shoe*; **tōh,** *tough*; **wōh,** *perverse, bad*; **seoh,** *see thou*; **sleah,** *slay thou*; **tēoh,** *pull thou.* **eolh,** *elk*; **holh,** *hollow*; **seolh,** *seal*; **sulh,** *plough*; **wealh,** *foreigner.* **feorh,** *life*; **furh,** *furrow*; **mearh,** *horse.*

Note.—Such forms as late WS. **blēoh,** *colour,* **ēoh,** *yew,* **frēoh,** *free,* beside **blēo, ēo, frēo,** owe their final **h** to the analogy of words like **feoh,** gen. **fēos.**

§ **329.** Medial **χ** disappeared:

1. Before **s** + consonant, as **fȳst** from ***fūχstiz,** *fist*; Nth. **se(i)sta,** *sixth,* beside WS. **siexta, syxta** which was a new formation from the cardinal; **sester** (Lat. **sextārius**), *vessel, pitcher, jar*; **þīsl** beside older **þīxl** (OHG. **dīhsala**), *wagon-pole*; **wæsma, wǣstm,** *growth,* beside **weaxan** (OHG. **wahsan**), *to grow.* But the **χ** remained in **χs** when it arose from vowel syncope, as **siehst,** *thou seest*; **hīehsta** from ***χauχist-,** *highest.*

2. Between a vowel and a following liquid or nasal, as **betwēonan, betwēonum,** *between,* cp. Goth. **tweihnái,** *two each*; **ēorod** from ***eohrād,** *troop*; **fīol, fēol** (OHG. **fīhala**),

*file*; **hēla** from ***hōhila,** *heel*; **lǣne** (OS. **lēhni**), *transitory*; **lēoma,** *ray of light*, cp. Goth. **liuhaþ,** *light*; **stīele** from ***staχlja-,** *steel* (§ **71**); **þwēal** (Goth. **þwahl**), *washing, bath*; masc. acc. sing. **wōne** beside nom. **wōh,** *perverse, bad*; **ȳmest** (Goth. **áuhmists**), *highest*; and similarly in compounds, as **hēalic,** *lofty*, **hēanes,** *height*, beside **hēah,** *high*; **nēalǣcan,** *to draw nigh*, **nēalic,** *near*, **nēawest,** *nearness*, beside **nēah,** *near*.

3. Between a liquid and a following vowel, as **fēolan** (Goth. **filhan**), *to penetrate, hide*; **þȳrel** from ***þurχil,** *opening, aperture*; sing. gen. **ēoles, fēares, fēores, hōles, mēares, sēoles, wēales,** beside nom. **eolh,** *elk*, **fearh,** *pig*, **feorh,** *life*, **holh,** *hole*, **mearh,** *horse*, **seolh,** *seal*, **wealh,** *foreigner*. See §§ **64,** Note 1; **66,** Note 3; **84,** Note 1; **106,** Note.

4. Between vowels, as **ēa** (OHG. **aha**), *water, river*; **ēam** (OHG. **ōheim**), *uncle*; **ēar** (Nth. **æhher,** OHG. **ahir**), *ear of corn*; **flēan** from ***fleahan,** older ***flahan,** *to flay*; and similarly **lēan,** *to blame*; **slēan** (Goth. **slahan**), *to slay*; **þwēan** (Goth. **þwahan**), *to wash*; **flēon** (OHG. **fliohan**), *to flee*; **fōn** (Goth. **fāhan**), *to seize*; **hōn** (Goth. **hāhan**), *to hang*; **līon, lēon** (OHG. **līhan**), *to lend*; **nēar** from ***nēahur,** *near*; **sēon** from ***seohan,** older ***sehan** (OHG. **sehan**), *to see*; **sīon, sēon** (OHG. **sīhan**), *to strain*; **slā** beside older **slāhæ** (OHG. **slēha**), *sloe*; **swēor** (OHG. **swehur**), *father-in-law*; **tā** beside older **tāhæ** (OHG. **zēha**), *toe*; **tēar** (Nth. **tæhher,** OHG. **zahar**), *tear*; **þīon, þēon** (Goth. **þeihan**), *to thrive*; sing. gen. **fēos, plēos,** beside nom. **feoh,** *cattle, property*, **pleoh,** *danger*; pl. nom. **hēa** from ***hēahe,** beside sing. **hēah,** *high*. In Anglian loss of **h** and contraction took place earlier than the syncope of **i(e)**, as **flīþ** from ***flīhiþ,** *he flees*, **fœ̄þ,** *he seizes*, **sīs(t)** from ***sihis,** *thou seest*, **sīþ** from ***sihiþ,** *he sees*, **hēsta** from ***hēhista,** *highest*, **nēsta** from ***nēhista,** *nearest*, beside WS. **flīehþ, fēhþ, siehst, siehþ, hīehsta, nīehsta.** See §§ **70, 87, 139, 141.**

# ACCIDENCE

## CHAPTER XI

### NOUNS

§ **330.** In OE. as in the oldest periods of the other Germanic languages, nouns are divided into two great classes, according as the stem originally ended in a vowel or a consonant, cp. the similar division of nouns in Sanskrit, Latin and Greek. Nouns whose stems originally ended in a vowel belong to the vocalic or so-called strong declension. Those whose stems originally ended in **-n** belong to the weak declension. All other consonantal stems will be put together under the general heading, 'Minor Declensions.'

§ **331.** Owing to the loss of final short vowels, and consonants, in prehistoric OE. (§§ **211–16**), several different kinds of stems regularly fell together in the nom. and acc. singular, so that, from the point of view of OE., the nom. and acc. singular end in consonants, and we are only able to classify such stems either by starting out from prim. Germanic, or from the plural, or from a comparison with the other old Germanic languages; thus the OE. nom. and acc. singular of **dæg,** *day*; **word,** *word*; **dǣl,** *part*; **hand,** *hand*; **lamb,** *lamb*, correspond to prim. Germanic ***đagaz, *đagan,** older **-os, -om**; ***wurđan,** older **-om**; ***đailiz, *đailin,** older **-is, -im**; ***χanđuz** (Goth. **handus**), ***χanđun** (Goth. **handu**), older **-us, -um**; ***lambaz,** older **-os** (cp. Lat. **genus,** gen. **generis**). The original distinction between the nom. and acc. singular of masculine and feminine nouns had disappeared in the oldest period of the English language except in the **ō**- and the **n**-stems. And the original distinction between the nom. and acc. plural of masculine and feminine nouns had also disappeared, as nom. acc. **dagas**, *days*, **ēste**, *favours*, **suna**, *sons*, but Goth. nom. **dagōs**, **ansteis**, **sunjus**; acc. **dagans**, **anstins**, **sununs**; **guman**, *men*, prim. Germanic nom. ***ʒumaniz**, acc. ***ʒuma-nunz**; **fēt**, *feet*, prim. Germanic nom. ***fōtiz**, acc. Goth. **fōtuns**. In like manner the original case endings of the **n**-stems, with the exception of the nom. singular and the gen. and dat. plural, had also disappeared in the oldest English, so that the element which originally formed part of the stem came to be regarded as a case ending (§§ **211–15**), cp. the similar process in the plural of the neuter **-os**-stems (§§ **419–20**). Before attempting the OE. declensions from a philological point of view, the student should master the chapter on the vowels of unaccented syllables, because it is impossible to restate in this chapter all the details dealt with there.

§ **332**. OE. nouns have two numbers: singular and plural; three genders: masculine, feminine, and neuter, as in the other old Germanic languages from which the gender of nouns in OE. does not materially differ; five cases: Nominative, Accusative, Genitive, Dative, and Instrumental. The dat. is generally used for the instr. in OE., so that this case is omitted in the paradigms, see § **334**, Note. The vocative is like the nominative. The nom. and acc. plural are always alike; in those declensions which would regularly have different forms for the nom. and acc., the acc. disappeared and the nom. was used in its stead. Traces of an old locative occur in what is called the uninflected dat. singular of **hām**, *home*. In Northumbrian both the declension and gender of nouns fluctuated considerably as compared with the other OE. dialects.

## A. The Vocalic or Strong Declension.

### 1. The a-declension.

§ **333**. The **a**-declension comprises masculine and neuter nouns only, and corresponds to the Latin and Greek **o**-declension (Lat. masc. **-us**, neut. **-um**, Gr. *-ος*, *-ον*), for which reason it is sometimes called the **o**-declension. The **a**-declension is divided into pure **a**-stems, **ja**-stems, and **wa**-stems.

#### *a*. Pure a-stems.

§ **334**. *Masculine.*

| | | | |
|---|---|---|---|
| Sing. | | | |
| Nom. Acc. | **stān**, *stone* | **dæg**, *day* | **mearh**, *horse* |
| Gen. | **stānes** | **dæges** | **mēares** |
| Dat. | **stāne** | **dæge** | **mēare** |
| Plur. | | | |
| Nom. Acc. | **stānas** | **dagas** | **mēaras** |
| Gen. | **stāna** | **daga** | **mēara** |
| Dat. | **stānum** | **dagum** | **mēarum** |

Note.—The gen. sing. ended in **-æs** in the oldest period of the language, and in late OE. occasionally in **-as**, **-ys**. The oldest ending of the dat. sing. is **-æ**. The dat. sing. is generally used for the instrumental, so that this case is omitted in the paradigms. In the oldest period of the language the instrumental (originally a locative) ended in **-i**, later **-y**, and corresponded to the Gr. loc. ending **οἴκ-ει**, *at home*, not to **οἴκ-οι** which would have become **-e** in OE. as in the dat. (§ **217**). In late OE. the dat. pl. ended in **-un**, **-on**, **-an** (§ **284**).

The prim. Germanic torms of **dæg** were: Sing. nom. ***đaʒaz**, acc. ***đaʒan**, gen. ***đaʒesa** or ***đaʒasa** (with pronominal ending, § **465**), dat. ***đaʒai**, instr. ***đaʒī**; Plural nom. ***đaʒōz** (cp. Goth. **dagōs**), acc. ***đaʒanz** (cp. Goth. **dagans**), gen. ***đaʒō̃n** (cp. Gr. *θεῶν*, *of gods*), dat. ***đaʒomiz**

(§ **218**, 1). From what has been said in chapter VI on the vowels of unaccented syllables it will be seen that all the forms of the singular and plural, except the nom. acc. pl., are regularly developed from the corresponding prim. Germanic forms. The regular nom. pl. ending corresponding to Goth. **-ōs** would be **-e** (cp. § **217**). The pl. ending **-as**, OS. **-os**, **-as**, beside OHG. **-a**, has never been satisfactorily explained. The most probable explanation is that it represents the ending of nouns which originally had the accent on the ending like Skr. **gharmás**, *heat* = Gr. θερμός, *hot*, and that this ending then came to be used also for nouns which originally had the accent on the stem. That some nouns had the accent on the ending in prim. Germanic is proved by such words as OE. **cēosan**, *to choose*, beside **cyre** from ***kuzís** (§ **252**), *choice*, which at a later period shifted the accent and dropped the final **-s** (? **-z**) after the analogy of nouns which originally had the accent on the stem. Upon this supposition the ending **-as** would regularly correspond to prim. Germanic pl. nom. **-ṓs** or acc. **-áns**. In like manner is to be explained the retention of the final **-s** in the second pers. sing. of the present tense of strong verbs in the West Germanic languages, cp. OE. **nimes(t)**, OS. OHG. **nimis**, beside Goth. **nimis**, *thou takest* (§ **476**). The usual explanation that **-as** corresponds to an early Aryan double plural ending **-āsas** from older **-ōses** with **-es** from the consonant stems, is not in accordance with our present knowledge of the history of short vowels in final syllables in the oldest period of the various Germanic languages. An original ending **-ōses** would have become **-or** in OE. It is possible, however, that the **-as** is a prim. OE. shortened pronominal form representing the **-ās** in **þās** (§ **466**), just as prim. Germanic had the pronominal ending of the gen. singular from the simple demonstrative pronoun, which accounts for the preservation of the final **-s** in both cases. For a similar pronominal ending of the nom. plural of these stems, cp. Lat. **lupī**, Gr. *λύκοι* with **-ī**, **-oi** = OE. **-ā** in **þā**, and Goth. **-ái** in **þái** (§ **465**).

§ **335**. Like **stān** are declined by far the greater majority of monosyllabic **a**-stems, as **ǣl**, *eel*; **ād**, *funeral pile*; **āþ**, *oath*; **bæst**, *bast*; **bār**, *boar*; **bāt**, *boat*; **bēag**, *ring, bracelet*; **bēam**, *tree*; **beard**, *beard*; **bearm**, *bosom*; **bēod**, *table*; **beorg**, *hill*; **beorn**, *warrior*; **bōg**, *bough*; **bolt**, *bolt*; **borg**, *pledge*; **brǣþ**, *odour*; **brand**, *firebrand*; **brōm**, *broom* (*the plant*); **būc**, *stomach*; **camb**, *comb*; **cēac**, *jug*; **cēap**, *price*; **cēol**, *ship*; **ceorl**, *churl*; **clām** (NE. dial. **cloam**), *mud*; **clāþ**, *cloth*; **clūt**, *patch*; **cniht**, *boy*; **cræft**, *skill, strength*; **cwealm**, *death*; **dōm**, *doom*; **drēam**, *joy, revelry*; **dweorg**, *dwarf*; **earm**, *arm*; **earn**, *eagle*; **eorl**, *nobleman*; **fisc**, *fish*; **flēam**, *flight*; **forsc**, *frog*; **forst**, *frost*; **fox**, *fox*; **gang**, *going*; **gāst**, *spirit*; **gēac**, *cuckoo*; **geard**, *yard*; **gielp**, *boasting*; **hæft**, *captive*; **hām**, *home*; **healm**, *haulm*; **heals**, *neck*; **helm**, *helmet*; **hlæst**, *burden*; **hlāf**, *loaf*; **hōf**, *hoof*; **hrēam**, *cry, shout, uproar*; **hrīm**, *rime*; **hring**, *ring*; **hund**, *dog*; **hwelp**, *whelp*; **lāst**, *footprint*; **mæst**, *mast*; **mōr**, *moor*; **mūþ**, *mouth*; **rāp**, *rope*; **rūm**, *room*; **sceaft**, *shaft*; **sēam**, *seam*; **stōl**, *stool*; **storm**, *storm*; **strēam**, *stream*; **torn**, *grief*; **þanc**, *thought*; **þēof**, *thief*; **þorp**, **þrop**, *farm, village*; **weg**, *way*; **wer**, *man*; **wulf**, *wolf*.

See § **259**, 1 on nouns whose stems ended in double consonants: **bucc**, *buck*; **cocc**, *cock*; **codd**, *cod, husk*; **coss**, *kiss*; **cnoll**, *knoll*; **cropp**, *sprout*; **hnæpp**, *cup*; **hwamm**, *corner*; **pott**, *pot*; **sceatt**, *property, money*; **smocc**, *smock*; **swamm**, *fungus*; **weall**, *wall*.

§ **336**. Like **dæg** are declined **pæþ**, *path*; **stæf**, *staff*; **hwæl**, *whale*, see §§ **54**, **57**. **mǣg**, *kinsman*, pl. **māgas** (§ **120**) beside **mǣgas** with **ǣ** from the singular.

§ **337**. Like **mearh** are declined **ealh**, *temple*; **eolh**, *elk*; **fearh**, *pig, boar*; **healh**, *corner*; **sealh**, *willow*; **seolh**, *seal* (*animal*); **wealh**, *foreigner*, see § **149**. **scōh**, *shoe*, gen. **scōs**, dat. **scō**, pl. **scōs**, gen. **scōna** with **-na** after the analogy of the **n**-stems (§ **400**), dat. **scōm, scōum**, see § **139**; and similarly **slōh** (also fem. and neut.), *slough, mire*; **eoh** (also neut.), *horse*, gen. **eōs**, dat. **ēo**. **horh** (also neut.), *dirt*, gen. **horwes**, dat. **horwe**, beside **hōres, hōre**; pl. **horwu** (neut.) beside **hōras**, see § **239**.

§ **338**. SING.

| | | | | |
|---|---|---|---|---|
| Nom. Acc. | **cyning**, *king* | **engel**, *angel* | **fugol**, *bird* | **heofon**, *heaven* |
| Gen. | **cyninges** | **engles** | **fugles** | **heofones** |
| Dat. | **cyninge** | **engle** | **fugle** | **heofone** |
| PLUR. | | | | |
| Nom. Acc. | **cyningas** | **englas** | **fuglas** | **heofenas** |
| Gen. | **cyninga** | **engla** | **fugla** | **heofena** |
| Dat. | **cyningum** | **englum** | **fuglum** | **heofenum** |

The vowel in the medial syllable generally disappeared in the inflected forms of dissyllabic words when the first syllable was long and the second short. It also generally disappeared when the first syllable was short and the second syllable ended in vocalic **l, m, n** in West Germanic (§ **219**). On the retention or the loss of the medial vowel in the inflected forms of dissyllabic words, see § **221**.

§ **339**. Like **cyning** are declined **æcer**, *field*; **cocer**, *quiver*; **hærfest**, *autumn*; **hengest**, *horse*. **brīdels**, *bridle*; **fǣtels**, *vessel, tub*; for other examples of nouns ending in **-els**, see § **598**. **æþeling**, *prince*; **cnæpling**, *youth*; **gædeling**, *companion*; **lȳtling**, *child*; for other examples of nouns ending in **-ling**, see § **607**.

§ **340**. Like **engel** are declined **ǣled**, *fire*; **angel**, *fish-hook*; **āþum**, *son-in-law*; **bealdor**, *prince*; **bīetel**, *mallet*; **blōstm**, *blossom*; **bolster** (also neut.), *bolster*; **bōsm**, *bosom*; **brēmel**, *bramble*; **dēofol**, *devil*; **dryhten**, *lord*; **ealdor**, *prince*; **finger**, *finger*; **hleahtor**, *laughter*; **māþum**, *treasure*; **morgen**, *morning*; **ōfer**, *shore*; **þȳmel**, *thimble, thumbstall*; **wæstm**, *growth*.

**botm,** *bottom*; **ellen** (also neut.), *zeal, courage, strength*; **fæþm,** *embrace*; **fugol,** *bird, fowl*; **hæg(e)l, hagol,** *hail*; **ofen,** *oven*; **nægl,** *nail*; **reg(e)n,** *rain*; **þeg(e)n,** *thane*.

But nouns like **bulluc,** *bullock*; **cassuc,** *sedge*; **langoþ,** *longing* (for other examples of nouns ending in **-oþ, -aþ,** see § **595**); **mattuc,** *mattock*; **pearroc,** *park*, generally retain the medial vowel.

§ **341.** Like **heofon** are declined **bydel,** *beadle*; **cradol,** *cradle*; **daroþ,** *dart, spear*; **eodor,** *enclosure*; **eofor,** *boar*; **hafoc, heafoc,** *hawk*; **hamor,** *hammer*; **heorot,** *stag, hart*; **metod,** *Creator*; **rodor,** *sky*; **sadol,** *saddle*; **stapol,** *pillar*; **þunor,** *thunder*. On the variation of the vowel in the medial syllable, see § **222**.

§ **342.** *Neuter.*

| | | | |
|---|---|---|---|
| SING. | | | |
| Nom. Acc. | **word,** *word* | **hof,** *dwelling* | **fæt,** *vessel* |
| Gen. | **wordes** | **hofes** | **fætes** |
| Dat. | **worde** | **hofe** | **fæte** |
| PLUR. | | | |
| Nom. Acc. | **word** | **hofu, -o** | **fatu, -o** |
| Gen. | **worda** | **hofa** | **fata** |
| Dat. | **wordum** | **hofum** | **fatum** |

The neuter **a**-stems had the same endings as the masculine except in the nom. and acc. plural. The prim. Germanic ending of the nom. acc. plural was **-ō** which became **-u** and then regularly disappeared after long stem-syllables (§ **215**). In the nouns with short stem-syllables the **-u** became **-o** at an early period, and then in late OE. **-a** (§ **215,** Note). In late OE. the long stems often had **-u** in the plural after the analogy of the short stems.

§ **343.** Like **word** are declined a large number of monosyllables with long stem, as **ār,** *brass*; **bǣl,** *funeral pile*; **bān,** *bone*; **bearn,** *child*; **bēor,** *beer*; **blōd,** *blood*; **bold,** *dwelling*; **bord,** *board*; **brēost,** *breast*; **corn,** *corn*; **dēor,** *wild animal*; **dūst,** *dust*; **fām,** *foam*; **fearn,** *fern*; **feax,** *hair*; **fleax,** *flax*; **folc,** *folk*; **gēar,** *year*; **gearn,** *yarn*; **gield,** *payment*; **gold,** *gold*; **hord** (also masc.), *treasure, hoard*; **horn,** *horn*; **hors,** *horse*; **hrēod,** *reed*; **hrīs,** *twig*; **hūs,** *house*; **īs,** *ice*; **lām,** *clay*; **land,** *land*; **lēaf,** *leaf*; **lēan,** *reward*; **lēoþ,** *song, poem*; **līc,** *body*; **līn,** *flax, linen*; **mān,** *crime*; **mōd,** *mind, courage*; **morþ,** *murder*; **nēat,** *ox*; **nest,** *nest*; **nīþ,** *enmity*; **sār,** *pain*; **scēap,** *sheep*; **seax,** *knife*; **sweord,** *sword*; **tōl,** *tool*; **þing,** *thing*; **weorc,** *work*; **weorþ,** *worth, price*; **wīf,** *woman*. And similarly words with a prefix, as **behāt,** *promise*; **gebeorc,** *barking*. See § **259,** 1 on nouns whose stems ended in double consonants: **fell,** *skin*; **full,** *cup*; **toll,** *tax, toll.*

§ **344.** Like **hof** are declined **broc,** *affliction*; **broþ,** *broth*; **ceaf,** *chaff*; **col,** *coal*; **dor,** *door*; **geoc,** *yoke*; **god,** *god* (*heathen*); **hol,** *hole*; **loc,** *lock*; **lot,** *deceit*; **sol,** *mud*; **spor,** *track*. And similarly words with a prefix, as **bebod, gebod,** *command.* **geat** (§ **72**), *gate*, pl. **gatu** beside **geatu** with **ea** from the singular.

Nouns which have **e, i** in the stem originally had **u-, o/a-**umlaut in the plural, as **gebeodu,** *prayers*, gen. **gebeoda,** dat. **gebeodum**; and similarly **geset,** *seat, dwelling*; **gesprec,** *speaking*, see § **48.** **cliofu,** *cliffs*, gen. **cliofa,** dat. **cliofum**; and similarly **brim,** *sea*; **hlid,** *lid*; **lim,** *limb*; **scip,** *ship*; **twig,** *twig*; **geflit,** *strife*; **gewrit,** *writing, letter.* **friþ** (OHG. **fridu**), *peace*, and **liþ** (Goth. **liþus**), *limb*, were originally masc. **u-**stems. See §§ **101-2.**

§ **345.** Like **fæt** are declined **bæc,** *back*; **bæþ,** *bath*; **blæc,** *ink*; **blæd,** *leaf*; **bræs,** *brass*; **cræt,** *cart*; **dæl,** *dale*; **fæc,** *period of time, space*; **fær,** *journey*; **fnæd, fnæs,** *fringe*; **gærs** from older **græs** (§ **280**), *grass*; **glæs,** *glass*; **græf,** *grave, cave*; **hæf,** *sea*; **sæp,** *sap*; **scræf,** *cave*; **swæþ,** *track*; **træf,** *tent*; **þæc,** *thatch, roof*; **wæd,** *water, sea*; **wæl,** *slaughter.* See §§ **54, 57.**

§ **346.** **flāh,** *fraud*, gen. **flās,** dat. **flā**; **þēoh,** *thigh*, gen. **þēos,** dat. **þēo,** pl. **þēo,** gen. **þēo** or **þēona** with **-na** after the analogy of the **n**-stems (§ **406**), dat. **þēom**; **pleoh**, *danger*, gen. **plēos**, dat. **plēo**, pl. **plēo**; **holh**, *hollow*, *hole*, gen. **hōles**, dat. **hōle**, pl. **holh**, see § **149**. **feoh**, *cattle*, originally belonged to the **u**-declension (§ **399**).

§ **347**. SING.

| | | | |
|---|---|---|---|
| Nom. Acc. | **tungol**, *star* | **wæter**, *water* | **hēafod**, *head* |
| Gen. | **tungles** | **wæteres** | **hēafdes** |
| Dat. | **tungle** | **wætere** | **hēafde** |
| PLUR. | | | |
| Nom. Acc. | **tungol** | **wæter** | **hēafodu** |
| Gen. | **tungla** | **wætera** | **hēafda** |
| Dat. | **tunglum** | **wæterum** | **hēafdum** |

Dissyllabic words which in West Germanic ended in vocalic **l**, **n**, **r** (§ **219**) syncopated the medial vowel in the gen. and dat. sing. and plural and lost the final **-u** in the nom. and acc. plural when the stem-syllable was long. So that the nom. acc. sing. and plural became alike just as in the monosyllabic long stems. Original trisyllabic words (§ **223**), and also dissyllabic words which in West Germanic ended in vocalic **n**, **r**, retained the medial vowel in the gen. and dat. sing. and plural, but lost the final **-u** in the nom. and acc. plural when the stem-syllable was short. Original trisyllabic words syncopated the medial vowel in the gen. and dat. sing. and plural, but retained the medial vowel and the final **-u** in the nom. and acc. plural when the stem-syllable was long. See §§ **216**, **223**.

NOTE.—In the later period of the language there was great fluctuation in the formation of the plural and in the loss or retention of the medial vowel, as nom. acc. plural **tunglu**, **wæt(e)ru**, **hēafdu** beside older **tungol**, **wæter**, **hēafodu**; gen. sing. **wætres** beside older **wæteres**.

§ **348**. Like **tungol** are declined **ātor**, *poison*; **bēacen**, *beacon*; **cnōsl**, *race*, *progeny*; **fācen**, *deceit*; **fōdor**, *fodder*; **spātl**, *saliva*; **tācen**, *token*; **wǣpen**, *weapon*; **wolcen**, *cloud*; **wuldor**, *glory*; **wundor**, *wonder*.

§ **349.** Like **wæter** are declined **brægen,** *brain*; **gamen,** *game, sport*; **leger,** *couch*; **mægen,** *strength*; **ofet,** *fruit*; **reced,** *house, hall*; **weder,** *weather*; **weorod, werod,** *troop*, pl. **weredu** (§ **222**) beside **werod. setl,** *seat*, pl. **setlu** beside **setl.**

§ **350.** Like **hēafod** are declined **clīewen, clīwen,** *ball of thread, clew*; **mǣden, mægden,** *maiden*; **nīeten,** *animal.*

### *b.* ja-STEMS.

§ **351.** *Masculine.*

| | | |
|---|---|---|
| SING. | | |
| Nom. Acc. | **secg,** *man* | **ende,** *end* |
| Gen. | **secges** | **endes** |
| Dat. | **secge** | **ende** |
| PLUR. | | |
| Nom. Acc. | **secg(e)as** | **endas** |
| Gen. | **secg(e)a** | **enda** |
| Dat. | **secg(i)um** (§ **319**) | **endum** |

It is necessary to distinguish between those stems which were originally long and those which became long by the West Germanic doubling of consonants (§ **254**). The **j** caused umlaut of the stem-vowel and then disappeared in the inflected forms except after **r** (§§ **271–2**). When the **j** came to stand finally after the loss of prim. Germanic **-az, -an** it became vocalized to **i** which remained in the oldest period of the language, and then later became **e** (§§ **215,** Note, **274**), cp. **here,** *army*, **ende,** *end*, beside Goth. acc. **hari, andi.** The OE. forms with double consonants in the nom. and accusative singular are all new formations from the inflected forms. The regular forms would be ***sege,** *man*; ***dyne,** *noise* = Goth. acc. ***sagi, *duni.**

§ **352.** Like **secg** are declined **bridd,** *young bird*; **cnyll,** *knell*; **dyn(n),** *noise*; **hlyn(n),** *loud sound*; **hrycg,** *back, ridge*; **hyll,** *hill*; **mæcg** (§ **55,** Note 3), *man*; **mycg,** *midge*; **wecg,** *wedge*. See § **259,** 1.

§ **353**. The j (written **i, g, ig**; also **ige** before a guttural vowel, § **268**) remained medially after **r** preceded by a short vowel, as nom. acc. **here,** *army*; gen. **heries, herges, heriges**; dat. **herie, herge, herige**; pl. nom. acc. **herias, hergas, herigas, herigeas**; gen. **heria, heriga, herigea**; dat. **herium, herigum.** Forms without j also occur occasionally, as gen. **heres,** dat. **here,** pl. **heras.**

§ **354**. Like **ende** are declined **esne,** *servant*; **hierde,** *shepherd*; **hwǣte,** *wheat*; **lǣce,** *physician*; **mēce,** *sword*; and the nomina agentis, as **bæcere,** *baker*; **biddere,** *petitioner*; **bōcere,** *scribe*; **sǣdere,** *sower*; for further examples see § **602**.

§ **355**. *Neuter.*

| | | | |
|---|---|---|---|
| SING. | | | |
| Nom. Acc. | **cyn(n),** *race* | **wīte,** *punishment* | **wēsten,** *desert* |
| Gen. | **cynnes** | **wītes** | **wēstennes** |
| Dat. | **cynne** | **wīte** | **wēstenne** |
| PLUR. | | | |
| Nom. Acc. | **cyn(n)** | **wītu** | **wēstennu** |
| Gen. | **cynna** | **wīta** | **wēstenna** |
| Dat. | **cynnum** | **wītum** | **wēstennum** |

As in the masc. **ja**-stems it is necessary to distinguish between those stems which were originally long and those which became long by the West Germanic doubling of consonants (§ **254**). The neuter **ja**-stems had the same endings as the masculine except in the nom. acc. plural. The nom. acc. plural ended in prim. Germanic in **-jō** which became **-ju** in prim. OE. The j regularly disappeared after causing umlaut of the preceding vowel. And then the **-u** being preceded by a long syllable also disappeared (§ **215**). The nom. acc. pl. of the originally short stems is regularly developed from the prim. Germanic form, as **cyn(n)** from ***kunjō.** But the **-u** in the originally long stems and in words containing a suffix is not the preservation of the prim. OE. **-u**. Such nouns owe their final **-u** to the analogy of the nom. acc. pl. of short **a**-stems (§ **342**). That forms like **wītu, wēstennu** are new formations is proved by the simple fact that from a prim. Germanic point of view these nouns ought to have the same ending in OE. as the nom. singular of the **jō**-stems (§ **374**). The OE. forms with double consonants in the nom. acc. singular are all new formations from the inflected forms, as **cyn(n), bedd, nett** for ***cyne, *bede, *nete** = Goth. **kuni, badi, nati**, see § **274**. On the final double consonants in the nom. acc. singular, see § **259**, 1. In late OE. the double consonants in words containing a suffix were generally simplified in the inflected forms, and the medial vowel was also occasionally syncopated, as gen. **wēstenes**, pl. **wēstenu**, beside **wēstnu**.

§ **356**. Like **cyn(n)** are declined **bedd**, *bed*; **bill**, *sword*; **denn**, *den*; **flett**, *floor*; **giedd**, *song*; **nebb**, *beak*; **nett**, *net*; **ribb**, *rib*; **webb**, *web*; **wedd**, *pledge*; **wicg**, *horse*; **witt**, *understanding*.

§ **357**. Like **wīte** are declined **ǣrende**, *errand*; **fēþe**, *walking, power of motion*; **ierfe**, *inheritance*; **ierre**, *anger*; **rīce**, *kingdom*; **rȳne**, *mystery*; **stīele**, *steel*; **wǣge**, *cup*; nouns with the prefix **ge-**, as **gefilde**, *plain*; **gefylce**, *troop*; **getīeme**, *yoke* (*of oxen*), *team*; **getimbre**, *building*; **gemierce**, *boundary*; **gewǣde**, *dress, clothing*; **geþīode, geþēode**, *language*. **flicce**, prim. Germanic ***flikkja-**, *flitch*; **stycce**, prim. Germanic ***stukkja-**, *piece*. See § **270**, Note, on nouns like **hīeg** (Goth. **hawi**), *hay*, **hīew, hīw** (Goth. **hiwi**), *shape, appearance*, **glīg, glīw** (Goth. ***gliwi**), *glee*, gen. **hīeges, hīewes (hīowes), glīges, glīwes**.

§ **358**. Like **wēsten** are declined **fæsten(n)**, *fortress*, cp. § **600**; **bærnet(t)**, *arson*; **nierwet(t)**, *narrowness*; **sǣwet(t)**, *sowing*; **þēowet(t)**, *slavery*; for further examples, see § **604**. To this class probably also belong the diminutives in **-incel**, which generally syncopate the **e** in the inflected forms, as **cofincel**, *little chamber*, gen. **cofincles**; and similarly **hæftincel**, *slave*; **hūsincel**, *little house*; **scipincel**, *little ship*; **sūlincel**, *small furrow*; for further examples, see § **606**. **fiþere**, *wing*.

c. **wa**-STEMS.

§ **359**. *Masculine.*

| | | |
|---|---|---|
| SING. | | |
| Nom. Acc. | **bearu, -o**, *grove* | **þēo**, *servant* |
| Gen. | **bearwes** | **þeowes** |
| Dat. | **bearwe** | **þeowe** |
| PLUR. | | |
| Nom. Acc. | **bearwas** | **þeowas** |
| Gen. | **bearwa** | **þeowa** |
| Dat. | **bearwum** | **þeowum** |

In the inflected forms the masc. **wa**-stems have the same endings as the pure **a**-stems. After the loss of prim. Germanic **-az, -an** in the nom. and acc. singular, the **w** being final became vocalized to **-u** which remained after short vowels followed by a consonant, but with a preceding short vowel it combined to form a diphthong (§§ **264–5**); thus prim. Germanic ***ƀarwaz, -an, *þewaz, -an** regularly became **bearu** (later **bearo**), **þēo**. After a long vowel the **-u** regularly disappeared, as in **snā**, *snow*, from ***snaiwaz, -an**. At a later period the **w** in the inflected forms was levelled out into the nom. acc. singular, whence **þēow, snāw** beside older **þēo, snā**. And then from **þēow** there was often formed a new gen. **þēowes** beside the regular form **þeowes** (§ **265**). On forms like gen. **bearuwes** beside **bearwes**, see § **220**.

§ **360**. Like **þēo, þēow** are declined **bēaw**, *gadfly*; **dēaw** (also neut.), *dew*; **lārēow** from **lār + þēow**, *teacher*; **lāttēow** from **lād + þēow**, *leader*; **þēaw**, *custom*; **brīw**

(Goth. ***breiws**), *pottage, porridge*; **gīw, gēow**, *griffin, vulture*; **īw, īow, ēow**, *yew*; **slīw** (Goth. ***sleiws**), *tench (a fish)*.

§ **361**. *Neuter.*

| | | |
|---|---|---|
| SING. | | |
| Nom. Acc. | **bealu, -o**, *evil* | **cnēo**, *knee* |
| Gen. | **bealwes** | **cneowes** |
| Dat. | **bealwe** | **cneowe** |
| PLUR. | | |
| Nom. Acc. | **bealu, -o** | **cnēo** |
| Gen. | **bealwa** | **cneowa** |
| Dat. | **bealwum** | **cneowum** |

The neuter **wa**-stems have the same endings as the masculine except in the nom. acc. plural. What has been said in § **359** about the history of the **w** also applies to the neuters. It should be noted that the nom. acc. plural **bealu, cnēo** are from older ***beal(w)u**, ***kne(w)u** (§ **266**), whereas the nom. acc. sing. **bealu, cnēo** are from older ***bealw-**, ***knew-** (§ **265**). On the svarabhakti vowel in the inflected forms like gen. **bealuwes** beside **bealwes**, see § **220**. Besides the regular nom. acc. pl. **cnēo**, there also occurs **cnēow** with **w** from the inflected forms; and also **cnĕowu** with **-u** from forms like **bealu**. In late OE. the pl. also ended in **-wa**, see § **215**, Note.

§ **362**. Like **bealu** are declined **c(w)udu**, *cud*; **teoru**, *tar*; **meolu, melu**, *meal, flour*; **searu**, *device*; **smeoru**, *fat*.

§ **363**. Like **cnēo, cnēow** are also declined **anclēow** (orig. masc.), *ankle*; **bēow**, *barley*; **gehlōw**, *lowing, bellowing*; **gehrēow**, *lamentation*; **hlēo(w)**, *protection, covering*; **sēaw** (also masc.), *juice*; **strēa(w)**, *straw*; **trēo(w)**, *tree*.

### 2. THE Ō-DECLENSION.

§ **364**. The **ō**-declension contains feminine nouns only, and corresponds to the Latin and Greek **ā**-declension, for which reason it is sometimes called the **ā**-declension. The **ō**-declension is divided into pure **ō**-stems, **jō**-stems, and **wō**-stems.

### *a.* Pure ō-stems.

§ **365.** Sing.

| | | |
|---|---|---|
| Nom. | **giefu, -o,** *gift* | **ār,** *honour* |
| Acc. | **giefe** | **āre** |
| Gen. | **giefe** | **āre** |
| Dat. | **giefe** | **āre** |
| Plur. | | |
| Nom. Acc. | **giefa, -e** | **āra, -e** |
| Gen. | **giefa, (-ena)** | **āra, (-na, -ena)** |
| Dat. | **giefum** | **ārum** |

The prim. Germanic forms were: Sing. nom. ***ȝeƀō**, acc. ***ȝeƀōn** (cp. Gr. χώρᾱν), gen. ***ȝeƀō̃z** (Goth. **gibōs**), dat. ***ȝeƀai** (Goth. **gibái**); Plur. nom. acc. ***ȝeƀō̃z** (Goth. **gibōs**), gen. ***ȝeƀō̃n** (Goth. **gibō**), dat. ***ȝeƀōmiz** (Goth. **gibōm**). The acc. gen. and dat. sing. and the nom. acc. pl. regularly fell together in **-æ** in prehistoric OE. (§ **217**). The **-æ** remained in the oldest period of the language and then later regularly became **-e**. In the nom. sing. the **-ō** became **-u** and then regularly disappeared after long stem-syllables (§ **215**). In late OE. the gen. sing. often ended in **-es** after the analogy of the masc. **a**-stems; and sometimes the nom. of the short stems was used for all cases of the singular. The regular ending of the gen. pl. is **-a**, but in late OE. the gen. pl. often ended in **-(e)na** after the analogy of the **n**-stems (§ **403**). On the ending **-um** of the dat. plural, see § **218**, 5. The normally developed ending of the nom. acc. pl. is **-e** which was regularly preserved in the Anglian dialects, whereas **-a** is the usual ending in WS. and Ken. Various attempts have been made to account for the **-a** in the nom. acc. pl. in WS. and Ken., and for the **-a** in the oblique cases of the fem. nouns ending in **-ung** in these dialects. Seeing that the gen. sing. and nom. pl. originally had the same ending **-ō̃z** and that both cases ended in **-æ** in the oldest OE., the **-a** in the nom. pl. cannot be a regular development from older **-æ**. It is sometimes assumed that **-a** is the regular development of prim. Germanic **-ō̃z** in OE., and that what is called the gen. sing. is morphologically the dat., but against this assumption it should be pointed out that in the oldest period of the language the gen. and dat. sing. and nom. plural had all the same ending. The ending **-a** in these dialects is doubtless due to the analogy of the feminine **u**-declension (§ **398**). After the analogy of words like **duru, hand**: pl. **dura, handa,** to words like **giefu, ār** were formed pl. **giefa, āra.** Short stems with **a** often have **æ** beside **a** in the acc. gen. and dat. sing. and nom. acc. pl., as **læþe, ræce,** beside **laþe, race.**

§ **366.** Like **giefu** are declined **caru,** *care*; **coþu,** *disease*; **cwalu,** *violent death*; **daru,** *injury*; **denu,** *valley*; **faru,** *journey*; **hogu,** *solicitude*; **laþu,** *invitation*; **lufu** (also weak), *love*; **nafu,** *nave* (*of wheel*); **notu,** *use*; **racu,** *account, narrative*; **rudu,** *redness*; **sacu,** *strife*; **sagu,** *saw*; **sc(e)amu,** *shame*; **scinu,** *shin*; **scolu,** *troop*; **snoru,** *daughter-in-law*; **stalu,** *theft*; **swaþu,** *track*; **talu,** *tale, number*; **þracu,** *violence, combat*; **waru,** *people*; **wracu,** *revenge*; &c.

§ **367.** Like **ār** are declined a large number of nouns, as **æsp,** *aspen-tree*; **bād,** *pledge*; **bǣr,** *bier*; **beorc,** *birch-tree*; **bōt,** *advantage*; **brōd,** *brood*; **eax,** *axis*; **eaxl,** *shoulder*; **fēol,** *file*; **gād,** *goad*; **glōf,** *glove*; **heall,** *hall*; **heord,** *herd, flock*; **hwīl,** *space of time*; **lād,** *way, journey*; **lāf,** *remnant*; **lār,** *learning*; **lēod,** *nation*; **lind,** *linden, shield*; **mearc,** *boundary*; **mēd, meord,** *reward*; **mund,** *hand*; **rād,** *ride, riding*; **reord,** *voice, language*; **rōd,** *cross*; **rūn,** *secret*; **scand,** *disgrace*; **scofl,** *shovel*; **sealf,** *ointment*; **sorg,** *sorrow*; **stund,** *period of time, hour*; **tang,** *tongs*; **þearf,** *need*; **þēod,** *nation*; **þrāg,** *time, period*; **wamb,** *stomach*;

**weard,** *protection*; **wund,** *wound*; &c. **brū,** *eyebrow,* has nom. acc. pl. **brūa** beside **brūwa,** gen. **brūna,** dat. **brūum** beside **brūwum.**

§ **368.** SING.

| | | |
|---|---|---|
| Nom. | **firen,** *crime* | **sāwol,** *soul* |
| Acc. | **firene** | **sāwle** |
| Gen. | **firene** | **sāwle** |
| Dat. | **firene** | **sāwle** |
| PLUR. | | |
| Nom. Acc. | **firena, -e** | **sāwla, -e** |
| Gen. | **firena** | **sāwla** |
| Dat. | **firenum** | **sāwlum** |

In originally trisyllabic words the final **-u** regularly disappeared in the nom. sing. when the stem and the medial syllable were short, but remained when the stem-syllable was long and the medial syllable short (§ **216**). Then after the analogy of words like **firen,** the final **-u** was also dropped in words like **sāwol.** The medial vowel regularly disappeared in the inflected forms after long stems, but remained after short (§ **221**). The nouns of this class do not have the ending **-(e)na** in the gen. plural.

§ **369.** Like **firen** are declined **bisen, bisn,** *example*; **byden,** *bushel*; **ciefes,** *concubine*; **feter,** *fetter*; **feþer,** *feather*; **netel,** *nettle*; **spinel,** *spindle*; **stefn,** *voice*; but **egenu,** *chaff.*

§ **370.** Like **sāwol** are declined **ādl,** *disease*; **ceaster,** *city, fortress*; **frōfor** (also masc.), *consolation*; **nǣdl,** *needle*; **wōcor,** *increase, usury.*

| | | |
|---|---|---|
| § **371.** Nom. | **strengþu, -o,** *strength* | **leornung,** *learning* |
| Acc. Gen. Dat. | **strengþe** | **leornunge, -a** |

The fem. abstract nouns ending in prim. Germanic **-iþō** (Goth. **-iþa, -ida,** OHG. **-ida**) regularly syncopated the medial **i** (§ **221**) and in the oldest period of the language retained the final **-u** in the nom. (§ **216**). Then at a later period the **-u** (**-o**) was often dropped after the analogy of words like **ār** (§ **367**). At a still later period the nom. with and without the final **-o** came to be used for all cases. The abstract nouns in **-ung** regularly syncopated the final **-u** in the nom. (§ **216**).

§ **372**. Like **strengþu, -o, strengþ** are declined **cȳþþu, cȳþ(þ)**, *native country*; **fǣhþ(u)**, *feud*; **gesǣlþ(u)**, *prosperity*; **hlīewþ(u)**, *shelter*; **mǣgþ(u)**, *family, kindred*; **þīefþ(u)**, *theft*; **wrǣþþ(u)**, *anger, wrath*; for further examples, see § **613**.

§ **373**. Like **leornung** are declined **ǣfnung**, *evening*; **ǣring**, *dawn*; **geþafung**, *consent*; **lēasung**, *falsehood*; **rihtung**, *direction*; **swinsung**, *melody*; **wēnung**, *hope, expectation*; for further examples, see § **615**.

*b*. **jō**-STEMS.

§ **374**. SING.

| | | |
|---|---|---|
| Nom. | **hen(n)**, *hen* | **gierd**, *rod* |
| Acc. | **henne** | **gierde** |
| Gen. | **henne** | **gierde** |
| Dat. | **henne** | **gierde** |
| PLUR. | | |
| Nom. Acc. | **henna, -e** | **gierda, -e** |
| Gen. | **henna** | **gierda** |
| Dat. | **hennum** | **gierdum** |

It is necessary to distinguish between those stems which were originally long and those which became long by the West Germanic doubling of consonants (§ **254**). The j regularly disappeared after causing umlaut of the preceding vowel, and then the **-u** in the nom. sing. being preceded by a long stem also disappeared (§ **215**), so that the endings of the **jō**-stems are the same as the long **ō**-stems except that the gen. pl. never has the ending **-(e)na** (§ **365**). On the final double consonants in the nom. singular, see § **259**, 1.

§ **375**. Like **hen(n)** are declined **benn**, *wound*; **brycg**, *bridge*; **bytt**, *flagon*; **cribb**, *crib*; **crycc**, *crutch*; **ecg**, *edge*;

**hell,** *hell*; **nytt,** *use, profit*; **sciell,** *shell*; **secg,** *sword*; **sibb,** *relationship*; **slecg,** *sledge-hammer*; **synn,** *sin*; **syll,** *sill, threshold*; **wynn,** *joy*. On **hæcc,** *gate, hatch*; **sæcc,** *strife*, see § **55,** Note 3.

§ **376.** Like **gierd** are declined **æx,** *axe*; **bend** (also masc. and neut.), *band*; **blīþs, bliss,** *bliss*; **hild,** *war, battle*; **hind,** *doe*; **līþs, liss,** *favour, kindness*; **milts,** *mercy, kindness*; **nift,** *niece*; **rest,** *rest*; **sprǣc,** *speech, language*; **wrǣc,** *vengeance*; **wylf,** *she-wolf*; **ȳþ,** *wave*. On the **g** in **cǣg,** *key*; **īeg,** *island*, see §§ **270, 272.**

§ **377.**

| | Sing. | Plur. |
|---|---|---|
| Nom. | **byrþen(n),** *burden* | **byrþenna, -e** |
| Acc. | **byrþenne** | **byrþenna, -e** |
| Gen. | **byrþenne** | **byrþenna** |
| Dat. | **byrþenne** | **byrþennum** |

In originally trisyllabic words the final **-u** in the nom. singular also regularly disappeared after the medial syllable which became long by the West Germanic doubling of consonants (§§ **216, 254**). The nouns ending in **-en(n)** sometimes took **-u** again in the nom. sing. after the analogy of the short ō-stems. In late OE. the double consonants were often simplified in the inflected forms.

§ **378.** Like **byrþen(n)** are declined **candel** (Lat. **candēla**), *candle*; **cnēoris(s),** *generation*; **hægtes(s),** *witch*; **biren,** *she-bear*; **fyxen,** *she-fox*; **gyden,** *goddess*; **þyften,** *female servant*; **wiergen,** *she-wolf*; **byrgen,** *tomb*; for further examples, see § **599.** **cōlnes(s),** *coolness*; **swiftnes(s),** *swiftness*; **þrīnes(s),** *trinity*; for further examples, see § **609.** **rǣden(n),** *arrangement, rule*; **hūsrǣden(n),** *household*; for further examples, see § **610.**

Note.—A few words simplified the double consonants at an early period and then added **-u** in the nom. singular after the analogy of the short ō-stems, as **hyrnetu** beside **hyrnet,** *hornet*; **ielfetu,** *swan*.

*c.* WŌ-STEMS.

§ **379.** SING.

| | | |
|---|---|---|
| Nom. | **beadu, -o,** *battle* | **mǣd,** *meadow* |
| Acc. Gen. Dat. | **beadwe** | **mǣdwe** |
| PLUR. | | |
| Nom. Acc. | **beadwa, -e** | **mǣdwa, -e** |
| Gen. | **beadwa** | **mǣdwa** |
| Dat. | **beadwum** | **mǣdwum** |

In the nom. singular the prim. Germanic ending **-wō** regularly became **-wu** (§ **214**), then the **w** disappeared before the **-u** (§ **266**). The **-u** remained after consonants preceded by an original short vowel, but disappeared after consonants preceded by a long vowel (§ **215**). When the **-u** was preceded by **a** it combined with it to form a diphthong, as **clēa** from ***cla(w)u,** *claw,* **þrēa** from ***þra(w)u,** *threat* (§ **75**), pl. nom. acc. **clēa,** dat. **clēam** from ***cla(w)um;** beside the regular nom. sing. forms **clēa, þrēa** new nominatives **clawu, þrawu** were made from the stem-form of the oblique cases. The final **-u** from older **-w** also regularly disappeared after long vowels and diphthongs (§ **215**), but the **w** was restored again from the inflected forms already in the oldest period of the language, as **hrēow,** *repentance*; **stōw,** *place*; **trēow** (§ **90**), *faith, truth.*

In the inflected forms the **wō**-stems had the same endings as the **ō**-stems except that they never had the ending **-(e)na** in the gen. plural. On the svarabhakti vowel in forms like gen. **beaduwe** beside **beadwe,** see § **220.**

§ **380.** Like **beadu** are declined **sinu, sionu,** *sinew*; **sceadu,** *shadow*; and the plurals **frætwa, -e,** *ornaments*; **geatwa, -e,** *armaments, armour.*

§ **381.** Like **mǣd** are declined **blōd(es)lǣs,** *blood-letting, bleeding*; **lǣs,** *pasture.*

### 3. Feminine Abstract Nouns in -īn.

§ **382.** This declension comprises the feminine abstract nouns formed from adjectives, as **brǣdu**, *breadth*: **brād**, *broad*; **strengu**, *strength*: **strang**, *strong*; Goth. **managei**, *multitude*: **manags**, *many*. The nouns of this category had originally the stem-ending **-īn** (§ **614**) and were declined according to the weak declension as in Gothic. The prim. Germanic stem- and case-endings were: Sing. nom. **-īn**, acc. **-īn-un**, gen. **-īn-az** or **-iz**, dat. **-īn-i**; Pl. nom. **-īn-iz**, acc. **-īn-unz**, gen. **-īn-ō̃n**, dat. **-īn-miz.** The **-īn**, **-īn-** regularly became **-i**, **-in-** in prehistoric OE. (§§ **211** (1), **214** (3), **218** (5)), and then the **i** caused umlaut of the stem-vowel. This **i**-umlaut of the stem-vowel is the only characteristic feature preserved in the historic period of the language of the nouns belonging to this class. The original declension was fairly well preserved in Gothic, as Sing. nom. **managei** for ***managi** with **-ei** from the oblique cases, acc. **managein**, gen. **manageins**, dat. **managein**; pl. nom. (also used for the acc.) **manageins**, gen., **manageinō**, dat. **manageim** which was formed direct from **managei-** with **-m** from the ending of the vocalic stems. But already in the prehistoric period of OE. this class of nouns was remodelled on analogy with the short **ō**-stems (§ **365**), so that the nom. came to end in **-u**, later **-o**, and the oblique cases of the singular in **-e.** At a later period the new nominative came to be used for all forms of the singular and for the nom. acc. plural. Few nouns belonging to this class have a plural.

| | Sing. | Plur. |
|---|---|---|
| Nom. | **strengu, -o**, *strength* | **strenga, -e**; **-u, -o** |
| Acc. | **strenge, -u, -o** | „ |
| Gen. | „ | **strenga** |
| Dat. | „ | **strengum** |

§ **383.** Like **strengu** are declined **bieldu**, *boldness*; **bierhtu**, *brightness*; **engu**, *narrowness*; **fyllu**, *fullness*;

**hǣlu**, *health*; **hǣtu**, *heat*; **hyldu**, *favour*; **ieldu**, *age*; **menigu**, **mengu**, *multitude*; **oferfierru**, *great distance*; **snytru**, *wisdom*; **þiestru**, *darkness*; **wlencu**, **wlenc(e)o**, *pride*. See §§ **563**, **614**.

### 4. The i-declension.

§ **384**. The **i**-declension comprises masculine, feminine and neuter nouns, and corresponds to the Lat. and Gr. **i**-declension (nom. masc. and fem. Lat. **-is**, Gr. *-ις*, acc. **-im**, *-ιν*; neut. nom. acc. **-e**, *-ι*).

#### *a. Masculine.*

§ **385**. Sing.

| | | |
|---|---|---|
| Nom. Acc. | **wine**, *friend* | **giest**, *guest* |
| Gen. | **wines** | **giestes** |
| Dat. | **wine** | **gieste** |
| Plur. | | |
| Nom. Acc. | **wine**, **-as** | **giestas** |
| Gen. | **wina**, **wini(ge)a**, | **giesta** |
| Dat. | **winum** | **giestum** |

The prim. Germanic forms were: Sing. nom. ***ʒastiz** (Goth. **gasts**), acc. ***ʒastin** (Goth. **gast**), gen. ***ʒastaiz** (cp. Goth. **anstáis**, *of a favour*), dat. (originally the locative) ***ʒastī** (cp. OHG. **ensti**) beside ***ʒastēi** (cp. Goth. **anstái**); Plur. nom. ***ʒastīz** older **-ijiz** = Indg. **-ejes** (Goth. **gasteis**), acc. ***ʒastinz** (Goth. **gastins**), gen. ***ʒast(i)jō̃n**, Indg. **-jō̃m**, **-ijō̃m** (cp. Gr. *τριῶν*, Lat. **trium**, *of three*, with regular loss of intervocalic **-j-**), dat. ***ʒastimiz** (Goth. **gastim**). The endings **-iz**, **-in** of the nom. acc. sing. regularly became **-i** in prehistoric OE. The **-i** caused umlaut of the stem-vowel and then disappeared after long stems (§ **215**), but remained after short stems and later became **-e** (§ **215**, Note). The regular ending of the gen. sing. would be **-e** (§ **217**), the **-es** is from the **a**-stems. The dat. sing. ended in **-i** (later **-e**) in the oldest OE. and corresponded to the dative ending **-ī**.

The prim. Germanic nom. pl. ending **-īz** regularly became **-i**, later **-e**, which remained in the oldest period of the language. But already at an early period the nom. pl. was re-formed after the analogy of the masc. **a**-stems and then later the old ending **-e** was only preserved in a few plurals, especially in names of peoples, as **Dene**, *Danes*; **Engle**, *the English*; **Mierce** (gen. **Miercna**), *Mercians*; **Norþhymbre**, *Northumbrians*; **Seaxe** (gen. **Seaxna**), *Saxons*; **ielde**, *men*; **ielfe**, *elves*; **līode, lēode**, *people*; **stede**, *places*. The ending **-(i)jō̃n** regularly became **-(i)ja** which has only been preserved in a few words with short stems, as **Deni(ge)a, wini(ge)a**. The ending **-a** is from the gen. pl. of the **a**- and consonantal stems. The dat. pl. would regularly have ended in **-im**, but it had **-um** from the other classes of nouns. Apart from the few words mentioned above, the long **i**-stems have the same endings as the masc. **a**-stems and are only distinguishable from them by the presence or absence of umlaut.

§ **386**. Like **wine** are declined a large number of nouns, as **bile**, *beak*; **bite**, *bite*; **bryce**, *breach*; **bryne**, *burning*; **byge**, *curve*; **byre**, *son*; **ciele**, *cold*; **cyme**, *advent*; **cyre**, *choice*; **cwide**, *saying, speech*; **dene**, *valley*; **drepe**, *stroke, blow*; **dryre**, *fall*; **dyne**, *din*; **flyge**, *flight*; **gripe**, *grasp*; **gryre**, *terror*; **gyte**, *pouring forth*; **hæle** (orig. a cons. stem, see § **414**), *man, hero*; **hefe**, *weight*; **hege**, *hedge*; **hrine**, *touch*; **hryre**, *fall*; **hyge**, *mind*; **hype**, *hip*; **hyse** (pl. **hys(s)as**), *youth, son*; **ile** (pl. **il(l)as**), *sole of the foot*; **lyge**, *falsehood*; **lyre**, *loss*; **mere** (orig. neut.), *lake, pool*; **mete** (pl. **mettas**), *food*; **myne**, *memory*; **ryge**, *rye*; **ryne**, *course*; **scyfe**, *shove*; **scyte**, *shooting*; **sele**, *hall*; **sice**, *sigh*; **slege**, *stroke, blow*; **slide**, *slip*; **slite**, *slit*; **snide**, *incision*; **stæpe** (see § **55**), *step*; **stede**, *place*; **stice**, *stitch*; **stige**, *ascent*; **stride**, *stride*; **swyle**, *swelling*; **þyle**, *orator*; **wlite**, *brightness, beauty*. **bēorscipe**, *feast*; for further examples, see § **611**. **bere** (Goth. ***baris**), *barley*; **ege**

(Goth. **agis**), *fear*; **hete** (Goth. **hatis**), *hate*; **mene**, *necklace*; **sige** (Goth. **sigis**), *victory*, originally belonged to the neuter **-os, -es**-declension (§ **419**). **hyse** (pl. **hys(s)as**), *youth, son*; **ile** pl. **il(l)as**, *sole of the foot*; **mete** (pl. **mettas**), *food*, form their plural after the analogy of the **ja**-stems (§ **351**). **ele** (Lat. **oleum**), *oil*, was also originally neuter.

§ **387.** Like **giest** are declined a large number of nouns, as **ǣrist** (also fem.), *resurrection*; **æsc** (see § **56**), *ash-tree*; **blǣd**, *blast, breath*; **blǣst**, *blast*; **brygd**, *brandishing*; **byht**, *bend*; **byrst**, *loss*; **cierm**, *clamour*; **cierr**, *turn, change*; **dǣl**, *part*; **drenc**, *drink*; **dynt**, *dint*; **ent**, *giant*; **feng**, *grasp*; **fiell**, *fall*; **fierst**, *period of time*; **flyht**, *flight*; **fyrs**, *furze*; **glǣm**, *gleam*; **gylt**, *guilt*; **hlīep**, *leap*; **hlyst** (also fem.), *sense of hearing*; **hwyrft**, *turning, circuit*; **hyht**, *hope*; **lǣst**, *track*; **lēc**, *sight, looking at*; **līeg**, *flame*; **list**, *skill, cunning*; **lyft** (also fem.), *air*; **mǣw**, *seagull*; **pliht**, *danger, peril*; **sǣl** (also fem.), *time*; **scenc**, *cup, draught*; **slieht**, *slaughter*; **smīec**, *smoke*; **stenc**, *odour*; **steng**, *pole*; **stiell**, *leap*; **streng**, *string*; **swēg**, *sound, noise*; **swylt**, *death*; **tyht**, *training, instruction*; **þyrs**, *giant*; **wǣg**, *wave*; **wiell**, *spring*; **wielm**, *boiling*; **wrenc**, *trick, stratagem*; **wyrm**, *worm*.

§ **388.** **sǣ**, prim. Germanic ***saiwiz**, *sea*, gen. **sǣs**, dat. **sǣ**, pl. nom. acc. **sǣs**, gen. ***sǣwa**, dat. **sǣm** beside **sǣwum** (a new formation); also fem. gen. dat. **sǣ** beside **sǣwe**; **drȳ**, *magician*, gen. **drȳs**, dat. **drȳ**, pl. nom. acc. **drȳas**, dat. **drȳum**. On the contracted forms, see §§ **139, 142**.

*b. Feminine.*

§ **389.** SING. PLUR.

| | Sing. | Plur. |
|---|---|---|
| Nom. Acc. | **cwēn**, *queen* | **cwēne, -a** |
| Gen. | **cwēne** | **cwēna** |
| Dat. | **cwēne** | **cwēnum** |

The masc. and fem. **i**-stems were originally declined alike in the sing. and plural as in Latin and Greek. The nom. acc. and gen. sing. were regularly developed from the corresponding prim. Germanic forms ***kwǣniz, *kwǣnin, *kwǣnaiz.** The dat. sing. had **-e** after the analogy of the **ō**-stems, the regular form would have been ***cwēn** (see §§ **214–15**). The nom. pl. **cwēne** for ***cwēn** had **-e** from the short **i**-stems. The gen. and dat. pl. were new formations as in the masc. **i**-stems. In early Nth. and then later also in WS. and Ken. the acc. sing. often had **-e** after the analogy of the **ō**-stems; and in like manner the nom. acc. pl. often had **-a** already in early OE. All the fem. short **i**-stems went over into the **ō**-declension in the prehistoric period of the language.

§ **390.** Like **cwēn** are declined **ǣht,** *property*; **ansīen,** *face*; **bēn,** *prayer*; **benc,** *bench*; **brȳd,** *bride*; **cȳf,** *tub*; **cyst,** *choice*; **dǣd,** *deed*; **dryht,** *troop*; **ēst** (Goth. **ansts**), *favour*; **fierd,** *army*; **fȳst,** *fist*; **glēd,** *live coal*; **hǣs,** *command*; **hȳd,** *hide, skin*; **hȳf,** *hive*; **hyrst,** *ornament*; **meaht, miht,** *might, power*; **nīed,** *need*; **scyld,** *guilt*; **spēd,** *success*; **sȳl,** *pillar*; **tīd,** *time*; **þrȳþ,** *strength*; **wǣd,** *garment*; **wēn,** *hope, expectation*; **wist,** *sustenance, food*; **wyrd,** *fate*; **wyrt,** *vegetable, herb*; **ȳst,** *storm.* **duguþ,** *strength,* **geoguþ,** *youth,* **ides,** *woman,* which originally belonged to this declension, went over into the **ō**-declension.

NOTE.—**ǣ,** prim. Germanic ***aiwiz,** *divine law,* generally remains uninflected in the sing. and in the nom. acc. plural, but beside the gen. dat. sing. **ǣ** there also exists **ǣwe** from which a new nom. **ǣw** was formed.

§ **391.** A certain number of nouns, which originally belonged to the fem. **i**-declension, partly or entirely became neuter and were then declined like **cynn** (§ **355**) or **hof** (§ **342**) in the singular, and like **hof** in the plural. Such nouns are: **fulwiht, fulluht,** *baptism*; **grīn,** *snare, noose*; **oferhygd,** *pride*; **wiht, wuht,** *thing, creature*; nouns with the prefix **ge-**, as **gebyrd,** *birth*; **gecynd,** *nature, kind*;

**gehygd,** *mind*; **gemynd,** *memory*; **gesceaft,** *creation*; **geþeaht,** *thought*; **geþyld,** *patience*; **gewyrht,** *merit, desert*; pl. **gedryhtu,** *elements*; **giftu,** *gifts*. In late OE. other fem. **i**-stems also sometimes took the neut. plural ending **-u** (**-o**).

*c. Neuter.*

§ **392.** SING. PLUR.

| | | |
|---|---|---|
| Nom. Acc. | **spere,** *spear* | **speru, -o** |
| Gen. | **speres** | **spera** |
| Dat. | **spere** | **sperum** |

The neuter **i**-stems had originally the same endings as the masculine except in the nom. acc. sing. and plural. The nom. acc. sing. ended in **-i** which regularly disappeared after long stems, but remained after short stems, and then later became **-e** (§ **215,** Note). The nom. acc. pl. ended in **-ī** which would regularly have become **-i** (§ **214**), later **-e,** after short stems, and disappeared after long stems. The nom acc. pl. ending **-u** (**-o**) was due to the influence of the short neuter **a**-stems. The endings of the other cases are of the same origin as those of the masc. short **i**-stems. The regular form of the nom. acc. singular would be ***spire** (§ **41**) if **spere** originally belonged to the neuter **i**-declension.

§ **393.** Like **spere** are declined **ofdæle,** *downward slope, descent*; **oferslege,** *lintel*; **orlege,** *fate*; **sife,** *sieve*. All these nouns probably belonged originally to the **-os-, -es-** declension (§ **419**).

A certain number of neuter nouns which originally belonged partly to the neut. **ja**-stems, and partly to the **-os-, -es-**stems are declined like **spere,** except that the stem-syllable being long the final **-e** disappeared in the nom. acc. singular. Such nouns are: **flǣsc,** *flesh*; **flīes,** *fleece*; **hǣl,** *health*; **hilt** (also masc.), *hilt*; **lǣn,** *loan*; **sweng,** *blow*.

**gefēg**, *joining, joint*; **gegrynd**, *plot of ground*; **gehield**, *watching, protection*; **gehlȳd**, *noise*; **gehnǣst**, **-āst**, *collision*; **genyht**, *sufficiency*; **geresp**, *blame*; **gewēd**, *fury, madness*; **geswinc**, *labour, affliction*.

### 5. The u-declension.

§ **394**. The **u**-declension comprises masculine, feminine and neuter nouns, and corresponds to the Lat. and Gr. **u**-declension (nom. masc. and fem. Lat. **-us**, Gr. *-υς*, acc. **-um**, *-υν*; neut. nom. acc. **-ū**, *-υ*). A large number of the masc. and fem. **u**-stems passed over entirely into the **a**- and **ō**-declensions respectively in the prehistoric period of the language, and the other masc. and fem. nouns ending in a consonant have the case-endings of the **a**- and **ō**-declensions beside the regular case-endings, especially in the gen. sing. and in the plural.

#### *a. Masculine.*

§ **395**. Sing.

| | | |
|---|---|---|
| Nom. Acc. | **sunu**, **-o**, *son* | **feld**, *field* |
| Gen. | **suna** | **felda** |
| Dat. | **suna** | **felda** |
| Plur. | | |
| Nom. Acc. | **suna** | **felda** |
| Gen. | **suna** | **felda** |
| Dat. | **sunum** | **feldum** |

The prim. Germanic forms were: Sing. nom. ***sunuz** (Goth. **sunus**), acc. ***sunun** (Goth. **sunu**), gen. ***sunauz** (Goth. **sunáus**), dat. ***suniwai** (***sunwai**), loc. ***suneu** (OHG. **suniu**) beside ***sunēu** (Goth. **sunáu**); Plur. nom. ***suniwiz** (Goth. **sunjus**), acc. ***sununz** (Goth. **sununs**), gen. ***sunuwō̃n** (***sunwō̃n**), dat. ***sunumiz** (Goth. **sunum**). The endings **-uz**, **-un** regularly became **-u** in prehistoric OE., and then disappeared after long stems (§§ **211**, **215**), but remained after short stems. This **-u** became **-o** at an early period and then in late OE. **-a** (§ **215**, Note). The prim. Germanic gen. sing. ending **-auz** regularly became **-a** in OE. (§ **217**). The OE. dat. sing. is originally the locative corresponding to Goth. **sunáu.** It is difficult to account for the ending **-a** of the nom. plural, which cannot be a normal development of prim. Germanic **-iwiz** = Indg. **-ewes.** The gen. pl. ending **-a** is from the **a-** and the consonantal stems. The dat. pl. ending **-um** is from older **-umiz.** At a later period the **-u** (**-o**) of the nom. acc. sing. was often extended to the dat. sing. and nom. acc. pl. in the short stems; and likewise the **-a** of the gen. and dat. sing. to the nom. acc. In late OE. the short stems also often formed their gen. sing. and nom. acc. pl. after the analogy of the masc. **a**-stems. Already at an early period the long stems were often declined entirely like the **a**-stems. Many nouns which originally belonged to this class went over into the **a**-declension in prehistoric OE. without leaving any trace of the **u**-declension, as **ār** (Goth. **áirus**), *messenger*; **dēaþ** (Goth. **dáuþus**), *death*; **feorh** (also neut.), *life*; **flōd**, *flood*; **grund**, *ground*; **lust**, *pleasure, desire*; **scield**, *shield*; **þorn**, *thorn*; **beofor**, *beaver*; **esol**, *ass*; **hungor**, *hunger*; **fiscoþ**, *fishing*; **huntoþ**, *hunting*: for further examples, see § **595**.

§ **396**. Like **sunu** are declined **bregu**, *prince, ruler*; **heoru**, *sword*; **lagu**, *sea, flood*; **magu**, *son, man*; **medu**, **meodu**, *mead* (gen. **meda** beside **medwes**); **sidu**, *custom*; **spitu**, *spit*; **wudu**, *wood*.

§ **397**. Like **feld** are declined **eard**, *native country*; **ford**, *ford*; **gār** (mostly in compounds), *spear*; **hād**, *rank, condition* (for compounds in **-hād**, see § **605**); **hearg**, *temple*; **sēaþ**, *pit, spring*; **weald**, *forest*; **sumor**, *summer*; **æppel** (gen. **æp(p)les**, pl. **ap(p)la** beside **æp(p)las**, and neut. **ap(p)lu**), *apple*; **winter** (pl. neut. **wintru** beside **winter**), *winter*.

*b. Feminine.*

§ **398.** Sing.

| | | |
|---|---|---|
| Nom. Acc. | **duru, -o,** *door* | **hand,** *hand* |
| Gen. | **dura** | **handa** |
| Dat. | **dura** | **handa** |
| Plur. | | |
| Nom. Acc. | **dura** | **handa** |
| Gen. | **dura** | **handa** |
| Dat. | **durum** | **handum** |

The masculine and feminine **u**-stems were originally declined alike as in Latin and Greek. In the short stems the nom. acc. sing. was also sometimes used for the dat. sing. and nom. acc. plural; and the gen. and dat. sing. often had **-e** after the analogy of the short **ō**-stems. Beside the regular gen. and dat. sing. **dura,** there also occurs **dyre, dyru** with **i**-umlaut after the analogy of the **i**-declension. In the long stems the nom. acc. sing. was sometimes used for the gen. and dative. To the short stems also belongs **nosu,** *nose*; and to the long stems: **cweorn** (also **ō**-declension), Goth **-qaírnus,** *hand-mill*; **flōr** (also masc.), *floor*; and originally also **cin(n)** (Goth. **kinnus,** Gr. **γένυς**), *chin.*

*c. Neuter.*

§ **399.** The neuter **u**-stems had originally the same endings as the masculine except in the nom. acc. sing. and plural, the former of which ended in **-u** and the latter in **-u.** Nth. **feolu, -o,** and the WS. isolated inflected form **fela, feola,** *much, many,* are the only remnants of this declension in OE. **feoh** (Goth. **faíhu**), *cattle,* went over into the **a**-declension in prehistoric OE.

## B. The Weak Declension (N-Stems).

The weak declension comprises masculine, feminine, and neuter nouns, and corresponds to the Latin and Greek declension of **n**-stems, as Lat. **homō** (OE. **guma**), *man*, **sermō**, *discourse*, acc. **homin-em** (OE. **guman**), **sermōnem**; Gr. nom. **ποιμήν**, *shepherd*, **ἡγεμών**, *leader*, acc. **ποιμένα**, **ἡγεμόν-α**.

*a. Masculine.*

§ **400.** Sing.

| | | |
|---|---|---|
| Nom. | **guma**, *man* | **frēa**, *lord* |
| Acc. | **guman** | **frēan** |
| Gen. | **guman** | **frēan** |
| Dat. | **guman** | **frēan** |
| Plur. | | |
| Nom. Acc. | **guman** | **frēan** |
| Gen. | **gumena** | **frēana** |
| Dat. | **gumum** | **frēa(u)m** |

The prim. Germanic forms were: Sing. nom. ***ʒumō̃**, acc. ***ʒumanun**, gen. ***ʒumenaz** (Goth. **gumins**), dat., properly locative, ***ʒumini** (Goth. **gumin**); Plur. nom. ***ʒumaniz** (Goth. **gumans**), acc. ***ʒumanunz**, gen. ***ʒumnō̃n** (cp. Goth. **aúhs-nē**, OE. **ox-na**, *of oxen*) beside West Germanic ***ʒumōnō̃n** (OHG. **gomōno**, OS. **gumono**) with -**ōnō̃n** from the fem. nouns, dat. ***ʒumunmiz** beside West Germanic ***ʒumō(n)miz** (OHG. **gomōm**) with -**ō**- from the genitive. In OE. the nom. and acc. sing. and the nom. pl. were regularly developed from the corresponding prim. Germanic forms. The regular form of the gen. and dat. sing. would be ***gumen**, ***gymen**, but OE. had levelled out the -**an** of the acc. sing. before the period of **i**-umlaut. The oldest OE. form of the gen. pl. was probably **gumana** from ***ʒumanō̃n** with **a** from the singular and the nom. plural, and the usual form **gumena** was a later weakening of -**an** to -**en**-. The endings -**ana**-, -**ona** (§ **59**) sometimes occur although not very frequently. The medial vowel of the ending was generally syncopated after long stems in poetry and in the names of peoples. The dat. pl. was formed direct from **ȝum-+-um**, the ending of the **a**-stems and the other consonantal stems, or else it was from West Germanic ***ȝumō(n)miz** (§ **218**, 4). On the loss of final **-n** in Nth., see § **288**.

From a morphological point of view the **n**-stems should be divided into **-an**, **-jan**, and **-wan** stems, but in OE. as in the other Germanic languages all three classes were declined alike. The **-jan** stems have **i**-umlaut in the stem-syllable and also gemination of consonants when the stem was originally short, as **dēma**, *judge*, **cȳta**, *kite*, **becca**, *pickaxe*, **brytta**, *distributor, prince*, from prim. Germanic ***đōmjō̃**, ***kūtjō̃**, ***ƀakjō̃**, ***ƀrutjō̃**.

§ **401**. Like **guma** are declined a large number of nouns, as **ācumba**, *oakum*; **ǣra**, *strigil*; **ǣrendra**, *messenger*; **āglǣca**, *monster*; **anda**, *envy*; **andsaca**, *adversary*; **anga**, *goad*; **apa**, *ape*; **assa**, *ass*; **bana**, *slayer*; **bēna**, *suppliant*; **beorma**, *barm, yeast*; **bera**, *bear*; **bes(e)ma**, *besom*; **bita**, *bit, morsel*; **blanca**, *horse*; **blōstma**, *blossom*; **boda**, *messenger*; **boga**, *bow*; **bolla**, *bowl*; **brōga**, *terror*; **bucca**, *he-goat*; **bylda**, *builder*; **byrga**, *surety*; **cleofa**, *cleft, cave*; **cnapa**, *boy*; **cnotta**, *knot*; **cofa**, *chamber*; **crabba**, *crab*; **cruma**, *crumb*; **cuma**, *guest, stranger*; **dogga**, *dog*; **dora**, *bumble-bee*; **dropa**, *drop*; **dwolma**, *chaos*; **eafora**, *son*; **fana**, *banner*; **fēþa**, *band of infantry*; **flīema**, *fugitive*; **flota**, *sailor*; **fola**, *foal*; **freca**, *warrior*; **frogga**, *frog*; **fruma**, *beginning*; **gāra**, *corner*; **gealga**, *gallows*; **gealla**, *gall*; **gefēra**, *companion*; **gehola**, *protector*; **gerēfa**, *reeve*; **gerūna**, *councillor*; **gesaca**, *adversary*; **geþofta**, *companion*; **gewuna**, *custom*; **haca**, *hook*; **hafela**, *head*; **hana**, *cock*; **hara**, *hare*; **hunta**, *hunter*; **inca**, *grudge*; **lēoma**, *ray of light*; **lida**, *sailor*; **loca**, *enclosure*; **maga**, *stomach*; **mōna**, *moon*; **naca**, *boat*; **nama**, *name*; **nefa**, *nephew*; **ōga**, *terror*; **ōretta**, *warrior*; **oxa** (pl. **œxen**, **exen**, beside **oxan**, § **107**), *ox*; **plega**, *play*; **pohha**, *pouch*, *bag*; **prica**, *prick, point*; **rima**, *rim*; **ryþþa**, *mastiff*; **sāda**, *cord, snare*; **scanca**, *shank*; **scaþa**, *foe, enemy*; **scrēawa**, *shrew-mouse*; **scucca**, *demon*; **scu(w)a**, *shadow*; **sefa**, *mind, heart*; **slaga**, *slayer*; **snaca**, *snake*; **sopa**, *sup*; **spāca**, *spoke of a wheel*; **spearwa**, *sparrow*; **staca**, *stake*; **stela**, *stalk*; **steorra**, *star*; **swēora**, *neck*; **swica**, *deceiver*; **swīma**, *giddiness*; **telga**, *branch*; **trega**, *grief, affliction*; **þearfa**, *pauper*; **þūma**, *thumb*; **wela**, *prosperity*; **wita**, *sage, wise man*; **wītega**, *prophet*; **wræcc(e)a** (§ **55**, Note 3), *exile*; **wyrhta**, *worker*; and the pl. **hīwan** (gen. **hīna** beside **hīwna**), *members of a household.*

§ **402**. Like **frēa** are declined **flēa**, *flea*; **gefā**, *foe*; **(ge)fēa**, *joy*; **lēo**, *lion*; **rā**, *roe*; **twēo**, *doubt*; **wēa**, *woe*; and the plural **Swēon**, *Swedes*. See § **139**.

*b. Feminine.*

§ **403**. Sing.

| | | |
|---|---|---|
| Nom. | **tunge**, *tongue* | **bēo**, *bee* |
| Acc. | **tungan** | **bēon** |
| Gen. | **tungan** | **bēon** |
| Dat. | **tungan** | **bēon** |
| Plur. | | |
| Nom. Acc. | **tungan** | **bēon** |
| Gen. | **tungena** | **bēona** |
| Dat. | **tungum** | **bēom** |

The feminine **n**-stems were originally declined like the masculine, as in Latin, Greek and Sanskrit, but already in the prehistoric period of the Germanic languages, they became differentiated in some of the cases by partly generalizing one or other of the forms; thus the nom. sing. originally ended in **-ō̃** or **-ōn** in both genders, the West Germanic languages restricted **-ō̃** to the masculine and **-ōn** to the feminine, but in Gothic the reverse took place. In the fem. Goth. O.Icel. OS. and OHG. levelled out the long vowel of the nom. into the oblique cases, whereas

OE. had the same forms as the masculine except in the nom. sing. -e from prim. Germanic **-ōn** (§ **217**). The general remarks made in § **400** concerning the masculine **n**-stems also apply to the feminine.

The fem. nouns with short stems began to form their nom. sing. after the analogy of the short **ō-stems** (§ **365**) already in early OE., as **cinu,** *chink,* **spadu,** *spade,* **wicu (wucu),** *week,* beside **cine, spade, wice (wuce).**

§ **404.** Like **tunge** are declined **ǣdre,** *artery, vein*; **ælmesse,** *alms*; **ǣsce,** *inquiry*; **ampre,** *sorrel*; **ar(e)we,** *arrow*; **asse,** *she-ass*; **asce,** *ash, cinders*; **āþexe,** *lizard*; **bæcestre** (also masc.), *baker* (for other examples containing the suffix **-estre,** see § **603**); **bēce,** *beech-tree*; **belle,** *bell*; **berige,** *berry*; **bīeme,** *trumpet*; **bicce,** *bitch*; **binde,** *head-band*; **blǣdre,** *bladder*; **blæse,** *blaze, firebrand, torch*; **burne,** *stream, brook*; **byrne,** *corslet*; **canne,** *can, cup*; **cēace,** *cheek, jaw*; **ceole,** *throat*; **cirice,** *church*; **clugge,** *bell*; **crāwe,** *crow*; **cuppe,** *cup*; **cūslyppe, -sloppe,** *cowslip*; **cwene,** *woman*; **docce,** *dock* (*plant*); **dūce,** *duck*; **eorþe,** *earth*; **fæcele,** *torch*; **faþe,** *aunt*; **fiþele,** *fiddle*; **flēoge,** *fly*; **flīete,** *cream*; **folde,** *earth*; **hacele,** *cloak*; **hearpe,** *harp*; **heofone,** *heaven*; **heorte** (orig. neut.), *heart*; **hlǣfdige,** *lady*; **hrūse,** *earth*; **loppe,** *flea*; **mǣge, māge,** *kinswoman*; **meowle,** *maiden*; **mīere,** *mare*; **mōdrige,** *maternal aunt*; **molde,** *earth*; **more,** *parsnip*; **moþþe,** *moth*; **nǣdre,** *snake*; **ōsle,** *ousel*; **panne,** *pan*; **pere,** *pear*; **pīpe,** *pipe*; **pirige,** *pear-tree*; **pise,** *pea*; **racente,** *chain*; **seohhe,** *sieve*; **sīde,** *side*; **slyppe,** *paste*; **smiþþe,** *smithy*; **sunne,** *sun*; **swealwe,** *swallow*; **swipe,** *scourge*; **þrote,** *throat*; **þyrne,** *thornbush*; **ūle,** *owl*; **wæcce** (§ **55,** Note 3), *vigil*; **wāse,** *mud*; **wicce,** *witch*; **wīse,** *way, manner*; **wice, wuce,** *week*; **wulle,** *wool*; **wuduwe,** *widow*; **ȳce,** *toad, frog*; and nomina agentis ending in **-estre,** as **hlēapestre,** *dancer*; **lǣrestre,** *teacher*; **sangestre,** *songstress*; for other examples, see § **603.**

§ **405.** Like **bēo** are declined **cēo,** *jackdaw, chough*; **flā,** *arrow*; **sēo,** *pupil of the eye*; **slā, slāh,** *sloe*; **tā,** *toe*; **þō,** *clay*. See § **139.**

*c. Neuter.*

§ **406.**

| | SING. | | PLUR. |
|---|---|---|---|
| Nom. Acc. | **ēage,** *eye* | | **ēagan** |
| Gen. | **ēagan** | | **ēagena** |
| Dat. | **ēagan** | | **ēagum** |

The neuter **n**-stems had originally the same endings as the masculine and feminine except in the acc. sing. and the nom. acc. plural. The nom. acc. sing. had **-ōn** which regularly became **-e** in OE. (§ **217**). The nom. acc. pl. had **-ōnə** in the Indg. parent language. This was changed in prim. Germanic into **-ōnō** with **-ō** from the neuter **a**-stems. **-ōnō** regularly became **-ōna** in Goth., as **áugō,** *eye*, nom. acc. pl. **áugōna.** The OE. ending **-an** was due to the analogy of the masc. and fem. **n**-stems.

§ **407.** Like **ēage** are declined only **ēare,** *ear*; **wange** (also with strong forms), *cheek*.

C. MINOR DECLENSIONS.

1. MONOSYLLABIC CONSONANT STEMS.

*a. Masculine.*

§ **408.**

| | SING. | | PLUR. |
|---|---|---|---|
| Nom. Acc. | **fōt,** *foot* | | **fēt** |
| Gen. | **fōtes** | | **fōta** |
| Dat. | **fēt** | | **fōtum** |

The prim. Germanic forms were: Sing. nom. **fōt** for older ***fōs(s)** (Gr. Dor. πώς) with **t** from the inflected forms (§ **240**), and similarly **tōþ** for older ***tōs(s)**, acc. ***fōtun** (Goth. **fōtu**), gen. ***fōtaz** or **-iz,** dat., properly loc., ***fōti**; Plur. nom. ***fōtiz,** acc. ***fōtunz** (Goth. **fōtuns**), gen. ***fōtō̃n,** dat. ***fōtumiz.** The OE. correspond to the prim. Germanic forms except in the gen. sing. which is a new formation after the analogy of the **a**-stems. The regular form would be ***fōt** or ***fēt**.

§ **409.** Like **fōt** are declined **tōþ**, *tooth*; **man(n)** (beside **manna**, acc. **mannan**, **n**-declension), *man*; and **wīfman**, **wimman**, *woman*.

*b. Feminine.*

§ **410.** SING.

| | | |
|---|---|---|
| Nom. Acc. | **bōc**, *book* | **hnutu**, *nut*. |
| Gen. | **bēc**; **bōce** | ***hnyte**; **hnute** |
| Dat. | **bēc** | **hnyte** |
| PLUR. | | |
| Nom. Acc. | **bēc** | **hnyte** |
| Gen. | **bōca** | **hnuta** |
| Dat. | **bōcum** | **hnutum** |

The prim. Germanic forms were: Sing. nom. ***bōk** (O.Icel. OS. **bōk**) which was a new formation for older ***bōχs** (§ **240**), acc. ***bōkun**, gen. ***bōkaz** or ***bōkiz** (= OE. **bēc**), dat., properly loc., ***bōki**; Plur. nom. ***bōkiz**, acc. ***bōkunz**, gen. ***bōkōn**, dat. ***bōkumiz**. With the exception of **bōce** all the OE. forms were regularly developed from the corresponding prim. Germanic forms. The gen. sing. **bōce** was a new formation after the analogy of the **ō**-stems. The regular nom. sing. of **hnutu** would be ***hnuss** (§ **240**), **hnutu** (prim. Germ. ***χnutun**) is the acc. used for the nominative. The gen. sing was formed after the analogy of the **ō**-stems; the dat. sing. and nom. pl. correspond to prim. Germanic ***χnuti**, ***χnutiz**, the final **-i** (later **-e**) being retained after a short stem (§ **215**).

In nouns belonging to this class the stem-vowels **ā**, **ō**, **u**, **ū** were regularly umlauted to **ǣ**, **ē** (Nth. **œ̄**), **y**, **ȳ** in the gen. dat. sing. and nom acc. plural. In nearly all the nouns belonging to this class, beside the gen. sing. with umlaut there exists a form ending in **-e** without umlaut which was made after the analogy of the **ō**-stems. In late OE. the dat. sing. was often like the nominative.

§ **411.** Like **bōc** are declined **āc,** *oak*; **brōc,** *trousers*; **burg,** *city* (gen. dat. sing. and nom. acc. pl. **byrig** beside **byrg,** § **220**; also declined like **cwēn** (§ **389**), but without i-umlaut); **cū,** *cow* (also gen. sing. **cūe, cūs**; nom. acc. pl. **cȳ, cȳe,** gen. **cūa, cūna, cȳna**); **dung,** *prison*; **gāt,** *goat*; **gōs,** *goose*; **grūt,** *coarse meal, groats*; **lūs,** *louse*; **meol(u)c,** *milk*; **mūs,** *mouse*; **neaht, niht,** *night* (also gen. dat. sing. **nihte**; adv. gen. **nihtes, ānes nihtes,** *at night, by night,* formed after the analogy of **dæges**); **turf,** *turf*; **furh,** *furrow* (gen. sing. **fūre** beside **fyrh,** pl. gen. **fūra,** dat. **fūrum,** § **115**); **sulh,** *plough* (gen. sing. **sūles** on analogy with the **a**-stems, pl. gen. **sūla,** dat. **sūlum**); **þrūh,** *trough* (dat. pl. **þrūm,** § **329,** 4); **wlōh,** *fringe*

§ **412.** Like **hnutu** are declined **hnitu,** *nit*; **studu, stuþu,** *pillar.*

### c. *Neuter.*

§ **413.** The only remnant of this class is **scrūd,** *garment,* dat. **scrȳd**; gen. **scrūdes** and late OE. dat. **scrūde** were formed after the analogy of the neuter **a**-stems, and also the nom. acc. pl. **scrūd**; gen. pl. **scrūda,** dat. **scrūdum.**

## 2. Stems in -þ.

§ **414.** Of the nouns which originally belonged to this declension only four have been preserved: masc. **hæleþ** (OHG. **helid**), **hæle,** *hero, man,* **mōnaþ** (Goth. **mēnōþs**), *month*; fem. **mæg(e)þ** (Goth. **magaþs**), *maiden*; neut. **ealu,** *ale.* **hæleþ, hæle, mōnaþ,** and **mæg(e)þ** originally had the same endings as the prim. Germanic forms of **fōt** (§ **408**) and **bōc** (§ **410**). The **þ** was reintroduced into the nom. sing. from the inflected forms. The old nom. acc. sing. has been preserved in **ealu.** The gen. and dat. sing. of **hæleþ** and **mōnaþ** were formed on analogy with the **a**-declension; and beside the nom. acc. pl. **hæleþ, mōnaþ,** there also exist **hæleþas, mōn(e)þas.** Those forms which did not originally have umlaut were generalized in OE. They are declined as follows:—

| SING. | | | | |
|---|---|---|---|---|
| Nom. Acc. | **hæle, hæleþ** | **mōnaþ** | **mæg(e)þ** | **ealu** |
| Gen. | **hæleþes** | **mōn(e)þes** | **mæg(e)þ** | **ealoþ** |
| Dat. | **hæleþe** | **mōn(e)þe** | **mæg(e)þ** | **ealoþ** |
| PLUR. | | | | |
| Nom. Acc. | **hæleþ** | **mōnaþ** | **mæg(e)þ** | |
| Gen. | **hæleþa** | **mōn(e)þa** | **mæg(e)þa** | **ealeþa** |
| Dat. | **hæleþum** | **mōn(e)þum** | **mæg(e)þum** | |

### 3. STEMS IN -r.

§ **415.** To this class belong the nouns of relationship: **fæder,** *father*; **brōþor,** *brother*; **mōdor,** *mother*; **dohtor,** *daughter*; **sweostor,** *sister*; and the collective plurals, **gebrōþor, gebrōþru,** *brethren*; **gesweostor, -tru, -tra,** *sisters*.

In the parent Indg. language the words for *father*, *mother*, and *daughter* had in the sing. nom. **-tēr**, acc. loc. **-ter-**, voc. **-ter**, gen. dat. **-tr-** (with consonantal **r**); Plur. nom. **-ter-**, acc. gen. **-tr-** (with consonantal **r**), dat. loc. **-tr-** (with vocalic **r**). The word for *brother* had sing. nom. **-tōr** or **-tēr** (cp. Gr. Dor. *φρᾱ́τωρ, φρᾱ́τηρ, member of a clan*), and the word for *sister* **-ōr** (cp. Lat. **soror** from older ***swesōr**) with short **-or-** or loss of **-o-** in the other cases just as in **-tēr, -ter-, -tr-**.

| SING. | | | |
|---|---|---|---|
| Nom. Acc. | **fæder** | **brōþor** | **mōdor** |
| Gen. | **fæder, -eres** | **brōþor** | **mōdor** |
| Dat. | **fæder** | **brēþer** | **mēder** |
| PLUR. | | | |
| Nom. Acc. | **fæderas** | **brōþor, -þru** | **mōdor, -dru, -dra** |
| Gen. | **fædera** | **brōþra** | **mōdra** |
| Dat. | **fæderum** | **brōþrum** | **mōdrum** |

| | | |
|---|---|---|
| SING. | | |
| Nom. Acc. | **dohtor** | **sweostor** |
| Gen. | **dohtor** | **sweostor** |
| Dat. | **dehter** | **sweostor** |
| PLUR. | | |
| Nom. Acc. | **dohtor, -tru, -tra** | **sweostor** |
| Gen. | **dohtra** | **sweostra** |
| Dat. | **dohtrum** | **sweostrum** |

Before the principal accent was shifted to the stem-syllable (see § **238**) the prim. Germanic forms of **fæder** were : Sing. nom. ***fađēr** (Gr. πατήρ), acc. ***fađerun** (Gr. πατέρα), gen. ***fađras** (Gr. πατρός) beside ***fađres** (Lat. **patris** from older ***patres**), dat., properly loc., ***fađri** (Gr. πατρί); Plur. nom. ***fađeriz** (Gr. πατέρες), acc. ***fađruns** (cp. Goth. **brōþruns**), gen. ***fađrō̃n** (Gr. πατρῶν), dat. ***fađrumis** (cp. Goth. **brōþrum**). After the principal accent was shifted to the stem-syllable during the prim. Germanic period the final **-s** became **-z** after the analogy of the inflected forms of the words for *brother* and *sister* and other consonantal stems which regularly had **-z** ; and the **-e-** in the gen. sing. ***fađrez,** older ***fađres,** and nom. pl. ***fađeriz** became **-i-** (§ **218**). And similarly in the prim. Germanic case-endings of ***mōđēr,** Indg. ***mātḗr,** *mother*. The OE. nom. acc. and gen. sing. **fæder** is normally developed from the corresponding prim. Germanic forms. On the gen. **fæder** from ***fađraz,** older ***fađras,** see § **219** ; **fæderes** was formed on analogy with the **a**-stems. The prim. Germanic pl. forms (except the acc.) regularly became ***fæder, fædra, fædrum,** the last two of which were common in the oldest period of the language ; then later **er** was levelled out into the gen. and dat., and the nom. pl. ***fæder** became **fæd(e)ras** on analogy with the **a**-stems.

The prim. Germanic case-endings of **brōþor, mōdor, dohtor,** and **sweostor** were the same as those of **fæder** except that **brōþor** and **sweostor** having originally the chief accent on the stem-syllable regularly had **-raz** in the gen. singular. The dat. forms ***ƀrōþri, *mōđri, *đoχtri** (older ***đuχtri**) with **o** from the nom. acc. and gen., ***swestri** (older ***swistri**) with **e** from the nom. acc. and gen., regularly became **brēþer, mēder, dehter, sweostor** (cp. § **219**). In late OE. the dat. **mēder, dehter** were often used for the gen. and vice versa. The gen. sing. ***ƀrōþraz, mōđraz, *đoχtraz, *swestraz,** regularly became **brōþor, mōdor, dohtor, sweostor** (§ **219**). The gen. and dat. pl. were regularly developed from the corresponding prim. Germanic forms. The nom. sing and pl. were in prim. OE. ***brōþer, *mōder, *doχter, *swestor,** then **-er** became **-or** (older **-ur**) through the influence of the guttural vowel in the stem (cp. § **219**), but the ending **-er** (rarely **-ar**) often occurs both in early and late OE. **sweostor** had **-or** in prim. Germanic, as nom. sing. ***swesor,** Indg. ***swesōr,** nom. pl. ***swesoriz,** Indg. ***swesores**; the **t** was developed between the **s** and **r** in the gen. sing. and pl. ***swestraz, *swestrōn,** and then became generalized (§ **250**).

**gebrōþor** and **gesweostor** were originally neuter collective nouns and were declined like **wīte** (§ **355**), whence the plural endings **gebrōþru, gesweostru, -tra,** which were afterwards extended to the plural of **mōdor** and **dohtor.**

### 4. The Masculine Stems in -nd.

§ **416.** Sing.

| | | |
|---|---|---|
| Nom. Acc. | **frēond,** *friend* | **wīgend,** *warrior* |
| Gen. | **frēondes** | **wīgendes** |
| Dat. | **frīend, frēonde** | **wīgende** |

Plur.

| | | |
|---|---|---|
| Nom. Acc. | **frīend, frēond, -as** | **wīgend, -e, -as** |
| Gen. | **frēonda** | **wīgendra** |
| Dat. | **frēondum** | **wīgendum** |

The nouns of this declension are old isolated present participles, like Lat. **ferēns,** *bearing,* gen. **ferentis,** and originally had the same case-endings as the other consonantal stems. But in OE. as in the other Germanic languages they underwent various new formations. The OE. present participles had passed over into the **ja**-declension of adjectives (§§ **433–4**) in the oldest period of the language.

The nom. sing. was a new formation with **d** from the inflected forms, cp. Lat. **ferēns** from ***ferenss** older ***ferents** (§ **240**). The gen. sing. **frēondes, wīgendes,** dat. **frēonde, wīgende,** nom. acc. pl. **frēondas, wīgendas** were formed after the analogy of the masc. **a**-stems. The dat. **frīend** with umlaut is from ***frīondi** older ***frijōndi**; and the nom. pl. **frīend** is also from ***frīondi** older ***frijōndiz** (Goth. ***frijōnds**). The nom. and gen. pl. endings **-e, -ra** are adjectival (§ **424**).

§ **417**. Like **frēond** are declined **fēond,** *enemy*; **tēond,** *accuser*; the compound noun **gōddōnd** (pl. **-dōnd,** beside **-dēnd**), *benefactor*; and the collective plurals **gefīend,** *enemies*; **gefrīend,** *friends,* which were originally neuter collective nouns and declined like **wīte** (§ **355**).

§ **418**. Like **wīgend** are declined **āgend,** *owner*; **beswīcend,** *deceiver*; **ēhtend,** *persecutor*; **hǣlend,** *Saviour*; **helpend,** *helper*; **hettend,** *enemy*; **ner(i)gend,** *Saviour*; **sēmend,** *arbitrator*; **wealdend,** *ruler*; for further examples, see § **601**.

### 5. Stems in -os, -es.

§ **419**. This class of nouns corresponds to the Gr. neuters in *-ος*, Lat. **-us,** as Gr. *γένος, race,* gen. *γένεος* older **γένεσος*, Lat. **genus,** gen. **generis,** pl. **genera.** A fairly large number of nouns originally belonged to this class, but owing to various levellings and new formations, of which some took place in the prehistoric period of all the Germanic languages, nearly all the nouns belonging here went over into other declensions in OE. The prim. Germanic forms of a word like **lamb** were: Sing. nom. acc. ***lambaz,** gen. ***lambezaz, *lambiziz,** dat. ***lambizi**; Plur. nom. acc. ***lambōzō** (for Indg. **-ōsə,** cp. § **406**), gen. ***lambezǭn,** dat. ***lambezumiz.** After the loss of the singular endings **-az, -iz, -i,** the following changes took place: from the gen. and dat. sing. a new nom. ***lambiz** beside **lamb** was formed. This accounts for the preservation of the **i** in Gothic in such words as **hatis** = OE. **hete,** *hate,* **sigis** = OE. **sige,** *victory,* which would have been ***hats** and ***sigs** in Gothic, had these words ended in **-iz** in prim. Germanic. The new nom. ending **-iz** regularly became **-i** in OE., then it caused umlaut in the stem-syllable and disappeared after long stems, but remained after short stems and later became **-e,** whence forms like nom. sing. **lemb, gǣst, hlǣw, hete, sige** beside **lamb, gāst, hlāw.** After medial **-z-** in the gen. and dat. sing. had become **r** (§ **252**) it was levelled out into the nom. sing. in some nouns, as ***dōȝr, *hālr** beside ***dōȝi, *hāli,** then later **dōgor, hālor,** older **-ur** (cp. § **219**), beside **dœ̄g** (Nth.), **hǣl.** All the nouns which underwent these new formations passed into other declensions partly with change of gender also. Thus, **gāst, gǣst,** *spirit, breath,* **sigor,** *victory,* went into the masc. **a**-declension; **hlǣw, hlāw,** *mound, hill,* **hrǣ(w), hrā(w),** also neut., *corpse, carrion,* into the masc. **wa**-declension; **dœ̄g** (Nth.), *day,* **ge-ban(n),** *summons,* **gefōg,** *joining, joint,* **geheald,** *keeping, custody,* **gehnāst,** *conflict, strife,* **gewealc,** *rolling,* **sæl,** *hall,* **dōgor,** *day,* **ēagor,** *flood, tide,* **ēar,** *ear of corn,* **hālor,** *salvation, health,* **hrīþer, hrȳþer,** *ox,* **salor,** *hall,* **stulor,** *theft,* pl. **hæteru,** *clothes,* into the neut. **a**-declension; **bere,** *barley,* **ege,** *fear,* **hete,** *hate,* **mene,** *necklace,* **sige,** *victory,* into the masc. **i**-declension; **oferslege,** *lintel,* **orlege,** *fate,* **sife,** *sieve,* **spere,** *spear,* **flǣsc,** *flesh,* **flīes,** *fleece,* **hǣl,** *health, salvation,* **hilt,** *hilt,* **lǣn,** *loan,* **sweng,** *blow,* into the neuter **i**-declension.

§ **420.** The few remaining nouns formed their gen. and dat. sing. after the analogy of the neuter **a**-stems. The cases of the plural were regularly developed from the corresponding prim. Germanic forms.

| | | | |
|---|---|---|---|
| SING. | | | |
| Nom. Acc. | **lamb**, *lamb* | **cealf**, *calf* | **ǣg**, *egg* |
| Gen. | **lambes** | **cealfes** | **ǣges** |
| Dat. | **lambe** | **cealfe** | **ǣge** |
| PLUR. | | | |
| Nom. Acc. | **lambru** | **cealfru** | **ǣgru** |
| Gen. | **lambra** | **cealfra** | **ǣgra** |
| Dat. | **lambrum** | **cealfrum** | **ǣgrum** |

Beside **lamb** there also occurs **lombor** and sometimes **lemb**; in late OE. the pl. was **lamb, lamba, lambum** after the analogy of the neuter **a**-stems. Beside the Anglian sing. **calf** there also occurs **cælf, celf** with **i**-umlaut.

Like **lamb** are declined **cild** (pl. **cild** beside **cildru**), *child*; **speld,** *splinter, torch*; pl. **brēadru,** *crumbs.*

# CHAPTER XII

## ADJECTIVES

### A. THE DECLENSION OF ADJECTIVES.

§ **421.** In the parent Indg. language nouns and adjectives were declined alike without any distinction in endings, as in Latin, Greek, and Sanskrit. What is called the uninflected form of adjectives in the Germanic languages is a remnant of the time when nouns and adjectives were declined alike. But already in Indo-Germanic the pronominal adjectives had partly nominal and partly pronominal endings as in Sanskrit. In prim. Germanic the endings of the pronominal adjectives were extended to all adjectives. These remarks apply to what is called in the Germanic languages the strong declension of adjectives.

The so-called weak declension of adjectives is a special Germanic formation by means of the suffixes **-en-**, **-on-**, which were originally used to form nomina agentis, and attributive nouns, as Lat. **edō** (gen. **edōnis**), *glutton*, OE. **slaga**, *slayer*, **wyrhta**, *worker*, gen. **slagan**, **wyrhtan**; Lat. adjectives **catus**, *sly*, *cunning*, **rūfus**, *red*, *red-haired*, **silus**, *pug-nosed*, beside the proper names **Catō** (gen. **Catōnis**), lit. *the sly one*, **Rūfō**, *the red-haired man*, **Silō**, *the pug-nosed man*; and similarly in OE. **blæc**, *black*, **frōd**, *wise*, *old*, **hālig**, *holy*, beside the proper names **Blaca**, **Frōda**, **Hālga**. In like manner Goth. **blinds**, OE. **blind**, *blind*, beside Goth. OE. **blinda**, which originally meant, *the blind man*; Goth. **ahma sa weiha**, lit. *ghost the holy one*. Such nouns came to be used attributively at an early period, and then later as adjectives. And already in prim. Germanic this weak declension became the rule when the adjective followed the definite article, as **Wulfmǣr se geonga**, *Wulfmǣr the Young*, OHG. **Ludowīg ther snello**, *Ludwig the Brave*, cp. NHG. **Karl der Grosse**. At a later period, but still in prim. Germanic, the two kinds of adjectives—strong and weak—became differentiated in use. When the one and when the other form was used in OE. is a question of syntax. There were adjectival **n**-stems in the parent Indg. language, but they did not have vocalic stems beside them as is the case in the Germanic languages. **eall**, *all*, **genōg**, *enough*, **manig**, *many*, and **ōþer**, *second*, were always declined according to the strong declension. Nearly all other adjectives can be declined according to either declension.

The strong form is used predicatively in the positive and superlative degrees; and when the adjective is used attributively without any other defining word, as **wæs sēo**

**fǣmne geong,** *the woman was young*; **þā menn sindon gōde,** *the men are good*; **þus wǣron þā latestan fyrmeste,** *thus were the last, first.* In the vocative the weak form exists beside the strong, as **þū lēofa dryhten,** *thou dear Lord*; **þū riht cyning,** *thou just king.*

The weak form is used after the definite article, and after demonstrative and possessive pronouns, as **se ofermōda cyning,** *the proud king*; **þæs ēadigan weres,** *of the blessed man*; **þes ealda mann,** *this old man*; **on þissum andweardan dæge,** *on this present day*; **mīn lēofa sunu,** *my dear son*; **þurh þīne æþelan hand,** *through thy noble hand.* In poetry the weak form often occurs where in prose the strong form would be used.

NOTE.—When the same adjective refers both to masc. and fem. beings, it is put in the neut. plural, as **Wit þus baru ne magon būtū ætsomne wesan,** *We* (*Adam and Eve*) *may not both together be thus here naked*; cp. Goth. **wēsun garaíhta ba in andwaírþja guþs,** O.Icel. **þau vǫro rētlǫt bǣþe fyr guþe,** OHG. **siu wārun rehtiu beidu fora gote,** *they* (*Zacharias and Elizabeth*) *were both righteous before God.*

§ **422.** In OE. the adjectives are declined as strong or weak. They have three genders, and the same cases as nouns with the addition of an instrumental in the masc. and neuter singular.

## 1. The Strong Declension.

§ **423.** The endings of the strong declension are partly nominal and partly pronominal; the latter are printed in italics for **glæd,** *glad,* and **blind,** *blind.* The nominal endings are those of the **a-, ō-**declensions. The strong declension is divided into pure **a-, ō-**stems, **ja-, jō-**stems, and **wa-, wō-**stems, like the corresponding nouns. The original **i-** and **u-**stems passed over almost entirely into this declension in prehistoric OE. In OE. the **ja-, jō-**stems and the **wa-, wō-**stems only differed from the pure

**a-, ō-**stems in the masc. and fem. nom. singular and the neut. nom. acc. singular.

### *a.* PURE **a-, ō-**STEMS.

**§ 424.**

| SING. | *Masc.* | *Neut.* | *Fem.* |
|---|---|---|---|
| Nom. | **glæd,** *glad* | **glæd** | **gladu, -o** |
| Acc. | **glæd***ne* | **glæd** | **glade** |
| Gen. | **glades** | **glades** | **glæd***re* |
| Dat. | **glad***um* | **glad***um* | **glæd***re* |
| Instr. | **glade** | **glade** | |
| PLUR. | | | |
| Nom. Acc. | **glad***e* | **gladu, -o** | **glada, -e** |
| Gen. | **glæd***ra* | **glæd***ra* | **glæd***ra* |
| Dat. | **gladum** | **gladum** | **gladum** |

| SING. | | | |
|---|---|---|---|
| Nom. | **blind,** *blind* | **blind** | **blind** |
| Acc. | **blind***ne* | **blind** | **blinde** |
| Gen. | **blindes** | **blindes** | **blind***re* |
| Dat. | **blind***um* | **blind***um* | **blind***re* |
| Instr. | **blinde** | **blinde** | |
| PLUR. | | | |
| Nom. Acc. | **blind***e* | **blind** | **blinda, -e** |
| Gen. | **blind***ra* | **blind***ra* | **blind***ra* |
| Dat. | **blindum** | **blindum** | **blindum** |

The prim. Germanic forms of **blind** were: Masc. sing. nom. ***ƀlinđaz** (Goth. **blinds**), acc. ***ƀlinđanōn** (Goth. **blindana**), gen. ***ƀlinđesa, -asa,** dat. **ƀlinđommō -ē** (Goth. **blindamma**), instr. (loc.) ***ƀlinđai**; plur. nom. ***ƀlinđai** (Goth. **blindái**), acc. ***ƀlinđanz** (Goth. **blindans**), gen. **ƀlinđaizǭn,** dat. ***ƀlinđomiz.** Neut. nom. acc. sing. ***ƀlinđan** (Goth. **blind**), nom. acc. pl. ***ƀlinđō** (Goth. **blinda**).

Fem. sing. nom. ***ƀlinđō** (Goth. **blinda**), acc. ***ƀlinđōn** (Goth. **blinda**), gen. ***ƀlinđizō̃z** (cp. Goth. **þizōs**, *of the*), dat. ***ƀlinđizai** (cp. Goth. **þizái,** *to the*); pl. nom. acc. ***ƀlinđō̃z** (Goth. **blindōs**), gen. ***ƀlinđaizō̃n,** dat. ***ƀlinđōmiz.** On the syncope of the medial vowel in **blindne, blindra, blindre,** see § **221;** after the analogy of such forms it was also dropped in adjectives with short stem-syllables. In late OE. **-era, -ere** are common after both long and short stem-syllables. The nom. acc. neut. pl. and nom. sing. fem. go back to prim. Germanic ***ƀlinđō,** the **-ō** of which became **-u** (§ **214**) and then disappeared after long stems (§ **215**), whence **blind** beside **gladu.** In late WS. the masc. nom. acc. pl. form was generally used for the neuter; and occasionally the **-u** of the short stems was extended to the long. On the **u** in **blindum,** see § **218;** the **-um** became **-un, -on, -an** in late OE. (§ **284**). **blindra** goes back to prim. OE. ***blindæra, *blindera,** with **æ, e** from the masc. and neut. gen. singular (cp. § **334,** Note). This form then came to be used for the feminine also. The remaining forms require no comment, as they are regularly developed from the corresponding prim. Germanic forms.

§ **425.** On the interchange between **æ** and **a** in the declension of **glæd,** see § **54,** Note 3. Like **glæd** are declined the monosyllabic adjectives with short stems, as **bær,** *bare*; **blæc,** *black*; **hræd,** *quick*; **hwæt,** *brisk, active*; **læt,** *slow*; **smæl,** *tender, small*; **sæd,** *satiated*; **wær,** *wary, cautious*; **dol,** *foolish*; **fram,** *active, bold*; **frec,** *bold*; **frum,** *original, first*; **gram,** *angry, fierce*; **hol,** *hollow*; **hnot,** *bald*; **til,** *good, useful*; **trum,** *firm, strong*; **wan,** *wanting, deficient.* Adjectives with the suffixes **-lic** and **-sum,** as **ānlic,** *solitary* (for other examples, see § **634**); **angsum,** *troublesome* (for other examples, see § **636**).

§ **426.** Like **blind** are declined the monosyllabic adjectives with long stems, as **beald,** *bold*; **beorht,** *bright*; **blāc,** *pale*; **brūn,** *brown*; **brād,** *broad*; **ceald,** *cold*; **cūþ,** *known, familiar*; **dēad,** *dead*; **dēaf,** *deaf*; **dēop,** *deep*; **deorc,** *dark*; **dumb,** *dumb*; **eald,** *old*; **earg,** *cowardly*; **earm,** *poor*; **forht,** *fearful, timid*; **frōd,** *wise, old*; **fūl,** *foul*; **fūs,** *ready*; **gefōg (gefōh),** *joint*; **genōg (genōh),** *enough*; **geong,** *young*; **georn,** *eager*; **gnēaþ,** *niggardly*; **gōd,** *good*; **grǣg,** *grey*; **grēat,** *large*; **hāl,** *whole, sound*; **hār,** *hoary*; **hās,** *hoarse*; **healt,** *halt, lame*; **hēan,** *lowly, despised*; **hold,** *gracious*; **hrōr,** *active, brave*; **hwīt,** *white*; **lang,** *long*; **lāþ,** *hateful*; **lēas,** *free from, faithless*; **lēof,** *dear*; **ranc,** *proud*; **rēad,** *red*; **riht,** *right, straight*; **rōf,** *brave, strong*; **rōt,** *glad, cheerful*; **rūm,** *roomy*; **sār,** *sore*; **scearp,** *sharp*; **scīr,** *bright, shining*; **scort,** *short*; **sēoc,** *sick*; **sōþ,** *true*; **stēap,** *steep, lofty*; **stearc,** *stiff*; **stīþ,** *stiff, rigid*; **strang,** *strong*; **swift,** *swift*; **swīþ,** *strong*; **torht,** *bright*; **trāg,** *lazy, bad*; **þearl,** *severe*; **wǣt,** *wet*; **wāc,** *weak*; **wealt,** *unsteady*; **wearm,** *warm*; **wīd,** *wide*; **wīs,** *wise*; **wlanc,** *proud*; **wōd,** *mad*; **wrǣst,** *firm, strong*; **wrāþ,** *wroth, angry*; **wund,** *wounded*; **fyrn** (orig. **i**-stem), *old, ancient*; **cōl** (orig. **u**-stem), *cool*; **heard** (orig. **u**-stem), *hard*. The double consonants were simplified in the inflected forms before other consonants (§ **259**) in words like **dunn,** *dun*; **eall,** *all*; **feorr,** *far*; **full,** *full*; **gewiss,** *certain, sure*; **grimm,** *grim*; **snell,** *ready, active*. For examples of adjectives like **æþelcund,** *of noble origin*; **ānfeald,** *single*; **ārfæst,** *virtuous*; **ārlēas,** *impious,* see Adjectival Suffixes, §§ **623, 627, 633.**

§ **427.**

| SING. | *Masc.* | *Neut.* | *Fem.* |
|---|---|---|---|
| Nom. | **hēah,** *high* | **hēah** | **hēa** |
| Acc. | **hēa(n)ne** | **hēah** | **hēa** |
| Gen. | **hēas** | **hēas** | **hēa(r)re** |
| Dat. | **hēa(u)m** | **hēa(u)m** | **hēa(r)re** |
| Instr. | **hēa** | **hēa** | |

| PLUR. | | | |
|---|---|---|---|
| Nom. Acc. | **hēa** | **hēa** | **hēa** |
| Gen. | **hēa(r)ra** | **hēa(r)ra** | **hēa(r)ra** |
| Dat. | **hēa(u)m** | **hēa(u)m** | **hēa(u)m** |

**hēanne, hēarra, hēarre** were due to the assimilation of **hn** and **hr**; and **hēane, hēara, hēare** arose from the regu lar loss of **h** before **n, r** (§ **329**, 2). In **hēaum** the **u** was restored after the analogy of forms like **gladum, blindum.** The instr., masc. and fem. nom. pl., and fem. acc. singular **hēa** was from older ***hēahe**; and the neut. nom. acc. pl. and fem. nom. singular from older ***hēahu**; masc. and neut. gen. sing. from ***hēahes.** See § **139.** Late OE. forms like gen. **hēages,** dat. **hēage,** nom. pl. **hēage** beside older **hēas, hēa(u)m, hēa** were formed after the analogy of such words as gen. **gefōges, genōges** beside nom. **gefōh, genōh** (§ **323**).

§ **428.** Like **hēah** are declined **fāh,** *hostile*; **flāh,** *deceitful*; **hrēoh,** *rude, rough, wild*; **nēah,** *nigh, near*; **rūh,** *rough*; **scēoh,** *shy*; **tōh,** *tough*; **wōh,** *crooked, bad.* **sceolh,** *awry, squinting*; **þweorh,** *cross, perverse,* dropped the **h** and lengthened the diphthong in the inflected forms, as gen. **scēoles, þwēores,** dat. **scēolum, þwēorum,** cp. § **149.**

§ **429.**

| SING. | *Masc.* | *Neut.* | *Fem.* |
|---|---|---|---|
| Nom. | **manig,** *many* | **manig** | **manig** |
| Acc. | **manigne** | **manig** | **manige** |
| Gen. | **maniges** | **maniges** | **manigre** |
| Dat. | **manigum** | **manigum** | **manigre** |
| Instr. | **manige** | **manige** | |
| PLUR. | | | |
| Nom. Acc. | **manige** | **manig** | **maniga, -e** |
| Gen. | **manigra** | **manigra** | **manigra** |
| Dat. | **manigum** | **manigum** | **manigum** |

| | | | |
|---|---|---|---|
| Sing. | | | |
| Nom. | **hālig,** *holy* | **hālig** | **hāligu, -o** |
| Acc. | **hāligne** | **hālig** | **hālge** |
| Gen. | **hālges** | **hālges** | **hāligre** |
| Dat. | **hālgum** | **hālgum** | **hāligre** |
| Instr. | **hālge** | **hālge** | |
| Plur. | | | |
| Nom. Acc. | **hālge** | **hāligu, -o** | **hālga, -e** |
| Gen. | **hāligra** | **hāligra** | **hāligra** |
| Dat. | **hālgum** | **hālgum** | **hālgum** |

Original short medial vowels in open syllables regularly remained in trisyllabic forms when the stem-syllable was short. They also remained in closed syllables irrespectively as to whether the stem-syllable was long or short. But they disappeared when the stem-syllable was long. See § **221.** Final **-u** regularly disappeared after a long medial syllable, and also when the stem and the medial syllable were short, but remained when the stem-syllable was long and the medial syllable short. See § **216.** There are many exceptions to the above rules due to analogical formations, as **yfles, hāliges, hālgu** beside older **yfeles, hālges, hāligu,** see § **223,** Note 1. In adjectives ending in **-en, -er,** the combinations **-enne** (masc. acc. sing.), **-erra** (gen. pl.), and **-erre** (fem. gen. dat. sing.) were often simplified to **-ene, -era, -ere** especially in late OE. (§ **259,** 4).

§ **430.** Like **manig** are declined the dissyllabic adjectives with short stems, as **atol,** *terrible, dire*; **bedol,** *suppliant*; **bræsen,** *of brass* (for examples of other adjectives ending in **-en,** see § **625**); **efen,** *even*; **etol,** *gluttonous*; **fægen,** *glad*; **fæger,** *fair*; **flacor,** *flickering*; **flugol,** *fleet, swift*; **forod,** *decayed*; **fracoþ,** *vile, bad*; **hnitol,** *given to butting*; **micel** (see § **223,** Note 1), *large, great*; **nacod,** *naked*; **open,** *open*; **plegol,** *playful*; **recen,** *ready, prompt*; **sicor,** *sure*; **sweotol,** *plain, evident*; **yfel,** *evil*; **wacor,** *vigilant*; **bysig,** *busy* (for other examples, see § **630**); past participles, as **boren**, *borne*; **coren**, *chosen*; **legen**, *lain*; &c.

§ **431**. Like **hālig** are declined the dissyllabic adjectives with long stems, as **ācol**, *timid, frightened*; **ǣt(t)ren**, *poisonous* (for examples of other adjectives ending in **-en**, see § **625**); **āgen**, *own*; **bēogol**, *agreeing*; **bit(t)er**, *bitter*; **brægden**, *deceitful*; **crīsten**, *christian*; **dēagol**, **dīegol** (cp. § **639**), *secret*; **ēacen**, *great, increased*; **earfoþ**, *difficult*; **frettol**, *greedy*; **geōmor**, *sad*; **gylden**, *golden*; **hādor**, *bright*; **hǣþen**, *heathen*; **hlūt(t)or**, *clear*; **īdel**, *vain*; **lȳtel**, *little*; **ōþer** (§ **223**), *second*; **snot(t)or**, *wise*; **stǣgel**, *steep*; **blōdig**, *bleeding*; **cræftig**, *skilful*; **ēadig**, *rich, happy* (for other examples, see § **630**); **cildisc**, *childish* (for other examples, see § **632**); past participles, as **bunden**, *bound*; **holpen**, *helped*, see § **442**.

### *b*. ja-, jō-STEMS.

§ **432**. In the **ja-**, **jō-**stems it is necessary to distinguish between those stems which were originally long and those which became long by the West Germanic doubling of consonants (§ **254**). The latter class were declined in OE. like the pure **a-**, **ō-**stems ending in double consonants (§ **426**); such are: **gesibb**, *akin, related*; **midd**, *middle*; **nytt**, *useful*. The regular form of the nom. sing. masc. and neut. of a word like **midd** would be ***mide**, see § **274**.

§ **433**.

| SING. | *Masc.* | *Neut.* | *Fem.* |
|---|---|---|---|
| Nom. | **wilde**, *wild* | **wilde** | **wildu**, **-o** |
| Acc. | **wildne** | **wilde** | **wilde** |
| Gen. | **wildes** | **wildes** | **wildre** |
| Dat. | **wildum** | **wildum** | **wildre** |
| Instr. | **wilde** | **wilde** | |
| PLUR. | | | |
| Nom. Acc. | **wilde** | **wildu**, **-o** | **wilda**, **-e** |
| Gen. | **wildra** | **wildra** | **wildra** |
| Dat. | **wildum** | **wildum** | **wildum** |

The only difference in declension between the original long **ja-, jō**-stems and the long pure **a-, ō**-stems is in the masc. nom. sing., neut. nom. acc. sing. and plural, and the fem. nom. singular. **wilde** (masc. nom. sing.) is regularly developed from prim. Germanic ***wilþjaz,** and the neut. nom. acc. sing. from ***wilþjan** (§**274**); **wildu** (fem. nom. sing. and neut. nom. acc. plural) was formed on analogy with the short pure **a**-stems (§ **424**), the regular form would be ***wild** (see § **215**). Double consonants were simplified before or after other consonants (§ **259**), as masc. acc. sing. **þynne,** *thin,* **fǣcne,** *deceitful,* **ierne,** *angry,* from ***þynnne, *fǣcnne, *ierrne;** fem. gen. dat. sing. **gīfre,** *greedy,* **ierre** from ***gīfrre, *ierrre.** When **n, r** came to stand between two consonants the first of which was not a nasal or liquid, they became vocalic and then developed an **e** before them, as masc. acc. sing. **gīferne** from ***gīfrne**; fem. gen. dat. sing. **fǣcenre** from ***fǣcnre.** Nearly all the old long **i**- and **u**-stems went over into this declension in prehistoric OE.

§ **434.** Like **wilde** are declined a large number of adjectives, as **æltǣwe,** *entire*; **æþele,** *noble*; **andfenge,** *acceptable*; **andrysne,** *terrible*; **ānlīepe,** *single*; **blīþe,** *joyful*; **brēme,** *famous*; **brȳce,** *useful*; **cēne,** *bold*; **clǣne,** *clean*; **cȳme,** *comely, beautiful*; **cynde,** *natural*; **dīere, dēore** (cp. § **138**), *dear*; **dierne,** *hidden*; **drȳge,** *dry*; **ēce,** *eternal*; **egle,** *troublesome*; **ēste,** *gracious*; **fǣcne,** *deceitful*; **fǣge,** *fated*; **fēowerfēte,** *four-footed*; **filde,** *level* (*of land*); **flēde,** *in flood*; **forþgenge,** *effective*; **frēcne,** *dangerous, wicked*; **frem(e)de,** *foreign*; **frēo** (§ **104**), *free*; **gecnǣwe,** *conscious of*; **gecwēme,** *pleasant*; **gedēfe,** *becoming, fit*; **gefēre,** *accessible*; **gehende,** *handy*; **gemǣne,** *common*; **genǣme,** *acceptable*; **gesīene,** *visible*; **getenge,** *near to*; **getrīewe,** *faithful*; **gīfre,** *greedy*; **grēne,** *green*; **hlǣne,** *lean*; **hnæsce,** *soft, tender*; **ierre,** *angry*; **īeþe,** *easy*; **lǣne,** *temporary*; **lætrǣde,** *deliberate*; **līþe,** *gentle*; **mǣre,** *famous*;

**manþwǣre**, *humane*; **medeme**, *moderate*; **mēþe**, *tired*; **milde**, *mild*; **mẏrge**, *merry*; **nīewe, nīwe** (§ **90**), *new*; **oferǣte**, *gluttonous*; **ofersprǣce**, *loquacious*; **ormǣte**, *immeasurable*; **rēþe**, *fierce*; **rīce**, *powerful*; **rīpe**, *ripe*; **sǣne**, *slow*; **sammǣle**, *agreed*; **scīene**, *beautiful*; **sēfte**, *soft*; **slīþe**, *cruel, savage*; **smēþe**, *smooth*; **smylte**, *mild, serene*; **stille**, *still*; **strenge**, *strong*; **swēte**, *sweet*; **swīge**, *silent*; **sȳfre**, *pure*; **þicce**, *thick*; **þīestre**, *dark, gloomy*; **þrifingre**, *three fingers thick*; **þrīste**, *rash, daring*; **þriwintre**, *three years old*; **þynne**, *thin*; **þyrre**, *withered*; **unhīere**, *horrible*; **ūþgenge**, *fugitive*; **wēste**, *waste, barren*; **wierþe**, *worthy*; **wrǣne**, *wanton*. In like manner are declined the present participles (§ **441**). For examples of adjectives like **æppelbǣre**, *apple-bearing*; **coppede**, *topped, polled*; **hālwende**, *healthful*, see Adjectival Suffixes, §§ **622, 624, 638**.

*c.* **wa-, wō-**STEMS.

§ **435.**

| | | *Masc.* | *Neut.* | *Fem.* |
|---|---|---|---|---|
| SING. | Nom. | **gearu, -o**, *ready* | **gearu, -o** | **gearu, -o** |
| | Acc. | **gearone** | **gearu, -o** | **gearwe** |
| | Gen. | **gearwes** | **gearwes** | **gearore** |
| | Dat. | **gearwum** | **gearwum** | **gearore** |
| | Instr. | **gearwe** | **gearwe** | |
| PLUR. | Nom. Acc. | **gearwe** | **gearu, -o** | **gearwa, -e** |
| | Gen. | **gearora** | **gearora** | **gearora** |
| | Dat. | **gearwum** | **gearwum** | **gearwum** |

**w** became vocalized to **u** (later **o**) when final and before consonants in prehistoric OE. (§ **265**); whence masc. nom. sing., neut. nom. acc. sing. **gearu** from ***ʒarw-az, -an.** The **u** had become **o** before consonants in the oldest period of the language, as **gearone, gearora.** The fem. nom. sing. and neut. nom. acc. pl. are from older ***ʒarwu** with loss of **w** before the following **u** (§ **266**). The dat.

**gearwum** for ***gearum** was a new formation made from forms like **gearwes, gearwe,** where the **w** was regular. On forms like gen. **gearuwes, gearowes** beside **gearwes,** see § **220**.

§ **436**. Like **gearu** are declined **basu, beasu,** *purple*; **calu,** *bald*; **cylu,** *spotted*; **fealu,** *fallow*; **geolu,** *yellow*; **hasu, heasu,** *grey, tawny*; **mearu,** *tender*; **nearu,** *narrow*; **salu, sealu,** *dusky, dark.*

§ **437**. The adjectives which had a long vowel or long diphthong in the stem reintroduced the **w** into the nominative from the inflected forms (§ **265**) and then came to be declined like pure long **a-, ō-**stems (§ **424**); such are: **gedēaw,** *dewy*; **gehlēow,** *sheltered*; **gesēaw,** *succulent*; **glēaw,** *wise*; **hnēaw,** *stingy*; **hrēaw,** *raw*; **rōw,** *quiet, calm*; **slāw,** *slow*; **þēow,** *servile*; **fēawe** (**fēa**), *few*, neut. **fēa** from ***fawu,** fem. **fēawa**; gen. **fēara, fēawera** (cp. § **220**), dat. **fēam, fēaum, fēawum.**

### *d.* i-STEMS.

§ **438**. Of the adjectives which originally belonged to this class, the long stems took final **-i** (later **-e**) from analogy with the short stems and then both classes went over into the **ja**-declension in prehistoric OE. The old short **i**-stems are still recognizable by the fact that they do not have double consonants in the stem-syllable. Examples are: **bryce,** *brittle*; **gemyne,** *remembering*; **swice,** *deceitful*; and of old long **i**-stems: **blīþe** (Goth. **bleiþs**), *joyful*; **brȳce** (Goth. **brūks**), *useful*; **clǣne,** *clean*; **gecwēme,** *pleasant*; **gedēfe** (Goth. **gadōfs**), *becoming, fit*; **gemǣne** (Goth. **gamáins**), *common*; **gesīene** (cp. Goth. **anasiuns**), *visible*; **grēne,** *green*; **scīene,** *beautiful*; **swēte,** *sweet*; &c.

### *e.* u-STEMS.

§ **439**. Of the adjectives which originally belonged to this class only two have preserved traces of the old

**u**-declension, namely nom. sing. **cwicu, c(w)ucu,** *alive,* masc. acc. sing. **cucone,** and nom. **wlacu,** *warm, tepid.* And even these two adjectives generally have nom. **cwic, wlæc** and are declined like short pure **a**-stems. Cp. § **399.** All the other adjectives passed over into the **a-, ja-,** or **wa**-declension in prehistoric OE., as **heard** (Goth. **hardus**), *hard*; **egle** (Goth. **aglus**), *troublesome*; **hnesce, hnæsce** (Goth. **hnasqus**), *soft, tender*; **twelfwintre** (Goth. **twalibwintrus**), *twelve years old*; **þyrre** (Goth. **þaúrsus**), *dry, withered*; **glēaw** (Goth. **glaggwus**), *wise.*

### 2. The Weak Declension.

§ **440.**

| Sing. | *Masc.* | *Neut.* | *Fem.* |
|---|---|---|---|
| Nom. | **blinda,** *blind* | **blinde** | **blinde** |
| Acc. | **blindan** | **blinde** | **blindan** |
| Gen. | **blindan** | **blindan** | **blindan** |
| Dat. | **blindan** | **blindan** | **blindan** |
| Plur. | | | |
| Nom. Acc. | **blindan** | **blindan** | **blindan** |
| Gen. | **blindra, -ena** | **blindra, -ena** | **blindra, -ena** |
| Dat. | **blindum** | **blindum** | **blindum** |

The weak declension of adjectives has the same endings as the weak declension of nouns, except that the adjectives generally have the strong ending **-ra** (§ **424**) instead of **-(e)na** in the gen. plural. Beside the regular dat. pl. ending **-um** there also occurs at an early period **-an** which was taken over from the nom. acc. plural. In trisyllabic adjectives the medial vowel remained after short stems, but disappeared after long stems, as **wacora, wacore,** *vigilant,* beside **hālga, hālge,** *holy* (§ **221**). On adjectives like **hēa,** *high,* gen. **hēan,** see § **427.** In like manner are declined the **ja-** and **wa-**stems, as **wilda, wilde,** *wild*; **gearwa, gearwe,** *ready*.

### 3. The Declension of Participles.

§ **441.** In the Indg. parent language the stem of the present participle ended in **-nt,** as in Lat. **ferent-,** Gr. φέροντ-, *bearing*. The masc. and neut. were originally declined like consonant stems (§ **416**). The fem. nom. originally ended in **-ī** which was shortened to **-i** (§ **214**) in prehistoric OE. (cp. Goth. **frijōndi,** fem. *friend*). The **-i** of the feminine was extended to the masculine and neuter, which was the cause of their passing over into the **ja-** declension (§ **433**). In OE. the pres. participle was declined strong or weak like an ordinary adjective. When used predicatively it often had the uninflected form for all genders in the nom. and accusative.

§ **442.** The past participle, like the present, was declined strong or weak like an ordinary adjective. When strong it was declined like **manig** or **hālig** (§ **429**) according as the stem-syllable was short or long; and similarly when it was declined weak (§ **440**). When used predicatively it generally had the uninflected form for all genders. A small number of past participles of strong verbs have **i-**umlaut of the stem-vowel, because in prim. Germanic, beside the ordinary ending **-énaz** = Indg. **-énos,** there also existed **-íniz** = Indg. **-énis,** hence forms like **ǣgen** beside **āgen,** *own*; **cymen** beside **cumen,** *come*; **slegen** beside **slægen, slagen,** *slain*; **tygen** from ***tuȝiniz** beside **togen** from ***tuȝenaz,** *drawn*. See § **483**.

## B. The Comparison of Adjectives.

### 1. The Comparative Degree.

§ **443.** The Indg. parent language had several suffixes by means of which the comparative degree was formed. But in the individual branches of the parent language, one of the suffixes generally became more productive than the rest, and in the course of time came to be the principal one from which the comparative was formed, the other suffixes only being preserved in isolated forms. The only Indg. comparative suffix which remained productive in the Germanic languages is **-is-**, which became **-iz-** (= Goth. **-iz-**, OHG. **-ir-**, OE. **-r-**) in prim. Germanic by Verner's law. To this suffix was added in prim. Germanic, or probably in the pre-Germanic period, the formative suffix **-en-**, **-on-**, as in Gr. *ἡδίων* from **σϝāδίσων*, gen. *ἡδίονος*, = Goth. **sŭtiza,** gen. **sŭtizins,** OHG. **suoȥiro,** gen. **suoȥiren,** (**-in**), OE. **swētra,** *sweeter*, gen. **swētran.** The original distinction in meaning between the Indg. suffix **-is-** and the extended form **-is-en, -is-on-** was that the former was adjectival and the latter substantival, but the substantival meaning became adjectival already in prim. Germanic (see § **421**), and similarly in Gr. *ἡδίων* which originally meant *the sweeter*. This explains why the comparative is declined weak in the oldest periods of the Germanic languages. Beside the suffix **-iz-** there was also in prim. Germanic a suffix **-ōz-** (Goth. **-ōz-**, OHG. **-ōr-**, OE. **-r-**) which did not exist in Indo-Germanic. This suffix is a special Germanic new formation, and arose from the comparative of adverbs whose positive originally ended in **-ō̆**, Indg. **-ō̆d** (§ **554**). And then at a later period it became extended to adjectives.

In OE. polysyllabic adjectives formed with derivative suffixes and compound adjectives had the Germanic suffix **-ōz-**; **ja**-stems the suffix **-iz-**; and uncompounded pure

**a**-stems mostly had **-ōz-**. Prim. Germanic **-izō̆** (= OHG. **-iro**) and **-ōzō̆** (= OHG. **-ōro**) fell together in **-ra** in OE., so that, except in the **ja**-stems, the presence or absence of umlaut is the only indication as to which of the two suffixes **-ra** goes back. The Goth. endings **-iza, -ōza** were from prim. Germanic **-izōn, -ōzōn,** see § **403.** Only a small number of adjectives have umlaut in OE., of which the most common are:

| | |
|---|---|
| **brād,** *broad* | **brǣdra** beside **brādra** |
| **eald,** *old* | **ieldra** (Goth. **alþiza**) |
| **feorr,** *far* | **fierra** |
| **geong,** *young* | **giengra, gingra** |
| **grēat,** *great* | **grīetra** |
| **hēah,** *high* | **hīehra, hīerra** beside **hēahra** |
| **lang,** *long* | **lengra** |
| **sceort,** *short* | **sciertra** |
| **strang,** *strong* | **strengra** |

Examples without umlaut in the comparative degree are: **ēadig,** *happy,* **earm,** *poor,* **fægen,** *glad,* **fæger,** *fair,* **gearu, -o,** *ready,* **glæd,** *glad,* **grimm,** *grim,* **hālig,** *holy,* **lēof,** *dear,* **nēah,** *near,* comparative **ēadigra, earmra, fægenra, fægerra, gearora, glædra, grimra, hāligra, lēofra, nēahra** (**nēarra**); and with umlaut in both the positive and superlative: **clǣne,** *clean,* **grēne,** *green,* **þynne,** *thin,* comparative **clǣnra, grēnra, þyn(n)ra,** see § **433.**

### 2. The Superlative Degree.

§ **444.** The superlative, like the comparative degree, was formed in the Indg. parent language by means of several suffixes. But in the individual branches of the parent language, one of the suffixes generally became more productive than the rest, and in the course of time came to be the principal one from which the superlative degree was formed, the other suffixes only being preserved in isolated forms. The only superlative suffix which remained productive in the Germanic languages is **-to-** in the combination **-isto-**, formed by adding the original superlative suffix **-to-** to the comparative suffix **-is-**, as in Sanskrit and Greek, as Gr. ἥδιστος = Goth. **sŭtists,** OHG. **suoȥisto,** OE. **swētest(a),** *sweetest.* The simple superlative suffix **-to-** has been preserved in Gr., Lat., and the Germanic languages in the formation of the ordinal numerals, as Gr. ἕκτος, Lat. **sextus,** Goth. **saíhsta,** OHG. **sehsto,** OE. **siexta,** *sixth.* The Germanic suffix **-ōst-** was a new formation like **-ōz-** in the comparative. **-ōst-, -ist-** regularly became **-ost-, -est-** in OE., and the medial vowel in the superlative being in a closed syllable remained (§ **221**). It is difficult to account for its early loss in **hīehst(a),** *highest,* and **nīehst(a),** *nearest* (see § **221**). In late OE. the medial vowel was often syncopated, as **lengsta, strengsta** (§ **223,** Note 2). On the interchange of the medial vowel in forms like **lēofesta** beside **lēofosta,** see § **222.** The adjectives which had **i**-umlaut in the comparative generally had **-est(a),** but sometimes also **-ost(a),** in the superlative, and those which did not have umlaut in the comparative generally had **-ost(a),** rarely **-ust(a), -ast(a),** as **ieldest(a), fierrest(a), giengest(a), gingest(a), grīetest(a), lengest(a), sciertest(a), strengest(a),** but **earmost(a), fægnost(a), gearwost(a), hāligost(a), lēofost(a),** &c.; and with umlaut in all three degrees: **clǣnest(a), grēnest(a), þynnest(a),** see § **433.**

In Gothic the superlative had both the strong and the weak declension, but in OE. it generally had only the latter except in the nom. acc. neut. which had both forms **-est, -ost,** beside **-este, -oste.**

### 3. Irregular Comparison.

§ **445.** The following adjectives form their comparatives and superlatives from a different root than the positive:—

| | | |
|---|---|---|
| **gōd**, *good* | { **bet(e)ra, bettra**<br>{ **sēlra, sēlla** | **bet(e)st, betsta** |
| **lȳtel**, *little* | **lǣssa** | **lǣst(a)** |
| **micel**, *great* | **māra** | **mǣst(a)** |
| **yfel**, *evil* | **wiersa** | **wierrest(a), wierst(a)** |

Note.—1. On the **tt** in **bettra** (Goth. **batiza**), see § **260**. **bet(e)st** = Goth. **batists**. **sēlla** with assimilation of **lr** to **ll** (§ **281**). **lǣssa** from ***lǣs(i)ra**, prim. Germanic ***laisizō̃** (§ **281**); **lǣst(a)** from ***lǣsist-**. **māra** (Goth. **máiza**); **mǣst(a)** (Goth. **máists**) with **ǣ** from analogy with **lǣst(a)**, Anglian **māst(a)**. **wiersa** (Goth. **wáirsiza**) from ***wiers(i)ra**; **wierrest(a)**, **wierst(a)** from ***wiersist-**.

2. In a few words comparative and superlative adjectives were formed from adverbs: **ǣr**, *before*, **ǣrra**, *former*, *earlier*, **ǣrest(a)**, *first*; **fyrest(a)** from ***furist-**, *first*, related to **fore**, *before*; **furþra**, *higher*, *greater*, related to **forþ**, *forth*.

§ **446.** In a number of words the comparative was formed from an adverb or preposition, with a superlative in **-um-**, **-uma** (prim. Germanic **-umō̃**), cp. Lat. **optimus**, *best*, **summus**, *highest*. The simple superlative suffix was preserved in OE. **forma** (Goth. **fruma**), *first*, beside **fore**, *before*; **hindema**, *last*, *hindmost*, beside **hindan**, *behind*; and **meduma, medema**, *midway in size*, related to **midd**, *middle*. But in prehistoric OE., as in Gothic, to **-um-** was added the ordinary superlative suffix **-ist-** which gave rise to the double superlative suffix **-umist-**, as Goth. **frumists**, *first*; **hindumists**, *hindmost*. In OE. **-umist-** became **-ymist-** (§ **47**), later **-imest-**, **-emest-**, **-mest-**, as

| | | |
|---|---|---|
| **æfter**, *after* | **æfterra** | **æftemest(a)** |
| **ēast**, *eastwards* | **ēasterra** | **ēastmest(a)** |
| **fore**, *before* | | **forma**, **fyrmest(a)** |

| | | |
|---|---|---|
| **inne**, *within* | **innerra** | **innemest(a)** |
| **læt**, *late* | **lætra** | **lætemest(a)** beside **lætest(a)** |
| **midd**, *middle* | | **medema, midmest(a)** |
| **nioþan**, *below* | **niþerra** | **ni(o)þemest(a)** |
| **norþ**, *northwards* | **norþerra, nyrþra** | **norþmest(a)** |
| **sīþ**, *late* | **sīþra** | **sīþemest(a)** |
| **sūþ**, *southwards* | **sūþerra, sȳþerra** | **sūþmest(a)** |
| **ufan**, *above* | {**uferra** / **yferra** | {**ufemest(a)** / **yfemest(a)** |
| **ūte**, *without* | {**ūterra** / **ȳterra** | {**ūt(e)mest(a)** / **ȳt(e)mest(a)** |
| **west**, *westwards* | **westerra** | **westmest(a)** |

## C. Numerals.

### 1. Cardinal and Ordinal.

**§ 447.**

| | |
|---|---|
| **ān**, *one* | {**forma, formest(a)** / **fyrmest(a), fyrest(a), ǣrest(a)** |
| **twā**, *two* | **ōþer, æfterra** |
| **þrī**, *three* | **þridda** |
| **fēower**, *four* | **fēo(we)rþa** |
| **fīf**, *five* | **fīfta** |
| **siex, six**, *six* | **siexta, sixta** |
| **seofon**, *seven* | **seofoþa** |
| **eahta**, *eight* | **eahtoþa** |
| **nigon**, *nine* | **nigoþa** |
| **tīen, tȳn, tēn**, *ten* | **tēoþa** |
| **en(d)le(o)fan**, *eleven* | **en(d)le(o)fta** |
| **twelf**, *twelve* | **twelfta** |
| **þrēotīene**, *thirteen* | **þrēotēoþa** |

| | |
|---|---|
| **fēowertīene,** *fourteen* | **fēowertēoþa** |
| **fīftīene,** *fifteen* | **fīftēoþa** |
| **siex-, sixtīene,** *sixteen* | **siex-, sixtēoþa** |
| **seofontīene,** *seventeen* | **seofontēoþa** |
| **eahtatīene,** *eighteen* | **eahtatēoþa** |
| **nigontīene,** *nineteen* | **nigontēoþa** |
| **twĕntig,** *twenty* | **twĕntigoþa** |
| **ān and twĕntig,** *twenty-one* | |
| **þrītig,** *thirty* | **þrītigoþa** |
| **fēowertig,** *forty* | **fēowertigoþa** |
| **fīftig,** *fifty* | **fīftigoþa** |
| **siextig,** *sixty* | **siextigoþa** |
| **hundseofontig,** *seventy* | **hundseofontigoþa** |
| **hundeahtatig,** *eighty* | **hundeahtatigoþa** |
| **hundnigontig,** *ninety* | **hundnigontigoþa** |
| **hundtēontig**<br>**hund, hundred** }, *hundred* | **hundtēontigoþa** |
| **hundendleofantig**<br>**hundendlufontig** }, 110 | **hundendleofantigoþa**<br>**hundendlufontigoþa** |
| **hundtwelftig,** 120 | **hundtwelftigoþa** |
| **tū hund, hundred,** 200 | |
| **þrēo hund, hundred,** 300 | |
| **þūsend,** *thousand* | |

**seox,** later **siex, six, syx** (§ 86). **seofon, nigon, tīen** (later **tȳn**) had their final **-n** from the inflected forms, as ***seƀuni-,** &c., or else they were formed, as in Goth. OS. and OHG., from the ordinals in prim. OE. before the **n** disappeared before **þ** (§ **286**). **nigon** from older ***nīon** (= Goth. OHG. **niun**); ***nīon** became dissyllabic and then between the two vowels a consonantal glide was developed (cp. § **270**). **tīen,** later **tȳn, tēn,** probably from an older inflected form ***tēoni-,** cp. **tēoþa. endleofan (endlefan, enlefan)** from older ***ǣnlefan, *ainina + liƀan-,** with excrescent **d** developed between the **n** and **l** and weak ending

-an. **twelf** = Goth. **twalif. endleofan** and **twelf** originally meant something like (*ten and*) *one left over*, (*ten and*) *two left over*, cp. Lithuanian **vënũlika,** *eleven*, **dvýlika,** *twelve*, &c., where Goth. **-lif** and Lith. **-lika** are from ***liqʷ-**, the weak form of the Indg. root **leiqʷ-**, *to leave*, and are ultimately related to OE. **līon (lēon)**, Goth. **leiƕan,** *to lend*, Gr. **λείπω**, Lat. **linquō,** *I leave*. The assimilation of ***-lih** to **-lif** first took place in **twalif** because of the preceding labial (§ **237**, Note), and then, at a later period, the **-lif** was extended to ***áinlif** (cp. dat. **áinlibim**) for older ***áinlih.** 13 to 19 were formed by the simple ordinals plus the inflected form **-tīene,** later **-tȳne, -tēne.**

The decades 20 to 60 were formed in prim. Germanic from the units 2 to 6 and the abstract noun ***teʒund-** = Indg. ***dekmt-**, *decade*, whence the Goth. stem-form **tigu-** which went over into the **u**-declension with a plural **tigjus,** as nom. **twái tigjus,** *twenty*, dat. **twáim tigum.** Prim. Germanic ***teʒunđ-** is a derivative of prim. Germanic ***teχun** (= Indg. ***dékm,** Gr. **δέκα**, Lat. **decem,** Goth. **taíhun,** OE. **tīen**) with change of χ to ʒ by Verner's law (§ **238**) and the loss of the final consonants (§ **211**). The stem ***teʒu-** regularly became **-tig** in OE. and OS., whence OE. **twēntig** from **twēgen + tig,** lit. *two decades*, **þrītig,** &c. with the following noun in the gen. case; **ān and twĕntig,** *twenty-one*, **twā and twĕntig,** *twenty-two*, &c. Many attempts have been made to explain the decades 70 to 120, but no satisfactory explanation of their morphology has ever yet been given, see Osthoff-Brugmann's *Morphologische Untersuchungen*, vol. V, pp. 11–17, 138–44, and Brugmann's *Grundriss*, vol. II, second ed. pp. 35–6. The decades could be used both substantively and adjectively. When used as substantives their gen. ended in **-es**; when used as adjectives they were either uninflected or formed their gen. in **-ra, -a,** and dat. in **-um.** Instead of **hundseofontig, hundeahtatig,** &c., the shorter forms

**seofontig, eahtatig,** were used when immediately preceded by **hund** = 100, as **hund and seofontig** = 170, but **hund and seofon and hundseofontig** = 177. At a later period the shorter forms became generally used in all positions. Besides the form **hundtēontig,** there were in OE. the two neuter nouns **hund** (= Gr. ἑ-κατόν, Lat. **centum,** Indg. ***kmtóm**), and **hundred, -reþ** (= O.Icel. **hundraþ**); the second element **-red, -reþ** is related to Gothic **raþjō,** *number.* 200 to 900 were generally expressed by the simple units and **hund** (also sometimes **hundred, hundtēontig**), as **twā hund, fīf hund,** &c. **hund** was usually uninflected, but occasionally it had a dat. ending **-e, -um. hundred** had a pl. form **hundredu,** when used absolutely. **þūsend** was a neuter noun and was often inflected as such.

The decades, and **hund, hundred,** and **þūsend,** being nouns, governed a following noun in the genitive case.

The forms for 'first' are old superlatives of adverbs (§§ **445,** Note 2, **446**). **ōþer** (Goth. **anþar,** cp. NE. *every other day*) was always declined according to the strong declension of adjectives (§ **429**). **þridda** (Goth. **þridja,** Gr. τρίτος) with weak stem-form from Indg. ***tri-** the weak form of ***trei-**, *three.* All the other ordinals were formed from the cardinals by means of the Indg. superlative suffix **-to-** (§ **444**), the **t** of which regularly remained unshifted in **fīfta, siexta, endleofta, twelfta** (§ **231,** Notes). In other positions the **t** became **þ** by the first sound-shifting (§ **231**), then **þ** became **d** by Verner's law (§ **238**) in those ordinals which did not originally have the chief accent immediately before the **þ,** and later **nd** became **nd** (§ **253**), as Goth. ***sibunda, niunda, taíhunda,** from Indg. ***septmtos, *neuntós, *dekmtós.** The regular forms of these would have been in OE. ***seofonda, *nigonda, *tēonda,** but OE. generalized those ordinal forms which in prim. Germanic had the chief accent immediately before the **þ,** whence the OE. new formations **seofoþa, nigoþa,**

**tēoþa** from older ***seƀunþō̃, *nijunþō̃, teχunþō̃**. In the decades the medial **o** may represent the older **u** in ***teȝu-** (see above). In compound ordinals the cardinal units were generally used, as **fēower and fīftigoþa,** *fifty-fourth*, but sometimes the ordinal forms of the units were used with the cardinal decades in the dative, as **fēo(we)rþa ēac fīftigum. hund, hundred,** and **þūsend** had no corresponding ordinals. All the ordinals, except **ōþer,** were declined according to the weak declension of adjectives.

§ **448.** In OE. the cardinals 1 to 3 were declinable in all cases and genders as in the other Germanic languages. **ān** was declined according to the strong (§ **424**) or weak declension (§ **440**) of adjectives. The strong masc. acc. sing. is generally **ǣnne** (shortened later to **ænne, enne**) from prim. Germanic ***aininōn,** beside the less common form **ānne** from ***ainanōn.** Strong pl. forms are rare, but they occur occasionally, meaning *each, all, every one*, **ānra gehwilc,** *each one*. When declined weak it means *alone, solus*.

| § **449.** | *Masc.* | *Neut.* | *Fem.* |
|---|---|---|---|
| Nom. Acc. | **twēgen** | **tū, twā** | **twā** |
| Gen. | **twēg(e)a**<br>**twēgra** | **twēg(e)a**<br>**twēgra** | **twēg(e)a**<br>**twēgra** |
| Dat. | **twǣm, twām** | **twǣm, twām** | **twǣm, twām** |

The formation of **twēgen** and of the genitive are difficult to explain. **twēg(e)a** cannot correspond to Goth. **twaddjē,** prim. Germanic ***twajjōn,** which would have become ***twǣg(e)a** in OE., cp. § **275. twǣm** from prim. Germanic ***twaimiz; twām** was a new formation from **twā. tū** from prim. Germanic ***twō** (§ **130**); **twā** corresponds to the Goth. masc. form **twái.**

§ **450.** Like **twēgen** is also declined **bēgen** (shortened later to **beggen**), **bū** (§ **130**), **bā** (Goth. masc. **bái**), *both*.

Also in the combination masc. and fem. **bā twā**, neut. **bū tū**, often written in one word **būtū**, *both*.

| § **451.** | *Masc.* | *Neut.* | *Fem.* |
|---|---|---|---|
| Nom. Acc. | **þrī, þrīe** | **þrīo, þrēo** | **þrīo, þrēo** |
| Gen. | **þrīora** / **þrēora** | **þrīora** / **þrēora** | **þrīora** / **þrēora** |
| Dat. | **þrim** | **þrim** | **þrim** |

**þrī** (Goth. **þreis**) from prim. Germanic ***þrijiz**; **þrīe** had its **e** from the adjectives (§ **424**). **þrīora** was formed from **þrīo** with the ending of the strong adjectives; the regular form would have been ***þrīa** from prim. Germanic ***þrijō̃n**. **þrim** (Goth. **þrim**) from ***þrimiz**; beside **þrim** there also occurs **þrīm** (cp. § **145**). Neut. **þrīo** (Goth. **þrija**) from ***þrīu** older ***þrijō**. Fem. **þrīo** from ***þrīu** older ***þrijō**.

§ **452.** The cardinal numbers 4 to 19 generally remained uninflected when they stood before a noun, whereas, if they stood after a noun or were used as nouns, they were declined according to the **i**-declension: nom. acc. masc. and fem. **-e**, neut. **-u** (**-o**); gen. **-a**, dat. **-um**, as of **fīf hlāfum**, *from five loaves*; **mid fēawum brōþrum, þæt is, seofonum oþþe eahtum**, *with seven or eight brothers*; **fīfa sum**, *one of five*.

## 2. Other Numerals.

§ **453.** In OE. the multiplicative numeral adjectives were formed from the cardinals and the Germanic suffix for *-fold*, Goth. **-falþs**, OHG. **-falt**, OE. **-feald** (§ **628**), as **ānfeald**, *single*, **twie-**, **twifeald**, *twofold*, **þrie-**, **þrifeald**, *threefold*, **fēowerfeald**, *fourfold*, &c., **manigfeald**, *manifold*, which were declined as ordinary adjectives. The first element of **twifeald**, **þrifeald** was sometimes inflected, as dat. **twǣmfealdum**, **þrimfealdum**.

§ **454.** Of the old adverbial multiplicatives only three occur: **ǣne** (rare in gen. form **ǣnes**), *once*; **tuwa**, **twiwa**,

**twywa,** *twice*; **þriwa, þrywa,** *thrice*. The remaining multiplicatives, and often also *once, twice, thrice*, were expressed by **sīþ,** *going, way*, and the cardinals, as **ǣne sīþa** or **on ǣnne sīþ, twǣm sīþum** (Goth. **twáim sinþam**), **fīf sīþum** (Goth. **fimf sinþam**), &c.

§ **455.** *For the first, second, third, &c. time*, were expressed by **sīþ** and the ordinals, as **forman sīþe, ōþre sīþe, þriddan sīþe, fīftan sīþe,** &c.

§ **456.** The distributive numerals were **ān-, ǣnlīepige,** *one each*; **be twǣm** or **twǣm** and **twǣm, be þrim** or **þrim** and **þrim, fēower** and **fēower, þūsendum** and **þūsendum,** &c. A remnant of the old distributive numeral corresponding to Gothic **tweihnái,** *two each*, has been preserved in the compound preposition **betwēonum,** *between*.

§ **457.** OE. also had numerals like NHG. **anderthalb, dritt(e)halb,** lit. (*one and*) *the second half*, (*two and*) *the third half*. This method of expressing numbers goes back to the prim. Germanic period, and was originally common in all the Germanic languages. Originally both elements of the compound were inflected, but at a later period the compound, when used before nouns, became uninflected like other cardinal numerals, as **ōþer healf hund daga,** 150 *days*; **þridda healf,** *two and a half*, **fēo(we)rþa healf,** *three and a half*; cp. Gr. τρίτον ἡμιτάλαντον, *two talents and a half*, lit. *third half talent*.

# CHAPTER XIII

## PRONOUNS

§ **458.** The most difficult chapter in works on comparative grammar is the one dealing with the pronouns. It is impossible to state with any degree of certainty how many pronouns the parent Indg. language had and what forms they had assumed at the time it became differentiated into the various branches which constitute the Indg. family of languages. The difficulty is rendered still more complicated by the fact that most of the pronouns, especially the personal and demonstrative, must have had accented and unaccented forms existing side by side in the parent language itself; and that one or other of the forms became generalized already in the prehistoric period of the individual branches of the parent language. And then at a later period, but still in prehistoric times, there arose new accented and unaccented forms side by side in the individual branches, as e.g. in prim. Germanic **ek, mek** beside **ik, mik.** The separate Germanic languages generalized one or other of these forms before the beginning of the oldest literary monuments and then new accented beside unaccented forms came into existence again. And similarly during the historic periods of the different languages. Thus, e.g. the OE. for **I** is **ic,** this became in ME. **ich** accented form beside **i** unaccented form, **ich** then disappeared in standard ME. (but it is still preserved in one of the modern dialects of Somersetshire) and **i** came to be used as the accented and unaccented form. At a later period it became **ī** when accented and remained **i** when unaccented. The former has become NE. **I,** and the latter has disappeared from the standard language, but it is still preserved in many northern Engl. dialects, as **i.** In these dialects **i** is regularly used in interrogative and subordinate sentences; the ME. accented form **ī** has become **ai** and is only used in the dialects to express special emphasis, and from it a new unaccented form **a** has been developed which can only be used in making direct assertions. Thus in one and the same dialect (Windhill, Yorks.) we arrive at three forms: **ai, a, i,** which are never mixed up syntactically by genuine native dialect speakers. Something similar to what has happened and still is happening in the modern dialects must also have taken place in the prehistoric and historic periods of all the Indg. languages; hence in the prehistoric forms of the pronouns given below, it must not be assumed that they were the only ones existing in prim. Germanic. They are merely given as the nearest ascertainable forms from which the OE. forms were descended.

### 1. Personal.

**§ 459.** *First Person.*

| | Sing. | Dual. | Plur. |
|---|---|---|---|
| Nom. | **ic**, *I* | **wit** | **wě̆** |
| Acc. | **mec, mě̆** | **uncit, unc** | **ūsic, ūs** |
| Gen. | **mīn** | **uncer** | **ūser, ūre** |
| Dat. | **mě̆** | **unc** | **ūs** |

**§ 460.** *Second Person.*

| | | | |
|---|---|---|---|
| Nom. | **þŭ̆**, *thou* | **git** | **gě̆** |
| Acc. | **þec, þě̆** | **incit, inc** | **ēowic, ēow, īow** |
| Gen. | **þīn** | **incer** | **ēower, īower** |
| Dat. | **þě̆** | **inc** | **ēow, īow** |

**§ 461.** *Third Person.*

Sing.

| | *Masc.* | *Neut.* | *Fem.* |
|---|---|---|---|
| Nom. | **hě̆**, *he* | **hit** | **hīo, hēo** |
| Acc. | **hine, hiene** | **hit** | **hīe** |
| Gen. | **his** | **his** | **hiere, hire** |
| Dat. | **him** | **him** | **hiere, hire** |

Plur. all Genders.

| | |
|---|---|
| Nom. Acc. | **hīe, hĭ̄** |
| Gen. | **hiera, hira, hiora, heora** |
| Dat. | **him** |

§ **462.** In the Indg. parent language the nom. was rarely used except to express emphasis (cp. Skr., Lat., and Gr.), because it was sufficiently indicated by the personal endings of the verb. Beside the accented form of each case of the personal pronouns, there also existed one or more unaccented forms just as in many modern dialects, where we often find three or even four forms for the nom. case of each pronoun. Most of the OE. forms of the personal pronouns represent prim. Germanic unaccented forms.

In forms marked with both long and short vowels, as in **mĕ, þĕ, gĕ,** &c., those with long vowels were the accented, and those with short vowels were the unaccented forms, see § **95.** In the pronouns of the first and second persons the gen. case singular, dual, and plural is the same as the uninflected forms of the corresponding possessive pronouns (§ **464**). The **c** in the acc. forms **mec, þec, ūsic, ēowic,** goes back to a prim. Germanic emphatic particle, ***ke** = Indg. ***ge,** which is found in Gr. pronominal forms like ἐμέγε. The acc. forms with **c** only occur in the oldest records and in poetry. **ic** is the old unaccented form, the accented form was preserved in O.Icel. **ek** (cp. Lat. **ego,** Gr. ἐγώ). The **e** in **me, þe** may represent Indg. **e,** cp. Gr. ἐμέ (μέ), τέ, but it is far more likely that **me, þe** are old datives used for the accusative. **þu** (OHG. **du**) beside **þū** (OHG. **dū**), NE. has preserved the old accented, and NHG. the old unaccented form. Dat. **me** (Goth. **mis,** OHG. **mir**), **þe** (OHG. **dir**), prim. Germanic ***mes,** ***þes** beside unaccented ***miz,** ***þiz,** with **-s, -z** from the dat. plural; OE. **me, þe** can represent either form, probably the latter, cp. **wĕ, gĕ.**

**wit** (Goth. OS. **wit**) and **git** (OS. **git**) were unaccented plurals with the addition of **-t** which is of obscure origin. There are grave phonological difficulties against assuming that the **-t** is related to the numeral for *two*. Acc. **uncit, incit** were formed from **unc, inc,** with **-it** from the nominative. **unc, inc** are old accusatives also used for the dative; **unc** (OS. **unc**) from **un** (which occurs in the acc. pl. **ūs** = Goth. **uns** = Indg. **ns** with vocalic **n**) + the particle ***ke** = prim. Germanic ***uŋki**; **inc** (OS. **ink**, cp. Goth. **igq-is**), prim. Germanic ***iŋq-** which is of unknown origin.

**we**, prim. Germanic ***wīs** (Goth. **weis**) beside the unaccented form ***wiz** (OHG. **wir**); ***wiz** became ***wi** in **prim.** OE. and then later **we**, from which a new accented form **wē** was formed. **gĕ** for ***gŭ** (= Goth. **jŭs**, prim. Germanic ***jūs** beside ***juz**) with **ĕ** from **wĕ**. **ūsic** from older ***unsek** (with **e** from **mec**); **ūs** (Goth. OHG. **uns**, Indg. **ns** with vocalic **n**). **ēowic** from older ***īuwek** (with **e** from **þec**); dat. **ēow** (OHG. **iu, eu**) from older ***īuw**, prim. Germanic ***iwwiz**; **ēow, īow** is the old dat. also used for the accusative.

The pronoun of the third person is originally a demonstrative pronoun formed from the Indg. stem ***ki-**, *this*, which occurs in Lat. **ci-s, ci-ter**, *on this side*. It has been preserved in Goth. in only a few isolated phrases, as **und hina dag**, *to this day*; **himma daga**, *on this day, to-day*; **und hita nu**, *till now*.

**hĕ**, prim. Germanic ***χis** beside unaccented ***χiz**; ***χiz** became ***χi** in prim. OE. and then later **he** from which a new accented **hē** was formed; **hine** (Goth. **hina**), prim. Germanic ***χinōn**, beside **hiene** with **ie** from **hiere, hiera**; **his** from ***χisa**; **him** from ***χimi** (orig. instrumental), **hit** (cp. Goth. **hita**, where the **t** = Lat. **-d** in **id**, *that*). **hīo** later **hēo**, formed from ***hi** + **ŭ** with **ŭ** from **sīo, sēo** (§ **465**); **hīe** later **hĭ, hў̆**, from ***hi** + **ōn**; gen. **hire** from ***χizōz**, dat. **hire** from ***χizai**; **hiere** had **ie** from the gen. plural; cp. the prim. Germanic endings of the fem. adjectives (§ **424**); the acc. form was often used for the nom. and vice versa. **hĭ** later **hў̆**, from ***χī**, unaccented ***χi**, beside **hīe** with **e** from the adjectives (§ **424**); **hī** was often written **hig** (see § **6**, Note) in late OE. The masc. form was used for all genders, but sometimes the old fem. sing. **hēo** was used instead of it; **hira** from ***χizōn,** beside **hiora, heora, hiera** with **o/a**-umlaut (§ **102**). **him** from ***χimiz,** beside late WS. **heom** with **eo** from the genitive. All the forms with **i** often had **y** in late WS.

## 2. Reflexive.

§ **463.** The reflexive pronoun originally referred to the chief person of the sentence (generally the subject), irrespectively as to whether the subject was the first, second, or third person singular or plural. This usage remained in Sanskrit, but in the Germanic languages the personal pronouns of the first and second person came to be used reflexively already in prim. Germanic, and then the original reflexive pronoun became restricted to the third person. But the prim. Germanic reflexive pronoun of the third person ***sek,** unaccented ***sik** (Goth. **sik,** OHG. **sih**) disappeared in OE., and the old genitive (Goth. **seina,** OHG. **sīn**) only remained as a possessive pronoun. So that the personal pronouns of the third person also came to be used reflexively in OE. When the personal pronouns were used reflexively **self,** *self* (declined strong and weak) was often added to emphasize them.

## 3. Possessive.

§ **464.** The possessive pronouns **mīn,** *my,* **þīn,** *thy,* **sīn** (mostly used in poetry), *his, her, its,* are originally old locatives, Indg. ***mei, *tei, *sei** with the addition of the nominal suffix **-no-,** whence prim. Germanic masc. nom. ***mīnaz, *þīnaz, *sīnaz**; fem. nom. ***mīnō, *þīnō, *sīnō,** which were declined in the sing. and plural, all genders, like **blind** (§ **424**); but instead of **sīn,** the gen. of the personal pronoun was often used as in Lat. **eius,** gen. pl. **eōrum, eārum.** The remaining possessive pronouns were formed from the personal pronouns by means of the Indg.

comparative suffix **-ero-**, prim. Germanic **-era-**, as **uncer** (Goth. ***ugkar**), *of us two*; **incer** (Goth. **igqar**), *of you two*; **ūser** (Goth. **unsar**), *our*; **ēower**, *your*, all of which were declined like **hālig** (§ **429**). **ūre**, *our*, was declined like **wilde** (§ **433**) except that the fem. nom. sing. was **ūre** not ***ūru**. It is difficult to account for the form **ūre**. In the fem. gen. and dat. sing. and gen. pl. **ūrre, ūrra**, the **rr** was often simplified to **r**. In those cases which had syncope of the medial vowel, the **sr** became **ss** (§ **281**) in the declension of **ūser**, and then the **ss** was sometimes extended by analogy to the other cases, as nom. sing. **ūsser**, masc. acc. sing. **ūsserne** beside the regular forms **ūser, ūserne.**

4. DEMONSTRATIVE.

§ **465.** In the parent Indg. language the nom. sing. masc. and fem. of the simple demonstrative was ***so, *sā** = Gr. ὁ, ἡ, Goth. **sa, sō**. All the other cases of the sing. and pl. were formed from the stems **te-, to-, toi-**; **tā-, tai-**, as acc. sing. Gr. τόν, τήν, Lat. **is-tum, is-tam**, Goth. **þan-a, þō**; nom. pl. Gr. τοί, ταί, Lat. **is-tī, is-tae**, Goth. **þái, þōs.**

| SING. | *Masc.* | *Neut.* | *Fem.* |
|---|---|---|---|
| Nom. | **sĕ**, *the, that* | **þæt** | **sīo, sēo** |
| Acc. | **þone** | **þæt** | **þā** |
| Gen. | **þæs** | **þæs** | **þǣre** |
| Dat. | **þǣm, þām** | **þǣm, þām** | **þǣre** |
| Instr. | | **þȳ, þon** | |

PLUR. ALL GENDERS.

| | |
|---|---|
| Nom. Acc. | **þā** |
| Gen. | **þāra, þǣra** |
| Dat. | **þǣm, þām** |

**se** was the unaccented form of prim. Germanic ***sa** (Goth. **sa**) to which a new accented form **sē** was made. (§ **144**); **þone** (Goth. **þana**) the unaccented form of prim. Germanic

***þanōn**, beside late OE. **þæne, þane; þæs** from prim. Germanic ***þasa** (§ 54), beside ***þesa** (Anglian **þes**, Goth. **þis**, OHG. **des**); **þǣm** from the prim. Germanic instrumental ***þaimi**, beside **þām** with **ā** from the plural **þā, þāra**, as in the dat. pl. **þām. þæt** (Goth. **þata**, Lat. **is-tud**, Indg. ***tod**); **þȳ, þon** are difficult to explain satisfactorily; they were chiefly used before the comparative of adverbs and as a factor in adverbial and conjunctional phrases like the Goth. instrumental **þē**, as **þon mā**, *the more*, cp. Gothic **ni þē haldis**, *none the more*; **for þȳ, for þon**, *because, on that account*. **sīo, sēo** does not correspond to Goth. **sō**, but like OHG. **siu**, *she*, it was a new formation from the prim. Germanic fem. pronoun ***sī** (= Gr. ἵ, Goth. **si**, OHG. **sĭ**), *she* + the Germanic fem. ending **-ō**; ***sīō** regularly became **sīo, sēo** through the intermediate stage of **sīu** which is found in the Anglian dialect. The reason why the new formation took place was probably due to the fact that the unaccented form of ***sī** would have become **sĕ** in OE. and thus have fallen together with the masc. nom. sing., cp. OE. **wĕ, hĕ** from the prim. Germanic unaccented forms ***wiz**, ***χiz** (§ 462); acc. **þā** (prim. Germanic ***þōn**, Goth. **þō**, Gr. Dor. *τάν*, Indg. ***tām**) is from the unaccented form ***þa** from which a new accented form **þā** was formed; gen. **þǣre** from ***þaizjō̃z** (cp. Skr. **tásyās**, Indg. ***tésjā̃s**) with **ai** from the gen. plural; and similarly in the dat. **þǣre** from ***þaizjai** (cp. Skr. **tásyāi** Indg. ***tésjā̃i**), beside **þāre** from ***þaizai**; for the gen. sing. Merc. and Ken. have **þere** (= Goth. **þizōs**), and for the dat. they have **þere** (= Goth. **þizái**). Pl. nom. masc. **þā** (= Goth. **þái**, Gr. *τοί*); the old nom. was also used for the nom. and acc. all genders; gen. **þāra** from prim. Germanic ***þaizō̃n**, Indg. ***toisō̃m** (cp. the Goth. gen. pl. of adjectives, as **blindaizē, -ō**), beside **þǣra** with **ǣ** from **þǣm; þǣm** (Goth. **þáim**) from prim. Germanic ***þaimiz**, beside **þām** with **ā** from the genitive, which became **þān** in late WS.

§ **466.** The compound demonstrative pronoun **þĕs, þis, þīos (þēos),** *this*, was originally formed from the simple demonstrative + the deictic particle **-se, -si** which is probably related to Goth. **sái,** OHG. **sē,** *lo!, behold!* Its earliest usage was that of an emphatic demonstrative pronoun and then later it came to be used also as a simple demonstrative adjective in much the same way that *this here, these here, that there, them there* (= *those*) are used in most Modern English dialects. Originally only the first element was inflected as in OHG. masc. nom. sing. **de-se,** gen. **des-se,** pl. **de-se.** At a later period the **-se** came to be inflected also, as masc. gen. sing. OHG. **des-ses** = OE. **þis-ses.** At this stage the gen. **þis-** (= Goth. **þis**) became extended to most of the other cases. And lastly the first element ceased to be inflected and the second element took in most cases the endings of the simple demonstrative. This compound demonstrative pronoun exists in all the Germanic languages except Gothic. The nom. sing. **þĕs, þīos (þēos)** were new formations made from the oblique stem-form with **þ** (§ **465**). The old nom. forms were preserved in the oldest Norse inscriptions, as masc. **sa-si,** fem. **su-si,** neut. **þat-si.**

| Sing. | *Masc.* | *Neut.* | *Fem.* |
|---|---|---|---|
| Nom. | **þĕs** | **þis** | **þīos, þēos** |
| Acc. | **þisne** | **þis** | **þās** |
| Gen. | **þis(s)es** | **þis(s)es** | **þisse** |
| Dat. | **þis(s)um** | **þis(s)um** | **þisse** |
| Instr. | | **þȳs, þīs** | |

Plur. all Genders.

| | |
|---|---|
| Nom. Acc. | **þās** |
| Gen. | **þissa** |
| Dat. | **þis(s)um** |

**þes** from older ***þe-se** (= OHG. **de-se**) was the unaccented form from which a new accented form **þēs** was made. **þīos** from **þīus** (preserved in the Anglian dialect), older ***þīū + se** (cp. **sīo,** § **465**). The fem. acc. sing., instr., and nom. pl. represent the simple demonstrative forms + **-se** which regularly became **-s.** The other cases singular and plural generalized the **þis-**, the **i** of which later became **y.** **ss** was often simplified to **s.** In the dat. sing. and pl. Anglian has **þios(s)um, þeos(s)um** with **u**-umlaut (§ **101**) beside **þis(s)um.** Fem. gen. and dat. sing. **þisse** from older ***þisre,** gen. pl. **þissa** from older ***þisra** (§ **281**); in late OE. there also occur **þissere, þissera** with **-re, -ra** from the simple demonstrative, beside **þisre, þisra** with syncope of the medial vowel and simplification of the **ss.**

§ **467.** **ilca,** *same,* which only occurs in combination with the def. art., as **sĕ ilca, þæt ilce, sēo ilce,** *the same,* is always declined weak.

**self, seolf, sylf, silf,** *self,* was declined according to the strong or weak declension of adjectives. In combination with the def. art., as **sĕ selfa, seolfa,** it meant *the selfsame.* See § **463.**

## 5. Relative.

§ **468.** A relative pronoun proper did not exist in prim. Germanic. The separate Germanic languages expressed it in various ways. In Goth. it was expressed by suffixing the relative particle **ei** to the personal pronouns for the first and second persons, and to the simple demonstrative for the third person; in O.Norse by the particles **sem** and **es** (later **er**) in combination with the simple demonstrative; in OS. and OHG. generally by the simple demonstrative; and in OE. by the relative particle **þĕ** alone or in combination with the personal or the simple demonstrative pronoun, and for the third person also by the simple demonstrative pronoun alone, as **se mon-dryhten, sē ēow þā māþmas geaf,** *the lord who gave you the treasures*; **þonne tōdǣlaþ hī his feoh þæt tō lāfe biþ,** *then they divide* *his property which is left.* **ic hit ēom, þe wiþ þē sprece,** *it is I who speak with thee*; **idesa scēnost þe on woruld cōme,** *the fairest one of ladies who came into the world*; **gē þe yfle synt,** *ye who are evil.* **sē þe brȳd hæfþ, sē is brȳdguma,** *he who hath the bride is the bridegroom*; **gehȳre, sē þe ēaran hæbbe,** *let him hear who hath ears*; **þæt þe ācenned is of flǣsce, þæt is flǣsc,** *that which is born of the flesh is flesh.* **wē þās word sprecaþ, þe wē in carcerne sittaþ,** *we who sit in prison speak these words*; **saga hwæt ic hātte, þe ic lond rēafige,** *say what I am called, I who lay waste the land*; **þæt se mon ne wāt, þe him on foldan fægrost limpeþ,** *the man to whom on earth the fairest happens knows not that.*

### 6. Interrogative.

§ **469.** The parent Indg. language had two stems from which the interrogative pronoun was formed, viz. **q$^{w}$o-** and **q$^{w}$i-** with labialized **q** (§ **237**). The former occurs in Gr. *πό-τερος, which of two?*, Goth. **ƕas,** OE. **hwă̄,** *who?*, from an original form ***q$^{w}$os;** Lat. **quod,** Goth. **ƕa,** O.Icel. **huat,** OS. **hwat,** OHG. **hwaȥ,** OE. **hwæt,** *what?*, from an original form ***q$^{w}$od.** And the latter occurs in Gr. *τίς*, Lat. **quis,** *who?*, from an original form ***q$^{w}$is;** Goth. **ƕileiks,** OE. **hwilc,** *what sort of?*

The OE. simple interrogative pronoun had no independent form for the feminine, and was declined in the singular only.

| | Masc. | Neut. |
|---|---|---|
| Nom. | **hwă̄** | **hwæt** |
| Acc. | **hwone** | **hwæt** |
| Gen. | **hwæs** | **hwæs** |
| Dat. | **hwǣm, hwām** | **hwǣm, hwām** |
| Instr. | | **hwȳ, hwī** |

On the long vowel in **hwā,** see § **79.** **hwone** (Goth. **ƕana**) from prim. Germanic ***χwanōn,** is the old unaccented form; beside this there rarely occurs the accented form **hwane,** and in late OE. **hwæne. hwæs** from prim. Germanic ***χwasa** beside Goth. **ƕis** from ***χwesa. hwǣm** from prim. Germanic ***χwaimi** (instrumental) beside **hwām,** a new formation from **hwǎ.** Beside the instr. **hwȳ, hwī** which are difficult to explain, there also occur **hwon,** in such adverbial phrases as **for hwon, tō hwon,** *why?,* and **hū** (§ 130), *how?*

§ **470. hwæþer** (Goth. **ƕaþar**), *which of two?,* and **hwelc, hwilc** (Goth. **ƕileiks**), *what sort of?,* were declined according to the strong declension of adjectives.

### 7. Indefinite.

§ **471.** OE. had the following indefinite pronouns:— **ǣghwā,** *each one, every one,* from **ā,** *ever* + **gi** + **hwa**; and similarly **ǣghwæþer,** *each of two, both*; **ǣghwelc, ǣghwilc,** *each one, every one.* **ǣlc,** *each, every*; **ǣnig,** *any,* **nǣnig,** *not any one, no one*; **æthwā,** *each*; **āhwā,** *any one*; **āhwæþer, ōhwæþer, āwþer, ōwþer,** *one of two,* **nāhwæþer, nōhwæþer, nāwþer, nōwþer,** *neither of two*; **ān,** *some one, a certain one,* in plur. *each, every, all,* **nān,** *no one,* **nānþing,** *nothing*; **āwiht, ōwiht, āwuht, ōwuht, āht, ōht,** *anything*; **nāwiht, nōwiht, nāwuht, nōwuht, nāht, nōht,** *nothing*; **gehwā,** *each one, every one*; **gehwæþer,** *each of two, both*; **gehwilc,** *each, every one*; **hwelchwugu,** *any, some, some one*; **hwæthwugu,** *somewhat, something*; **lōc, lōca** + pronoun **hwā, hwæþer,** as **lōc hwæþer þāra gebrōþra,** *whichever of the two brothers,* **bide me lōce hwæs þū wille,** *ask me for whatever thou wilt*; **man,** *one*; **nāt** + **hwā, hwelc,** *some one I know not who, which*; **samhwilc,** *some*; **sum,** *some one*; **swā . . . swā,** as **swā hwā swā,** *whosoever, whoever,* **swā hwæt swā,** *whatsoever, whatever,* **swā hwæþer swā,** *whichever of two,* **swā hwelc swā,** *whichever*; **swelc, swilc,** *such*; **þyslic, þuslic, þyllic, þullic,** *such.*

# CHAPTER XIV

## VERBS

§ **472.** In the parent Indg. language the verbs were divided into two great classes: athematic and thematic. In the athematic verbs the personal endings were added to the bare root which had the strong grade form of ablaut in the singular, but the weak grade in the dual and plural. Thus for example the singular and plural of the verbs for *to be* and *to go* were: ***és-mi, *és-si, *és-ti, *s-més** or ***s-mós, *s-té, *s-énti**; ***éi-mi, *éi-si, *éi-ti, *i-més** or ***i-mós, *i-té, *j-énti.** Verbs of this class are often called **mi**-verbs because the first person singular ends in **-mi.** The Germanic languages have only preserved a few traces of the **mi**-conjugation (§ **547**). Nearly all the verbal forms, which originally belonged to this class, passed over into the **ō**-conjugation in the prim. Germanic period.

In the thematic verbs the stem-vowel, which could be either of the strong or weak grade of ablaut, remained unchanged throughout the present; in the former case they are called imperfect presents (as **cēosan,** *to choose*; **helpan,** *to help*; **etan,** *to eat*; &c.), and in the latter case aorist presents (as OE. **lūcan,** *to close*; **murnan,** *to mourn*; &c.). The present was formed by means of the thematic vowels, **e, o,** which came between the root and the personal endings, and the accent was on the root or the thematic vowel according as the root contained the strong or weak grade of ablaut, thus the present singular and plural of the verbs for *to bear* and *to come* were: ***bhérō, *bhér-e-si, *bhér-e-ti, *bhér-o-mes,** (**-mos**), ***bhér-e-te, *bhér-o-nti,** but ***gʷmṓ** (with vocalic **-m-** throughout the present), ***gʷm-é-si, *gʷm-é-ti, *gʷm-ó-mes,** (**-mos**), **gʷm-é-te, *gʷm-ó-nti.** Verbs of this class are generally called **ō**-verbs because the first person singular ends in **-ō.** The **-ō** in

***bhérō** is generally regarded as the personal ending, but in reality it is simply the lengthened ablaut-grade of the thematic vowel. In the early period of the parent Indg. language the base ***bher-o-** was used for the first pers. singular, and then at a later period the thematic vowel became lengthened. It is sometimes assumed that the **-ō** arose from the contraction of the thematic vowel **-o-** + **-a** (the original ending of the perfect, as in Gr. *οἶδα, I know*), but this would have become **-ō̃** not **-ṓ** (§ **9**). The old distinction between the **mi-** and the **ō-**conjugation was fairly well preserved in Greek, as *εἰμί, I am, εἶμι, I go, δίδωμι, I give*; *μένω, I remain, πείθω, I persuade*; *τρί́βω, I rub, τῡ́φω, I smoke.*

§ **473.** In treating the history of the verbal forms in OE. it is advisable to start out partly from prim. Germanic and partly from the oldest OE. The Indg. verbal system underwent so many radical changes in prim. Germanic that it would be necessary to treat here in detail the verbal system of the non-Germanic languages such as Sanskrit, Greek, and Latin in order to account for all the changes.

In the Germanic languages the verbs are divided into two great classes:—Strong and Weak. The strong verbs form their preterite (originally perfect) and past participle by means of ablaut (§ **224**). The weak verbs form their preterite by the addition of a syllable containing a dental (Goth. **-da, (-ta)**, OE. **-de, -te**), and their past participle by means of a dental suffix (Goth. **-þ, (-t)**, OE. **-d, (-t)**).

Besides these two great classes of strong and weak verbs, there are a few others which will be treated under the general heading of *Minor Groups.*

The strong verbs were originally further sub-divided into reduplicated and non-reduplicated verbs, as Goth. **haldan,** *to hold,* **lētan,** *to let,* preterite **haíhald, laílōt**; **niman,** *to take,* **hilpan,** *to help,* preterite **nam, halp.** In OE. the reduplication almost entirely disappeared in the prehistoric period of the language (§ **511**). The non-reduplicated verbs are divided into six classes according to the six ablaut-series (§ **226**). The originally reduplicated verbs are put together in this book and called class VII.

§ **474.** The OE. verb has the following independent forms:—one voice (active), two numbers, three persons, two tenses (present and preterite), two complete moods (indicative and subjunctive, the latter originally the optative), besides an imperative which is only used in the present tense; one verbal noun (the present infinitive), a present participle with active meaning, and one verbal adjective (the past participle).

The simple future was generally expressed by the present tense as in the oldest periods of the other Germanic languages, but already in OE. the present forms of **bēon,** *to be,* **sculan,** *shall,* **willan,** *will,* with the infinitive began to be used to express the future. In the oldest OE. the perfect of transitive verbs was formed by means of the forms of **habban,** *to have,* and the past participle, and that of intransitive verbs by means of **wesan,** *to be,* and the past participle. At a later period **habban** came to be used to form the perfect of intransitive verbs also. The only trace of the old passive voice preserved in OE. is **hātte** (Goth. **háitada**), *is* or *was called,* pl. **hātton.** Otherwise the passive was expressed by the forms of **bēon, wesan,** *to be,* occasionally also **weorþan,** *to become,* and the past participle.

## A. Strong Verbs.

§ **475.** We are able to conjugate a strong verb in OE. when we know the four stems, as seen (1) in the infinitive or first pers. sing. pres. indicative, (2) first pers. sing. pret. indicative, (3) pret. pl. indicative, (4) the past participle. The pret. subjunctive and the second pers. pret. indicative have the same stem-vowel as the pret. pl. indicative. The conjugation of **beran,** *to bear,* **helpan,** *to help,* **bindan,** *to* *bind*, **rīdan,** *to ride*, **cēosan,** *to choose*, **weorpan,** *to throw*, **faran,** *to go*, **biddan,** *to pray*, **feallan,** *to fall*, **tēon,** *to draw*, **slēan,** *to slay*, **fōn,** *to seize*, will serve as models for all strong verbs, because in addition to verbal endings, one or other of them illustrates such phenomena as umlaut, the interchange between **i** and **e** in the pres. indic. of verbs belonging to classes III, IV, and V, breaking, vowel contraction, vowel syncope, the simplification of double consonants, Verner's law, and the consonant changes in the second and third pers. sing. of the pres. indicative.

*Present.*

Indicative.

| | | | | | |
|---|---|---|---|---|---|
| Sing. | 1. | **bere** | **helpe** | **binde** | **rīde** |
| | 2. | **bir(e)st** | **hilpst** | **bintst** | **rītst** |
| | 3. | **bir(e)þ** | **hilpþ** | **bint** | **rīt(t)** |
| Plur. | | **beraþ** | **helpaþ** | **bindaþ** | **rīdaþ** |

Subjunctive.

| | | | | | |
|---|---|---|---|---|---|
| Sing. | | **bere** | **helpe** | **binde** | **rīde** |
| Plur. | | **beren** | **helpen** | **binden** | **rīden** |

Imperative.

| | | | | | |
|---|---|---|---|---|---|
| Sing. | 2. | **ber** | **help** | **bind** | **rīd** |
| Plur. | 2. | **beraþ** | **helpaþ** | **bindaþ** | **rīdaþ** |

Infinitive.

| | | | | |
|---|---|---|---|---|
| | **beran** | **helpan** | **bindan** | **rīdan** |

Participle.

| | | | | |
|---|---|---|---|---|
| | **berende** | **helpende** | **bindende** | **rīdende** |

*Preterite.*

Indicative.

| | | | | | |
|---|---|---|---|---|---|
| Sing. | 1. | **bær** | **healp** | **band** | **rād** |
| | 2. | **bǣre** | **hulpe** | **bunde** | **ride** |
| | 3. | **bær** | **healp** | **band** | **rād** |
| Plur. | | **bǣron** | **hulpon** | **bundon** | **ridon** |

Subjunctive.

| | | | | | |
|---|---|---|---|---|---|
| Sing. | | **bǣre** | **hulpe** | **bunde** | **ride** |
| Plur. | | **bǣren** | **hulpen** | **bunden** | **riden** |

Participle.

| | | | | | |
|---|---|---|---|---|---|
| | | **boren** | **holpen** | **bunden** | **riden** |

*Present.*

Indicative.

| | | | | | |
|---|---|---|---|---|---|
| Sing. | 1. | **cēose** | **weorpe** | **fare** | **bidde** |
| | 2. | **cīest** | **wierpst** | **fær(e)st** | **bitst** |
| | 3. | **cīest** | **wierpþ** | **fær(e)þ** | **bit(t)** |
| Plur. | | **cēosaþ** | **weorpaþ** | **faraþ** | **biddaþ** |

Subjunctive.

| | | | | | |
|---|---|---|---|---|---|
| Sing. | | **cēose** | **weorpe** | **fare** | **bidde** |
| Plur. | | **cēosen** | **weorpen** | **faren** | **bidden** |

Imperative.

| | | | | | |
|---|---|---|---|---|---|
| Sing. | 2. | **cēos** | **weorp** | **far** | **bide** |
| Plur. | 2. | **cēosaþ** | **weorpaþ** | **faraþ** | **biddaþ** |

Infinitive.

| | | | | | |
|---|---|---|---|---|---|
| | | **cēosan** | **weorpan** | **faran** | **biddan** |

Participle.

| | | | | | |
|---|---|---|---|---|---|
| | | **cēosende** | **weorpende** | **farende** | **biddende** |

*Preterite.*

Indicative.

| | | | | | |
|---|---|---|---|---|---|
| Sing. | 1. | **cēas** | **wearp** | **fōr** | **bæd** |
| | 2. | **cure** | **wurpe** | **fōre** | **bǣde** |
| | 3. | **cēas** | **wearp** | **fōr** | **bæd** |
| Plur. | | **curon** | **wurpon** | **fōron** | **bǣdon** |

Subjunctive.

| | | | | | |
|---|---|---|---|---|---|
| Sing. | | **cure** | **wurpe** | **fōre** | **bǣde** |
| Plur. | | **curen** | **wurpen** | **fōren** | **bǣden** |

Participle.

| | | | | | |
|---|---|---|---|---|---|
| | | coren | worpen | faren | þeden |

*Present.*

Indicative.

| | | | | | |
|---|---|---|---|---|---|
| Sing. | 1. | fealle | tēo | slēa | fō |
| | 2. | fielst | tīehst | sliehst | fēhst |
| | 3. | fielþ | tīehþ | sliehþ | fēhþ |
| Plur. | | feallaþ | tēoþ | slēaþ | fōþ |

Subjunctive.

| | | | | | |
|---|---|---|---|---|---|
| Sing. | | fealle | tēo | slēa | fō |
| Plur. | | feallen | tēon | slēan | fōn |

Imperative.

| | | | | | |
|---|---|---|---|---|---|
| Sing. | 2. | feall | tēoh | sleah | fōh |
| Plur. | 2. | feallaþ | tēoþ | slēaþ | fōþ |

Infinitive.

| | | | | | |
|---|---|---|---|---|---|
| | | feallan | tēon | slēan | fōn |

Participle.

| | | | | | |
|---|---|---|---|---|---|
| | | feallende | tēonde | slēande | fōnde |

*Preterite.*

Indicative.

| | | | | | |
|---|---|---|---|---|---|
| Sing. | 1. | fēoll | tēah | slōh, slōg | fēng |
| | 2. | fēolle | tuge | slōge | fēnge |
| | 3. | fēoll | tēah | slōh, slōg | fēng |
| Plur. | | fēollon | tugon | slōgon | fēngon |

Subjunctive.

| | | | | | |
|---|---|---|---|---|---|
| Sing. | | fēolle | tuge | slōge | fēnge |
| Plur. | | fēollen | tugen | slōgen | fēngen |

Participle.

| | | | | | |
|---|---|---|---|---|---|
| | | feallen | togen | slægen | fangen |

## The Endings of Strong Verbs.

§ **476.** Pres. indicative: The Indg. and prim. Germanic ending of the first pers. sing. was **-ō** (cp. Lat. **ferō**, Gr. φέρω, Indg. ***bhérō**, *I bear*) which became **-u** (later **-o**) in prim. OE. (§ **214**). The **-u** (**-o**) regularly remained after short stems and disappeared after long stems, as **beru, -o** beside ***help, *bind** (§ **215**), but already in prehistoric OE. the verbs with long stems took **-u** again after the analogy of those with short stems. The Anglian dialect mostly preserved the **-u** (**-o**), but in early WS. and Ken. its place was taken by **-e** from the pres. subjunctive.

The prim. Germanic forms of the second pers. sing. of **beran** and **bindan** were ***ƀirizi, *ƀinđizi** = Indg. ***bhéresi, *bhéndhesi,** which would regularly have become ***birir, *bindir,** later ***birer, *binder** in OE. (§§ **218**, 3, **252**), but already in prehistoric OE. the second pers. sing. of strong verbs was remodelled on the analogy of the first class of weak verbs which did not have the chief accent on the stem in prim. Germanic (see Note and § **239**, Note 2). The oldest OE. forms were **biris, bindis** which regularly became later **bires, bindes.** The ending **-st** arose partly from analogy with the preterite-present forms **wāst, þearft, scealt,** &c. and partly from a false etymological division of the pronoun from the verb to which it was often attached enclitically, thus **birisþu** became **biristu,** from which **birist** was extracted as the verbal form, cp. the similar process in OHG. The ending **-st** occurs earliest in the contracted verbs, **tīehst, sliehst,** &c.

The prim. Germanic forms of the third pers. sing. of **beran** and **bindan** were ***ƀiriđi** (= OS. **birid,** OHG. **birit**), ***ƀinđiđi** = Indg. ***bhéreti, *bhéndheti,** which would regularly have become ***bired,** older ***birid,** and ***bind(d)** in OE., but already in prehistoric OE. the third pers. sing. like the second was remodelled on analogy with the first class of weak verbs. The oldest OE. forms were **biriþ, bindiþ**, later **bir(e)þ, bint** (§ **300**). The **-eþ** appears as **-es** in late Nth.

In the second and third pers. sing. the **-i-** (**-e-**) was regularly syncopated after long stems, as **hilpst, hilpþ, rītst, rīt(t), tīehst, tīehþ**, &c., and remained after short stems, as **birest, bireþ, færest, færeþ**, &c. (§ **221**), but there are many exceptions to this rule, especially in WS. and Ken., owing to new formations in both directions, as **bindest, bindeþ, hilpest, hilpeþ**, &c., and on the other hand **birst, birþ, færst, færþ**, &c. In Anglian the forms without syncope were almost entirely generalized, but in WS. and Ken. syncope was practically general, especially after voiceless consonants and after **d, f** (= **ƀ**), and **g**, but as a rule not after a single liquid or a nasal.

The loss of **-e-** in the second and third pers. sing. gave rise to various consonantal changes: Double consonants were simplified before the personal endings (§ **259**), as **fielst, fielþ, spinst, spinþ**, beside inf. **feallan, spinnan.**

**d** became **t** before **-st**, as **bintst, bitst, rītst, wieltst** beside **wealdan**, *to wield.* **d** and **t** + **-þ** became **tt** (common in the older period), later **t**, as **bint, bit(t), rīt(t)**; **birst, it(t)**, beside inf. **berstan**, *to burst*, **etan**, *to eat*, see §§ **300, 305.** Forms like **bindest, bidst, wieldst**; **bindeþ, bid(e)þ**, &c. were new formations after the analogy of forms which regularly had **d.**

After a long vowel, diphthong, or liquid, **g** became **h** before **-st, -þ** (§ **320**, Note), as **stīhst, stīhþ**, inf. **stīgan**, *to ascend*, **flīehst, flīehþ**, inf. **flēogan**, *to fly*, **swilhst, swilhþ**, inf. **swelgan**, *to swallow*, but the **g** was often restored from forms which regularly had **g.**

**s, ss, st** + **-st, -þ** became **-st** (§§ **259, 305**), as **cīest**; **cyst** beside inf. wv. **cyssan**, *to kiss*, **birst** beside **birstest, birsteþ** (new formations); **x** (= **hs**) + **-st, -þ** became **xt**, as **wiext** beside inf. **weaxan**, *to grow.* In verbs of this type the second and third pers. singular regularly fell together.

þ disappeared before **-st** (§ **305**), as **cwist, wierst,** beside inf. **cweþan,** *to say,* **weorþan,** *to become.* Forms like **cwiþst, wierþst, snīþst** (inf. **snīþan,** *to cut*), were new formations after the analogy of the other forms of the present. **þ + -þ** became **þ,** as **cwiþ, wierþ.**

The forms of the first and second pers. plural had disappeared already in the oldest period of the language, their place having been taken by the form of the third person. The prim. Germanic forms of the third pers. pl. of **beran, bindan** were ***ƀeranđi, *ƀinđanđi** = Indg. ***bhéronti** (Gr. Doric φέροντι), ***bhéndhonti,** which would regularly have become in OE. ***berand, *bindand** = Goth. **baírand, bindand,** but, as in the second and third pers. singular, the third pers. pl. was remodelled on analogy with the first class of weak verbs which regularly had **-ánþi** in prim. Germanic. **-ánþi** became **-aþ** in OE. through the intermediate stages **-anþ, -onþ, -ōþ** (§ **218**). **-aþ** appears as **-as** in late Nth. This **-s** plural has been preserved in the Modern northern dialects when the subject is not a simple personal pronoun placed immediately before or after the verb.

Note.—The personal endings of the second and third pers. singular and the third pers. plural of strong verbs which originally had the principal accent on the stem-syllable were in prim. Germanic **-zi, -đi, -nđi** = Indg. **-si, -ti, -nti,** but the personal endings of the corresponding persons of the aorist presents (see § **472**) and of the first class of weak verbs were **´-si, ´-þi, ´-nþi,** which became generalized in prehistoric OE., cp. § **239,** Note 2.

§ **477.** Pres. subjunctive: This tense is properly an old optative which came to be used in place of the original subjunctive in prim. Germanic. The original forms of the singular and plural of **beran** were ***bhéroi-, *bhérois,**

***bhéroit, *bhéroim-, *bhéroite, *bhéroint.** The final **-t** was regularly dropped in prim. Germanic (§ **211**) and the **oi** became **ai** during the same period (§ **30**). Then **ai** became **ǣ** which was shortened to **æ** (§ **217**). The **æ** was preserved in the oldest period of the language and afterwards became **e.** In OE. the original forms of the singular regularly fell together in **bere.** The old forms of the first and second pers. plural disappeared and their place was taken by the third pers. **beren** (Goth. **baíráin-a**). Beside **-en** there also occurs in late WS. **-an,** and also **-un, -on** taken over from the pret. pl. indicative. On the loss of final **-n** in Nth., see § **288**. The final **-n** also disappeared in WS. and Ken. when a personal pronoun of the first or second person came immediately after the verb, as **bere wĕ̄, wit, gĕ̄, git.** Then **bere wĕ̄,** &c., came to be used also for the indicative and imperative.

§ **478**. Imperative: The original ending of the second pers. sing. was **-e** which regularly disappeared without leaving any trace of its former existence (§ **213**), whence OE. **ber** = Gr. φέρε, Indg. ***bhére.** On the **-e** in **bide** beside its absence in **ber, bind,** &c., see § **273**. In OE. the third pers. plural of the pres. indicative was used for the second pers. plural. A form in **-an,** as **beran, bindan,** was occasionally used in the oldest period of the language for the first pers. plural. This form was originally identical with the first pers. pl. pres. indic. which disappeared in OE. The first pers. pl. is generally expressed by the pres. subjunctive, as **beren, binden,** &c.

§ **479**. Pres. participle: In the Indg. parent language the stem of the pres. participle ended in **-nt,** as in Lat. **ferent-,** Gr. φέροντ-, Indg. ***bhéront-** = OE. **berend-e,** Goth. **baírand-s.** The masc. and neut. were originally declined like consonant stems (§ **416**). The fem. nom. sing. originally ended in **-ī** which was shortened to **-i** (§ **214**) in prehistoric OE., cp. Goth. fem. **frijōndi,** *friend.*

The -i of the feminine was extended to the masc. and neut. which was the cause of their passing over into the **ja**-declension (§ **433**). See § **441.** The oldest OE. ending is **-ændi, -endi,** later **-ende.**

§ **480.** Infinitive: The inf. was originally a nomen actionis, formed by means of various suffixes in the different Indg. languages. The suffix **-ono-,** to which was added the nom. acc. neuter ending **-m,** became generalized in prim. Germanic, thus the original form of **beran** was ***bhéronom,** the **-onom** of which regularly became **-an** in OE. Goth. OS. and OHG. On the loss of the final **-n** in Nth., see § **288.** In prim. West Germanic the inf. was inflected in the gen. and. dat. like an ordinary noun of the **ja**-declension (§ **355**), gen. **-ennes,** dat. **-enne.** The inflected forms of the inf. are sometimes called the gerund. The gen. disappeared in prehistoric OE. The dat. **tō berenne** generally became **-anne** through the influence of the inf. ending **-an.** Beside **-enne, -anne** there also occur in late OE. **-ene, -ane,** and **-ende** with **d** from the present participle.

§ **481.** Pret. indicative: The pret. indic. is morpho logically an old perfect, which already in prim. Germanic was chiefly used to express the past tense. The original endings of the perf. singular were **-a, -tha, -e,** cp. Gr. *οἶδα, οἶσθα, οἶδε*. The **-a** and **-e** regularly disappeared in prehistoric OE. (§§ **212**–**13**), whence OE. first and third pers. singular **bær, band,** &c. The ending of the second pers. singular would regularly have become **-þ** (§ **233**) in OE. OS. O.Icel. and Goth., except after prim. Germanic **s, f, χ** where it regularly became **t** (§ **231,** Notes), as in Goth. **last,** *thou didst gather,* **slōht,** *thou didst slay,* **þarft** (OE. **þearft**), *thou needest.* This **-t** became generalized in prim. Germanic, as Goth. O.Icel. **namt,** *thou tookest.* But in the West Germanic languages the old ending was only preserved in the preterite-present verbs, as OE. **þearft,** *thou needest,* **scealt,** *thou shalt,* **meaht,** *thou mayest,* &c. See §§ **486, 539** ff. The third pers. plural ended in the parent language in **-nt** (with vocalic n) which regularly became **-un** in prim. Germanic (§§ **35, 211**). **-un** remained in the oldest OE. and then later became **-on,** and in late OE. **-an** beside **-on** occurs, whence **bǣron, bundon,** &c.

§ **482.** Pret. subjunctive: The original endings were: singular **-jēm, -jēs, -jēt,** plural **-īm-, -īte, -īnt,** consisting of the optative element **-jē-,** (**-ī-**) and the personal endings. Already in prim. Germanic the **-ī-** of the plural was levelled out into the singular. The new sing. endings **-īm, -īs, -īt** would regularly have become **-i** (§§ **214, 218**) in the oldest OE. The **-i** would have caused umlaut in the stem. syllable and then have disappeared after long stems and have remained (later **-e**) after short stems. Regular forms would have been ***bynd, *hylp, *fēr,** &c., but ***cyre, *tyge,** &c. The pl. ending **-īnt** would regularly have become **-in** (later **-en**) with umlaut in the stem-syllable, as ***bynden, *cyren,** &c. But real old pret. subjunctive forms have only been preserved in OE. in a few isolated instances as in the preterite-presents, **dyge, scyle, þyrfe.** In OE. the old endings of the pres. subjunctive came to be used for the preterite some time before the operation of i-umlaut. This accounts for the absence of umlaut in the pret. subjunctive in OE., as **bunde, bunden,** &c. Already in early OE. the pret. subjunctive began to take the endings of the pret. indicative. On the loss of the final **-n** in Nth., see § **288.** The final **-n** also disappeared in WS. and Ken. when a personal pronoun of the first or second person came immediately after the verb, as **bǣre wĕ̄, wit, gĕ̄, git.** Then later **bǣre wĕ̄,** &c., came to be used also for the indicative.

§ **483.** Past participle: The past participle was formed in various ways in the parent language. In prim. Germanic the suffix **-éno-, -óno-** became restricted to strong verbs, and the suffix **-tó-** to weak verbs. In the strong verbs OE. and O.Icel. generalized the form **-éno-**, and Goth. OS. and OHG. the form **-óno-**. Beside the suffix **-éno-**, **-óno-** there also existed in prim. Germanic **-ini-** = Indg. **-éni-** which was preserved in a few OE. past participles with umlaut in the stem-syllable, see § **442**. Prim. Germanic **-énaz**, **-íniz** = Indg. **-énos**, **-énis** regularly fell together in **-en** in OE., but they were still kept apart in the oldest period of the language, the former being **-æn** (**-en**) and the latter **-in**.

### General Remarks on the Strong Verbs.

§ **484.** Present indicative: On the interchange between **i** in the second and third pers. sing. and **e** in the other forms of the present in verbs belonging to classes III, IV, and V, as **hilpst, hilpþ**: **helpan**, *to help*; **bir(e)st, bir(e)þ**: **beran**, *to bear*; **cwist, cwiþ**: **cweþan**, *to say*, see § **41**. **i**-umlaut took place in the second and third pers. sing. of all verbs containing a vowel or diphthong capable of being umlauted. On the **i**-umlaut in verbs of class VI, as **fær(e)st, fær(e)þ**, see § **55**, Note 2. On the Anglian forms of the second and third pers. sing. of verbs like **cēosan**, **tēon**, see § **138**. The regular forms of the second and third pers. sing. were often remodelled on analogy with the other forms of the present, especially in the Anglian dialect, as **help(e)st, help(e)þ**; **fealst, fealþ, feallest, fealleþ**; **weorpest, weorpeþ**, beside older **hilpst, hilpþ**; **fielst, fielþ**; **wierpst, wierpþ**.

On **u-** or **o/a**-umlaut of **a, e** in the first pers. sing., and the pl. in the non-WS. dialects, see § **48**. On the breaking of Germanic **a** to **ea**, as in **feallan, healp, wearp**, and of **e** to **eo**, as in **weorpan**, see § **49**. On the vowel contraction in the present of the contracted verbs, see § **139**.

Strong verbs like **biddan**, *to pray*, **hliehhan**, *to laugh*, **licgan**, *to lie down*, **sittan**, *to sit*, had single medial consonants in the second and third pers. sing., because the **j**, which caused the doubling of the consonants in the other forms of the present, had disappeared before the West Germanic doubling of consonants took place, whence **bitst, bit(t)**; **hliehst, hliehþ**; **lig(e)st, lig(e)þ**; **sitst, sit(t)**.

§ **485**. Infinitive: On the **o/a**-umlaut in the non-WS. dialects, see § **48**.

§ **486**. Pret. indicative: The West Germanic languages only preserved the old pret. (originally perfect) of the second pers. sing. in the preterite-present verbs (see §§ **481, 539**). In all other strong verbs the OE. second pers. sing. was formed direct from the pret. subjunctive, which accounts for the absence of **i**-umlaut in the stem syllable and the preservation of the final **-e** after both short and long stems, as **ride, cure**, &c., and **bǣre, hulpe, bunde**, &c. The regular forms would have been **ride, *cyre**, and ***bǣr, *hylp, *bynd**. These and similar forms were originally augmentless aorists which had in Indo-Germanic the ending **-es** and the same grades of ablaut in the stem-syllable as in the OE. pret. pl. indicative (see § **224**, Notes 3–5).

On the question of **u**-umlaut in the plural of verbs belonging to class I, see § **101**.

§ **487**. Pret. subjunctive: If the OE. pret. subjunctive had been normally developed from the corresponding prim. Germanic forms, it would have had **i**-umlaut in the stem-syllable as in O. Icelandic. But this tense took the endings of the pres. subjunctive in the prehistoric period of the language before the operation of **i**-umlaut. See § **482**.

§ **488**. Past Participle: The ending of the past participle has already been explained in § **442**. In prim. Germanic the prefix ***ʒi-** was added to the past participle to impart to it a perfective meaning. Verbs which were already perfective in meaning, such as **bringan**, *to bring*, **cuman**, *to come*, **findan**, *to find*, **niman**, *to take*, **weorþan**, *to become*, did not originally have it. But in OE. the simple past participle generally had **ge-**, irrespectively as to whether it was perfective or imperfective in meaning. On past participles which have **i**-umlaut, see § **442**.

§ **489**. On the parts of strong verbs which exhibit Verner's law in OE., see § **238**.

## The Classification of the Strong Verbs.

### Class I.

§ **490**. The verbs of this class belong to the first ablaut-series (§ **226**) and therefore have **ī** in all forms of the present, **ā** in the first and third pers. sing. of the preterite, and **i** in the preterite plural and past participle, thus:

| | | | |
|---|---|---|---|
| **bīdan**, *to await* | **bād** | **bidon** | **biden** |
| Goth. **beidan** | **báiþ** | **bidun** | **bidans** |

And similarly **ætwītan**, *to blame, reproach*; **ācwīnan**, *to dwindle away*; **behlīdan**, *to cover*; **belīfan**, *to remain*; **bescītan**, *to befoul*; **besmītan**, *to pollute*; **bītan**, *to bite*; **blīcan**, *to shine*; **cīnan**, *to crack*; **clīfan**, *to stick, adhere*; **cnīdan**, *to beat*; **drīfan**, *to drive*; **dwīnan**, *to dwindle*; **flītan**, *to strive, quarrel*; **gewītan**, *to depart*; **gīnan**, *to yawn*; **glīdan**, *to glide*; **gnīdan**, *to rub together*; **grīpan**, *to seize*; **hnītan**, *to knock*; **hrīnan**, *to touch*; **hwīnan**, *to whizz*; **nīpan**, *to grow dark*; **rīdan**, *to ride*; **sīcan**, *to sigh*; **scīnan** (§ **133**, Note 2), *to shine*; **scrīfan**, *to prescribe*; **slīdan**, *to slide*; **slītan**, *to slit*; **snīcan**, *to crawl*; **spīwan** (§ **265**), *to spew, spit*; **strīcan**, *to stroke*; **strīdan**, *to stride*; **swīcan**, *to cease from*; **swīfan**, *to sweep*; **tōslīfan**, *to split*; **þwīnan**, *to grow soft*; **þwītan**, *to hew*; **wīcan**, *to yield, give way*; **wlītan**, *to gaze*; **wrīdan**, *to grow, flourish*; **wrītan**, *to write*. **stīgan**, *to ascend*, pret. sing. **stāg** beside **stāh** (§ **323**); and similarly **hnīgan**, *to incline*; **mīgan**, *to make water*; **sīgan**, *to sink*.

§ **491.** **snīþan,** *to cut* **snāþ** **snidon** **sniden**

And similarly **līþan,** *to go*; **scrīþan,** *to go, proceed.* See § **239.** In **ārīsan,** *to arise*; **gerīsan,** *to befit*; **mīþan,** *to avoid*; **wrīþan,** *to twist,* the **s, þ** of the present was extended to all forms of the verb.

§ **492.** **tīon, tēon,** *to accuse* **tāh** **tigon** **tigen**

**tīon, tēon,** from older ***tīohan, *tīhan** (§ **127**); on the **g** in the pret. pl. and past participle, see § **239.** In the pres. the **ēo** from older **īo** regularly fell together with the **ēo** from Germanic **eu** (§ **137**) which was the cause of verbs of this type often forming their preterite and past participle after the analogy of class II (§ **495**), as **tēah, tugon, togen;** and similarly **lēon,** *to lend*; **sēon,** *to strain*; **þēon,** *to thrive*; **wrēon,** *to cover.* **þēon** from prim. Germanic ***þiŋχanan** (§ **41**) originally belonged to class III; the regular principal parts in OE. would have been **þēon, *þōh** (§ **40**), **þungon, þungen,** all of which occur except ***þōh.** The regular past participles of **lēon** (Goth. **leihvan**) and **sēon** (prim. Germanic ***sīχwan-**) were ***liwen, siwen** with **w** from prim. Germanic **ʒw** (§ **241**); **ligen, sigen** were formed on analogy with the other verbs of this type.

### Class II.

§ **493.** The verbs of this class belong to the second ablaut-series (§ **226**) and therefore have **ēo** in the present, **ēa** in the first and third pers. sing. of the preterite, **u** in the pret. plural, and **o** in the past participle, thus:

| | | | | |
|---|---|---|---|---|
| | **bēodan,** *to command* | **bēad** | **budon** | **boden** |
| Goth. | **biudan** | **báuþ** | **budun** | **budans** |

And similarly **āþrēotan,** *to tire of*; **brēotan,** *to break, destroy*; **clēofan,** *to cleave asunder*; **crēopan,** *to creep*; **drēopan,** *to drip*; **flēotan,** *to flow*; **gēopan,** *to take to oneself*; **gēotan,** *to pour*; **grēotan,** *to weep*; **hlēotan,** *to cast* *lots*; **lēodan,** *to grow*; **nēotan,** *to use, enjoy*; **rēocan,** *to smoke, reek*; **rēodan,** *to redden*; **rēotan,** *to weep*; **scēotan,** *to shoot*; **smēocan,** *to smoke*; **þēotan,** *to howl.* **drēogan,** *to endure,* pret. sing. **drēag** beside **drēah** (§ **323**); and similarly **flēogan,** *to fly*; **lēogan,** *to tell lies.* **brēowan,** *to brew,* pret. sing. **brēaw** (§ **265**); and similarly **cēowan,** *to chew*; **hrēowan,** *to repent of, rue.*

§ **494.** **cēosan,** *to choose* **cēas** **curon** **coren**

And similarly **drēosan,** *to fall*; **forlēosan,** *to lose*; **frēosan,** *to freeze*; **hrēosan,** *to fall*; **sēoþan** (**sudon, soden**), *to boil.* See § **239.** **ābrēoþan,** *to perish, ruin,* extended the **þ** to all parts of the verb.

§ **495.** **tēon,** *to draw* **tēah** **tugon** **togen**

**tēon** (Goth. **tiuhan**) from ***tēohan** (§ **139**); on the **g** in the pret. plural and past participle, see § **239**; and similarly **flēon,** *to flee.*

§ **496.** Here belong also the aorist presents with weak grade vowel in all forms of the present (§ **472**).

**brūcan,** *to use* **brēac** **brucon** **brocen**

And similarly **dūfan,** *to dive*; **hrūtan,** *to snore*; **lūcan,** *to lock*; **lūtan,** *to incline, bow down*; **scūfan,** *to push, shove*; **slūpan,** *to slip*; **sūcan,** *to suck*; **sūpan,** *to sup*; **strūdan,** *to pillage*; **þūtan,** *to howl.* **būgan,** *to bend,* pret. sing. **bēag** beside **bēah** (§ **323**); and similarly **smūgan,** *to creep*; **sūgan,** *to suck.*

### Class III.

§ **497.** The verbs of this class belong to the third ablaut-series (§ **226**), and include the strong verbs having a medial nasal or liquid + consonant, and a few others in which the vowel is followed by two consonants other than a nasal or liquid + consonant.

§ **498.** Verbs with nasal + consonant had **i** in all forms of the present, **a, o** (§ **59**) in the first and third pers. sing. of the preterite, and **u** in the preterite pl. and past participle, thus:

| | | | |
|---|---|---|---|
| **bindan,** *to bind* | **band** (**bond**) | **bundon** | **bunden** |
| Goth. **bindan** | **band** | **bundun** | **bundans** |

And similarly **ācwincan,** *to vanish*; **climban,** *to climb*; **clingan,** *to shrink*; **crimman,** *to insert*; **crincan, cringan,** *to fall, succumb*; **drincan,** *to drink*; **gelimpan,** *to happen*; **grimman,** *to rage*; **grindan,** *to grind*; **hlimman,** *to resound*; **hrindan,** *to push*; **linnan,** *to cease*; **onginnan,** *to begin*; **rinnan,** *to run, flow*; **scrincan, scringan,** *to shrink*; **sinnan,** *to meditate*; **slincan,** *to slink, creep*; **spinnan,** *to spin*; **springan,** *to leap*; **stincan,** *to stink*; **stingan,** *to sting*; **þindan,** *to swell*; **þringan,** *to throng, press*; **þrintan,** *to swell*; **windan,** *to wind*; **winnan,** *to toil, fight*; **wringan,** *to wring*. On **sincan** (Goth. **sigqan**), *to sink*; **singan** (Goth. **siggwan**), *to sing*; **swincan,** *to toil*; **swindan,** *to disappear*; **swingan,** *to swing*; **swimman,** *to swim*, see § **249.** The regular principal parts of **findan** (Goth. **finþan**) would have been ***fīþan** (§ **97**), ***fōþ** (§ **61**), **fundon, funden** (§ **239**); the present and the pret. sing. **fand** were formed on analogy with verbs like **bindan**; beside **fand** there occurs **funde** which is the second pers. sing. also used for the first and third. On **biernan** (Goth. **brinnan**), *to burn*, **barn** (Goth. **brann**), **born** (later **bearn**), **burnon, burnen**; and **iernan** (Goth. **rinnan**, see above), *to run*, **arn** (Goth. **rann**), **orn** (later **earn**), **urnon, urnen,** see § **98,** Note 3.

§ **499.** Verbs with **l**+cons. except **lc** (§ **84**) have **e** in the present, **ea** (§ **64**) in the first and third pers. sing. of the preterite, **u** in the pret. plural, and **o** in the past participle (§ **43**), thus:

| | | | |
|---|---|---|---|
| **helpan,** *to help* | **healp** | **hulpon** | **holpen** |
| Goth. **hilpan** | **halp** | **hulpun** | **hulpans** |

And similarly **belgan,** *to swell with anger*; **bellan,** *to bellow*; **beteldan,** *to cover*; **delfan,** *to dig*; **meltan,** *to melt*; **swelgan,** *to swallow*; **swellan,** *to swell*; **sweltan** (§ **249**), *to die.* **gieldan** (§ **91**), *to yield,* **geald, guldon, golden**; and similarly **giellan,** *to yell*; **gielpan,** *to boast.*

§ **500.** Verbs with **lc, r** or **h** + consonant have **eo** in the present (§§ **83–6**), **ea** in the first and third pers. sing. of the preterite, **u** in the preterite plural, and **o** in the past participle. On the verbs with the combination **weo** in the present, see § **94.**

| | | | |
|---|---|---|---|
| **weorpan,** *to throw* | **wearp** | **wurpon** | **worpen** |

And similarly **āseolcan,** *to languish*; **beorcan,** *to bark*; **beorgan,** *to protect*; **ceorfan,** *to cut, carve*; **deorfan,** *to labour*; **hweorfan,** *to turn, go*; **feohtan,** *to fight*; **meolcan,** late WS. also **melcan,** *to milk*; **sceorfan,** *to gnaw*; **sceorpan,** *to scrape*; **steorfan,** *to die*; **sweorfan,** *to rub*; **sweorcan,** *to become dark.* **weorþan,** *to become,* **wearþ, wurdon, worden** (§ **239**).

§ **501. fēolan** from ***feolhan** (§ **84,** Note 1), *to enter, penetrate,* **fealh** (§ **64**), **fulgon** (§ **239**) beside the more common form **fǣlon** made after the analogy of verbs of class IV, **folgen**; pret. pl. and pp. also **fūlon** from ***fulhon, fōlen** from ***folhen** with **h** from the pres. ***feolhan.**

§ **502.**

| | | | |
|---|---|---|---|
| **bregdan,** *to brandish* | **brægd** | **brugdon** | **brogden** |
| **stregdan,** *to strew* | **strægd** | **strugdon** | **strogden** |
| **berstan,** *to burst* | **bærst** | **burston** | **borsten** |
| **þerscan,** *to thresh* | **þærsc** | **þurscon** | **þorscen** |
| **frignan,** *to ask* | **frægn** | **frugnon** | **frugnen** |
| **murnan,** *to mourn* | **mearn** | **murnon** | |
| **spurnan,** *to spurn* | **spearn** | **spurnon** | **spornen** |

In **bregdan** and **stregdan,** beside the forms with **g** there also occur forms with loss of **g** and lengthening of the preceding vowel, as **brēdan** (§ **80**, Note 2), **brǣd** (§ **54**, Note 2), **brūdon, brōden** (§ **106**, Note). **berstan** (OHG. **brestan**) and **þerscan** (OHG. **dreskan**) have metathesis of **r** (§ **280**), hence the absence of breaking in the present and pret. singular. The **i** in **frignan** is due to the influence of the **gn**; beside **frignan** there also occurs **frīnan** (§ **96**, Note 1) to which a new pret. sing. **frān** was formed after the analogy of verbs of class I; the **n** belonged originally to the present only, and the **g** to the pret. plural and past participle; the **n** and **g** were extended to all forms of the verb, cp. Goth. **fraíhnan, frah, frēhun** for ***frēgun, fraíhans** for ***frigans**; the Goth. shows that the OE. verb originally belonged to class V and that the principal parts would regularly have been ***freohnan** (***frēonan**, § **329**, 2), ***freah**, ***frāgon** (§ **120**), ***fregen**; beside the pret. pl. **frugnon** there also occur **frungon** with metathesis of **gn**, and **frūnon** with loss of **g**; and beside the pp. **frugnen** there also occur **frūnen** with loss of **g**, and **frognen**. **murnan** and **spurnan** (also **spornan**) are properly aorist presents (§ **472**).

## Class IV.

§ **503**. The verbs of this class belong to the fourth ablaut-series (§ **226**), which includes the strong verbs whose stems end in a single liquid or nasal. They have **e** in the present, **æ** in the first and third pers. sing. of the preterite, **ǣ** in the pret. plural, and **o** in the past participle, thus:

| | | | |
|---|---|---|---|
| **beran**, *to bear* | **bær** | **bǣron** | **boren** |
| Goth. **baíran** | **bar** | **bērun** | **baúrans** |

And similarly **cwelan**, *to die*; **helan**, *to conceal*; **stelan**, *to steal*; **teran**, *to tear*; **þweran**, *to stir*. **scieran** (§ **91**), *to shear*, **scear** (§ **72**), **scēaron** (§ **124**), **scoren**.

§ **504**.

| | | | |
|---|---|---|---|
| **cuman**, *to come* | **c(w)ōm** | **c(w)ōmon** | **cumen (cymen)** |
| **niman**, *to take* | **nōm** | **nōmon** | **numen** |

From the regular forms of the second and third pers. sing. pres. indic. **cym(e)st, cym(e)þ**, the **y** was often extended to other forms of the pres., especially to the pres. subjunctive as **cyme** beside **cume**; **cuman** is an aorist present (§ **472**) from older ***kwoman** with regular loss of **w** before **u** (§§ **109, 266**), after the analogy of which it was often dropped in the preterite; **c(w)ōm** for ***cwam, *cwom,** was a new formation from the plural where **ō** was regular (§ **121**); **cumen** from older ***kwomen**; on **cymen,** see § **442. niman** from older ***neman** (§ **81**); **nōm** was a new formation from the plural which regularly had **ō** (§ **121**); beside **nōm, nōmon** there also occur the new formations **nam, nāmon**; **numen** from older ***nomen** (§ **109**).

### Class V.

§ **505.** The verbs of this class belong to the fifth ablaut-series (§ **226**), which includes the strong verbs whose stems end in a single consonant other than a liquid or a nasal. They have **e** in the present, **æ** in the first and third pers. sing. of the preterite, **ǣ** in the pret. plural, and **e** in the past participle, thus:

| | | | |
|---|---|---|---|
| **metan,** *to measure* | **mæt** | **mǣton** | **meten** |
| Goth. **mitan** | **mat** | **mētun** | **mitans** |

And similarly **brecan** (pp. **brocen** after the analogy of class IV), *to break*; **cnedan,** *to knead*; **drepan** (pp. also **dropen** after the analogy of class IV); **screpan,** *to scrape*; **sprecan,** late OE. **specan,** *to speak*; **swefan,** *to sleep*; **tredan,** *to tread*; **wefan,** *to weave* · **wegan** (pret. pl. **wǣgon** beside **wāgon,** see § **120**), *to carry*; **wrecan,** *to avenge*. **giefan** (§ **91**), *to give*, **geaf** (§ **72**), **gēafon** (§ **124**), **giefen**; and similarly **forgietan,** *to forget*. **etan,** *to eat*, and **fretan** (Goth. **fra-itan,** pret. sing. **frēt**), *to devour*, had **ǣ** in the pret. sing. already in prim. Germanic, cp. Goth. **ēt,** O.Icel. OS. **āt,** OHG. **āʒ** (§ **119**). **cweþan,** *to say*, **cwæþ, cwǣdon,**

**cweden**; **wesan,** *to be,* pret. pl. **wǣron** (§ **239**). **genesan,** *to be saved,* and **lesan,** *to collect, gather,* have extended the **s** of the present and pret. sing. to all forms of the verb.

§ **506.** **sēon** (Goth. **saíƕan**) from ***seohan** (§ **87**), *to see,* **seah** (§ **68**), **sāwon** beside **sǣgon** (§ **241**), **sewen** (§ **241**) beside **sawen** with **a** difficult to account for, and Anglian **gesegen** with **g** from the pret. plural; and similarly **gefēon,** *to rejoice,* **gefeah,** pret. pl. **gefǣgon**; **plēon,** *to risk,* pret. sing. **pleah.**

§ **507.** To this class also belong **biddan,** *to pray*; **licgan,** *to lie down*; **sittan,** *to sit,* which originally had **j** in the present (§ **254**): **biddan** (Goth. **bidjan**), **bæd** (Goth. **baþ**), **bǣdon** (Goth. **bēdun**), **beden** (Goth. **bidans**). The pret. pl. of **licgan** is **lāgon** beside **lǣgon** (§ **120**). **þicgan,** *to receive,* is a weak verb in WS.; in poetry it has the strong forms **þeah** (**þāh**), **þǣgon, þegen. fricgan,** *to ask, inquire,* with strong pp. **gefrigen, gefrugen** (cp. § **502**).

## Class VI.

§ **508.** The verbs of this class belong to the sixth ablaut-series (§ **226**), and have **a** in the present, **ō** in the pret. sing. and plural, and **æ** beside **a** in the past participle. There is a good deal of fluctuation between **æ** and **a** in the past participle, as **færen, græfen, sæcen, slægen** beside **faren, grafen, sacen, slagen.** The regular development of Germanic **a** when followed by a palatal vowel in the next syllable is **æ** (§ **54**), so that forms with **a** like **faren,** &c., are new formations with **a** from the present, see § **54,** Note 3.

On the origin of the **a, ō** in verbs belonging to this class, see §§ **224,** Note 5, **228.**

| | | | |
|---|---|---|---|
| **faran,** *to go* | **fōr** | **fōron** | **færen, faren** |
| Goth. **faran** | **fōr** | **fōrun** | **farans** |

And similarly **alan,** *to grow*; **bacan,** *to bake*; **calan,** *to be cold*; **galan,** *to sing*; **grafan,** *to dig*; **hladan,** *to lade,* *load*; **sacan,** *to strive, quarrel*; **wacan,** *to awake, be born*; **wadan,** *to go*; **wascan,** *to wash.* **gnagan** (pret. sing. **gnōg** beside **gnōh,** § **323**), *to gnaw*; and similarly **dragan,** *to draw.* **scacan, sceacan** (§ **57,** Note), *to shake,* **scōc, sceōc** (§ **128,** Note), **scacen, sceacen**; and similarly **scafan, sceafan,** *to shave, scrape.* **standan** (Goth. **standan**), *to stand,* **stōd, stōdon, standen** with **n** from the present. **spanan,** *to allure,* pret. **spōn** beside **spēon** which was formed after the analogy of verbs of class VII.

§ **509.**

| | | | |
|---|---|---|---|
| **slēan,** *to strike* | **slōg, slōh** | **slōgon** | **slægen, slagen** |

**slēan** (Goth. **slahan**) from ***sleahan** (§ **70**); **slōg** with **g** from the plural, beside **slōh** (§ **323**), **slōgon** (§ **239**); beside **slægen, slagen** there also occurs **slegen** with **i**-umlaut (§ **442**); and similarly **flēan,** *to flay*; **lēan,** *to blame*; **þwēan,** *to wash.*

§ **510.** To this class also belong **hebban** (Goth. **hafjan**), *to raise*; **hliehhan** (Goth. **hlahjan**), *to laugh*; **sceþþan** (Goth. **skaþjan**), *to injure,* cp. § **526**; **scieppan** (Goth. **ga-skapjan**), *to create*; **stæppan** beside **steppan** (§ **55,** Note 3), *to step, go*; **swerian,** *to swear,* which originally had **j** in the present (§ **271**).

| | | | |
|---|---|---|---|
| **hebban** | **hōf** | **hōfon** | **hæfen, hafen** |
| **hliehhan** | **hlōg, hlōh** | **hlōgon** | |
| **sceþþan** | **scōd** | **scōdon** | |
| **scieppan** | **scōp** | **scōpon** | **sceapen** |
| **stæppan** | **stōp** | **stōpon** | **stæpen, stapen** |
| **swerian** | **swōr** | **swōron** | **sworen** |

**hebban** has also weak pret. and pp. in late WS. (**hefde, hefod**); beside **hæfen** there also occurs **hefen** (§ **442**). **hlōg** with **g** from the plural beside **hlōh** (§ **323**) The regular WS. form of **sceþþan** would be **scieþþan** (§ **73**); **scōd** with **d** from **scōdon.** On **sceō-** beside **scō-,** see § **128,**

Note. On **sceapen**, see § **57**, Note. **sworen** with **o** from analogy of verbs of class IV as in OHG. **gisworan.**

## Class VII.

§ **511.** To this class belong those verbs which originally had reduplicated preterites like Goth. **haíhald, laílōt, faíflōk, haíháit, raírōþ, laíláik,** inf. **haldan,** *to hold,* **lētan,** *to let,* **flōkan,** *to complain,* **háitan,** *to call,* **rēdan,** *to advise,* **láikan,** *to leap.* Traces of the old reduplicated preterites have been preserved in Anglian and in poetry, viz. **hĕht** (also WS.), **leolc, leort, ondreord, reord,** beside inf. **hātan, lācan, lǣtan, ondrǣdan, rǣdan,** see below. This class of verbs is divided into two sub-divisions according as the preterite had **ē** or **ēo.** Much has been written about the stem-vowel in the preterite of these verbs, but little or nothing is really known of how it came about. It is usually assumed to be due to the old reduplicated syllable having undergone contraction with the stem-syllable, but this assumption leaves many phonological difficulties unexplained. The preterite sing. and pl. have the same stem-vowel. The stem-syllable of all verbs belonging to this class is long.

### Sub-division 1.

§ **512.** **hātan,** *to call* **hēt** **hāten**

And similarly **lācan,** *to play*; **scādan, sceādan** (§ **133,** Note 2), *to separate,* pret. **scēd** beside **scēad.**

§ **513.** **lǣtan,** *to let, allow* **lēt** **lǣten**

And similarly **ondrǣdan** (WS. also weak pret. **ondrǣdde**), *to dread, fear*; **rǣdan** (pret. and pp. mostly weak in WS.: **rǣdde, gerǣdd**), *to advise*; **slǣpan** (WS. also weak pret. **slǣpte**), *to sleep.* **blandan,** *to mix,* pret. **blēnd,** pp. **blanden.**

§ **514.** **fōn** (§ **117**), *to seize* **fēng** (§ **239**) **fangen**

And similarly **hōn,** *to hang.*

Sub-division 2.

§ **515.** **bannan,** *to summon* **bēon(n)** **bannen**

And similarly **gangan** (pret. also **gīeng**), *to go*; **spannan,** *to join, clasp.*

§ **516.** **fealdan** (§ **64**), *to fold* **fēold** **fealden**

And similarly **feallan,** *to fall*; **healdan,** *to hold*; **stealdan,** *to possess*; **wealcan,** *to roll*; **wealdan,** *to rule*; **weallan,** *to boil*; **weaxan** (originally belonged to class VI), *to grow.*

§ **517.** **blāwan,** *to blow* **blēow** (§ **265**) **blāwen**

And similarly **cnāwan,** *to know*; **crāwan,** *to crow*; **māwan,** *to mow*; **sāwan,** *to sow*; **swāpan,** *to sweep*; **þrāwan,** *to turn, twist*; **wāwan,** *to blow.*

§ **518.** **bēatan,** *to beat* **bēot** **bēaten**

And similarly **āhnēapan,** *to pluck off*; **hēawan,** *to hew*; **hlēapan,** *to leap.*

§ **519.** **blōtan,** *to sacrifice* **blēot** **blōten**

And similarly **blōwan,** *to bloom, blossom*; **hrōpan,** *to shout*; **hwōpan,** *to threaten*; **flōwan,** *to flow*; **grōwan,** *to grow*; **hlōwan,** *to low, bellow*; **rōwan** (pret. pl. **rēon** beside **rēowon,** § **266**), *to row*; **spōwan,** *to succeed*; **wēpan** (Goth. **wōpjan**), *to weep.* The pret. of **flōcan,** *to clap, strike*; **swōgan,** *to sound*; **wrōtan,** *to root up,* do not occur.

B. Weak Verbs.

§ **520.** The weak verbs, which for the most part are derivative and denominative, form by far the greater majority of all OE. verbs. They are divided into three classes according to the endings of the infinitive, pret. indicative, and past participle. These endings are:—

| | Inf. | Pret. | P.P. |
|---|---|---|---|
| Class I. | **-an** | **-ede, -de, -te** | **-ed, -d, -t** |
| | (Goth. **-jan**) | (Goth. **-ida, -ta**) | (Goth. **-iþs, -ts**) |

| | | | |
|---|---|---|---|
| Class II. | **-ian** | **-ode** | **-od** |
| | (Goth. **-ōn**) | (Goth. **-ōda**) | (Goth. **-ōþs**) |
| Class III. | **-an** | **-de** | **-d** |
| | (Goth. **-an**) | (Goth. **-áida**) | (Goth. **-áiþs**) |

The weak preterite is a special Germanic formation, and many points connected with its origin are still uncertain. Some scholars are inclined to regard it as a periphrastic formation which was originally confined to denominative verbs, and then at a later period became extended to primary verbs as well. The OE. endings **-de, -des(t)**, **-de,** pl. **-don** (older **-dun**), would thus represent an old aorist formed from the root ***dhē-**, *put, place* (Gr. *τί-θη-μι*), which stands in ablaut relation to OE. **dōn,** *to do.* The old preterite (perfect) of this verb has been preserved in the preterite plural of Gothic weak verbs, as **háusi-dēdum** (*we heard*), **-dēduþ, -dēdun** = OHG. **tātum, tātut, tātun** (OS. **dādun**), the pret. pl. of **tuon,** *to do.* But it is also probable that the dental in the OE. preterite stands in close relationship to the dental in the past participle, where the **-d** = prim. Germanic **-đás** = Gr. *-τό-ς*. Prim. Germanic **-đōn (đǣn)**, **-đǣs, -đǣ(þ)**, pl. third pers. **-đun(þ)** from Indg. ***-dhn̥t** with vocalic **n̥,** regularly became **-de, -des(t), -de, -don** older **-dun** in OE. The personal endings of the present indicative are the same as those of strong verbs (§ **476**). The endings **-e, -en** of the pres. and pret. subjunctive are of the same origin as in strong verbs (§§ **477, 482**). The present participle was declined like an ordinary **ja**-stem (§ **441**), and the past participle like **manig** or **hālig** according as the stem-syllable was short or long (§§ **429, 440**). Three stems are to be distinguished in the conjugation of a weak verb: the stem of the present, preterite, and past participle, which mostly agrees with that of the preterite.

Note.—Many points concerning the inflexion of weak verbs in the oldest periods of the Germanic languages have never been satisfactorily explained. For a summary and discussion of the various explanations which have been suggested by scholars the student should consult: Brugmann, *Kurze vergleichende Grammatik der indogermanischen Sprachen*, p. 550, also *Beiträge zur Geschichte der deutschen Sprache und Literatur*, herausgegeben von W. Braune, vol. xxxix, pp. 84–97; Kluge, *Vorgeschichte der altgermanischen Sprachen* in Paul's *Grundriss der germanischen Philologie*, third ed., pp. 168–72; Streitberg, *Urgermanische Grammatik*, pp. 334–42; Collitz, *Das schwache Präteritum und seine Vorgeschichte*, where the whole subject is treated in great detail.

## Class I.

§ **521.** In OE. the verbs of this class are divided into two sub-divisions: (*a*) verbs which originally had a short stem-syllable; (*b*) polysyllabic verbs and those which originally had a long stem-syllable. Nearly all the verbs belonging to this class are causative and denominative. On the personal and other endings, see §§ **273, 476–83.**

### Sub-division (*a*).

§ **522.** Formation of the present stem: The present stem of verbs ending in a single consonant, except **r**, became long (except in the second and third pers. sing. pres. indicative, and second pers. sing. imperative) by the West Germanic law of the doubling of consonants (§ **254**). The **j** had already disappeared in these persons before the operation of the law, for which reason they had single consonants in OE. (§ **254**, Note).

§ **523.** Formation of the pret. and past participle: The **j**, which caused the doubling of the final consonants in the present stems, never existed in the preterite or past participle, so that these stems ended in single consonants. The pret. generally had the ending **-ede** from prim. Germanic **-iđōn**, but verbs whose present stems ended in **dd**, **tt** (= West Germanic **dj**, **tj**) had **-de**, **-te** on analogy with the verbs which originally had long stems (§ **528**). On many verbs whose present stems ended in **cc, ll** (= West Germanic **kj, lj**), see § **534**.

The past participle generally ended in **-ed** from older **-id**, prim. Germanic **-iđaz** from older **-iđás**, Indg. **-itós**, as **genered, gefremed** (see § **442**). But in WS. and Ken. the verbs whose stems ended in **d, t** had vowel syncope and assimilation of consonants, as **geset(t)**, masc. acc. sing. **gesetne**, dat. **gesettum**, fem. gen. dat. sing. **gesetre**, beside Anglian **geseted, gesetedne, gesettum, gesetedre**; **gehredd** beside Anglian **gehreded,** *rescued*. See § **300**.

§ **524.** The full conjugation of **nerian** (Goth. **nasjan**), *to save*; **fremman** (Goth. ***framjan**), *to perform*; **settan** (Goth. **satjan**), *to set*, will serve as models for this class.

*Present.*

Indicative.

| | | | | |
|---|---|---|---|---|
| Sing. | 1. | **nerie** | **fremme** | **sette** |
| | 2. | **neres(t)** | **fremes(t)** | **setst** |
| | 3. | **nereþ** | **fremeþ** | **set(t)** |
| Plur. | | **neriaþ** | **fremmaþ** | **settaþ** |

Subjunctive.

| | | | | |
|---|---|---|---|---|
| Sing. | | **nerie** | **fremme** | **sette** |
| Plur. | | **nerien** | **fremmen** | **setten** |

Imperative.

| | | | | |
|---|---|---|---|---|
| Sing. | 2. | **nere** (§ **214**) | **freme** | **sete** |
| Plur | 2. | **neriaþ** | **fremmaþ** | **settaþ** |

Infinitive.

| | | |
|---|---|---|
| **nerian** | **fremman** | **settan** |

Participle.

| | | |
|---|---|---|
| **neriende** | **fremmende** | **settende** |

*Preterite.*

Indicative.

| | | | | |
|---|---|---|---|---|
| Sing. | 1. | **nerede** | **fremede** | **sette** |
| | 2. | **neredes(t)** | **fremedes(t)** | **settes(t)** |
| | 3. | **nerede** | **fremede** | **sette** |
| Plur. | | **neredon** | **fremedon** | **setton** |

Subjunctive.

| | | | |
|---|---|---|---|
| Sing. | **nerede** | **fremede** | **sette** |
| Plur. | **nereden** | **fremeden** | **setten** |

Participle.

| | | |
|---|---|---|
| **genered** | **gefremed** | **geseted, geset(t)** |

§ **525.** On forms like **nergan, nerigan, nerigean**, see § **271.** Like **nerian** are conjugated **āmerian,** *to purify*; **andswerian,** *to answer*; **berian,** *to make bare*; **bescierian,** *to deprive*; **byrian,** *to pertain to, belong to*; **derian,** *to injure*; **erian,** *to plough*; **ferian,** *to carry*; **gewerian,** *to clothe*; **herian,** *to praise*; **onhyrian,** *to emulate*; **scierian,** *to allot*; **snyrian,** *to hasten*; **spyrian,** *to pursue*; **styrian,** *to stir*; **werian,** *to defend.*

In late WS. many of the verbs of this type went over into class II owing to the ending of the infinitive being the same in both classes.

§ **526.** Like **fremman** are conjugated **āswebban,** *to kill*; **clynnan,** *to sound*; **cnyssan,** *to knock*; **dynnan,** *to make a noise*; **gremman,** *to anger, provoke*; **hlynnan,** *to roar*; **hrissan,** *to shake*; **sceþþan** (also sv. § **510**), *to injure*; **sweþþan,** *to swathe*; **temman,** *to tame*; **trymman,** *to strengthen*; **þennan,** *to stretch*; **þicgan** (in poetry also strong pret. **þeah, þāh**), *to receive*; **wecgan,** *to agitate*; **wennan,** *to accustom*; **wreþþan,** *to support.*

In WS. and Ken. most of the verbs whose stems ended in **l, m, n, s, þ** were remodelled on analogy with verbs like

**nerian** with single consonant, as **clynian, fremian, helian,** *to conceal,* **sylian,** *to sully,* **sweþian,** and then later often went over into class II. On the pret. and past participle of verbs whose stems ended in **þ**, see § **305**.

§ **527**. Like **settan** are conjugated **ātreddan,** *to search out*; **cnyttan,** *to bind, knit*; **hreddan,** *to rescue, save*; **hwettan,** *to whet, incite*; **lettan,** *to hinder*; **spryttan,** *to sprout*; and **lecgan,** *to lay.*

Sub-division (*b*).

§ **528**. The preterite generally ended in **-de** from older **-ide,** the **i** of which caused umlaut in the stem-syllable and then disappeared (§ **221**). The following points should be noted in regard to the consonants: (1) Germanic double consonants were simplified before **-de,** as **fyllan** (Goth. **fulljan**), *to fill,* pret. **fylde** (§ **259**), pp. **gefylled**; (2) **þ** + **d** became **dd** in late WS., as **cȳþan,** *to make known,* pret. **cȳþde,** pp. **gecȳþed,** later **cȳdde** (§ **305**), pp. **gecȳd(d)** with **dd** from the inflected forms; (3) **-de** became **-te** after voiceless consonants (§ **300**), as **cyssan,** *to kiss,* pret. **cyste,** pp. **gecyssed**; **grētan,** *to greet,* pret. **grētte,** pp. **gegrēt(ed)**; (4) the **d** in **-de** disappeared after consonant + **d** or **t** (§ **259**, 3), as **sendan,** *to send,* pret. **sende,** pp. **gesend(ed)**; **fæstan,** *to make fast,* pret. **fæste,** pp. **gefæst(ed)**. Verbs which would regularly have vocalic **l, n, r** in the pret. generally have **-ede,** especially in the combination long syllable + **l, n, r,** as **hyngran,** *to hunger,* **dīeglan,** *to hide,* pret. **hyngrede, dīeglede** (§ **221**); but in the combination short syllable + **l, n, r** they generally had **-de** in the oldest period of the language and then later **-ede,** as **eglan,** *to trouble,* pret. **eglde** beside later **eglede**; the verbs of this type often went over into class II (cp. § **222**).

The uninflected form of the past participle generally ended in **-ed** from older **-id,** prim. Germanic **-iđás** just as in sub-division (*a*). In those cases where the **e** was regularly syncopated in the inflected forms (see § **222**), the same consonantal changes took place as in the preterite, as gen. sing. **gefyldes, gedrenctes, gesendes, gegrēttes, gefæstes,** &c. beside nom. sing. **gefylled, gedrenced, gesend(ed), gegrēt(ed), gefæst(ed).** See § **442.**

§ **529.** The full conjugation of **dēman** (Goth. **dōmjan**), *to judge*, **drencan** (Goth. **dragkjan**), *to submerge*, **hyngran** (Goth. **huggrjan**), *to hunger*, and **gierwan** from ***ȝearwjan**, *to prepare*, will serve as models for this class.

*Present.*

Indicative.

| | | | | | |
|---|---|---|---|---|---|
| Sing. | 1. | **dēme** | **drence** | **hyngre** | **gierwe** |
| | 2. | **dēm(e)st** | **drenc(e)st** | **hyngrest** | **gierest** |
| | 3. | **dēm(e)þ** | **drenc(e)þ** | **hyngreþ** | **giereþ** |
| Plur. | | **dēmaþ** | **drencaþ** | **hyngraþ** | **gierwaþ** |

Subjunctive.

| | | | | |
|---|---|---|---|---|
| Sing. | **dēme** | **drence** | **hyngre** | **gierwe** |
| Plur. | **dēmen** | **drencen** | **hyngren** | **gierwen** |

Imperative.

| | | | | | |
|---|---|---|---|---|---|
| Sing. | 2. | **dēm** (§ **215**) | **drenc** | **hyngre** | **giere** |
| Plur. | 2. | **dēmaþ** | **drencaþ** | **hyngraþ** | **gierwaþ** |

Infinitive.

| | | | |
|---|---|---|---|
| **dēman** | **drencan** | **hyngran** | **gierwan** |

Participle.

| | | | |
|---|---|---|---|
| **dēmende** | **drencende** | **hyngrende** | **gierwende** |

*Preterite.*

Indicative.

| | | | | | |
|---|---|---|---|---|---|
| Sing. | 1. | **dēmde** | **drencte** | **hyngrede** | **gierede** |
| | 2. | **dēmdes(t)** | **drenctes(t)** | **hyngredes(t)** | **gieredes(t)** |
| | 3. | **dēmde** | **drencte** | **hyngrede** | **gierede** |
| Plur. | | **dēmdon** | **drencton** | **hyngredon** | **gieredon** |

Subjunctive.

| | | | | |
|---|---|---|---|---|
| Sing. | **dēmde** | **drencte** | **hyngrede** | **gierede** |
| Plur. | **dēmden** | **drencten** | **hyngreden** | **giereden** |

Participle.

| | | | | |
|---|---|---|---|---|
| | **gedēmed** | **gedrenced** | **gehyngred** | **gegier(w)ed** |

§ **530.** Like **dēman** are conjugated a large number of verbs, as **ǣlan,** *to set on fire*; **ærnan,** *to gallop, cause to run*; **āflīegan,** *to put to flight*; **ālīefan,** *to allow*; **āwyrgan,** *to strangle, kill*; **bǣdan,** *to compel*; **bærnan,** *to burn up, cause to burn*; **benǣman,** *to deprive of*; **bīegan,** *to bend*; **brǣdan,** *to broaden*; **byrgan,** *to taste*; **byrgan,** *to bury*; **cēlan,** *to cool*; **cemban,** *to comb*; **cīegan** (§ **270**), *to call*; **cwielman,** *to kill*; **dǣlan,** *to share*; **dīedan,** *to kill*; **drǣfan,** *to drive out*; **drēfan,** *to stir up*; **drȳgan,** *to dry*; **ēaþmēdan,** *to humble*; **fēdan,** *to feed*; **fēgan,** *to join*; **fēran,** *to go, journey*; **flīeman,** *to put to flight*; **fylgan,** *to follow*; **fȳsan,** *to hasten*; **gefrēdan,** *to feel, perceive*; **gelīefan,** *to believe*; **geþīedan,** *to join together*; **gīeman,** *to heed*; **giernan,** *to desire, yearn for*; **glengan,** *to adorn*; **hǣlan,** *to heal*; **hǣman,** *to marry*; **hīenan,** *to humiliate, ill-use*; **hīeran,** *to hear*; **hlȳdan,** *to make a noise*; **hringan,** *to ring, sound*; **hwierfan,** *to convert*; **hȳdan,** *to hide*; **lǣdan,** *to lead*; **lǣfan,** *to leave*; **lǣnan,** *to lend*; **lǣran,** *to teach*; **lengan,** *to require*; **līesan,** *to set free*; **mǣnan,** *to moan, complain*; **mǣran,** *to proclaim*; **mengan,** *to mix*; **nemnan** (pret. **nemde,** pp. **genem(n)ed**), *to name*; **nīedan,** *to compel*; **rǣran,** *to raise*; **rǣsan,** *to rush*; **rȳman,** *to make room*; **sǣgan,** *to lay low*; **sǣlan,** *to bind with a rope*; **scrȳdan,** *to clothe*; **sengan,** *to singe*; **sprǣdan,** *to spread*; **sprengan,** *to burst*; **stīeran,** *to steer*; **strīenan,** *to acquire*; **swēgan,** *to make a sound*; **tǣlan,** *to blame*; **tǣsan,** *to pull, tear*; **tengan,** *to hasten*; **tȳnan,** *to enclose*; **wēdan,** *to rage*; **wēnan,** *to expect*; **wiernan,** *to refuse*; **wrēgan,** *to accuse.* The contracted verbs **hēan** (pret. **hēade**, pp. **hēad**), *to heighten, raise*; and similarly **rȳn**, *to roar*; **tȳn**, *to teach*; **þēon**, *to perform, do*; **þȳn** (also in form **þȳwan**), *to press.* **cȳþan** (pret. **cȳþde**, later **cȳdde**), *to make known*; and similarly **āhȳþan**, *to destroy, lay waste*; **cwīþan**, *to lament*; **læþan**, *to hate, abuse*; **nēþan**, *to venture on*; **oferswīþan**, *to overcome*; **sēþan**, *to testify*; **wrǣþan**, *to be angry, get angry.* **fyllan** (pret. **fylde**), *to fill*; and similarly **āfierran**, *to remove*; **cennan**, *to bring forth*; **cierran**, *to turn*; **clyppan**, *to embrace*; **cyssan** (pret. **cyste**), *to kiss*; **fiellan**, *to fell*; **mierran**, *to mar*; **pyffan**, *to puff*; **spillan**, *to destroy*; **stillan**, *to still*; **wemman**, *to defile.* **ieldan** (pret. **ielde**), *to delay*, **sendan** (pret. **sende**), *to send*, **gyrdan** (pret. **gyrde**), *to gird*; and similarly **behyldan**, *to flay*; **gewieldan**, *to overpower*; **gyldan**, *to gild*; **onhieldan**, *to incline*; **scildan**, *to protect*; **spildan**, *to destroy*; **wieldan**, *to control, subdue*; **bendan**, *to bind*; **blendan**, *to blind*; **lendan**, *to land, arrive*; **ontendan**, *to kindle*; **pyndan**, *to shut up, confine*; **scendan**, *to put to shame*; **wendan**, *to turn*; **andwyrdan**, *to answer*; **āwierdan**, *to destroy*; **hierdan**, *to harden*; **onbyrdan**, *to inspire, incite.* **fæstan** (pret. **fæste**), *to make fast*; and similarly **ācræftan**, *to devise, plan*; **āfyrhtan**, *to frighten*; **āgyltan**, *to be guilty*; **āwēstan**, *to lay waste*; **efstan**, *to hasten*; **ēhtan**, *to pursue, persecute*; **fylstan**, *to help*; **gedæftan**, *to put in order*; **gehlæstan**, *to load*; **gehyrstan**, *to equip*; **grimettan**, *to roar, rage* (for other examples of verbs in **-ettan**, see § **657**); **hæftan**, *to hold captive*; **hierstan**, *to roast*; **hiertan**, *to hearten, encourage*; **hlystan**, *to listen*; **hyhtan**, *to hope*; **lǣstan**, *to perform*; **līehtan**, *to give light*; **lystan**, *to please*; **mæstan**, *to feed with mast*; **myntan**, *to intend, think*; **restan**, *to rest*; **rihtan**, *to set right*; **scyrtan**, *to shorten*; **tyhtan**, *to incite, allure*; **þyrstan**, *to thirst.*

§ **531.** Like **drencan** are conjugated **ācwencan**, *to quench*; **ādwæscan**, *to quench*; **āstīepan**, *to bereave*;

**bǣtan**, *to bridle*; **berīepan**, *to despoil*; **bētan**, *to atone for, amend*; **cēpan**, *to keep*; **cīepan**, *to buy*; **cyspan**, *to bind, fetter*; **drīepan**, *to let drop, moisten*; **gewlencan**, *to make proud*; **geswencan**, *to injure*; **grētan**, *to greet*; **hǣtan**, *to heat*; **hwītan**, *to whiten*; **hyspan**, *to mock*; **īecan** (see § **534**, Note 2), *to increase*; **līexan**, *to shine*; **mētan**, *to meet*; **nǣtan**, *to afflict*; **oftyrfan**, *to stone*; **ofþryscan**, *to beat down*; **rētan**, *to cheer*; **scencan**, *to pour out*; **scierpan**, *to sharpen*; **screncan**, *to cause to tumble*; **sencan**, *to cause to sink*; **spǣtan**, *to spit*; **swǣtan**, *to sweat*; **swencan**, *to vex, afflict*; **tōstencan**, *to scatter*; **yppan**, *to open, manifest*; **wǣtan**, *to wet*; **wierpan**, *to recover*; **wȳscan**, *to wish*.

§ **532**. Like **hyngran** are conjugated **bīecnan**, *to make a sign*; **dīeglan**, *to conceal*; **forglendran**, *to devour*; **frēfran**, *to comfort*; **symblan**, *to feast*; **timbran**, *to build*; **wrixlan**, *to change, exchange*. **efnan** (pret. **efnde**, later **efnede**, § **528**), *to level, perform*; and similarly **bytlan**, *to build*; **eglan**, *to trouble, afflict*; **ræfnan**, *to perform*; **seglan**, *to sail*; **þrysman**, *to suffocate*. The verbs of this type often went over into class II (cp. § **222**).

§ **533**. **gierest**, **giereþ**, **gierede** from older ***gierwis**, ***gierwiþ**, ***gierwide** with regular loss of **w** (§ **266**). At a later period the verbs of this type mostly generalized the forms with or without **w**, and often went over into class II. The verbs with a long vowel or a long diphthong in the stem generally had **w** in all forms of the verb. Like **gierwan** are conjugated **hierwan**, *to despise, ill-treat*; **nierwan**, *to constrain*; **sierwan**, *to contrive, plot*; **smierwan**, *to anoint, smear*. **lǣwan** (pret. **lǣwde**), *to betray*; and similarly **forslǣwan**, *to delay, be slow*; **getrīewan**, *to trust*; **hlēowan**, **hlīewan**, *to shelter, warm*; **īewan**, *to show, disclose*.

**sīowan**, **sēowan** (Goth. **siujan**, OHG. **siuwen**) from older ***siuwjan** (cp. § **138**), *to sew*, pret. **siowede**, **seowede** from older ***siwide**; from the pret. was formed a new inf.

**si(o)wian** after the analogy of class II, with preterite **siowode, seowode. spīowan, spēowan** from ***spiuwjan** older ***spiwwjan** (§ **254**), *to spit*, pret. **spiowede, speowede** from ***spiwide,** beside **spīode, spēode,** formed direct from the present; from the pret. **spiowede** was formed a new inf. **spi(o)wian** after the analogy of class II. **streowan** (Goth. ***stráujan**), *to strew*, pret. **streowede** beside **strewede** (Goth. **strawida**), § **77**, from which a new inf. **streowian, strewian** was formed after the analogy of class II, pret. **streowode.**

§ **534.** A certain number of verbs belonging to class I formed their preterite and past participle already in prim. Germanic without the medial vowel **-i-**, as **bycgan** (Goth. **bugjan**), *to buy*, pret. **bohte** (Goth. **baúhta**), pp. **geboht** (Goth. **baúhts**); **þencan** (Goth. **þagkjan**), *to think*, pret. **þōhte** (Goth. **þāhta,** § **40**), pp. **geþōht** (Goth. **þāhts**), whence the absence of **i**-umlaut in the pret. and past participle of verbs of this type. See § **539.** In addition to a few verbs which had long stems originally, they embrace verbs whose present stems end in **cc, ll** from West Germanic **kj** and **lj** (§ **254**). On the interchange between **c, cc** from **kj, cg** from **ʒj,** and **h,** see § **240.** At a later period the preterite and pp. of verbs with **-ecc-** in the present were re-formed with **e** from the present, as **cweccan, cwehte, gecweht**; and similarly **rǣcan, tǣcan,** prim. Germanic ***raikjan, *taikjan,** generally had pret. **rǣhte, tǣhte** with **ǣ** from the present, beside the regular forms **rāhte, tāhte.** The verbs with **ll** in the present often formed the pret. and pp. on analogy with the verbs of sub-division (*a*) especially in late OE., as **dwelede, -ode,** beside older **dwealde.** Beside **sellan** (Goth. **saljan**) there also occurs **siellan** (later **syllan**) from ***sealljan** with **ea** borrowed from the pret. and pp. in prehistoric OE. **bringan,** *to bring*, is the strong form (cp. § **498**); the regular weak form **brengan** is rare in OE.

| | | |
|---|---|---|
| **bycgan**, *to buy* | **bohte** | **geboht** |
| **cweccan**, *to shake* | **cweahte** | **gecweaht** |
| **dreccan**, *to afflict* | **dreahte** | **gedreaht** |
| **leccan**, *to moisten* | **leahte** | **geleaht** |
| **reccan**, *to narrate* | **reahte** | **gereaht** |
| **streccan**, *to stretch* | **streahte** | **gestreaht** |
| **þeccan**, *to cover* | **þeahte** | **geþeaht** |
| **weccan**, *to awake* | **weahte** | **geweaht** |
| **cwellan**, *to kill* | **cwealde** | **gecweald** |
| **dwellan**, *to hinder* | **dwealde** | **gedweald** |
| **sellan**, *to sell* | **sealde** | **geseald** |
| **stellan**, *to place* | **stealde** | **gesteald** |
| **tellan**, *to count* | **tealde** | **geteald** |
| **rǣcan**, *to reach* | **rǣhte, rāhte** | **gerǣht** |
| **tǣcan**, *to teach* | **tǣhte, tāhte** | **getǣht, getāht** |
| **sēcan**, *to seek* | **sōhte** | **gesōht** |
| **bringan**, *to bring* | **brōhte** | **gebrōht** |
| **þencan**, *to think* | **þōhte** | **geþōht** |
| **þyncan**, *to seem* | **þūhte** | **geþūht** |
| **wyrcan**, *to work* | **worhte** | **geworht** |

Note.—1. The presents **reccan** for ***rēcan** (pret. **rōhte**), *to care for, reck*; and **læccan** for ***lǣcan** (pret. **lǣhte**, pp. **gelǣht**), *to seize*, are difficult to account for.

2. Especially in late OE. verbs with medial **c, cc** often formed their pret. and pp. in **-hte, -ht** after the analogy of the above type of verbs, but with the retention of **i**-umlaut, as **bepǣcan**, *to deceive*, **bepǣhte, bepǣht**, beside older **bepǣcte, bepǣct**; and similarly **gewǣcan**, *to weaken*; **īecan**, *to increase*; **nēalǣcan**, *to approach* (for further examples of verbs with **-lǣcan**, see § **658**); **ōleccan**, *to flatter*; **sȳcan**, *to suckle*; **þryccan**, *to press, crush*; **wleccan**, *to warm*.

## Class II.

§ **535**. With the exception of a few primary verbs all the verbs belonging to this class are denominative. The former originally belonged to the athematic and the latter to the thematic conjugation, and the endings of the two types of verbs were: Sing. **-ā́-mi, -ā́-si, -ā́-ti,** Plur. **-ā́-mes,** (**-mos**), **-ā́-te, -ā́-nti**; Sing. **-ā-jṓ, -ā-jé-si, -ā-jé-ti,** Plur. **-ā-jó-mes,** (**-mos**), **-ā-jé-te, -ā-jó-nti.** The denominative verbs were originally formed from nouns belonging to the Germanic ō-declension (cp. §§ **23, 364**), as Lat. **plantō,** older ***plantājō**: **planta,** *plant*; Gr. τῑμάω, older *τῑμάjω, Indg. **-ājṓ**: τῑμᾱ́, -ή, *honour.* In Goth. and OHG. the athematic endings became generalized, and similarly in OE. except the first person singular and the third person plural which was also used for the first and second persons (§ **476**), cp. OHG. **salbōm** from **-ōmi,** beside OE. **sealfie** from **-ōjō,** *I anoint*; OHG. **salbōnt,** Goth. **salbōnd** from **-ōnđi,** beside OE. **sealfiaþ** from **-ōjanþi.** A large number of the verbs which originally belonged to class III went over into this class in prehistoric OE. On the verbs of class I which went over into this class, see §§ **525–6, 533.**

The full conjugation of **sealfian,** *to anoint,* will serve as a model for the verbs of this class.

*Present.*

| | | Indic. | Subj. | Imper. |
|---|---|---|---|---|
| Sing. | 1. | **sealfie** | **sealfie** | |
| | 2. | **sealfas(t)** | ,, | **sealfa** |
| | 3. | **sealfaþ** | ,, | |
| Plur. | | **sealfiaþ** | **sealfien** | **sealfiaþ** |

Infinitive.

**sealfian**

Participle.

**sealfiende**

*Preterite.*

| | | | |
|---|---|---|---|
| Sing. | 1. | **sealfode** | **sealfode** |
| | 2. | **sealfodes(t)** | „ |
| | 3. | **sealfode** | „ |
| Plur. | | **sealfodon** | **sealfoden** |

Participle.

**gesealfod**

The corresponding prim. Germanic forms of the pres. indicative were: ***salƀōjō**, ***salƀōsi** (Goth. **salbōs**), ***salƀōþi** (Goth. **salbōþ**), pl. ***salƀōjanþi** (§ **218**, 5). In OE. **-ōj-** regularly became **-i-** (§ **273**) which not being original did not cause **i**-umlaut in the stem-syllable. The **-i-** was often written **-ig-**, also **-ige-** before guttural vowels, as **sealfige, sealfigan, sealfigean,** beside **sealfie, sealfian,** see § **273.** On the ending **-e** in the first pers. sing. of the present, see § **476.** The ending **-a** in the imperative second pers. sing. was from **sealfas(t)**; a form corresponding to Goth. **salbō** would have become in OE. ***sealf** from older ***sealƀū** (§ **215**). Inf. **sealfian** is from prim. Germanic ***salƀōjanan.**

The corresponding prim. Germanic forms of the pret. indicative were: ***salƀōđōn** (Goth. **salbōda**), ***salƀōđǣs** (Goth. **salbōdēs**), ***salƀōđǣ(þ)** (Goth. **salbōda**), pl. **salƀōđun(þ)**. The medial **-ō-** was regularly shortened to **-u-** in prehistoric OE. (§ **218**) and then later became **-o-**, **-a-**, the former of which is usual in WS. and the latter in Anglian and Ken. On **-e-** beside **-o-**, **-a-**, see § **222.** And similarly in the past participle WS. **-od**, Anglian and Ken. **-ad,** prim. Germanic **-ōđaz** from older **-ōđás,** Indg. **-ātós,** cp. Lat. **-ātus,** Gr. Doric dial. *-ᾱτός*.

§ **536.** Like **sealfian** are conjugated a large number of verbs, as **ācealdian,** *to become cold*; **ārian,** *to honour*; **āscian,** *to ask*; **āswefecian,** *to eradicate*; **bedecian,** *to beg*;

**behōfian**, *to have need of*; **bodian**, *to announce*; **cēapian**, *to buy*; **ceorian**, *to complain*; **costian**, *to try, prove*; **cunnian**, *to try, test*; **dysigian**, *to be foolish*; **dwolian**, *to err*; **eahtian**, *to esteem, consider*; **eardian**, *to dwell, inhabit*; **earnian**, *to earn*; **endian**, *to end*; **fæg(e)nian**, *to rejoice*; **fæstnian**, *to fasten*; **fandian**, *to try, search out*; **folgian**, *to follow*; **fullian**, *to fulfil*; **fundian**, *to strive after*; **gearcian**, *to prepare*; **gearwian** (§ **533**), *to prepare*; **gedafenian**, *to beseem*; **gemīdlian**, *to bridle, restrain*; **gemyndgian**, *to remember*; **geōmrian**, *to be sad, lament*; **gestrangian**, *to make strong*; **grāpian**, *to grope, feel*; **hafenian**, *to hold*; **hālgian**, *to hallow*; **hangian**, *to hang*; **hatian**, *to hate*; **hef(i)gian**, *to make heavy*; **hergian** (cp. § **525**), *to harry*; **hīgian**, *to hasten*; **hnappian**, *to doze*; **hopian**, *to hope*; **hwearfian**, *to wander*; **ieldcian**, *to delay*; **lācnian**, *to heal*; **langian**, *to long for*; **latian**, *to be slow, sluggish* or *torpid*; **laþian**, *to invite*; **lēanian**, *to reward*; **lēasian**, *to tell lies*; **līcian**, *to please*; **lōcian**, *to look*; **lofian**, *to praise*; **losian**, *to lose*; **lufian**, *to love*; **macian**, *to make*; **manian**, *to exhort*; **meldian**, *to announce*; **met(e)gian**, *to measure*; **offrian**, *to offer*; **op(e)nian**, *to open*; **rēafian**, *to plunder*; **samnian**, *to collect, gather*; **sārgian**, *to cause pain*; **sārian**, *to grieve, be sad*; **scamian**, *to be ashamed*; **scēawian**, *to look*; **scyld(i)gian**, *to sin*; **sīþian**, *to travel*; **sorgian**, *to sorrow, grieve*; **sparian**, *to spare*; **syngian**, *to sin*; **tiohhian**, **teohhian**, *to think, consider*; **þaccian**, *to stroke*; **þancian**, *to thank*; **þolian**, *to suffer*; **þrōwian**, *to suffer*; **wacian**, *to be awake*; **wæcnian** (also as sv. **wæcnan**, pret. **wōc**), *to waken, arise, spring up*; **wandrian**, *to wander*; **war(e)nian**, *to beware, take heed*; **warian**, *to beware*; **wealwian**, *to roll, wallow*; **welegian**, *to enrich*; **weorþian**, *to honour*; **wērgian**, *to grow weary*; **wilnian**, *to desire*; **wincian**, *to wink*; **wīsian**, *to guide*; **wītgian**, *to prophesy*; **wītnian**, *to punish, torment*; **wuldrian**, *to glorify*; **wundian**, *to wound*; **wundrian**, *to wonder*; **wunian**, *to dwell*. **bletsian**, *to bless*;

**blīþsian, blissian,** *to rejoice*; **clǣnsian,** *to cleanse*; **efesian,** *to shear*; **eg(e)sian,** *to frighten, terrify*; **gītsian,** *to covet*; **grimsian,** *to rage*; **hrēowsian,** *to repent of, rue*; **iersian,** *to be angry*; **mǣrsian,** *to make famous*; **miltsian,** *to have mercy*; **rīcsian, rīxian,** *to rule, govern*; **unrōtsian,** *to be sad*; **untrēowsian,** *to defraud, deceive,* see § **659.**

On the second and third pers. sing. pres. indic., imperative sing., and pret. indicative of verbs like **bifian,** *to tremble*; **clifian,** *to adhere, cleave*; **clipian,** *to call*; **ginian,** *to yawn, gape*; **hlinian,** *to lean, recline*; **stician,** *to prick, stab*; **tilian,** *to strive after, labour,* see §§ **101–2.**

§ **537.** **twēogan,** Anglian **twīogan,** from ***twiχōjan** (§§ **98, 139**), *to doubt*; pres. indic. **twēoge, twēost, twēoþ**; pres. part. **twēonde** (poetical) beside **twēogende**; pret. indic. **twēode,** Anglian **twīode,** from ***twiχōđōn**; pp. **twēod.** And similarly in WS. the following verbs which originally belonged to class III: **fēog(e)an,** *to hate*; **frēog(e)an,** *to love, make free*; **smēag(e)an,** *to ponder, consider*; **þrēag(e)an,** *to reprove, rebuke.*

## Class III.

§ **538.** Nearly all the verbs of this class were originally primary verbs which partly belonged to the thematic and partly to the athematic conjugation. The stem of both types of verbs was dissyllabic. The thematic type had the endings: Sing. **-ē-jō, -ē-je-si, -ē-je-ti,** Plur. **-ē-jo-mes, (-mos), -ē-je-te, -ē-jo-nti.** The stem of the athematic type ended in **-ē(i)-** beside the weak grade of ablaut **-ĭ-** (**-j-** before vowels) which belonged to all forms of the present, as Sing. **-ĭ-mi, -ĭsi, -ĭ-ti,** Plur. **-ĭ-mes, (-mos), -ĭ-te, -j-enti.** And the **-ē(i)-** belonged to the non-present forms. The original athematic inflexion of the present became partly or entirely thematic in the prehistoric period of all the Indg. languages, see Wright, *Comparative Grammar of the Greek Language,* §§ **458, 481.**

The prim. Germanic inflexion of the present of OE. **habban**, Goth. **haban**, OHG. **habēn**, OS. **hebbian**, O.Icel. **hafa**, Lat. **habē-re**, *to have*, was: Sing. *χaƀǣjō (Lat. **habeo** from *habējō), *χaƀǣjizi (Goth. **habáis**), *χaƀǣjiđi (Goth. **habáiþ**). Plur. *χaƀǣjomiz (cp. § **218**, 1) *χaƀǣjiđi (Goth. **habáiþ**), *χaƀǣjanđi; beside Sing. *χaƀjō (OE. **hæbbe**, OS. **hebbiu**), *χaƀizi, *χaƀiđi, Plur. *χaƀimiz, *χaƀiđi, *χaƀjanđi (OE. **habbaþ**, OS. **hebbiad**). In the infinitive the prim. Germanic **-ǣj-** like **-ōj-** (§ **273**) in class II regularly became **-i-** in OE., which is the reason why nearly all the verbs of class III went over into class II in the prehistoric period of the language, cp. **hatian** (Goth. **hatan**, OHG. **haʒʒēn**) from prim. Germanic *χatǣjanan, *to hate*. In OE. OS. and O.Icel. the preterite and past participle were formed from *χaƀ- without a medial vowel, as OE. **hæfde, gehæfd**, OS. **haƀda, gihabd**, O.Icel. **hafþa, hafþr**, beside Goth. **habáida, habáiþs**, OHG. **habēta, gihabēt**. The chief verbs are: **habban**, *to have*; **libban**, *to live*; **secgan**, *to say*; and **hycgan**, *to think*.

*Present.*

Indicative.

| | | | | | |
|---|---|---|---|---|---|
| Sing. | 1. | **hæbbe** | **libbe** | **secge** | **hycge** |
| | 2. | **hafas(t)**, **hæfst** | **liofas(t)** | **sagas(t)**, **sægst** | **hogas(t)**, **hyg(e)st** |
| | 3. | **hafaþ**, **hæfþ** | **liofaþ** | **sagaþ**, **sægþ** | **hogaþ**, **hyg(e)þ** |
| Plur. | | **habbaþ** | **libbaþ** | **secg(e)aþ** | **hycg(e)aþ** |

Subjunctive.

| | | | | |
|---|---|---|---|---|
| Sing. | **hæbbe** | **libbe** | **secge** | **hycge** |
| Plur. | **hæbben** | **libben** | **secgen** | **hycgen** |

Imperative.

| | | | | |
|---|---|---|---|---|
| Sing. 2. | **hafa** | **liofa** | **saga, sæge** | **hoga, hyge** |
| Plur. 2. | **habbaþ** | **libbaþ** | **secg(e)aþ** | **hycg(e)aþ** |

Infinitive.

| | | | | |
|---|---|---|---|---|
| | **habban** | **libban** | **secg(e)an** | **hycg(e)an** |

Participle.

| | | | | |
|---|---|---|---|---|
| | **hæbbende** | **libbende** | **secgende** | **hycgende** |

*Preterite.*

Indicative.

| | | | | |
|---|---|---|---|---|
| Sing. 1. | **hæfde** | **lifde** | **sægde** | **hogde** |
| 2. | **hæfdes(t)** | **lifdes(t)** | **sægdes(t)** | **hogdes(t)** |
| 3. | **hæfde** | **lifde** | **sægde** | **hogde** |
| Plur. | **hæfdon** | **lifdon** | **sægdon** | **hogdon** |

Subjunctive.

| | | | | |
|---|---|---|---|---|
| Sing. | **hæfde** | **lifde** | **sægde** | **hogde** |
| Plur. | **hæfden** | **lifden** | **sægden** | **hogden** |

Participle.

| | | | | |
|---|---|---|---|---|
| | **gehæfd** | **gelifd** | **gesægd** | **gehogod** |

The endings **-as(t)**, **-aþ** of the second and third pers. sing. pres. indicative, and **-a** of the imperative sing., were from verbs of class II; the endings corresponding to Goth. **-áis**, **-áiþ**, **-ái** would have become **-es(t)**, **-eþ**, **-e** in OE. The regular form of **hæbbe** would be ***hebbe** (OS. **hebbiu**) from West Germanic ***χabbjō**, but the **a** of the second and third pers. sing. was extended to the first and then **a** became **æ** by i-umlaut, cp. § **55**, Note 2. On the **æ** beside **a** in the second and third pers. singular, see §§ **54**, **57**. **hafas(t)**, **hafaþ** are rare in pure WS., the usual forms are **hæfst**, **hæfþ**; and similarly with **sægst**, **sægþ**; **hyg(e)st**, **hyg(e)þ**. **habbaþ**, **habban** (West Germanic ***χabbjanþi**, ***χabbjanan**, OS. **hebbiad**, **hebbian**, § **254**) had the **a** in the stem-syllable from **hafas(t)**, **hafaþ**. On forms like **næbbe** from **ne hæbbe**, see § **325**, Note.

**libbe** (OS. **libbiu**), **libban** (OS. **libbian**), from West Germanic ***libbjō**, ***libbjanan**. Beside **libban** there was also

**lifian**, common in Anglian and Ken., which was inflected like **sealfian** (§ **535**) in the present. On the **io** in **liofas(t)** and **liofaþ**, see § **102.**

**secge** (OS. **seggiu**), **secg(e)an** (OS. **seggian**), from West Germanic ***saggjō, *saggjanan.** In the present the **e** as in **secge, secg(e)an** was often extended to forms which regularly had **æ,** and vice versa. In late WS. the **e** was extended to all forms of the present. On forms like pret. **sǣde** beside **sægde,** see § **54,** Note **2.**

On the **y** in **hycg(e)an** beside the **o** in **hogde,** see § **43.** In the pret. this verb was also inflected like class II, **hogode,** &c.; cp. also the past participle **gehogod** for ***gehogd.**

Note.—Traces of the old inflexion of verbs which originally belonged to class III are seen in such forms as **bȳa** (Nth.), *to dwell*, **fylg(e)an,** *to follow*, **onscynian** (Anglian), *to shun*, **wæccende,** *being awake*, beside **būan, folgian, onscunian, waciende; hettend,** *enemy*, beside **hatian,** *to hate*; pret. **plægde, trūde,** beside **plagode,** *he played*, **trūwian,** *to trust.*

## C. Minor Groups.

### A. Preterite-Presents.

§ **539.** These verbs were originally unreduplicated perfects, which acquired a present meaning like Skr. **vḗda,** Gr. *οἶδα*, Latin **nōvī,** *I know.* In prim. Germanic a new weak preterite, an infinitive, a pres. participle, and in some verbs a strong past participle, were formed. They are inflected in the present like the preterite of strong verbs, except that the second pers. singular has the same stem-vowel as the first and third persons, and has preserved the old ending **-t** (§ **481**). It should be noted that the ending of the weak past participles of verbs belonging to the preterite-presents goes back to Indg. **-tós,** and not **-itós** as in the first class of weak verbs (§ **523**), as **ge-wiss** from

Indg. ***wid + tós** (see § **240**), **cūþ** (Goth. **kunþs**) from prim. Germanic ***kúnþaz,** Indg. ***gntós** with vocalic **n** (§ **542,** Note); and similarly with the weak past participles in the other Germanic languages. This is no doubt the reason why the preterites do not have the medial **-i-** which is found in the preterites and past participles of the first class of weak verbs, as **nerede** (Goth. **nasida**), **genered** (Goth. **nasiþs**); and similarly with the preterites **bohte** (Goth. **baúhta**), **þōhte** (Goth. **þāhta**), &c. and the past participles, see § **534.**

The following verbs, many of which are defective, belong to this class:—

§ **540.** I. Ablaut-Series.

**wāt,** *I know, he knows,* 2 sing. **wāst** (§ **240**), pl. **witon** beside **wioton, wieton** (§ **101**), **wuton** (§ **103**); subj. **wite,** pl. **witen;** imperative sing. **wite,** pl. **witaþ** with **-aþ** from the pres. indic. 3. pers. pl. of other verbs (§ **476**); inf. **witan** beside **wiotan, wietan** (§ **102**); pres. part. **witende** beside **weotende;** pret. **wisse, wiste** (§ **240**); pp. **gewiten;** participial adj. **gewiss,** *certain.* On forms like **nāt** beside **ne wāt,** see § **267.**

§ **541.** II. Ablaut-Series.

**dēag** (Anglian **dēg**) beside later **dēah** (§ **323**), *I avail, he avails,* pl. **dugon;** subj. **dyge** beside the more common form **duge** (§ **482**); inf. **dugan,** pres. part. **dugende;** pret. **dohte** (§ **43**).

§ **542.** III. Ablaut-Series.

**an(n), on(n),** *I grant,* pl. **unnon;** subj. **unne;** imperative **unne;** inf. **unnan;** pres. part. **unnende;** pret. **ūþe** (§ **113**); pp. **geunnen.**

**can(n), con(n),** *I know, can,* 2 sing. **canst, const** with **-st** from forms like **dearst,** pl. **cunnon;** subj. **cunne,**

pl. **cunnen**; inf. **cunnan**; pret. **cūþe** (Goth. **kunþa**); pp. **-cunnen**; participial adj. **cūþ** (Goth. **kunþs**), *known*.

NOTE.—The preterite and past participle of these verbs present difficulties in all the Germanic languages. The pp. OE. **cūþ**, OS. **kūþ**, O.Fris. **kūth**, O.Icel. **kūþr** (**kunnr**), OHG. **kund**, Goth. **kunþs** all go back to prim. Germanic ***kúnþaz**, Indg. ***gntós** with vocalic **n**. The regular prim. Germanic form would have been ***kunđás**, but the separate languages show that the accent must have been shifted from the ending to the stem some time prior to the operation of Verner's law, and that then a preterite was formed direct from the base ***kunþ-** + the endings **-ōn**, (**-ǣn**), **-ǣs**, **-ǣ**, &c. (§ **520**), whence OE. **cūþe**, O.Icel. **kunna** from older ***kunþa**, OHG. **konda**, Goth. **kunþa**; and similarly OE. **ūþe**, O.Icel. **unna** from older ***unþa**, OHG. **onda**, all from prim. Germanic ***unþōn**.

**þearf**, *I need, he needs*, 2. sing. **þearft**, pl. **þurfon**; subj. **þyrfe** beside the more common form **þurfe** (§ **482**); inf. **þurfan**; pres. part. **þurfende** beside participial adj. **þearfende** (formed from **þearf**), *needy*; pret. **þorfte**.

**dear(r)** (Goth. **ga-dars**), *I dare, he dares*, with **rr** from the plural, 2. sing. **dearst**, pl. **durron** (Goth. **ga-daúrsum**) with **rr** from Germanic **rz** by Verner's law (§ **239**); subj. **dyrre** beside the more common form **durre** (§ **482**); pret. **dorste** (Goth. **ga-daúrsta**).

§ **543**. IV. Ablaut-Series.

**sceal**, *I shall, owe*, 2. sing. **scealt**, pl. **sculon** (see § **224**, Note 4) beside **sceolon** (§ **116**); subj. **scyle**, later **scule**, **sceole**; inf. **sculan**, **sceolan**; pret. **sc(e)olde** (§ **110**).

**man**, **mon**, *I think, he thinks*, 2. sing. **manst**, **monst** with **-st** from forms like **dearst**, pl. **munon** (see § **224**, Note 4); subj. **myne** beside the more common form **mune** (§ **482**), pl. **munen**; imperative **-mun** beside **-myne**, **-mune**; inf. **munan**; pres. part. **munende**; pret. **munde** (Goth. **munda**); pp. **gemunen**.

§ **544.** V. Ablaut-Series.

**mæg,** *I, he can,* 2. sing. **meaht** later **miht,** pl. **magon;** subj. **mæge,** pl. **mægen;** inf. **magan;** pres. part. **magende;** pret. **meahte, mehte** (§ **68,** Note 2), later **mihte;** participial adj. **meaht** later **miht,** *mighty, powerful,* cp. Goth. **mahts,** *possible.*

**be-neah** (Goth. **bi-nah**), **ge-neah** (Goth. **ga-nah**), *it suffices,* pl. **-nugon;** subj. **-nuge;** pret. **-nohte** (§ **43**).

§ **545.** VI. Ablaut-Series.

**mōt,** *I, he may,* 2. sing. **mōst** (§ **240**), pl. **mōton;** subj. **mōte,** pl. **mōten;** pret. **mōste,** pl. **mōsten** (§ **240**).

§ **546.** The following verb probably belonged originally to the seventh class of strong verbs (§ **512**): **āg** later **āh** (§ **323**), *I have, he has,* 2. sing. **āhst** with **-st** from forms like **dearst,** pl. **āgon;** subj. **āge,** pl. **āgen;** imperative **āge;** inf. **āgan;** pret. **āhte,** pl. **āhton;** pp. **āgen, ǣgen** (§ **442**), *own.*

B. Verbs in **-mi.**

§ **547.** The first pers. sing. pres. indicative of the Indo-Germanic verb ended either in **-ō** or **-mi** (cp. Greek verbs in -ω and -μι, like φέρω, *I bear,* τίθημι, *I place*). See § **472.** To the verbs in **ō** belong all the regular Germanic verbs; of the verbs in **-mi** only scanty remains have been preserved; they are distinguished by the fact that the first pers. sing. pres. indicative ended in **-m.** Here belong the following OE. verbs:—

§ **548.** 1. The Substantive Verb.

The full conjugation of this verb is made up out of several distinct roots, viz. **es-; er-** (perfect stem-form **or-**); **bheu-** (weak grade form **bhw-**); and **wes-.** From **es-** and **or-** were formed a pres. indicative and subjunctive; from **bhw-** a pres. indicative (also with future meaning), pres.

subjunctive, imperative, infinitive, and present participle; and from **wes-** an infinitive, present participle, imperative, and a pret. indicative and subjunctive.

*Present.*

Indicative.

| | | WS. | Anglian. | WS. | Anglian. |
|---|---|---|---|---|---|
| Sing. | 1. | **eom** | **eam, am** | **bīo, bēo** | **bīom** |
| | 2. | **eart** | **earþ, arþ** | **bist** | **bis(t)** |
| | 3. | **is** | **is** | **biþ** | **biþ** |
| Plur. | | **sint sindon, -un** | **sint, sind sindon, -un earon, aron, -un** | **bīoþ, bēoþ** | **bīoþ bi(o)þon, -un** |

Subjunctive.

| | | | |
|---|---|---|---|
| Sing. | **sīe, sī** | **sīe** | **bīo, bēo** |
| Plur. | **sīen, sīn** | **sīen** | **bīon, bēon** |

Imperative.

| | | |
|---|---|---|
| Sing. | **bīo, bēo** | **wes** |
| Plur. | **bīoþ, bēoþ** | **wesaþ** |

Infinitive.

**bīon, bēon** **wesan**

Participle.

**bīonde, bēonde** **wesende**

*Preterite.*

Indic. **wæs, wǣre, wæs,** pl. **wǣron** (§ **505**)
Subj. **wǣre,** pl. **wǣren**

Pres. indicative: **eom** was the unaccented form of ***ēom** with **ēo** from **bēo** (cp. the opposite process in Anglian **bīom**); the regular form would have been ***im** = Goth. **im**; **eart, earþ, arþ,** and pl. **earon, aron** are old perfects from the root **er-**, perfect stem-form **or-**, prim. Germanic **ar-**, of which nothing further is known; on the **-þ** in **earþ, arþ**, see § **481**; **is** with loss of **-t** from older ***ist** = Goth. **ist**, Lat. **est**; **sind** from prim. Germanic ***sinđi** = Indg. ***sénti** (§ **472**); **sint** was the unaccented form of **sind**; **sindon, -un**, with the ending of the pret. pl. added on (§ **481**); beside **sint, sindon** there also occur in WS. **sient, siendon**. **bīo** later **bēo** (cp. § **104**), from ***biju** (cp. § **138**), Indg. ***bhwĭjō**, Lat. **fīō**; Anglian **bīom** with **m** from **eom**; **bist** from older **bis**, Indg. ***bhwĭsi**, Lat. **fīs**; **biþ** from older ***biþi**, Indg. ***bhwĭti**, Lat. **fit**; Anglian **bioþon** with **u**-umlaut (§ **101**) was a new formation from **biþ**; **bīoþ** from ***bijanþi**.

Pres. subjunctive: **sīe, sīen** later **sī** (OS. OHG. **sī**), **sīn** (OS. OHG. **sīn**), beside **sīo, sēo** with **īo, ēo** from **bīo, bēo**.

§ **549**. 2. The Verb **dōn**, *to do*.

*Present.*

| | Indic. | Subj. | Imper. |
|---|---|---|---|
| Sing. 1. | **dō** | **dō** | |
| 2. | **dēst** | „ | **dō** |
| 3. | **dēþ** | „ | |
| Plur. | **dōþ** | **dōn** | **dōþ** |

Infinitive **dōn**

Participle **dōnde**

*Preterite.*

| | Indic. | Subj. |
|---|---|---|
| Sing. 1. | **dyde** | **dyde** |
| 2. | **dydes(t)** | „ |
| 3. | **dyde** | „ |
| Plur. | **dydon** | **dyden** |

Participle **gedōn**

Anglian has the older form **dōm** for the first pers. singular; **dēst**, Nth. **dœ̄s(t)**; **dēþ**, Nth. **dœ̄þ**, **dœ̄s**, from ***dō·is**, ***dō·iþ** (§ **47**); **dōþ** from ***dō·anþi**; Anglian often has longer forms in the present, as imper. **dōa**, **dōaþ**, inf. **dōa(n)**. The **y** from older **u** in the pret. indic. and subj. is of obscure origin; in poetry there occurs the real old pret. pl. indic. **dǣdon**, corresponding to OS. **dādun**, OHG. **tātun**, Goth. **-dēdun** which has only been preserved in the pret. of weak verbs (§ **520**). Pret. subj. **dyde**, **dyden** from ***dudī-**, ***dudīn** (§ **482**); beside **dyde** there also occurs in poetry **dǣde**, corresponding to OS. **dādi**, OHG. **tāti**, and Goth. **-dēdi**. Beside the pp. **-dōn** there also occurs in poetry **-dēn**, Nth. **-dœ̄n** (§ **442**).

§ **550**. 3. The Verb **gān**, *to go*.

*Present.*

| | | Indic. | Subj. | Imper. |
|---|---|---|---|---|
| Sing. | 1. | **gā** | **gā** | |
| | 2. | **gǣst** | „ | **gā** |
| | 3. | **gǣþ** | „ | |
| Plur. | | **gāþ** | **gān** | **gāþ** |

Infinitive **gān**. Past participle **gegān**.

**gǣst**, **gǣþ**, from older ***ʒā·is**, ***ʒā·iþ** (§ **47**). The pret. indic. and subjunctive were supplied by **ēode** from older ***īode** (§ **275**) which was a defective verb inflected like the pret. of **nerian** (§ **524**).

§ **551**. 4. The Verb **willan**, *will*.

The present tense of this verb was originally an optative (subjunctive) form of a verb in **-mi**, which already in prim. Germanic came to be used indicatively. To this was formed in OE. a new infinitive, present participle, and weak preterite.

*Present.*

| | Indic. | Subj. | Infin. |
|---|---|---|---|
| Sing. 1. | **wille** | **wille, wile** | **willan** |
| 2. | **wilt** | ,, | |
| 3. | **wile, wille** | ,, | Participle. |
| | | | **willende** |
| Plur. | **willaþ** | **willen** | |

The pret. indic. and subjunctive **wolde** was inflected like the pret. of **nerian** (§ **524**). **wilt** was a new formation with **-t** from the preterite-present verbs, cp. OHG. **wili**, Goth. **wileis**, Lat. **velīs**; **wile**, indic. and subj. = Goth. OHG. **wili**, Lat. **velit**; **willaþ** was a new formation with the ordinary ending of the pres. indic. (§ **476**), the old form was preserved in Goth. **wilein-a** = Lat. **velint.** The various forms of this verb often underwent contraction with the negative particle **ne**, as **nille, nylle, nelle** (especially in late WS.), pret. **nolde**.

# CHAPTER XV

## ADVERBS, PREPOSITIONS, AND CONJUNCTIONS

### 1. Adverbs.

§ **552.** We shall here chiefly deal with the formation of adverbs from adjectives, and with the inflected forms of nouns and adjectives used adverbially.

§ **553.** The **-e**, generally used to form adverbs from adjectives, is originally a locative ending and is identical with the **-e** (= prim. Germanic **-ai**, § **217**) in the instrumental case of adjectives (§ **424**). Examples are: **dēop**: **dēope**, *deeply*; **nearu, -o** (cp. § **435**): **nearwe**, *narrowly, closely*; **yfel**: **yf(e)le**, *wickedly*; and similarly **bit(e)re**, *bitterly*; **cāfe**, *quickly, boldly*; **cūþe**, *clearly*; **earge**, *badly*;

**earme,** *wretchedly*; **gearwe,** *completely*; **georne,** *eagerly*; **grame,** *angrily*; **hāte,** *hotly*; **hēane,** *ignominiously*; **hearde,** *fiercely*; **hlūde,** *loudly*; **holde,** *graciously, loyally*; **late,** *slowly*; **micle,** *much*; **rihte,** *rightly*; **scearpe,** *sharply*; **singale,** *always, continually*; **smicere,** *elegantly*; **snūde,** *quickly*; **sōþe,** *truly*; **strange,** *violently*; **sweotole,** *clearly, evidently*; **swīþe,** *exceedingly, very*; **syndrige,** *separately*; **þearle,** *severely*; **ungemete,** *excessively*; **wīde,** *widely*; **wrāþe,** *angrily.*

When the adjective ends in **-e** (§ **434**) the adverb and adjective are alike in form, as **blīþe,** *joyful*: **blīþe,** *joyfully*; and similarly **brēme,** *famously, gloriously*; **clǣne,** *fully, entirely*; **ēce,** *eternally*; **fǣcne,** *deceitfully*; **frēcne,** *dangerously, fiercely*; **gedēfe,** *fitly*; **gehende,** *at hand, near*; **milde,** *mercifully*; **myrge,** *merrily*; **swegle,** *clearly, brightly*; **þicce,** *thickly.* A few adverbs, the corresponding adjectives of which did not originally belong to the **ja-** or **i-**declension, do not have umlaut in the stem-syllable, as **ange,** *anxiously,* **smōþe,** *smoothly,* **sōfte,** *gently, softly,* **swōte,** *sweetly,* beside the adjectives **enge, smēþe, sēfte, swēte.**

In adverbs like **cræftlī̆ce,** *skilfully*; **dollī̆ce,** *foolishly*; **frēondlī̆ce,** *kindly*; **gelīce,** *as, similarly*; **loflī̆ce,** *gloriously*; **hetelī̆ce,** *violently,* which were regularly formed from adjectives ending in **-lic** (see § **634**), the **lī̆ce** came to be regarded as an abverbial ending, and was then used in forming adverbs from adjectives which did not end in **-lic,** as **eornostlī̆ce,** *earnestly*; **holdlī̆ce,** *graciously*; **hwætlī̆ce,** *quickly*; **lætlī̆ce,** *slowly*; **spēdlī̆ce,** *prosperously*; **stearclī̆ce,** *vigorously,* &c.

§ **554.** The adverbial ending in the other Germanic languages, as Goth. **-ō,** OS. OHG. **-o,** goes back to the Indg. ablative ending **-ō̆d** which regularly became **-a** in OE. (§§ **211, 217**). This **-a** was only preserved in a few isolated forms, as **sōna,** *soon*; **twiwa,** *twice*; and in a few adverbs ending in **-inga** (= Goth. **-iggō**), **-unga** (= OS. **ungo**), **-linga, -lunga** (cp. §§ **607, 615**), as **dearnunga, -inga,** *secretly*; **eallunga, -inga,** *entirely*; and similarly **ēawunga,** *openly, publicly*; **ednīwunga,** *anew*; **fǣrunga,** *quickly, suddenly*; **gegnunga,** *straight forwards*; **hōlunga,** *in vain, without cause*; **sim(b)lunga,** *always, continually*; **unwēnunga** (Goth. **unwēniggō**), *unexpectedly*; **wēnunga,** *perhaps, by chance*. **ierringa,** *angrily*; **nēadinga, nīedinga,** *by force, against one's will*; **orsceattinga,** *gratuitously*; **stierninga,** *sternly*. **grundlunga, -linga,** *to the ground, completely*; and similarly **midlunga,** *moderately*; **nēadlunga,** *by force, against one's will*.

§ **555.** The comparative and superlative degrees of the adverbs in **-e** generally ended in **-or** (prim. Germanic **-ōz,** § **443**), and **-ost** (prim. Germanic **-ōst-,** § **444**), as **earme,** *wretchedly*, **earmor, earmost; hearde,** *fiercely*, **heardor, heardost; holdlīce,** *graciously*, **holdlicor, holdlicost; strange,** *violently*, **strangor, strangost;** but **seldan,** *seldom*, **seld(n)or, seldost.**

§ **556.** A certain number of adverbs had originally **-iz** (Goth. **-is, -s,** cp. the **-is** in Lat. **magis,** *more*) in the comparative and **-ist** (Goth. **-ist, -st**), rarely **-ōst,** in the superlative (cp. §§ **443–4**), as **ēaþe,** *easily*, **īeþ** from ***auþiz, ēaþost; feorr,** *far*, **fierr** from ***ferriz, fierrest; lange,** *long*, **leng** from ***langiz, lengest; sōfte,** *softly*, **sēft** from ***samftiz; tulge,** *strongly, firmly*, **tylg** from ***tulʒiz, tylgest; ǣr** from ***airiz** (Goth. **áiris**), *earlier, formerly*; **sīþ** from ***sīþiz** (Goth. **þana-seiþs,** *further, more*), *later*. The following form their comparative and superlative from a different word than the positive :—**lȳt, lȳtle,** *little*, **lǣs** from ***laisiz, lǣst; micle,** *much*, **mā** (Goth. **máis,** Anglian **mǣ**), **mǣst; wel,** *well*, comp. **bet** from ***ƀatiz,** with loss of **-e** after the analogy of comparatives with long stems, beside **sēl** from ***sōliz,** superl. **betst, sēlest; yf(e)le,** *badly, wretchedly*, **wiers, wyrs,** from ***wirsiz** (Goth. **waírs,** OHG. **wirs**), **wierrest, wyrrest, wyrst.**

§ **557.** A large number of OE. adverbs consist of the various cases of nouns and adjectives used adverbially, as acc. sing. **ealne weg, ealneg,** *always*; **āwiht, āwuht,** *at all, by any means*; **bæcling,** *back, behind.* **eal mǣst,** *almost*; **eall tela,** *quite well*; **ēast norþ,** *north-east*; **ēaþ,** *easily*; **fela, feola,** *very much*; **full,** *perfectly, very*; **fyrn,** *formerly*; **geador,** *together, jointly*; **gefyrn,** *once, long ago, formerly*; **genōg,** *enough, sufficiently*; **hēah,** *high*; **lȳthwōn,** *little*; **mǣst,** *mostly*; **samen,** *together*; **sīþ,** *late*; **sundor,** *asunder, apart*; **tela, teola,** *well, befittingly*; **ungefyrn,** *not long ago*; **untela,** *amiss*; **west,** *westward*; **west lang,** *extending westwards.* Compounds of **-weard,** as **forweard,** *continually, always*; **hindanweard,** *hindwards, at the end*; **norþweard,** *northward*; **sūþweard,** *southward*; **ūpweard,** *upwards*; **tōweard,** *towards,* see § **637.**

Gen. sing., as **ānstreces,** *continuously*; **dæges,** *daily, by day*; **gewealdes,** *willingly, intentionally*; **hū gēares,** *at what time of year*; **hū gerādes,** *how*; **īdæges,** *on the same day*; **innanbordes,** *at home*; **īsīþes,** *at that time*; **orcēapes,** *without payment*; **orþances,** *heedlessly*; **samtinges,** *immediately, forthwith*; **selfwilles,** *voluntarily*; **sundorlīepes,** *separately*; **sunganges,** *moving with the sun*; **þances,** *gladly, voluntarily*; **ungemetes,** *excessively, immeasurably*; **ungewealdes,** *involuntarily*; **unþances,** *unwillingly*; **willes,** *willingly*; the **-es** was sometimes extended to fem. nouns, as **endebyrdes,** *in an orderly manner*; **nīedes,** *of necessity, needs*; **nihtes** (cp. NHG. **nachts**), *at night, by night.* **ǣghwæs,** *altogether, in every way*; **dæglanges,** *during a day*; **elles,** *otherwise, else*; **ealles,** *entirely, wholly*; **endemes,** *equally, in like manner*; **gehwæþeres,** *on all sides*; **nealles,** *not at all, by no means*; **nihtlanges,** *all night long*; **simbles,** *ever, always*; **singales,** *always, ever*; **sōþes,** *truly, verily*; **sumes,** *somewhat, to some extent*; **þæs,** *after*; **þwēores,** *athwart, transversely*; **ungewisses,** *unconsciously*; **hām-weardes,** *homewards*; **norþweardes,** *northwards*; **niþer-**

**weardes,** *downwards*; **tōweardes,** *towards*. A preposition was sometimes prefixed to the genitive, as **in·stæpes,** *instantly, at once*; **tō·ǣfenes,** *till evening*; **tō·emnes,** *alongside, beside*; **tō·gēanes,** *towards, against*; **tō·geflites,** *in emulation*; **tō·gifes,** *freely, gratis*; **tō·middes,** *amidst, among*.

Gen. pl., as **ǣnge þinga,** *anyhow, in any way*; **gēara,** *of yore, formerly*; **hū meta,** *how, in what way*; **hū nyta,** *wherefore*; **nǣnge, nānge þinga,** *not at all*; **ungēara,** *not long ago, recently*.

Dat. and instrumental sing., as **bearhtme,** *instantly*; **elne,** *strongly, vigorously*; **fācne,** *exceedingly*; **hlūdswēge,** *loudly*; **nīede,** *of need, necessarily*; **nēode,** *zealously, diligently*; **nīwan stefne,** *anew, again*; **recene,** *instantly, at once*; **torne,** *grievously*; **wihte,** *at all*. **ealle,** *entirely*; **hēo·dæg** (cp. NHG. **heute** from OHG. **hiu tagu**), *to-day*; **hwēne,** *somewhat*. **dæg·hwǣm,** *daily*; **furþum,** *even, indeed*; **gegnum,** *forwards, straight on*; **lēofwendum,** *ardently*; **wrāþum,** *fiercely*.

Dat. pl., as **dæg·tīdum,** *by day*; **fir(e)num,** *excessively, very*; **gēardagum,** *formerly, in days of old*; **geþyldum,** *patiently*; **hwīl·tīdum,** *at times, sometimes*; **hwīlum,** *sometimes*; **of(e)stum,** *speedily, hastily*; **searwum,** *skilfully*; **snyttrum,** *cunningly, wisely*; **spēdum,** *speedily*; **stundum,** *from time to time*; **tīdum,** *at times, occasionally*; **þingum,** *powerfully, violently, purposely*; **þrymmum,** *powerfully*; **ungemetum,** *excessively*; **unsnyttrum,** *foolishly*; **unsynnum,** *guiltlessly*; **unwearnum,** *irresistibly*; **unwillum,** *unwillingly*; **wundrum,** *wonderfully*; **wynnum,** *joyfully, pleasantly*; compounds with **-mǣlum,** as **byrþenmǣlum,** *by loads*; **dǣlmǣlum,** *piecemeal*; **dropmǣlum,** *drop by drop*; **flitmǣlum,** *contentiously*; **floccmǣlum,** *in troops*; **fōtmǣlum,** *step by step*; **hēapmǣlum,** *in troops*; **hīdmǣlum,** *by hides*; **limmǣlum,** *limb by limb*; **nammǣlum,** *name by name*; **snǣdmǣlum,** *bit by bit*; **stundmǣlum,** *gradually*;

**styccemǣlum**, *piecemeal*; **sundormǣlum**, *singly*; **þrāgmǣlum**, *from time to time*; **þrēatmǣlum**, *in crowds*; **wornmǣlum**, *in troops*.

By nouns, &c. in conjunction with prepositions, as **ætforan**, *beforehand*; **ætgædere**, *together*; **æthindan**, *behind*; **æt-hwōn**, *almost*; **æt-nīehstan**, *at last*; **æt-rihte**, *nearly, almost*; **ætsamne**, *together*; **be ungewyrhtum**, *undeservedly*; **for hwon**, *wherefore*; **in-stæpe**, *forthwith*; **in-stede**, *at once*; **ofdūne**, *down*; **onbæc**, *backwards*; **onbæcling**, *behind*; **onbūtan**, *about*; **onefn**, *close by*; **onforan**, *before, afore*; **on scipwīsan**, *like a ship*; **onsundrum**, *singly, separately*; **onweg**, *away*; **tō-dæg(e)**, *to-day*; **tō-ēacen**, *besides*; **tō hwon**, *wherefore*; **tō-morgen**, *to-morrow*; **tōsamne**, *together*; **tō-sōþan**, *in truth, in sooth*; **tō wissum**, *with certainty*; **underbæc**, *backwards*; **underneoþan**, *underneath*; **wiþæftan**, *behind*; **wiþforan**, *before*; **wiþinnan**, *within*; **wiþneoþan**, *beneath*; **wiþūtan**, *outside of, without*.

§ **558.** The following are the chief adverbs of place :—

| *Rest.* | *Motion towards.* | *Motion from.* |
|---|---|---|
| **feorr(an)**, *far, afar* | **feorr** | **feorran** |
| **foran, fore**, *before* | **forþ** | **foran** |
| **hēr**, *here* | **hider** | **hionan** |
| **hindan**, *behind* | **hinder** | **hindan** |
| **hwǣr**, *where* | **hwider** | **hwanon** |
| **inne, innan**, *within* | **in(n)** | **innan** |
| **nēah**, *near* | **nēar** | **nēan** |
| **nioþan**, *beneath* | **niþer** | **nioþan** |
| **þǣr**, *there* | **þider** | **þanan, þonan** |
| **uppe**, *up, above* | **up(p)** | **uppan** |
| **ūte, ūtan**, *outside* | **ūt** | **ūtan** |

**sūþ**, *southwards*, **sūþan**, *from the south*; and similarly **ēast, ēastan**; **norþ, norþan**; **west, westan**; **æftan**, *from behind*; **ufan**, *from above*; **ūtane**, *from without*; **wīdan**, *from far.* **ǣghwǣr, ǣghwider, gehwǣr,** *everywhere, in all directions*; **ǣghwanon,** *from all parts*; **āhwǣr, āwer, ōwer,** *anywhere*; **āhwanon,** *from anywhere*; **nāhwǣr, nāwer, nōwer,** *nowhere*; **welhwǣr, welgehwǣr, gewelhwǣr,** *nearly everywhere*; **hider-geond,** *thither*; **hidres þidres,** *hither and thither.*

§ **559.** 2. PREPOSITIONS.

(1) With the accusative: **geond,** *throughout, during*; **geondan,** *beyond*; **underneoþan,** *underneath, below*; **wiþgeondan,** *beyond*; **ymb,** *around, about, at*; **ymbūtan,** *around, about*; **oþ** (more rarely dat.), *to, up to, as far as, until*; **þurh** (more rarely dat. or gen.), *through, during.*

(2) With the genitive: **andlang, andlanges,** *alongside.*

(3) With the dative: **æfter,** *behind, after, along, during, through, according to, in consequence of*; **ǣr,** *before*; **ætforan,** *before, in the presence of*; **bī (be),** also with instr., *by, along, in*; **bæftan,** *behind*; **beheonan,** *on this side of*; **beneoþan,** *beneath, below*; **binnan,** *within, in, into*; **ēac,** *in addition to, besides*; **fram (from),** also with instr., *from, by*; **gehende,** *near*; **mid,** also with instr., *together with, among*; **nēah** (also comp. **nēar,** superl. **nīehst),** *near*; **of,** *from, away from, out of*; **ongemang, onmang,** *among*; **oninnan,** *in, within, into, among*; **onufan,** *upon*; **samod,** *together with, at (of time)*; **til** (NE. dial. **tul**), *to*; **tō-emnes,** *alongside, on a level with*; **tōforan,** *before, in front of*; **tōmiddes,** *in the midst of*; **wiþæftan,** *behind*; **wiþforan,** *before*; **wiþūtan,** *outside, without, except.* The following also sometimes govern the acc.: **æt,** *at, by, in, on, upon*; **beforan,** *before, in the presence of*; **būtan,** *outside, without, free from*; **fore,** *before, in the sight of*; **tō** (also occasionally gen. and instr.), *to, into, at, by*; **wiþinnan,** *within.*

(4) With the accusative and dative: **ābūtan, onbūtan,** *around, about (of time)*; **begeondan,** *beyond*; **behindan,** *behind*; **betwēonan, betwēonum,** *between, among*; **be-**

**tweox, betweoh, bet(w)uh, betwih, betwix,** *between, among*; **bufan,** *above, away from*; **for** (also instr.), *before, in the sight of, during, for, on account of, instead of*; **gemang,** *among, into the midst of*; **in,** *in, into, on, among, during*; **ofer,** *over, above, beyond, contrary to*; **on** (also instr.), *on, in, into, on to, to, among*; **ongēan, ongeagn, ongegn, ongēn,** *opposite, in front of, against*; **onuppan,** *on, upon*; **tōgēanes, tōgegnes, tōgēnes,** *towards, against*; **under,** *under, beneath, among*; **uppan,** *on, above.*

(5) With the genitive and dative: **tōweard, tōweardes,** *towards.*

(6) With the accusative, genitive, and dative: **innan,** *within, in, into*; **wiþ,** *against, towards, to, opposite, near.*

**§ 560.** 3. Conjunctions.

(1) Co-ordinate: **ac,** *but*; **and,** *and*; **ǣgþer . . . and, ǣgþer . . . ge,** *both . . . and*; **ēac,** *also*; **ēac swelc (swylc), swelc ēac,** *as also*; **for þǣm (þām), for þon, for þȳ, þonne,** *therefore*; **ge,** *and*; **ge . . . ge,** *both . . . and*; **hwæþ(e)re, þēah, swa þēah, swā þēah hwæþ(e)re,** *however*; **ne . . . ne, ne . . . ne ēac, nāhwæþer ne . . . ne,** *neither . . . nor*; **oþþe,** *or*; **oþþe . . . oþþe,** *either . . . or*; **samod . . . and,** *both . . . and.*

(2) Subordinate: **æfter þǣm (þām) þe,** *after*; **ǣr þām þe,** *before*; **būtan,** *unless, unless that*; **for þǣm (þām) þe, for þon þe, for þȳ þe,** *because*; **gelīc and,** *as if*; **gif,** *if, whether*; **hwæþer,** *whether*; **hwæþer þe . . . þe,** *whether . . . or*; **mid þȳ þe, mid þām þe,** *when, although*; **nemne, nefne, nymþe,** *unless, except*; **nū þe,** *now that*; **oþ, oþ þæt, oþ þe,** *until, until that*; **swā . . . swā,** *so . . . as*; **swā swā . . . ealswā,** *just . . . as*; **swā sōna swā,** *as soon as*; **swā þæt, tō þon þæt,** *so that*; **tō þon þe,** *in order that*; **þæs þe, siþþan þe,** *after, since*; **þæt, þætte,** *that, in order that*; **þā, þā þe,** *when*; **þā hwīle þe,** *whilst, so long as*; **þēah,**

*although*; **þēah þe . . . swā þēah, hwæþ(e)re,** *although . . yet*; **þenden,** *while*; **þonne,** *when*; **þȳ,** *because*; **þȳ þe,** *so that.*

# CHAPTER XVI

## WORD-FORMATION

§ **561.** By far the greater part of the word-forming elements, used in the parent language, were no longer felt as such in the oldest period of the English language. In this chapter we shall chiefly confine ourselves to those word-forming elements which were felt as such in OE., such as prefixes and suffixes.

### NOUNS.

§ **562.** Nouns may be divided into simple, derivative, and compound. Examples of simple nouns are: **āc,** *oak*; **bān,** *bone*; **bōc,** *book*; **burg,** *city*; **cǣg,** *key*; **cild,** *child*; **dæl,** *dale*; **dēor,** *deer*; **ende,** *end*; **feld,** *field*; **folc,** *folk*; **fōt,** *foot*; **gold,** *gold*; **hām,** *home*; **hand,** *hand*; **hūs,** *house*; **land,** *land*; **lim,** *limb*; **līc,** *body*; **lof,** *praise*; **mann,** *man*; **molde,** *mould*; **mūs,** *mouse*; **nama,** *name*; **nett,** *net*; **oxa,** *ox*; **pytt,** *pit*; **rūm,** *room*; **sǣ,** *sea*; **scield,** *shield*; **spere,** *spear*; **tīma,** *time*; **trēo,** *tree*; **þēof,** *thief*; **þing,** *thing*; **weg,** *way*; **wēn,** *hope*; **weorc,** *work*; **word,** *word*; **wyrm,** *worm*; **ȳþ,** *wave.*

Many simple nouns are related to the various classes of strong verbs (§§ **490–519**), as **bite,** *cutting, bite*; **lād,** *way, course*; **lāf,** *remnant*; **lida,** *sailor*; **rād,** *riding*; **ridda,** *rider*; **slide,** *slip*; **snǣd,** *morsel, slice*; **snide,** *incision*; **wita,** *wise man.*

**boga,** *bow*; **bryce,** *use*; **cyre,** *choice*; **flēoge,** *fly*; **flota,** *sailor*; **loc,** *lock*; **lyre,** *loss*; **notu,** *use*; **scēat,** *region.*

**bend,** *band*; **bryne,** *burning*; **drenc,** *drink*; **feoht,** *battle, fight*; **gield,** *payment*; **ryne,** *running, course*; **stenc,** *odour*; **steng,** *pole*; **wyrd,** *fate.*

**bǣr**, *bier*; **bryce**, *breaking*; **byre**, *son*; **cuma**, *guest*; **cwalu**, *killing*; **cyme**, *advent*; **stalu**, *theft*.

**sprǣc**, *speech*; **wǣg**, *wave*.

**faru**, *journey*; **fōr**, *journey*; **slege**, *blow*.

**gang**, *going*; **heald**, *protection*; **hlīep**, *jump*; **rǣd**, *counsel*. See § **225**.

§ **563**. Derivative nouns are formed in a great variety of ways:—

1. From adjectives, as **bieldu**, *boldness*; **brǣdu**, *breadth*; **cieldu**, *cold*; **fyllu**, *fullness*; **hǣlu**, *health*; **hǣtu**, *heat*; **hyldu**, *favour, grace*; **ieldu**, *old age*; **lengu**, *length*; **menigu**, *crowd*; **snytru**, *wisdom*; **strengu**, *strength*. See §§ **383**, **614**.

2. By means of various suffixes which were no longer felt as such in OE., as **bydel**, *messenger*; **fugol**, *bird*; **gafol**, *tribute*; **hagol**, *hail*; **nǣdl**, *needle*; **nǣgl**, *nail*; **segl**, *sail*; **setl**, *seat*; **staþol**, *foundation*; **tungol**, *star*. **ǣþm**, *breath*; **botm**, *bottom*; **māþm**, *treasure*; **wæstm**, *growth*. **dryhten**, *lord*; **heofon**, *heaven*; **morgen**, *morning*; **þegen**, *thane*; **wǣpen**, *weapon*. **brōþor**, *brother*; **fæder**, *father*; **finger**, *finger*; **fōdor**, *food*; **hamor**, *hammer*; **sweostor**, *sister*; **þunor**, *thunder*; **winter**, *winter*.

3. From verbs by means of a dental suffix, as **blǣd**, *blowing*; **cyst**, *virtue, excellence*; **dǣd**, *deed*; **fierd**, *army*; **flyht**, *flight*; **gebyrd**, *birth*; **genyht**, *sufficiency*; **gesceaft**, *creation*; **geþeaht**, *plan*; **gift**, *price of a wife*; **glēd**, *live coal*; **hæft**, *captivity*; **hyht**, *hope*; **lāst**, *track*; **meaht**, *power*; **mǣþ**, *mowing*; **sǣd**, *seed*; **slieht**, *slaughter*; **spēd**, *success*; **weft**, *weft*.

4. From verbs with inseparable particles, as **bebod**, *command*; **beclȳsing**, *cell*; **bedelfing**, *digging round*; **begang**, *practice*; **behāt**, *promise*; **belāf**, *remainder*; **belimp**, *occurrence*; **begīemen**, *care, attention*. **forbod**, *prohibition*; **forhæfednes**, *temperance*; **forlor**, *destruction*; **forwyrd**, *fate, destruction*. **gebann**, *decree, proclamation*; **gebed**,

*prayer*; **geblōt,** *sacrifice*; **gebrec,** *clamour, noise*; **gefeoht,** *fight, battle.* **ofcyrf,** *cutting off*; **ofslegennes,** *destruction*; **ofsprǣc,** *utterance.*

5. By means of various prefixes. Some of the forms given as prefixes below are in reality independent words forming the first elements of compounds. They have been included among the real prefixes for purely practical purposes. It should be noted that the examples given below include both nouns and adjectives:—

PREFIXES.

§ **564.** **ā-,** Goth. **áiw,** *ever,* as **ābrēmende,** *ever celebrating*; **ālibbende,** *everlasting*; **āwunigende,** *continual.*

§ **565.** **ǣ-,** privative prefix denoting *without,* like the **ā** in OHG. **āmaht,** *without power,* as **ǣfelle,** *without skin*; **ǣgilde,** *without compensation*; **ǣmen(ne),** *depopulated*; **ǣmōd,** *out of heart, dismayed*; **ǣwēne,** *hopeless.*

§ **566.** **æf-,** stressed form of **of-,** *off,* as **æfest,** *envy*; **æfþanc(a),** *grudge*; **æfweard,** *absent.*

§ **567.** **æfter-,** *after,* as **æftergenga,** *successor*; **æftergield,** *after-payment*; **æfterfolgere,** *follower*; **æfterweard,** *following*; **æfterlēan,** *recompense*; **æfterieldo,** *old age*; **æfterlic,** *second.*

§ **568.** **an-,** stressed form of the preposition **on,** *on,* as **anfilte,** *anvil*; **anginn,** *beginning*; **ansīen,** *countenance*; **anweald,** *authority.* **anbrucol,** *rugged*; **anforht,** *alarmed*; **ansund,** *entire, sound.*

§ **569.** **and-** (Goth. **and-,** OHG. **ant-**; Gr. ἀντί, *against,* Lat. **ante,** *before*), the stressed form of **on-** (§§ **59,** Note, **654**), as **andcwis(s),** *answer*; **andfenga,** *taker up, defender*; **andgiet,** *intelligence*; **andsaca,** *adversary*; **andswaru,** *answer*; **andweald,** *power*; **andwlita,** *countenance*; **andwyrde,** *answer.* **andfenge,** *acceptable*; **andgietol,** *intelligent*; **andlang,** *continuous*; **andweard,** *present*; **andwrāþ,** *hostile.*

§ **570.** **bī-** (OHG. **bī**), the stressed form of the preposition and adverb **bī**, *by*, of which the unstressed form is **be-** (§ 647), as **bīcwide**, *proverb*; **bīfylce**, *neighbouring people*; **bīgeng**, *practice*; **bīgyrdel**, *girdle, purse*; **bīleofa**, *sustenance*; **bīspell**, *example*; **bīwist**, *sustenance*; **bīword**, *proverb*.

§ **571**. **ed-** (Goth. **id-**, OHG. **ita-**, **it-**), *back, again, re-*, as **edcierr**, *return*; **edgield**, *repayment*; **edgift**, *restitution*; **edgrōwung**, *regrowing*; **edlēan**, *reward*; **edroc**, *rumination*; **edwīt** (Goth. **idweit**), *reproach*. **edgeong**, *growing young again*; **ednīwe**, *renewed*.

§ **572**. **fore-** (Goth. **faúra**, OHG. **fora**), the stressed form of the preposition and adverb **fore**, *before, fore-*, as **forebēacen**, *foretoken*; **foreduru**, *vestibule*; **foregīsl**, *preliminary hostage*; **forespreca**, *advocate*; **foreþanc**, *forethought*. **forehālig**, *very holy*; **foremǣre**, *illustrious*.

§ **573**. **fram-** (Goth. OHG. **fram**), the stressed form of the preposition and adverb **fram**, *from*, as **framcyme**, *progeny*; **framlād**, *retreat*; **framsīþ**, *departure*. **framweard**, *turned from*.

§ **574**. **ge-** (Goth. **ga-**, OHG. **ga-**, **gi-**), originally a preposition meaning *together*, which already in prim. Germanic was no longer used as an independent word. It was especially used in forming collective nouns, but at a later period it often had only an intensitive meaning or no special meaning at all, as **gebedda**, *consort*; **gebrōþor**, *brethren*; **gefēra**, *companion*; **gefylce**, *army*; **gegaderung**, *gathering*; **gehāda**, *brother minister*; **gemæcca**, *mate*; **gemōt**, *meeting*; **gesceaft**, *creation*; **gesīþ**, *comrade*; **gewider**, *bad weather*. **gebyrd**, *birth, descent*; **geweorc**, *work*; **gewita**, *witness*; **gewuna**, *custom*. **ge-æþele**, *congenial*; **gecynde**, *innate, natural*; **gedēfe**, *befitting*; **gelīc**, *similar*; **gemyndig**, *mindful*; **gemǣne**, *common*; **gesund**, *healthy, sound*.

§ **575**. **in-**, the stressed form of the preposition **in**, *in*, as **inādl**, *internal disease*; **inbūend**, *inhabitant*; **incniht**, *house-servant*; **incofa**, *inner chamber*; **infær**, *entrance*; **infaru**, *invasion*; **inhere,** *home army*; **insegl,** *seal, signet.* **inþicce,** *very thick, coarse.*

§ **576. mid-** (Goth. **miþ,** OS. **mid,** OHG. **mit**), the stressed form of the preposition **mid,** *with,* as **midspreca,** *advocate*; **midwist,** *presence, society*; **midwunung,** *living in company*; **midwyrhta,** *co-operator.*

§ **577. mis-** (Goth. **missa-,** OHG. **missa-, missi-**), originally a participial adjective meaning *lost,* the same word as OHG. **missi,** *different,* as **misfadung,** *misconduct*; **mislār,** *bad teaching*; **misrǣd,** *misguidance.* **misboren,** *misshapen at birth*; **mishworfen,** *perverted.*

§ **578. ofer-** (Goth. **ufar,** OHG. **ubar,** Gr. ὑπέρ, Skr. **upári**), the stressed form of the preposition **ofer,** *over,* as **oferǣt,** *gluttony*; **oferbrū,** *eyebrow*; **oferdrenc,** *drunkenness*; **oferhygd,** *pride*; **ofermægen,** *superior force*; **oferslop,** *surplice*; **ofersprǣc,** *loquacity*; **oferþearf,** *extreme need*; **oferweorc,** *tomb.* **oferhlūd,** *overloud*; **ofermǣte,** *excessive*; **ofermicel,** *overmuch*; **ofermōdig,** *overbearing.*

§ **579. on-,** in late formations with the preposition **on,** *on,* of which the real stressed form is **an,** see above. Examples are: **onbring,** *instigation*; **onbryce,** *inroad*; **onflǣscnes,** *incarnation*; **onstīgend,** *rider*; **onsting,** *authority.* **onæþele,** *natural to.*

§ **580. or-,** originally a preposition meaning *out,* preserved as an independent word in Goth. **us,** OHG. **ur,** cp. also NHG. **urteil** beside **erteilen.** Examples are: **ordāl,** *ordeal*; **orsorg,** *without anxiety*; **orþanc,** *skill, intelligence*; **orweorþ,** *ignominy.* **orcēas,** *free from complaint*; **orcnāwe,** *easily recognized*; **oreald,** *very old*; **orgiete,** *manifest*; **orgilde,** *unpaid for*; **orhleahtre,** *blameless*; **ormǣte,** *excessive*; **ormōd,** *despairing*; **orsāwle,** *lifeless*; **ortȳdre,** *barren*; **orwēne,** *despairing.*

§ **581. sam-,** related to the adverb Goth. **samana,** OHG. **saman,** OE. **samen,** *together,* Gr. preposition ἅμα, *together with,* as **samhīwan,** *members of a family*; **samwist,** *living* *together*; **samwrǣdnes,** *union, combination*; **samheort,** *unanimous*; **sammǣle,** *agreed*; **samwinnende,** *contending together.*

§ **582. sam-,** a prim. OE. shortening of ***sāmi-,** older ***sǣmi-** = OHG. **sāmi-,** Lat. **sēmi-,** Gr. ἡμι-, *half,* the unshortened form of which would have been **sōmi-** (§ **121**), as **sambærned,** *half-burnt*; **samcucu,** *half-dead*; **samhāl,** *in bad health*; **samgrēne,** *half-green*; **samlǣred,** *half-taught*; **samsoden,** *half-cooked*; **samwīs,** *dull, foolish.*

§ **583. sin-** (Goth. OHG. **sin-**), *ever, perpetual,* as **sindrēam,** *everlasting joy*; **sinhere,** *immense army*; **sinhīwan,** *married couple*; **sinniht,** *eternal night*; **sinscipe,** *marriage, wedlock*; **sinsorg,** *continual sorrow.* **sinceald,** *ever cold*; **sinfulle,** **singrēne,** *houseleek*; **singrim,** *ever fierce.*

§ **584. tō-,** the preposition **tō,** *to,* as **tōcyme,** *approach, arrival*; **tōhlystend,** *listener*; **tōhyht,** *hope*; **tō-īecnes,** *increase*; **tōnama,** *surname*; **tōsprǣc,** *conversation*; **tōtyhting,** *instigation.* **tōcumende,** *foreign, strange*; **tōheald,** *inclined, leaning*; **tō-iernende,** *approaching*; **tō-weard,** *facing, approaching.*

§ **585. twi-** (OHG. **zwi-,** Lat. **bi-,** Gr. δι- from *δϝι-), *two,* as **twibill,** *two-edged axe*; **twigilde,** *double payment*; **twiweg,** *place where two roads meet*; **twibēte,** *needing double compensation*; **twifeald,** *twofold*; **twifēre,** *accessible by two ways*; **twifēte,** *two-footed*; **twifingre,** *two fingers thick*; **twihēafode,** *two-headed*; **twi-hwēole,** *two-wheeled*; **twi-nihte,** *two days old*; **twirǣde,** *irresolute*; **twisprǣce,** *double-tongued, false in speech*; **twiwintre,** *of two years.*

§ **586. þri-** (OHG. **dri-,** Lat. **tri-,** Gr. δρι-), *three,* as **þridæglic,** *lasting three days*; **þridǣled,** *tripartite*; **þri-feald,** *threefold*; **þrifēte,** *having three feet*; **þriflēre,** *three-storied*; **þrilēafe,** *trefoil*; **þrinihte,** *three days old*; **þrirēþre,** *having three banks of oars*; **þrisciete,** *triangular.*

§ **587. þurh-,** the preposition **þurh,** *through,* as **þurh-beorht,** *very bright*; **þurhbitter,** *very bitter*; **þurhfēre,** *penetrable*; **þurhhālig,** *very holy*; **þurhscīnendlic,** *splendid*; **þurhscyldig,** *very guilty*; **þurhspēdig,** *very wealthy*; **þurh-wacol,** *sleepless.*

§ **588. un-** (Goth. OHG. **un-**, Lat. **en-**, Gr. *ἀ-*), a negative particle, *un-*, sometimes used intensitively with the meaning *bad, evil,* &c., as **unār,** *dishonour*; **unbealo,** *innocence*; **uncyst,** *vice*; **unfriþ,** *war*; **unhǣlo,** *sickness.* **uncræft,** *evil practice*; **undǣd,** *crime*; **ungeþanc,** *evil thought*; **ungield,** *excessive tax*; **unlagu,** *evil law, injustice*; **unlār,** *false doctrine*; **unswefn,** *bad dream*; **unwrītere,** *careless scribe.* **unæþele,** *plebeian*; **unāgiefen,** *unpaid*; **unandgiet-full,** *unintelligent*; **unbeald,** *timid*; **unclǣne,** *unclean*; **undēadlic,** *immortal*; **undēop,** *shallow*; **undierne,** *manifest*; **unfæger,** *ugly*; **ungeorne,** *reluctantly*; **unlēof,** *hated*; **unmǣre,** *inglorious*; **unriht,** *wrong*; **unslāw,** *active*; **unsōþ,** *untrue*; **unswēte,** *sour*; **unsynnig,** *innocent*; **ungewiss,** *uncertain.*

§ **589. under-,** same word as the preposition **under,** *under,* as **underburg,** *suburb*; **undercyning,** *viceroy*; **underdiacon,** *sub-deacon*; **underling,** *underling.*

§ **590. ūp-,** the preposition **ūp,** *up,* as **ūpcyme,** *rising, origin*; **ūpende,** *upper end*; **ūpflēring,** *upper floor*; **ūpgang,** *rising, sunrise*; **ūpheofon,** *sky*; **ūplyft,** *upper air*; **ūpstige,** *ascent*; **ūpstīgend,** *rider*; **ūpweg,** *way to heaven.* **ūpcund,** *celestial*; **ūphēah,** *uplifted*; **ūplendisc,** *rural, rustic*; **ūpriht,** *upright, erect.*

§ **591. ūt-,** the preposition **ūt,** *out,* as **ūtcwealm,** *utter destruction*; **ūtdrǣf,** *expulsion*; **ūtfær,** *exit*; **ūtgang,** *exit*; **ūtgefeoht,** *foreign war*; **ūtgemǣre,** *extreme boundary*; **ūthere,** *foreign army*; **ūtlagu,** *outlaw.* **ūtlendisc,** *strange, foreign*; **ūtlic,** *external, foreign.*

§ **592. wan-,** the same word as the adjective Goth. **wans,** OE. OHG. **wan,** *wanting, lacking, deficient,* as **wanhǣlþ,** *weakness*; **wanhafa,** *poor person*; **wanhoga,** *thoughtless person*; **wanhygd,** *carelessness*; **wanspēd,** *poverty.* **wansælig,** *unhappy*; **wanscrȳdd,** *poorly clad*; **wanspēdig,** *poor.*

§ **593. wiþer-,** the preposition Goth. **wiþra,** OHG. **widar,** OE. **wiþer,** *against,* as **wiþercwide,** *contradiction*; **wiþerlēan,** *requital*; **wiþersaca,** *adversary*; **wiþersæc,** *opposition*; **wiþertrod,** *retreat.* **wiþerrǣde,** *adverse.*

§ **594. ymb-,** the preposition **ymb** (OHG. ***umb,** Gr. ἀμφί), *around,* and related to the adverb **ymbe,** OHG. **umbi,** both from an older **umb + bĭ,** literally *around by.* Examples are: **ymbfær,** *circuit*; **ymbgang,** *circumference*; **ymbhoga,** *consideration.*

## Suffixes.

§ **595. -aþ, -oþ** (Goth. **-ōþu-,** OHG. **-ōd,** Lat. **-atu-,** Gr. -ητύ-), used in forming masc. abstract nouns from the second class of weak verbs, as **drohtaþ,** *way of life*; **drūgoþ,** *dryness, drought*; **fiscoþ,** *fishing*; **fugeloþ,** *fowling*; **huntoþ,** *hunting*; **langoþ,** *longing, desire*; **sweoloþ, swoloþ,** *heat, burning.* Often extended to **-noþ** with **n** from the verbal forms, as **drohtnian,** *to pass life*; **hæftnian,** *to take captive*; whence **fiscnoþ, fugelnoþ**; **sǣdnoþ,** *sowing*; &c.

§ **596. -bora,** also used as an independent noun, *one who bears* or *sustains the charge of anything, a ruler,* related to **beran,** *to bear,* as **æscbora,** *spear-bearer*; **cǣgbora,** *key-bearer*; **mundbora,** *protector*; **rǣdbora,** *counsellor*; **rōdbora,** *cross-bearer*; **strǣlbora,** *archer*; **wǣpenbora,** *warrior*; **wōþbora,** *poet*; **wrōhtbora,** *accuser.*

§ **597. -dōm** (OHG. **-tuom**), also used as an independent word, Goth. **dōms,** OE. **dōm,** *judgment*; OHG. **tuom,** *state, condition,* as **abbuddōm,** *abbacy*; **campdōm,** *contest, war*; **cynedōm,** *kingdom*; **ealdordōm,** *authority*; **frēodōm,** *freedom*; **hæftedōm,** *captivity*; **hlāforddōm,** *lordship*; **lǣcedōm,** *medicine*; **lārēowdōm,** *office of teacher*; **reccenddōm,** *rule, governance*; **swīcdōm,** *deceit*; **þēowdōm,** *service.*

§ **598. -els** from older **-isl** by metathesis (§ **277**), West

Germanic **-islja-** = OHG. **-isli,** used in forming masculine nouns, as **brǣdels,** *covering, carpet*; **brīdels,** *bridle*; **byrgels,** *tomb*; **cnyttels,** *sinew*; **fǣtels,** *tub*; **gyrdels,** *girdle*; **hȳdels,** *hiding-place, cave*; **mǣrels,** *mooring-rope*; **miercels,** *mark*; **rǣdels,** *riddle*; **rēcels,** *incense*; **smierels,** *ointment*; **sticels,** *goad*; **wrigels,** *covering.*

§ **599.** **-en** (OHG. **-in,** acc. **-inna**), prim. Germanic **-inī, -injō-** (West Germanic **-innjō-,** § **254**), mostly used to form the feminine from nouns denoting male beings; also used to form fem. abstract and concrete nouns, as **fyxen,** *she-fox*; **gyden,** *goddess*; **menen,** *female slave*; **mynecen(n),** *nun*; **þēowen(n),** *servant*; **þignen, þinen,** *handmaid*; **wiergen(n),** *she-wolf.* **gīemen(n),** *care, responsibility*; **hæften,** *custody*; **hengen,** *hanging*; **lygen,** *falsehood*; **scielden(n),** *protection*; **selen, sellen,** *gift*; **strēowen,** *bed*; **tyhten(n),** *incitement.*

§ **600.** **-en** (Goth. **-ein,** OHG. **-īn**), West Germanic **-īn-** beside **-innja-,** used in forming neuter nouns often with diminutive meaning, as **clīewen, clȳwen,** *clew*; **cȳcen,** *chicken*; **embren,** *bucket*; **fæsten,** *fortress*; **filmen,** *film*; **gǣten,** *little goat, kid*; **mægden, mǣden,** *maiden*; **ticcen,** *kid*; **wēsten(n),** *desert.*

§ **601.** **-end** (**-nd**), originally the ending of the present participle of verbs (§ **441**), used in forming nomina agentis, as **fēond,** *enemy*; **frēond,** *friend*; **galend,** *enchanter*; **hǣlend,** *Saviour*; **hettend,** *enemy*; **hlystend,** *listener*; **lǣstend,** *doer*; **līþend,** *sailor, traveller*; **metend,** *measurer*; **reccend,** *ruler*; **rīdend,** *rider*; **scēotend,** *warrior*; **secgend,** *speaker*; **sellend,** *giver*; **tǣlend,** *reprover*; **wealdend,** *ruler*; **wīgend,** *warrior*; **wrecend,** *avenger.*

§ **602.** **-ere** (Goth. **-areis,** OHG. **-ări,** Lat. **-ārius**), originally used to form nomina agentis from other nouns, and then later from verbs also, as **bæcere,** *baker*; **costere,** *templer*; **crēopere,** *cripple*; **drēamere,** *musician*; **drincere,** *drinker*; **etere,** *eater*; **folgere,** *follower*; **fugelere,** *fowler*; **gītsere,** *miser*; **godspellere,** *evangelist*; **hearpere,** *harper*;

**hordere**, *steward, treasurer*; **hwistlere**, *piper*; **lǣnere**, *lender*; **lēasere**, *hypocrite*; **lēogere**, *liar*; **leornere**, *disciple, learner*; **mǣþere**, *mower*; **mangere**, *merchant, trader*; **rēafere**, *robber*; **reccere**, *ruler*; **sǣdere**, *sower*; **sangere**, *singer*; **scipere**, *sailor*; **sēamere**, *tailor*; **sūtere**, *shoemaker*; **tollere**, *tax-gatherer*; **wrītere**, *writer*.

§ **603**. **-estre** from older **-istræ**, prim. Germanic **-istrjōn-** beside **-astrjōn-**, used in forming fem. nomina agentis from verbs, also occasionally from nouns, as **bæcestre**, *baker*; **cempestre**, *female novice*; **fylgestre**, *follower*; **hlēapestre**, *dancer*; **huntigestre**, *huntress*; **lǣrestre**, *teacher*; **loppestre**, *lobster*; **lufestre**, *lover*; **rǣdestre**, *reader*; **sangestre**, *songstress*; **sēamestre**, *sempstress*; **tæppestre**, *tavern-keeper*; **webbestre**, *weaver*; **wītegestre**, *prophetess*.

§ **604**. **-et(t)** (Goth. **-iti**, OHG. **-izzi**), prim. Germanic **-itja-** beside **-atja-**, used in forming neut. verbal and denominative abstract nouns, as **bærnet**, *arson*; **bealcet(t)**, *belching*; **emnet**, *plain*; **hīewet**, *cutting*; **nierwet(t)**, *narrowness*; **rēwet**, *rowing*; **rȳmet**, *space, extent*; **sǣwet**, *sowing*; **sweofot**, *sleep*; **þēowet**, **-ot**, *slavery*; **þiccet(t)**, *thicket*.

§ **605**. **-hād** (OHG. **-heit**), used to form masc. abstract nouns from nouns and adjectives, also used as an independent word, Goth. **háidus**, *way, manner*, OE. **hād**, OHG. **heit**, *grade, rank*. Examples are: **abbudhād**, *rank of an abbot*; **camphād**, *warfare*; **cildhād**, *childhood*; **cnihthād**, *boyhood*; **fulwihthād**, *baptismal vow*; **geoguþhād**, *youth*; **hēalichād**, *loftiness*; **mægdenhād**, *maidenhood*; **mǣgþhād**, *relationship*; **munuchād**, *monastic state*; **prēosthād**, *priesthood*; **þēowhād**, *service*; **werhād**, *manhood, male sex*; **wīfhād**, *womanhood*.

§ **606**. **-incel** (cp. OHG. **-inklīn**), a neuter diminutive suffix of uncertain origin, as **cofincel**, *little chamber*; **hæftincel**, *slave*; **hūsincel**, *little house*; **liþincel**, *little joint*; **rāpincel**, *cord, string*; **scipincel**, *little ship*; **stānincel**, *little stone*; **tūnincel**, *small estate*; **þēowincel**, *young slave*; **weargincel**, *butcher-bird*.

§ **607**. **-ing** (O.Icel. **-ingr**, OHG. **-ing**), used in forming masc. concrete nouns, especially patronymics, as **æþeling**, *son of a noble, prince*; **cyning**, *king*; **Ealdulfing**, **Scēfing**, **Scylding**. **bīesting**, *first milk of a cow after calving*; **cāsering**, *a coin*; **scilling**, *shilling*; **hǣring**, *herring*; **hearding**, *hero, bold man*; **hemming**, *shoe of hide*; **ierming**, *poor wretch*; **silfring**, *silver coin*; **swertling**, *titlark*. From nouns like **æþeling** beside the adj. **æþele**, *noble*; and **lȳtling**, *child*, beside **lȳtel**, *little*, was extracted the suffix **-ling** which became common especially in forming nouns denoting persons, as **cnæpling**, *youth*; **dēorling**, *favourite, darling*; **fēorþling**, *fourth part, farthing*; **fōstorling**, *foster-child*; **geongling**, *youth*; **gesibling**, *kinsman*; **hæftling**, *prisoner*; **hēafodling**, *equal, companion*; **hȳrling**, *hireling*; **ierþling**, *ploughman*; **nīedling**, *slave, bondman*; **rǣpling**, *prisoner*; **þēowling**, *slave*.

§ **608**. **-lāc**, used in forming neuter nouns. Also used as an independent word, Goth. **láiks**, *dance*, O.Icel. **leikr**, *play*, OHG. **leih**, *play, song*. The original meaning seems to have been '*motion in general*', but in OE. **lāc** means *battle*; *offering, sacrifice*; *gift, present*. Examples are: **ǣfenlāc**, *evening sacrifice*; **brēowlāc**, *brewing*; **brȳdlāc**, *marriage gift*; **feohtlāc**, *fighting*; **rēaflāc**, *robbery, booty*; **sǣlāc**, *gift* or *offering from the sea*; **scīnlāc**, *magic*; **wedlāc**, *wedlock*; **wītelāc**, *punishment*; **wrōhtlāc**, *accusation*.

§ **609**. **-nes(s)**, **-nis(s)** (OHG. **-nessi**, **-nissi**), used in forming fem. abstract nouns from adjectives, as **æþelnes**, *nobility*; **biternes**, *bitterness*; **blindnes**, *blindness*; **cēlnes**, *coolness*; **clǣnnes**, *purity*; **drēorignes**, *sadness*; **ēadignes**, *prosperity*; **fæstnes**, *firmness*; **glēawnes**, *sagacity*; **grēnnes**, *greenness*; **hǣlnes**, *salvation*; **heardnes**, *hardness*; **īdelnes**, *idleness*; **lufsumnes**, *amiability*; **mildheortnes**, *mercy*; **oferetolnes**, *gluttony*; **slæcnes**, *slackness*; **strangnes**, *strength*; **wærnes,** *prudence*; **wæterseōcnes,** *dropsy*; **wōdnes,** *madness.*

§ **610.** **-rǣden(n),** used in forming fem. abstract nouns denoting a state or condition. Also used as an independent word, **rǣden(n),** *state, condition,* related to the verb **gerǣdan,** *to arrange, put in order.* Examples are: **geferrǣden,** *companionship*; **geþēodrǣden,** *fellowship*; **hīwrǣden,** *family, household*; **holdrǣden,** *loyalty*; **hūsrǣden,** *household*; **hyldrǣden,** *fidelity*; **mǣdrǣden,** *grass mown on a meadow*; **mǣgrǣden,** *relationship*; **man(n)rǣden,** *allegiance, homage*; **tēonrǣden,** *injury*; **trēowrǣden,** *fidelity*; **þingrǣden,** *intercession*; **wīterǣden,** *punishment.*

§ **611.** **-scipe** (related to Goth. **skapjan,** OE. **scieppan,** *to create*), used in forming masc. abstract nouns, as **bēorscipe,** *feast*; **burgscipe,** *township*; **cāfscipe,** *activity*; **dryhtscipe,** *sovereignty*; **fracodscipe,** *vileness*; **fēondscipe,** *hostility*; **frēondscipe,** *friendship*; **gēapscipe,** *deceit*; **geferscipe,** *companionship*; **gemǣnscipe,** *fellowship, communion*; **gōdscipe,** *goodness*; **hǣþenscipe,** *paganism*; **hlāfordscipe,** *lordship*; **holdscipe,** *loyalty*; **hwætscipe,** *bravery*; **manscipe,** *humanity*; **prūtscipe,** *pride*; **sinscipe,** *wedlock*; **tūnscipe,** *inhabitants of a village*; **þēodscipe,** *nation*; **wærscipe,** *prudence.*

§ **612.** **-stafas,** the plural of **stæf,** *staff, stick,* used to form masc. abstract nouns, as **ārstafas,** *kindness*; **fācenstafas,** *treachery*; **hearmstafas,** *trouble, affliction*; **sorgstafas,** *sorrow, affliction*; **wrōhtstafas,** *crime*; **wyrdstafas,** *destiny.*

§ **613.** **-þo, -þ,** older **-þu** (Goth. **-iþa,** OHG. **-ida,** prim. Germanic **-iþō**), used in forming fem. abstract nouns from adjectives (§ **371**), as **fȳlþ,** *filth*; **hīehþ(o),** *height*; **hīenþ(o),** *humiliation*; **hlīewþ,** *covering, shelter*; **hrīefþ(o),** *scurfiness*; **iermþ(o),** *poverty*; **iergþ(o),** *cowardice*; **lǣþþo,** *hatred*; **lengþ(o),** *length*; **mǣrþ(o),** *fame, glory*; **myr(i)gþ,** *mirth*; **sǣlþ,** *happiness*; **slǣwþ,** *sloth*; **strengþ(o),** *strength*;

**trēowþ, trīewþ,** *fidelity*; **trymþ,** *firmness*; **þiefþ,** *theft*; **wræþþ(o),** *wrath*. On the **t** in words like **gescentu,** *disgrace*; **gesyntu,** *health*; **ofermēttu,** *pride*, see § **305.** In nouns formed from adjectives ending in **-lēas,** the **-þ** became **-t** after the **s** (§ **305**), as **lārlēast, -līest,** *ignorance*; **līflēast,** *death*; **andgietlēast,** *folly*; **slǣplēast,** *sleeplessness*; **gīemelīest,** *carelessness, negligence*; **hlāflēast,** *want of bread*; **hygelēast,** *thoughtlessness*.

§ **614.** **-u, -o,** embracing fem. abstract nouns formed from adjectives. In prim. Germanic the stem of this class of nouns ended in **-īn,** cp. Goth. **managei,** *multitude*, gen. **manageins** (§ **382**). The OE. nouns have **-u, -o** from the ō-declension (§ **365**), as **menniscu, -o,** *humanity, human state*; **micelu,** *size*; **wæstmbǣru,** *fertility*; **wlencu,** *pride*. For further examples, see § **563,** 1.

§ **615.** **-ung,** more rarely **-ing** (O.Icel. **-ung, -ing**; OHG. **-ung, -unga**), used in forming fem. abstract nouns, especially from the second class of weak verbs (§§ **535–6**), as **ābīdung,** *waiting*; **āscung,** *interrogation*; **bīegung,** *curvature*; **blācung,** *pallor*; **brocung,** *affliction*; **cēapung,** *trading*; **costung,** *temptation*; **deorcung,** *twilight*; **gemiltsung,** *pity*; **glōmung,** *gloaming*; **handlung,** *handling*; **hārung,** *hoariness*; **hearpung,** *harping*; **langung,** *longing*; **lēasung,** *lying, leasing*; **murcnung,** *murmuring*; **niþerung,** *humiliation*; **scēawung,** *contemplation*; **scotung,** *shooting*; **strūdung,** *robbery*; **swīgung,** *silence*; **tācnung,** *signification*; **tēoþung,** *tithing*; **þegnung,** *ministration*; **þingung,** *intercession*; **warnung,** *warning*; **wiccung,** *witchcraft*; **wunung,** *dwelling*. **ærning,** *riding, racing*; **grēting,** *greeting*; **ielding,** *delay*; **rǣding,** *reading*; **wending,** *turning*.

§ **616.** **-wist,** used in forming fem. abstract nouns. Also used as an independent word. Goth. **wists,** OHG. OE. **wist,** *being, existence, substance*, the verbal abstract noun of OE. **wesan,** *to be*. Examples are: **hūswist,** *household*; **loswist,** *perdition, loss*; **midwist,** *presence*; **nēawist,** *neighbourhood*; **onwist,** *dwelling in a place*; **samwist,** *living together*; **stedewist,** *steadiness, constancy.*

## Compound Nouns.

§ **617.** In compound nouns formed by composition, the second element is always a noun, but the first element may be a noun, adjective, or a particle. The declension and gender of compound nouns are determined by the final element. Examples are:

**ācleāf,** *oak-leaf*; **ǣfenmete,** *supper*; **æppelwīn,** *cider*; **bǣlfȳr,** *funeral fire*; **bāncofa,** *body*; **bōccræft,** *literature*; **borggielda,** *debtor*; **brōþorsunu,** *nephew*; **brȳdguma,** *bridegroom*; **campstede,** *battle-field*; **cornhūs,** *granary*; **cūhierde,** *cow-herd*; **dōmdæg,** *doomsday*; **earmbēag,** *bracelet*; **fæderslaga,** *parricide*; **feldhūs,** *tent*; **fierdlēoþ,** *war-song*; **flǣschama,** *body*; **folctoga,** *general*; **gārbēam,** *spear-shaft*; **godspell,** *gospel*; **gūþfana,** *banner*; **hāmstede,** *homestead*; **handgeweorc,** *handiwork*; **lārhūs,** *school*; **mōthūs,** *court-house*; **rīmcræft,** *arithmetic*; **sangbōc,** *hymn-book*; **sǣcyning,** *sea-king*; **scōhnægl,** *shoe-nail*; **stæfcræft,** *grammar*; **stānbrycg,** *stone-bridge*; **tungolcræft,** *astronomy*; **wæterādl,** *dropsy*; **weorcdæg,** *workday*; **wīfman,** *woman*; **woruldcaru,** *worldly care.*

**ānhaga,** *recluse*; **beorhtrodor,** *heaven*; **blæcgimm,** *jet*; **brādbrim,** *ocean*; **cwicǣht,** *live-stock*; **dimhūs,** *prison*; **ealdormann,** *magistrate*; **ealdsprǣc,** *tradition*; **fæder(e)nmǣg,** *paternal kinsman*; **fēowergield,** *fourfold payment*; **frēobearn,** *freeborn child*; **hēahsynn,** *deadly sin*; **lēasgielp,** *vainglory*; **middelniht,** *midnight*; **nēahmǣg,** *near relation*; **rihthand,** *right hand*; **sorglufu,** *sad love*; **sōþword,** *true word*; **wansceaft,** *misfortune*; **wīdsǣ,** *open sea*; **wōhgod,** *false god.*

**angbrēost,** *asthma*; **eftcyme,** *return*; **ellorsīþ,** *departure, death*; **gēosceaft,** *destiny*; **hidercyme,** *arrival*; **niþergang,** *descent*; **samodsprǣc,** *colloquy.*

§ **618.** The first element of a compound noun regularly retained its final vowel, when it was a short **i-**, **u-**, or **wa-** stem. The final vowel generally remained in **ja-**stems whether the stem-syllable of the first element was long or short. On the other hand it regularly disappeared in **n-**, and short **ō-**stems. Examples are: **berelāf,** *barley loaf*; **cwidegiedd,** *song*; **elebēam,** *olive-tree*; **merewīf,** *water-witch*; **selegiest,** *hall-guest*; **winemǣg,** *kinsman.* **duru-weard,** *door-keeper*; **felawyrdnes,** *loquacity*; **hagosteald,** *bachelor*; **heoruword,** *fierce word*; **magorinc,** *warrior*; **medudrēam,** *mead-joy*; **wudubearo,** *grove.* **beadocræft,** *skill in war*; **bealoþanc,** *evil thought.*

**endelāf,** *last remnant*; **hierdebōc,** *pastoral book*; **ierfe-weard,** *heir*; **wītestōw,** *place of torment.* **cynerīce,** *king-dom*; **herefolc,** *army.*

**bangār,** *deadly spear*; **gumcynn,** *mankind*; **frumbearn,** *firstborn child*; **nambōc,** *register*; **steorscēawere,** *astro-nomer*; **swēorbān,** *neck bone.* **ciricbōc,** *church-book*; **heortcoþu,** *heart-disease*; **moldgræf,** *grave*; **nunmynster,** *convent, nunnery*; **sunbēam,** *sunbeam.* **ēarwicga,** *earwig.* **cargāst,** *sad spirit*; **giefstōl,** *throne*; **luftācen,** *love token.*

§ **619.** Sometimes the first element of compounds appears in its inflected form, as **dægesēage,** *daisy*; **gēacessūre,** *wood-sorrel*; **hādesmann,** *member of a particular order*; **stēoresmann** beside **stēormann,** *steersman*; **Tīwesdæg,** *Tuesday.* **hellebryne,** *hell-fire*; **hellewīte,** *hell-torment*; **hildestrengo,** *warlike strength*; **rōdehengen(n),** *crucifixion.* **mōnanǣfen,** *Sunday evening*; **mōnandæg** beside **mōndæg,** *Monday*; **nunnanmynster** beside **nunmynster,** *nunnery*; **sunnandæg,** *Sunday*; **sunnanniht,** *Saturday evening.* **ǣgerfelma,** *film of an egg*; **ǣgergeolu,** *yolk of egg,* beside **ǣgsciell,** *egg-shell.* **Englaland,** *England*; **witenagemōt,** *parliament.*

## Adjectives.

§ **620.** Adjectives, like nouns, may be conveniently divided into three classes: simple, derivative, and compound. Examples of simple adjectives are: **beald,** *bold*; **blæc,** *black*; **ceald,** *cold*; **dēop,** *deep*; **eald,** *old*; **earm,** *poor*; **full,** *full*; **geolu,** *yellow*; **geong,** *young*; **hāl,** *whole, sound*; **heard,** *hard*; **læt,** *slow*; **lang,** *long*; **lēof,** *dear*; **mǣre,** *famous*; **nīewe,** *new*; **rēad,** *red*; **scearp,** *sharp*; **smæl,** *small*; **strang,** *strong*; **trum,** *firm*; **þicce,** *thick*; **wāc,** *weak*; **wīs,** *wise*.

§ **621.** Derivative adjectives often have the same inseparable prefixes as nouns (§§ **564–94**), as **andfenge,** *acceptable*; **ansund,** *entire, sound*; **edgeong,** *growing young*; **gecynde,** *innate, natural*; **sammǣle,** *agreed*; **unsynnig,** *innocent*.

## Suffixes.

§ **622.** **-bǣre** (OHG. **-bāri,** Lat. **-fer** in **lūcifer,** *light-bearing*; originally a verbal adj. from **beran,** *to bear*), as **æppelbǣre,** *apple-bearing*; **ātorbǣre,** *poisonous*; **cwealmbǣre,** *deadly*; **feþerbǣre,** *winged*; **fȳrbǣre,** *fiery*; **grambǣre,** *passionate*; **hālbǣre,** *wholesome*; **hornbǣre,** *horned*; **lēohtbǣre,** *bright, splendid*; **lustbǣre,** *desirable*; **mannbǣre,** *producing men*; **tungolbǣre,** *starry*; **wæstmbǣre,** *fruitful*; **wīgbǣre,** *warlike*.

§ **623.** **-cund** (Goth. **-kunds,** OHG. **-kunt,** denoting *kind, sort, origin*; originally a participial adj., related to **cennan,** *to bring forth, beget*), as **æþelcund,** *of noble origin*; **dēofolcund,** *diabolical*; **eorlcund,** *noble*; **eorþcund,** *earthly*; **feorrcund,** *foreign*; **gāstcund,** *spiritual*; **godcund,** *divine*; **heofoncund,** *heavenly*; **innancund,** *internal, inward*; **sāwolcund,** *spiritual*; **weoroldcund,** *worldly*; **yfelcund,** *evil*.

§ **624.** **-ede** (OHG. **-ōti**), denoting *provided with, furnished with*, used in forming adjectives from nouns, as **coppede,** *topped, polled*; **hēalede**, *ruptured*; **hōcede**, *shaped like a hook*; **hoferede**, *humpbacked*; **hringed(e)**, *furnished with rings*; **micelhēafdede**, *big-headed*; **sūrēagede**, *blear-eyed*; **þrihēafdede**, *three-headed.*

§ **625**. **-en** (Goth. **-ein**, OHG. **-īn**, prim. Germanic **-īnaz** = Lat. **-īnus**), used in forming adjectives denoting the material of which a thing is made, as **æscen**, *made of ash-wood*; **bræsen**, *of brass*; **fellen**, *of skins*; **flǣscen**, *of flesh*; **fȳren**, *fiery*; **gǣten**, *of goats*; **gielpen**, *boastful*; **gylden**, *golden*; **hǣren**, *of hair*; **hwǣten**, *wheaten*; **hwīlen**, *transitory*; **hyrnen**, *made of horns*; **lēaden**, *leaden*; **picen**, *of pitch*; **rygen**, *of rye*; **seolfren**, *of silver*; **sīden**, *silken*; **stǣnen**, *stony, of stone*; **sweflen**, *sulphurous*; **trēowen**, *wooden*; **tunglen**, *of the stars.*

Note.—Forms like **bræsen**, **fellen**, **lēaden**, **trēowen**, for ***bresen**, ***fillen**, ***līeden**, ***trīewen**, are new formations made direct from the corresponding nouns without umlaut.

§ **626**. **-erne** (prim. Germanic **-rōnja-**), used in forming adjectives denoting *direction*, as **ēasterne**, *east, eastern*; **norþerne**, *northern*; **sūþerne**, *southern*; **westerne**, *western.*

§ **627**. **-fæst**, same word as the adj. **fæst**, *fast, fixed, firm*, as **ǣrendfæst**, *bound on an errand*; **ārfæst**, *virtuous*; **bīdfæst**, *stationary*; **blǣdfæst**, *glorious*; **eorþfæst**, *fixed in the earth*; **gieffæst**, *gifted*; **hogfæst**, *prudent*; **hūsfæst**, *having a home*; **hygefæst**, *wise*; **mægenfæst**, *vigorous*; **sigefæst**, *victorious*; **stedefæst**, *steadfast*; **trēowfæst**, *faithful.*

§ **628**. **-feald** (Goth. **-falþs**, OHG. **-falt**, related to **fealdan**, *to fold*), used in forming adjectives from other adjectives, especially from numerals, as **ānfeald**, *single*; **felafeald**, *manifold*; **hundfeald**, *hundredfold*; **manigfeald**, *manifold*; **seofonfeald**, *sevenfold*; **twĕntigfeald**, *twentyfold.*

§ **629**. **-full**, sometimes weakened to **-fol**, same word as the adj. **full**, *full*, used in forming adjectives, especially from abstract nouns, as **andgietfull**, *intelligent*; **bealofull**, *wicked*; **bismerfull,** *disgraceful*; **forhtfull,** *timorous*; **gelēaffull,** *believing*; **geornfull,** *eager*; **hyhtfull,** *joyful*; **mōdfull,** *arrogant, proud*; **scyldfull,** *guilty*; **þancfull,** *thoughtful*; **wordfull,** *wordy*; **wundorfull,** *wonderful.*

§ **630.** **-ig** (Goth. **-ag, -eig,** OHG. **-ag, -ĭg**). The two Germanic suffixes **-ag, -īg,** can only be distinguished in OE. by the presence or absence of umlaut in the stem-syllable of the derivative adjective. Examples are: **andig,** *envious*; **cræftig,** *strong*; **cystig,** *bountiful*; **dēawig,** *dewy*; **fyrstig,** *frosty*; **gesǣlig,** *happy, prosperous*; **geþyldig,** *patient*; **grēdig,** *greedy*; **hungrig,** *hungry*; **mōdig,** *brave, bold*; **ōmig,** *rusty*; **scyldig,** *guilty*; **stǣnig** beside **stānig,** *stony*; **þornig,** *thorny*; **þurstig** beside **þyrstig,** *thirsty*; **wordig,** *wordy*; **ȳstig,** *stormy.*

§ **631.** **-iht** (OHG. **-aht(i), -oht(i),** NHG. **-icht**) has much the same meaning or force as **-ig,** as **cambiht,** *crested*; **croppiht,** *bunchy*; **finiht,** *finny*; **hǣriht,** *hairy*; **hǣþiht,** *heathy*; **hrēodiht,** *reedy*; **īfiht,** *covered with ivy*; **sandiht,** *sandy*; **stǣniht** beside **stāniht,** *stony*; **þorniht** beside **þyrniht,** *thorny*; **wudiht,** *wooded, forest-like.*

§ **632.** **-isc** (Goth. **-isk,** OHG. **-isc, -isk**), generally connoting the quality of the object denoted by the simplex, as **centisc,** *Kentish*; **cildisc,** *childish*; **denisc,** *Danish*; **englisc,** *English*; **entisc,** *of giants*; **eorlisc,** *noble*; **folcisc,** *popular*; **heofonisc,** *heavenly*; **inlendisc,** *native*; **mennisc,** *human*; **scyttisc,** *Scotch*; **wīelisc,** *foreign, Welsh.*

Note.—1. Forms like **eorlisc, folcisc** for ***ierlisc, *fylcisc,** are new formations made direct from the corresponding nouns without umlaut.

2. Adjectives of this kind are sometimes used as nouns, as **īedisc,** *property*, **hīwisc,** *family, household*; **mennisc,** *mankind, people.*

§ **633.** **-lēas** (Goth. **-láus,** OHG. **-lōs**). Also used as an independent word Goth. **láus,** *empty*; OE. **lēas,** OHG. **lōs,** *devoid of.* Examples are: **ārlēas,** *impious, cruel*; **bānlēas,** *boneless*; **beardlēas,** *beardless*; **carlēas,** *careless*; **cwidelēas,** *speechless*; **fæderlēas,** *fatherless*; **gīemelēas,** *heedless*; **hāmlēas,** *homeless*; **hrōflēas,** *roofless*; **mægenlēas,** *powerless*; **saclēas,** *innocent*; **sprǣclēas,** *speechless*; **tōþlēas,** *toothless*; **weorþlēas,** *worthless.*

§ **634.** **-lic** (Goth. **-leik,** OHG. **-līh, -līch**). Also preserved as an independent word in Goth. **ga-leiks,** OHG. **gi-līch,** OE. **ge-līc,** *like*; originally the same word as Goth. **leik,** OE. **līc,** *body*. Examples are: **ǣnlic,** *unique*; **ānlic,** *solitary*; **cildlic,** *infantine*; **cynelic,** *royal*; **dæglic,** *daily*; **dēadlic,** *deadly*; **ealdlic,** *venerable*; **forhtlic,** *afraid*; **gēarlic,** *yearly*; **gesinsciplic,** *conjugal*; **heofonlic,** *heavenly*; **hetelic,** *hostile*; **loflic,** *praiseworthy*; **mennisclic,** *human*; **mǣrlic,** *famous*; **nytlic,** *useful*; **stōwlic,** *local*; **tīdlic,** *temporary*; **wīflic,** *womanly.*

§ **635.** **-ol** (Goth. **-ul,** OHG. **-al**), mostly used in forming adjectives from verbal forms, as **andgietol,** *intelligent*; **beswicol,** *deceitful*; **etol,** *voracious*; **hetol,** *hostile*; **hlagol,** *apt to laugh*; **meagol,** *earnest, vigorous*; **numol,** *capacious*; **nyttol,** *useful*; **rēafol,** *rapacious*; **slāpol,** *somnolent, sleepy*; **sprecol,** *talkative*; **þancol,** *thoughtful*; **wacol,** *vigilant*; **witol,** *wise.*

§ **636.** **-sum** (OHG. **-sam**; Goth. **-sam** only preserved in **lustu-sams,** *longed for, much desired*). Also used as an independent word Goth. **sama,** *same,* OHG. **sama,** *in like manner,* OE. **swā same,** *similarly.* **-sum** stands in ablaut-relation to OHG. **-sam.** Examples are: **angsum,** *troublesome*; **ānsum,** *whole*; **friþsum,** *pacific*; **fremsum,** *beneficial*; **gelēafsum,** *credible, faithful*; **genyhtsum,** *abundant*; **gesibbsum,** *peaceable, friendly*; **langsum,** *lasting, tedious*; **lufsum,** *amiable*; **wilsum,** *pleasant*; **wynsum,** *winsome.*

§ **637.** **-weard** (OHG. **-wert,** Goth. **-waírþs,** originally a verbal adjective and related to **weorþan,** *to become*), used in forming adjectives denoting *position* or *direction,* as **æfterweard,** *following*; **andweard,** *present*; **forþweard,** *inclined* *forward*; **heononweard**, *transitory, going hence*; **hiderweard**, *hitherward*; **innanweard**, *inward, internal*; **niþerweard**, *downward*; **norþ(e)weard**, *northward*; **ongēanweard**, *going towards*; **tōweard**, *toward, about to come*.

§ **638**. **-wende**, related to **wendan**, *to turn*, used in forming adjectives from nouns and other adjectives, as **hālwende**, *healthful, wholesome*; **hātwende**, *hot, burning*; **hwīlwende**, *transitory, temporary*; **lāþwende**, *hateful, hostile*; **lēofwende**, *loving, friendly*; **lufwende**, *amiable*.

§ **639**. Suffixes, which were no longer felt as such in OE., are omitted, e.g. the **-od**, **-ol** (**-el**), **-en**, **-er** (**-or**) in adjectives like **forod**, *broken, decayed*; **nacod**, *naked*. **ācol**, *timid*; **dēagol** (prim. Germanic ***đauʒalaz**), **dīegol** (prim. Germanic ***đauʒilaz**), *secret*; **īdel**, *vain*; **lȳtel**, *little*; **sweotol**, *plain, evident*; **yfel**, *evil*. **efen**, *even*; **fægen**, *glad*; **open**, *open*. **bitter**, *bitter*; **fæger**, *fair*; **sicor**, *sure*; **snottor**, *wise*; **wacor**, *vigilant, watchful*. On the suffixes in the present and past participles, see §§ **520**, **601**.

## Compound Adjectives.

§ **640**. In compound adjectives formed by composition, the second element is always an adjective or used as an adjective, but the first element may be a noun, adjective, verb, or particle. On the loss or retention of the final vowel in the first element of compounds, see § **618**. Examples are: **ǣhtspēdig**, *wealthy*; **ælfsciene**, *beautiful as a fairy*; **bæcslitol**, *slandering*; **beadocræftig**, *skilful in war*; **blōdrēad**, *blood-red*; **brimceald**, *sea-cold*; **brūnfāg**, *brown-coloured*; **brynehāt**, *burning hot*; **cynegōd**, *noble*; **dǣdcēne**, *bold in deeds*; **dēaþfæge**, *fated to die*; **dēopþancol**, *thoughtful*; **dōmgeorn**, *ambitious*; **druncengeorn**, *drunken*; **dūnlendisc**, *hilly*; **eallgōd**, *perfectly good*; **ecgheard**, *hard of edge*; **efeneald**, *contemporary*; **ellenrōf**, *brave*; **ellorfūs**, *ready to depart*; **fæstrǣd**, *steadfast*; **felasynnig**, *very guilty*;

**feohstrang,** *opulent*; **folcmǣre,** *celebrated*; **friþgeorn,** *pacific*; **gærsgrēne,** *grass-green*; **gearoþancol,** *ready-witted*; **healfcwic,** *half-dead*; **heteþancol,** *hostile*; **limhāl,** *sound in limb*; **luftīeme,** *loving, benevolent*; **mōdcearig,** *anxious*; **namcūþ,** *celebrated*; **rǣdsnotor,** *wise*; **seldcūþ,** *unfamiliar*; **sigorēadig,** *victorious*; **snāhwīt,** *snow-white*; **þancsnotor,** *wise*; **wīdcūþ,** *widely known*. The present and past participles often form the second element of compounds, as **eallwealdende,** *omnipotent*; **glēawhycgende,** *thoughtful*; **healfslǣpende,** *half-asleep*; **lēohtberende,** *luminous*; **rihtwillende,** *well-meaning*; **sǣdberende,** *seed-bearing*; **tēargēotende,** *tearful*. **æfterboren,** *posthumous*; **ælfremede,** *foreign*; **ǣrboren,** *first-born*; **cyneboren,** *of royal birth*; **goldhroden,** *adorned with gold*; **healfsoden,** *half-cooked*; **rihtgefremed,** *orthodox*.

§ **641.** In addition to the class of compound adjectives given above, the parent language had a class, the second element of which was originally a noun. Such compounds are generally called bahuvrīhi or possessive compounds, as Lat. **longipēs,** *having a long foot, long-footed*; Gr. δυσμενής, *having an evil mind, hostile*; Goth. **hráinjahaírts,** *having a pure heart, pure-hearted*. In OE. the most common adjectives of this kind are those ending in **-heort** and **-mōd,** as **clǣnheort,** *pure in heart*; **gramheort,** *hostile-minded*; **mildheort,** *gentle*; **stearcheort,** *stout-hearted*; **wulfheort,** *savage*; **drēorigmōd,** *sad*; **fæstmōd,** *constant*; **glædmōd,** *cheerful*; **grammōd,** *fierce*; **ierremōd,** *angry*; **langmōd,** *patient*; **micelmōd,** *magnanimous*; **strangmōd,** *resolute*; **sārigmōd,** *sad*; **þancolmōd,** *thoughtful*; **wrāþmōd,** *wrathful*. Other examples are: **brūnecg,** *brown-edged*; **glēawferhþ,** *prudent*; **gyldenfeax,** *golden-haired*; **stīelecg,** *steel-edged*; **yfelsprǣce,** *evil-speaking*.

VERBS.

§ **642.** From a morphological point of view, all verbs may be divided into two great classes: simple and compound. Simple verbs are sub-divided into primary and denominative verbs. To the former sub-division belong the strong verbs and a certain number of weak verbs, and to the latter the denominative verbs. The simple primary verbs are here left out of further consideration, as their formation belongs to the wider field of comparative grammar. Compound verbs are of various kinds: (1) those formed from simple verbs by means of separable or inseparable particles, (2) those formed from nouns and adjectives with verbal prefixes or suffixes. Separable verbs call for no further comment, because they merely consist of the juxtaposition of two independent words.

§ **643.** Simple verbs are formed direct from nouns and adjectives or from the corresponding strong verbs, as **ǣrendian,** *to go on an errand*; **andswerian,** *to answer*; **andwyrdan,** *to answer*; **ārian,** *to honour*; **baþian,** *to bathe*; **cwielman,** *to torture, kill*; **cyssan,** *to kiss*; **dēman,** *to judge*; **fēdan,** *to feed*; **flīeman,** *to put to flight*; **gelīefan,** *to believe*; **hiertan,** *to hearten, encourage*; **lǣran,** *to teach*; **līehtan,** *to give light*; **mengan,** *to mix*; **nemnan,** *to name*; **rēafian,** *to plunder*; **rȳman,** *to make clear, enlarge*; **sǣlan,** *to bind*; **scendan,** *to put to shame*; **scrȳdan,** *to clothe*; **sīþian,** *to travel*; **sorgian,** *to grieve*; **swǣtan,** *to sweat*; **tȳnan,** *to enclose.*

**brǣdan,** *to broaden*; **cēlan,** *to cool*; **cȳþan,** *to make known*; **fægnian,** *to rejoice*; **fullian,** *to fulfil*; **fyllan,** *to fill*; **hǣlan,** *to heal*; **hlȳdan,** *to make a noise*; **ieldan,** *to delay*; **lēasian,** *to tell lies*; **mǣran,** *to proclaim*; **nearwian,** *to become narrow*; **openian,** *to open*; **scierpan,** *to sharpen.*

**ærnan,** *to cause to run*; **bærnan,** *to burn*; **bīegan,** *to bend*; **cwellan,** *to kill*; **drencan,** *to submerge*; **fiellan,**

*to fell*; **geswencan,** *to injure*; **gewieldan,** *to overpower*; **lǣdan,** *to lead*; **lecgan,** *to lay*; **nerian,** *to save*; **rǣran,** *to raise*; **sǣgan,** *to lay low*; **sencan,** *to submerge*; **sengan,** *to singe*; **settan,** *to set*; **swebban,** *to lull to sleep*.

§ **644.** Compound verbs are formed from simple verbs, nouns, and adjectives, by means of various prefixes. See below.

PREFIXES.

§ **645.** From the list of prefixes given below are excluded such words as **æt, ofer, þurh, under, wiþ, wiþer,** and **ymb(e),** which were separable or inseparable according as they were stressed or unstressed.

§ **646.** **ā-** (OHG. **ar-, ir-**), the unstressed form of **or-** (§ **580**), as **āberan,** *to remove*; **ābēodan,** *to announce*; **ābīdan,** *to abide*; **ābītan,** *to devour*; **āblinnan,** *to cease*; **āceorfan,** *to cut off*; **ādōn,** *to send away*; **ādrīfan,** *to expel*; **āfaran,** *to depart*; **āgiefan,** *to repay*; **āhēawan,** *to hew off*; **ālǣtan,** *to relinquish*; **ārīsan,** *to arise*; **āscūfan,** *to shove off*; **āstīgan,** *to climb*.

**ācwellan,** *to destroy*; **ādrencan,** *to submerge*; **āfæstnian,** *to confirm*; **āflīeman,** *to banish*; **āfrēfran,** *to console*; **ālǣdan,** *to lead away*; **ālīehtan,** *to illuminate*; **ālīesan,** *to redeem*; **ālibban,** *to survive*; **ārǣran,** *to rear, lift up*.

§ **647.** **be-** (OHG. **bi-**), the unstressed form of **bī-** (§ **570**), as **bebrecan,** *to break off*; **bebūgan,** *to encompass*; **beclingan,** *to enclose*; **becuman,** *to become, happen*; **becweþan,** *to bequeath*; **bedrincan,** *to drink in, absorb*; **behealdan,** *to behold*; **behēawan,** *to cut off*; **belicgan,** *to surround*; **belimpan,** *to happen*; **belūcan,** *to lock up*; **bemurnan,** *to bewail*; **benēotan,** *to deprive*; **besingan,** *to bewitch*; **beslēan,** *to deprive of*; **beþringan,** *to surround*; **bewindan,** *to bind round*.

**bebycgan,** *to sell*; **bebyrgan,** *to bury*; **befæstan,** *to make fast*; **behēafdian,** *to behead*; **behelian,** *to cover over*;

**belǣwan,** *to betray*; **belendan,** *to deprive of land*; **beswǣlan,** *to scorch*; **beþencan,** *to consider*; **bewēpan,** *to bewail.*

§ **648. ed-,** *re-, again* (§ **571**), as **edgieldan,** *to repay.* **edbyrdan,** *to regenerate*; **edhiertan,** *to encourage*; **edlǣcan,** *to repeat*; **edlǣstan,** *to repeat*; **edstaþelian,** *to re-establish*; **edwierpan,** *to recover.*

§ **649. for-** (Goth. **faír-**, late OHG. and MHG. **ver-**). The real unstressed form is **fer-**, corresponding to Goth. **faír-** and German **ver-**, but already at an early period the originally stressed form **for-** came to be used in place of **fer-**. The old stressed form has been preserved in **fórwyrd,** *destruction,* beside **forwéorþan,** *to perish.* Examples are: **forbēodan,** *to forbid*; **forbrecan,** *to destroy*; **forcweþan,** *to rebuke*; **fordōn,** *to destroy*; **fordrīfan,** *to expel*; **forfaran,** *to perish*; **forfōn,** *to seize, take away*; **forgān,** *to forgo*; **forgiefan,** *to forgive*; **forgieldan,** *to repay*; **forlācan,** *to lead astray*; **forlēosan,** *to lose*; **formeltan,** *to melt away*; **forniman,** *to take away*; **forrǣdan,** *to plot against*; **forscrīfan,** *to proscribe*; **forsēon,** *to despise*; **forswerian,** *to swear falsely*; **forweorþan,** *to perish.*

**forbryttan,** *to break in pieces*; **forcierran,** *to turn aside*; **fordǣlan,** *to deal out*; **fordēman,** *to condemn*; **forealdian,** *to become old*; **forgīeman,** *to neglect*; **forhabban,** *to restrain*; **forherigan,** *to ravage*; **forhogian,** *to despise*; **forlǣdan,** *to mislead*; **forsendan,** *to banish*; **forwyrcan,** *to do wrong.*

§ **650. ful(l)-** (OHG. **folle-**), originally the adj. **full,** *full,* used adverbially, as **fullberstan,** *to break completely*; **fullbrecan,** *to violate*; **fuldōn,** *to satisfy*; **fulgān,** *to accomplish*; **fullgrōwan,** *to grow to maturity*; **fullþungen,** *fully grown.*

**fulbētan,** *to make full amends*; **fullendian,** *to complete*; **fullfremman,** *to fulfil*; **fullfyllan,** *to fulfil*; **fullǣstan,** *to give aid*; **fultrūwian,** *to confide in.*

§ **651. ge-** (OHG. **gi-**, unstressed form of OHG. Goth. **ga-**), originally a prep. meaning *together* (§ **574**), as **gebelgan,** *to* *provoke*; **gebēodan**, *to command*; **gebeorgan**, *to protect*; **geberan**, *to bring forth*; **gebindan**, *to bind*; **gecēosan**, *to choose*; **gefaran**, *to go*; **gefrignan**, *to learn by asking*; **gehātan**, *to promise*; **gelimpan**, *to happen*; **gerinnan**, *to congeal*; **gestīgan**, *to mount*; **gewinnan**, *to win*.

**ge-ærnan**, *to gain by running*; **ge-āgnian**, *to claim as one's own*; **ge-āscian**, *to learn by asking*; **gebǣdan**, *to compel*; **gebǣran**, *to behave*; **gebētan**, *to improve*; **ge-hefigian**, *to make heavy*; **gehycgan**, *to think*; **gelīefan**, *to believe*; **gemētan**, *to discover*; **gerǣcan**, *to obtain*; **gesec-gan**, *to say, tell*; **geþēodan**, *to join together*.

§ **652. mis-** (Goth. **missa-**, OHG. **missa-**, **missi-**, § **577**), as **misbēodan**, *to ill-treat*; **miscweþan**, *to speak incorrectly*; **misdōn**, *to transgress*; **misfaran**, *to go astray*; **misfōn**, *to make a mistake*.

**misfadian**, *to arrange wrongly*; **misfēran**, *to go astray*; **misgīeman**, *to neglect*; **misgrētan**, *to insult*; **mishīeran**, *to disregard*; **mislǣran**, *to advise wrongly*; **misrǣcan**, *to revile*; **miswendan**, *to pervert*.

§ **653. of-**, the unstressed form of **æf-** (§ **566**), as **ofbēatan**, *to beat to death*; **ofgān**, *to exact*; **ofgiefan**, *to give up*; **ofmunan**, *to call to mind*; **ofsittan**, *to oppress*; **ofslingan**, *to stab to death*; **ofswingan**, *to scourge to death*; **oftēon**, *to withdraw*; **ofþringan**, *to press upon*.

**ofāscian**, *to find out by asking*; **ofclipian**, *to obtain by calling*; **ofearmian**, *to have pity on*; **offēran**, *to overtake*; **offiellan**, *to kill*; **ofsendan**, *to send for*; **ofsteppan**, *to trample upon*; **ofstician**, *to stab to death*; **ofwundrian**, *to be astonished*.

§ **654. on-** (OHG. **int-**), the unstressed form of **and-** (§ **569**), as **onbēodan**, *to bid*; **onberan**, *to carry off*; **on-bindan**, *to unbind*; **oncnāwan**, *to perceive*; **onfealdan**, *to unfold*; **onfindan**, *to discover*; **ongietan**, *to perceive*; **onlūcan**, *to unlock*; **onsīgan**, *to sink*; **onspannan**, *to un-fasten*; **onwindan**, *to unwind*; **onwrēon**, *to uncover*;

**onwrīþan,** *to uncover.* **onsǣlan,** *to untie*; **onscrȳdan,** *to undress*; **ontȳnan,** *to unclose, open*; **onwendan,** *to change.*

§ **655.** **oþ-,** *from, away* (Goth. **unþa-** in **unþaþliuhan,** *to escape*), the unstressed form of **ūþ-,** preserved in **ūþgenge,** *departing*; **ūþmǣte,** *immense.* Examples are: **oþberan,** *to carry away*; **oþberstan,** *to escape*; **oþcwelan,** *to die*; **oþflēon,** *to flee away*; **oþglīdan,** *to glide away*; **oþhebban,** *to exalt*; **oþiernan,** *to run away*; **oþswerian,** *to deny on oath.*

**oþfæstan,** *to inflict upon*; **oþhȳdan,** *to hide from*; **oþlǣdan,** *to lead away*; **oþstillan,** *to stop*; **oþwendan,** *to turn away.*

§ **656.** **tō-** (OHG. **zar-, zir-,** MHG. **zer-**). The real unstressed form is **te-, ti-,** corresponding to OHG. **zar-, zir-,** but already at an early period the originally stressed form **tō-** came to be used in place of **te-.** The old stressed form is preserved in OHG. **zur-** in compound nouns, Goth. **tus-,** *asunder, apart,* and Gr. **δυς-,** *hard, bad, ill,* as in **δυσμαθής,** *hard to learn.* Examples are: **tōberstan,** *to burst asunder*; **tōblāwan,** *to blow to pieces*; **tōbrecan,** *to break to pieces*; **tōceorfan,** *to cut in pieces*; **tōclēofan,** *to cleave asunder*; **tōfeallan,** *to fall to pieces*; **tōflōwan,** *to flow apart*; **tōlūcan,** *to pull asunder*; **tōniman,** *to separate*; **tōscūfan,** *to push apart*; **tōsittan,** *to be separated*; **tōsnīþan,** *to cut up*; **tōstandan,** *to stand apart*; **tōweorpan,** *to scatter.*

**tōbrȳsan,** *to crush in pieces*; **tōcnyssan,** *to shatter*; **tōdǣlan,** *to sunder*; **tōdrǣfan,** *to disperse*; **tōfēran,** *to separate*; **tōfiellan,** *to cause to fall asunder*; **tōhaccian,** *to hack to pieces*; **tōrendan,** *to tear asunder*; **tōtwǣman,** *to divide.*

## Suffixes.

§ **657.** **-ettan** (Goth. **-atjan,** OHG. **-azzen,** later **-ezen**), used in forming intensitive verbs, as **grimettan,** *to roar, rage*; **hlēapettan,** *to leap up*; **hoppettan,** *to leap, throb*;

**lēasettan,** *to feign, pretend*; **licettan,** *to flatter*; **lyffettan,** *to flatter*; **sārettan,** *to lament*; **scofettan,** *to drive hither and thither*; **scrallettan,** *to sound loudly*; **sicettan,** *to sigh*; **spornettan,** *to kick*; **stammettan,** *to stammer*; **sworettan,** *to sigh, pant.*

§ **658.** **-lǣcan,** also used as an independent verb, **lǣcan,** *to move quickly, spring,* cp. § **608.** Examples are: **ǣfen-lǣcan,** *to become evening*; **dyrstlǣcan,** *to dare, presume*; **efenlǣcan,** *to imitate*; **gēanlǣcan,** *to unite, join*; **loflǣcan,** *to praise*; **nēalǣcan,** *to approach*; **rihtlǣcan,** *to put right*; **sumorlǣcan,** *to draw on towards summer*; **þrīstlǣcan,** *to embolden*; **winterlǣcan,** *to grow wintry.*

§ **659.** **-(e)sian.** From verbs like Goth. **hatizōn,** *to hate,* beside **hatis,** *hatred*; OE. **eg(e)sian,** OHG. **egisōn,** *to terrify,* beside Goth. **agis,** OHG. **egiso,** OE. **egesa,** *fear,* was extracted the ending Goth. OHG. **-isōn,** OE. **-(e)sian,** which then came to be used in forming verbs from nouns and adjectives which did not originally contain **-is-,** as **bletsian** older **blētsian,** *to bless*; **blīþsian, blissian,** *to rejoice*; **clǣnsian,** *to cleanse*; **gītsian,** *to covet*; **grimsian,** *to rage*; **hrēowsian,** *to rue*; **iersian,** *to rage, be angry*; **mǣrsian,** *to celebrate*; **miltsian,** *to pity, have mercy on*; **rīcsian, rīxian,** *to rule.*

# INDEX

*The numbers after a word refer to the paragraphs in the Grammar.*